Brigham Young University

Brigham Young University

The First One Hundred Years

Volume 4

Ernest L. Wilkinson
Editor

Leonard J. Arrington
Bruce C. Hafen
Associate Editors

Brigham Young
University Press

Library of Congress Catalog Card Number: 75-669
International Standard Book Number: 0-8425-0708-6
© 1976 by Brigham Young University Press. All rights reserved
Brigham Young University Press, Provo, Utah 84602
Printed in the United States of America
7/76 3.2M 16679

Contents

Acknowledgments and Valedictory

Until one has written a history of the one hundred years of Brigham Young University, he has no comprehension of the task involved. When my name was suggested for the project, I was told that one of the General Authorities of the Church commented that I would be an excellent selection because I had already written most of the history in preparing the address I delivered at a testimonial honoring Brigham Young University given by the Newcomen Society of North America on 2 April 1971. In writing the four-volume history, I found several mistakes even in that comparatively short address.

Our original resolution was to read everything ever written about BYU. When we were about half way through the project, the school archivist and the Centennial staff estimated that nearly one million documents had been handled by the Centennial History Committee up to that point. This involved combing through 1,000 document cases of presidential papers in the BYU Archives, as well as 600 cases of other administrative papers, minutes of official business, and hundreds of primary and secondary sources, in addition to scores of papers in the LDS Church Archives, Utah State Historical Society, a mass of papers stored in the basements of the old

Church Office Building and the Provo Tabernacle, and dozens of diaries given or loaned to the Centennial Committee (*Provo Herald,* 25 May 1975). The *Provo Herald* suggested that there must have been around 30,000 negatives of photographs which had been screened. Although we were unable to keep our original resolution, we have read everything that promised a comprehensive and balanced view of the history. Although we have attempted to be careful and judicious, there will inevitably be inaccuracies and deficiencies. For these we apologize.

We do not pretend that even four capacious volumes give a complete history of BYU. Even in four volumes, space did not permit proper recognition of the scores of individuals who served BYU during its first century. Those of us who have been here during the last quarter-century will never be able to repay earlier stalwarts for their sacrifices, which in large measure made possible the school we have today.

It has been our continuing prayer that we have caught the scope and validity of the vision and mission of the school and that we have accurately portrayed and done justice to both its history and its destiny.

The editor thanks the original advisory committee, consisting of Leonard J. Arrington, Edwin Butterworth, Jr., James R. Clark, LeRoy R. Hafen, Wayne B. Hales, John Clifton Moffitt, Ernest L. Olson, Kiefer B. Sauls, Hollis Scott, W. Cleon Skousen, and Vasco M. Tanner, for advice with respect to the overall organization of the subject matter of the history. The editor also expresses his warm appreciation to the First Presidency of The Church of Jesus Christ of Latter-day Saints, the LDS Church Historian, and the Utah State Historical Society for making many journals and other primary documents available for research for the first time. The editor also had the benefit of historical information coming from the deans or their assistants concerning their respective colleges.

Those on the Centennial History staff who did the research work and assisted in the original drafting of the history were Dr. James R. Clark, who began as the editor's first assistant and later resigned to assume a full teaching load, Richard E.

Bennett, Eugene T. Thompson, Harvard S. Heath, and Janet W. Hansen, who worked at various times on the original project. Later, Glenn V. Bird, with the help of Linda C. Gravley, assisted in research work and did the documentation for Volumes 3 and 4. William G. Hartley made the original draft of chapter 40, "Education of Native Americans." The editor is especially indebted to Roy K Bird for his skillful revision and editing for the typesetters of most of the four volumes. A part of Volume 3 also was edited by Jean R. Paulson.

Since the one-volume edition of this history was founded on the present four-volume edition, its staff was not large. It consisted of Ernest L. Wilkinson, editor; W. Cleon Skousen, associate editor; Glenn V. Bird; and Orson Scott Card of the University Press. Although some of the material in the one-volume history was new, most of it was taken from the first two volumes of the four-volume history, which were then completed, and from drafts of chapters of the last two volumes of that history, which were not then completed. W. Cleon Skousen, associate editor, wrote most of the initial drafts, which were reviewed and revised by the editor. Sometimes, verbatim extracts were taken from the above sources. It required considerable condensation to reduce the four-volume work of approximately 2,800 pages to the one-volume book of approximately 900 pages. Bird verified the documentation, and Card did the editing for the typesetters.

Persons not on the staff for either the four-volume or the one-volume editions, but who were of constant and valuable help, were Hollis Scott, University archivist, and his staff, in particular, Beverly R. Green; Marvin Wiggins, head of Reference and Research Services for the BYU Library; Edwin Butterworth, director of the BYU News Bureau, who supplied many of the photographs and assisted in other ways; M. Ephraim Hatch of the BYU Department of Physical Plant; Ben E. Lewis, executive vice-president of BYU; Lyman E. Durfee, director of the BYU Office of Financial Services; Kiefer B. Sauls, who came to the University as a student in 1911, was placed on the University staff in 1921 by Franklin S.

Harris, and who was retired only three years ago (1973); Wayne B. Hales, who began as a student at the University in 1912 and is now professor emeritus of physics; Helen Candland Stark, a former student and gifted writer; Richard L. Gunn, who prepared the montage for the end sheets of the one-volume history; Lorin F. Wheelwright, assistant to the president and Centennial Director; Marianne C. Sharp, counselor to Belle S. Spafford, former president of the Relief Society of the Church; Anna Boss Hart, a former faculty member; Fern Eyring Fletcher, widow of Carl Eyring and now wife of Harvey Fletcher, who researched and edited manuscripts pertaining to important women in the history of the University; and Truman G. Madsen, who contributed valuable information for Chapter 54 — "A Fruitful Tree: A Century of Love, Truth and Service."

Of great satisfaction to the editors has been the acquisition by BYU of important diaries and journals, including the diary of James E. Talmage, who began teaching at Brigham Young Academy at the age of seventeen and would have succeeded Karl G. Maeser as principal of BYA except that he was assigned by the First Presidency to be principal of LDS Academy in Salt Lake City. These diaries were donated by John R. Talmage and Helen Talmage Perry, his son and daughter; the diary of Walter E. Wolfe, second in command of the Cluff Expedition to South America, donated by Arthur C. Wolfe, a relative living in Michigan; the diary of David John, counselor to President Abraham O. Smoot of Utah Stake and later president of the same stake, contributed by his children, W. Clarence John, Lorenda John Openshaw, and Howard D. John; the diary of Horace H. Cummings, superintendent of Church schools during the early part of the twentieth century, donated by his son, Harold M. Cummings; a history contributed by Colonel Robert Kelly Dusenberry entitled "Warren Newton Dusenberry: Prominent Utah Pioneer, Educator, Judge, and Public Servant," which gives historical information concerning his great-grandfather, the first principal of BYA. Other diaries and material of historical significance also were contributed.

The editor and his staff wrote the first two volumes. The editor is grateful to Leonard J. Arrington, LDS Church Historian and Lemuel H. Redd Professor of Western History at BYU, for being coeditor of the third volume. Much of the manuscript also was read by Robert K. Thomas, academic vice-president of BYU; Frank W. Fox, assistant professor of history at BYU; and President Dallin H. Oaks. Leonard Arrington and Bruce C. Hafen, assistant to President Oaks for special projects, were associate editors of the fourth volume. Hafen wrote the original text, assisted by George R. Ryskamp and Bruce T. Reese. The text was reviewed by President Oaks and Robert K. Thomas, who made a number of suggestions. Most, but not all, of the suggestions made by the reviewers were accepted, and the editor takes full responsibility for the complete edition.

The editor is indebted to Brigham Young University Press for its unusual service. Despite delays in receiving the manuscript on schedule, the Press succeeded in getting the first and second volumes ready before Founders Day of 1975 and in having the one-volume edition ready for distribution by April Commencement of 1976. It is contemplated that the other two of the four volumes will be ready for distribution before Founders Day of 1976, the one hundredth year from the time BYA classes originally began. In particular, Ernest L. Olson, director of the University Press, gave the printing of these editions priority over other matters, and Frank Haymore, assistant director, was personally responsible for coordinating the typesetting with Column Type Co., Inc., and the binding with Mountain States Bindery, both of Salt Lake City, and for the exceptional speed with which the one-volume edition was printed by BYU Press. This required working around the clock during the last weeks of the project. Gail W. Bell, managing editor of BYU Press, was always responsive. Stephanie J. Bird and Kathryn B. Jenkins, head proofreaders for the Press; McRay Magleby and the Graphics Department at the Press; Hanna M. Horton, in charge of distribution; and Kenneth G. Trane, in charge of publicity, also rendered unusual service. There were many others, both named and unnamed, who rendered assistance and deserve the commendation of the University and all those who read the histories.

I am grateful to Linda W. Lee, who spent more than three years in devoted service as secretary of the Centennial History Project, and Edith Johnson, who worked on the project in addition to her other duties as the editor's personal secretary. Together, they typed and retyped some of the ninety-seven chapters of the one- and four-volume histories as many as a dozen times and made hundreds of memoranda. Without their help the history never would have been completed. In addition, the following temporary and/or part-time secretaries have served along the way: Nanette B. Bame, Carolyn F. Baum, Patricia D. Bennett, Karen E. Edwards, Pamela K. Fugate, Dori T. Lewis, Robyn G. Liddiard, Klea C. Lundgreen, and Phyllis L. Thompson.

Finally, as stated in the acknowledgments to Volume 1 of the four-volume history, the editor expresses appreciation to his sweetheart, Alice, who, after twenty-eight busy years as wife of a law student and lawyer and twenty years as wife of a president of BYU, had anticipated that the editor would at long last devote a good part of his time to her and to their family, but who, because of this history, has endured or enjoyed an additional four years of "widowhood." Mrs. Wilkinson also assisted in editing parts of the manuscript.

Ernest L. Wilkinson

Brigham Young University

45

A President for the 1970s

In his 1936 history of Harvard University, Samuel Eliot Morison apologizes to his readers when he realizes that he has begun writing about events that took place in the twentieth century.[1] He quotes his predecessor, Josiah Quincy, Harvard's historian of 1836, who wrote when his history reached the year 1780, "The history of Harvard University has now been brought down to our times; to a period too near to be viewed in just historical perspective."[2] Undeterred, however, Morison offered this much encouragement for the historian who writes of current times at a university: "As this story approaches our own times, the difficulty of threading one's way among the mass of material increases. It will be best to consider the rest of this book as a personal impression, subject to correction in fact, and to revision as perspective lengthens."[3]

---

1. Chapters 45 to 53, which treat the Oaks Administration, were written by Bruce Hafen, assistant to President Oaks and associate editor of this volume. These chapters have, however, been edited by Ernest L. Wilkinson and Leonard J. Arrington, coeditors of volume 3 (Arrington is also an associate editor for this volume).
2. Samuel Eliot Morison, *Three Centuries of Harvard* (Cambridge: Harvard University Press, 1936), p. 439.
3. Ibid.

Morison's caution to his readers is even more applicable to this concluding segment of the centennial history of Brigham Young University. There have been but five years between the announcement of Dallin Oaks's appointment and the date of this publication. Since nearly every issue and every person who has played some role in the events of these five years is still alive, everything said in the following pages must be regarded as tentative.[4] Further, as Morison suggested, history so current must necessarily be impressionistic.

Nevertheless, it has been the decision of the editors of the centennial history that, in spite of the limitations inherent in writing of times so current, some story about these times should be told. And thus is the story offered, "subject to correction in fact, and to revision as perspective lengthens."

A Successor to President Wilkinson

The acceptance of Ernest L. Wilkinson's resignation by the Board of Trustees was announced in a student body assembly on 9 March 1971.

The resignation letter had been handwritten and sent to the First Presidency by President Wilkinson in June 1970. The decision to appoint Neal A. Maxwell as Commissioner of Church Education was being made by the First Presidency during that same month, though the appointment was not made effective until 1 August 1970. The letter of resignation recited Wilkinson's view that the new First Presidency (organized immediately after President McKay's death on 18 January 1970) should be given an opportunity to appoint a new BYU president of their own choosing. There were sev-

4. Another effect of the writing of current history is the difficulty of providing comprehensive footnote coverage of detailed source materials. Much that is written in the chapters dealing with the Oaks Administration is within the personal knowledge of the writers. Much else is based on current conversations with those who have been involved. Where citations of authority are available, however, they are provided as seems reasonably necessary. Little of the Oaks correspondence has been read by Ernest L. Wilkinson and Leonard J. Arrington, but much of it has been scrutinized by Bruce Hafen and his assistants, Bruce T. Reese and George Ryskamp.

Joseph Fielding Smith,
President of the LDS Church
from 1970 to 1972.

eral other factors that suggested the inevitability of a change in the University's leadership. By 1970, President Wilkinson was seventy-one years old. The Board of Trustees had recently adopted a policy of retirement at age sixty-five for all Church employees except General Authorities.[5] In addition, Wilkinson's health was declining, as evidenced by his open heart surgery within two months after his successor took office. Further, the 25,000 enrollment ceiling appeared to signal an end to the era of rapid physical expansion, and the long and significant McKay-Wilkinson relationship had ended. Moreover, the appointment of Maxwell as commissioner reflected an emerging set of new priorities for Church education generally. Total Church membership had nearly tripled from 1,111,134 in 1950 to 2,930,810 in 1970, with large segments of that growth coming outside the United States and among the college-age population. Growth and internationalization had become the Church's primary problems. Brigham Young was to remain the only university in the Church Educational System, but, even with its inevitable position of leadership within the system, its role was to be that of team member rather than player-coach. Only with a team relationship was it thought possible for BYU and the remaining elements of the Educational System to pursue singlemindedly their differing roles, competing for limited available resources and creating effective diversity to meet the increasingly complex needs of the system.

In that larger context, new leaders were appointed within the first ten months of Maxwell's administration, not only for BYU, but also for Ricks College, Church College of Hawaii, and the Church seminaries and institutes — constituting virtually a complete change of educational leadership.

---

5. As early as 1954, Wilkinson was given the authority to retire faculty members and others at the end of the school year in which they became sixty-five years of age. During the first part of the Oaks Administration, this policy of discretionary retirement was changed to mandatory retirement. *See* minutes of a joint meeting of the Church Board of Education and the BYU Board of Trustees, 26 February 1954, BYU Archives.

The selection of Dallin H. Oaks as Ernest Wilkinson's successor, as well as the selections made for other key positions within the Educational System, can best be understood with the benefit of some understanding of Neal Maxwell's position at the time of his own appointment. By this time Maxwell had established himself as an unusually articulate and effective spokesman, both for the Church and for Utah higher education. Appointed executive vice-president of the University of Utah in 1964, he had been called as one of the original Regional Representatives of the Twelve in 1967. During the middle and late 1960s, he and Harold B. Lee, then a senior member of the Council of the Twelve, associated on a number of Church and civic matters, eventually establishing a close relationship characterized by high mutual trust and thorough communication. Elder Lee was one of the leading figures in encouraging a general willingness by the Church to reexamine its programs in the early 1970s. As an established educator of some sophistication and reputation in the Church intellectual community, Maxwell understood, communicated with, and commanded the respect of that community to a unique degree.

Well in advance of the public announcement of the Wilkinson resignation, Commissioner Maxwell had quietly secured the approval of the First Presidency for the creation of a "search committee" made up of General Authorities to assist in finding and recommending a new BYU president, as well as new leaders elsewhere within the Educational System. In addition to Maxwell, the committee included Marion G. Romney, one of the Twelve, who acted as chairman of the committee; Boyd K. Packer of the Council of the Twelve; and Marion D. Hanks, an Assistant to the Twelve. Elder Romney was later to become a counselor to President Lee in the First Presidency. The committee began soliciting suggestions and interviewing prospective candidates for the BYU position as soon as the resignation was announced.

When the work of the search committee began, Dallin Oaks's name was not at the top of any lists. The committee had some general ideas about criteria — strong religious faith, proven scholarship, personal leadership skills — but no favorite candidates. Already aware of many general student and faculty attitudes, the committee conveyed its openmindedness by seeking and receiving suggestions from the University community. Having received encouragement to interview Oaks from unusually divergent sources,[6] Commissioner Maxwell telephoned Oaks soon after the committee search was announced in order to arrange an early meeting. Oaks was unable to meet with the committee, however, until the end of the second week of committee deliberations. By then, Maxwell had departed for Europe to complete a previously arranged teaching assignment. At the time of his departure, the commissioner did not feel the committee had found the right man.

The manner of interviewing by the committee was described by President Lee at the inauguration of Dallin Oaks as "a diligent and prayerful search." Neal Maxwell had said publicly at the outset that the search would be an "open, quiet" one that would range "as widely as we need to" in order to "get information and blend it with inspiration so that the decision [will be one] in which we all can rejoice."[7] Some time after the Oaks appointment, Marion Romney described his chairmanship role to have been essentially the same approach he would have taken in making an ecclesiastical appointment — thorough, spontaneous interviewing, characterized by a constant seeking for spiritual impressions.

After Dallin Oaks and all the other prospective candidates had been seen by the committee, the list of prospects was narrowed to five and then three. Elder Romney and Commissioner Maxwell shared their views by telephone, as Maxwell, who had never met Oaks personally, was still in England when the final decision was made. It soon became clear, however,

6. His predecessor, Ernest L. Wilkinson, urged that he be interviewed. In addition, University of Utah Academic Vice-President Jerry R. Andersen, an able, tough-minded, and politically liberal law professor who probably did not consider himself a great fan of BYU, also urged that he be considered.
7. "Neal Maxwell Outlines Policy; Search for Successor Begins," BYU *Daily Universe,* 10 March 1971.

Dallin H. Oaks, president of
BYU since 1971.

that Oaks was the first choice of the search committee. His name was recommended unanimously by the committee to the First Presidency. President Lee called to offer him the position on 27 March 1971, and he accepted. He was told that the appointment was not a "calling" in the Mormon ecclesiastical sense; rather, it was to be viewed as a professional opportunity, even though the search had been conducted as it was. The new president was presented to the Board of Trustees on 4 May 1971. The Board gave unanimous approval to the decision of the First Presidency. Later that day, the appointment was announced at a BYU student body assembly. President Oaks publicly accepted his appointment as both a tremendous challenge and a personal compliment. On 1 August 1971, twelve days before his thirty-ninth birthday, the new president assumed his duties.

Oaks's Early Years

Even though he had been away from Provo for nearly twenty years prior to his appointment as president, Dallin Harris Oaks was no stranger to BYU.[8] He was born in Provo on 12 August 1932. His mother, Stella Harris, was herself a graduate of BYU, as had been her father, Silas Albert Harris, a student of Karl G. Maeser. Oak's maternal great-grandfather and the father of former BYU president Franklin S. Harris were brothers. The brothers were nephews of Martin Harris, one of the three witnesses to the authenticity of the Book of Mormon. Dallin's father, Lloyd E. Oaks, a native of Vernal, Utah, had come to Provo in the year of Dallin's birth to begin his practice as an ophthalmologist. He had obtained his medical training in Pennsylvania, after completing his premedical studies at BYU.

Symbolic of the significance of culture in the philosophy of Dr. and Mrs. Oaks was the impetus for the choice of a name for their first-born son. Not many days before Dallin's birth, a

8. The primary sources of information for the biographical material in this section are the correspondence, journals, and scrapbooks of Dallin H. Oaks, supplemented by interviews with Oaks himself, along with members of his family.

Utah-born sculptor of eminent national reputation named Cyrus E. Dallin returned to his native Utah County to present his famous statue of "The Pioneer Mother" to Springville. The ceremonies incident to that occasion praised the role of art in the pioneer communities of Utah, as well as mentioning the distinction brought to those communities by the great accomplishments of their children. The event and its implications, as well as the intrinsic appeal of the name, sparked the imagination of the new parents. Even after leaving Provo, the Oaks family regularly returned to visit the annual Springville Art Show as a means of both uplifting and teaching their children. Along with good books, much original art held a prominent place in the Oaks home.

After practicing three years in Provo in partnership with his brother, Dr. L. Weston Oaks, Lloyd Oaks moved his family to Twin Falls, Idaho, where he continued in his practice for five years until he was stricken with tuberculosis, which took his life after a struggle of six months. At the time of his death, Dr. Oaks was thirty-seven. Dallin was not yet eight; his brother, Merrill, was four; and his sister, Evelyn, was one. Well in advance of his passing, Dr. Oaks and his wife had established a common dream for the education of their youngsters. The plan included a year or two for Dallin at Oxford. The tragic death seemed to shatter these hopes, as the young doctor's widow was left with large debts incurred by her husband in medical school and in buying the equipment for his practice.

As part of a family history written while he was teaching in Chicago, Dallin recalled that he never remembered having felt bitter about the early death of his father. He attributed his optimistic outlook to the faith and assurance provided by his mother and grandparents, whose attitudes reinforced the sweetness of his memories and the continuing influence of his father's philosophy of devotion to the Church, to aesthetic values, and to education. That difficult lesson in optimism seems to have been learned well by Stella and all her children. Buoyancy and cheerfulness are family traits that have played a part wherever Dallin Oaks has been.

Reassured by local Church leaders whose blessing and

Dallin Oaks and his wife, June (on Oaks's right), chatting with a guest at a BYU reception.

counsel she firmly trusted, Stella resolved that her children would not be deprived of the finest educational opportunities. Sher returned to her parents' home in Payson, Utah, where her children remained while she interspersed several years of school teaching with extended trips to New York City for further education. In 1942 she moved her family to Vernal, where they lived for seven years while she taught and continued her education. In 1946 she received a master's degree from Columbia University. After Dallin finished his sophomore year in high school, the family moved back to Provo, where Stella accepted a position as supervisor of adult education in the Provo City schools. She has remained a vigorous and influential educator in Utah County since that time. She is also one of the few women ever to serve on the Provo City Council, having been elected to two terms in that office beginning in 1955.

Gradually came the fulfillment of what was for Stella a divine promise about the education of her children. After graduating from Brigham Young High School and then BYU, Dallin was awarded the first National Honor Scholarship (full tuition for three years) given to a BYU student by the University of Chicago Law School. A few years later, Merrill was given Utah's first National Health Foundation medical school scholarship. He graduated from the University of Rochester, completed a residency in St. Louis, and has since established himself in Provo as a specialist in his father's field. Meanwhile, Evelyn was granted an Elks Club scholarship for her college tuition, and she went on to receive a grant for attendance at Detroit's Merrill Palmer Institute in family life studies.

Marriage and Education

Determination to receive an education was also a dominant characteristic of June Dixon, the daughter of True Call and Utah County banker Charles H. Dixon. June became Mrs. Dallin Oaks in 1952. Because her husband was but a college junior and she was a sophomore when their first child was born, June's own college education was available only a piece at a time. After the passage of several years, her degree was something of a family project. It was in early 1965 that eight-year-old Lloyd presented a shirt with a missing button and meekly asked, "Mother, when you graduate will you please sew on this button?" She received her degree from BYU in June of that year.

Dallin and June first met after a high school basketball game when June was a high school senior. Dallin, having just entered BYU, was present as the sportscaster for a Utah County radio station. He had earned his radio engineer's license at age sixteen, and by age seventeen was billed by the Provo *Daily Herald* as the "youngest combination man [engineer-announcer] in radio." By the time he was nineteen, the *Herald* proclaimed in a feature article that his "life's work was tied up in radio." Learning to ad lib before a microphone provided an early and helpful foundation for Dallin's poise. June was something of a local celebrity herself because of the dance routines she did throughout the county with her twin sister, Jean.

Dallin was unable to serve as a Mormon missionary because of stringent missionary quotas and his membership in the Utah National Guard at the time of the Korean conflict. When his unit had not yet been called to active duty after a tense year of waiting and June had come into his life, he began making payments at a Provo jewelry store on a diamond engagement ring. The day he made the final payment, he proposed, and she accepted. He began to detect a noticeable improvement in his scholastic performance from the time of his marriage.

By the time of his college graduation in 1954, Dallin had earned grades which placed him in the top three percent of the first BYU class to graduate after four academic years under the presidency of Ernest Wilkinson. He had decided to major in accounting; his plans for a career in law materialized gradually. He had shown an early talent for writing and an interest in literature. His father-in-law was a major source of encouragement toward law as a field that would call upon all his gifts and interests.

Once the decision had been made to attend law school,

Dallin sought out President Wilkinson for some counsel about where in the East one might find the best training in corporate law. This early conversation was the beginning of a relationship that continued over the years as President Wilkinson followed Dallin's career with real interest.

The awarding of the Chicago scholarship, together with Wilkinson's advice that Chicago was one of the country's best law schools, made it easy for the young Oaks family (now with two daughters, Sharmon and Cheri) to decide to move to Illinois. From the day their stuffed car and trailer headed east, Dallin and June assumed they would one day return and settle in Utah. As time went on, that assumption receded somewhat but never really left them.

Dallin's natural optimism was heavily tempered as he began law school — he confided to his journal that he knew he would have to "work like crazy" to get B's and C's. Characteristically making up his mind to be happy with whatever came of his best efforts, he established at the outset not only a regular study pattern, but also a habit of not studying on Sundays and a determination to stay close to his family and serve as called in Church positions. No one was more astonished than the young father who had not previously been east of Denver when Dean Edward H. Levi of the law school invited him to lunch soon after the end of his first year to advise him that his first year record was not only the best in his class, but the best in some years at Chicago. This comparative level of performance on law school examinations indicated more about Dallin's capabilities than the obvious ability to memorize or the discipline to study hard. The grading standards placed a premium on instinct and judgment in the identification and analysis of pivotal questions in large and complex factual situations. The analysis portion also required innate capacity for written expression. From that time on, he began to drink deeply of all that could be learned by intimate associations with Dean Levi (who later became president of the University of Chicago; one of the country's most highly regarded educational leaders; and, in 1975, U.S. Attorney General), with the world of serious scholarship on the school's *Law Review,* and with numerous faculty members and fellow students who were then or were to become major figures in the legal profession.

With the Supreme Court

By his senior year, Dallin's academic record and his writing and administrative abilities earned his appointment as editor-in-chief of the *Law Review*. He received considerable encouragement to apply for a position as a clerk to a Supreme Court justice. When his prospects for a position with Justice John Harlan began to look somewhat dim, he asked Dean Levi if anyone at the law school knew Chief Justice Warren well enough to recommend him for a clerkship with the Chief Justice, to whom he had also made application. No one did. He then found Ernest L. Wilkinson taking an active enough interest to encourage one of Wilkinson's Washington law partners named Carl Hawkins, himself a BYU graduate and a former clerk to Warren's predecessor, Chief Justice Fred Vinson, to give appropriate endorsement to the Oaks application.[9] Early in 1957, Dallin was informed of his one-year appointment as one of three law clerks to Chief Justice Earl Warren. The honor of a second BYU alumnus receiving such an appointment did not pass unnoticed in Provo.

Dallin's experience with the Warren Court, and particularly with Warren himself, had a heavy impact on his development. His reverence for the awesome institution of the Supreme Court continued, but it became tempered with a healthy realism. He gained new insight, for example, into the way legal theory must be successfully blended with common sense and social reality. Through Warren's expansive view of justice and equality for the common man, he gained new appreciation for the plight of those in disadvantaged positions. He was also inspired by Warren's lofty sense of public trust, his strongly held views on the confidentiality of the inner workings of the Court, his unusual personal style of private warmth and courtesy, and his great affection for children and family

9. Hawkins is now acting dean of the J. Reuben Clark School of Law.

life. He also noted the way in which public impressions of the Court's judges and decisions were at times inaccurate and misinformed. As he listened to and openly evaluated the views of those responsible to decide matters of national importance, and as his own views on such matters were heard, he gained new confidence in his own instincts and renewed assurance about the value of free and candid debate among close associates.

The journal he maintained during the year with Warren records that in one of many personal conversations with the Chief Justice he stated that his plans were to practice law in Chicago for a few years and then "return to Provo and public life." Not long afterward, he declined an invitation to join the faculty of the University of Pennsylvania Law School. In a letter expressing disappointment at that decision, a law teacher from that school closed with this admonition: "Please do not consider this impertinent. Don't go and bury yourself in Provo, Utah."

The Return to Chicago

When Dallin left the Court in 1958 and began his career as a practicing lawyer with the large Chicago firm of Kirkland, Ellis, Hodson, Chaffetz, and Masters, Utah was important primarily because it was the home of his and June's parents. It was partly to be reasonably close to their families in Utah that they declined offers on the East Coast and chose to remain in Chicago to begin practice. Other serious possibilities had been Cleveland, New York, and Washington. They also were influenced by having lived in Chicago three years and having worked for Kirkland and Ellis during two summers. In addition, the firm offered him a full diet of large corporate litigation matters, which was his first choice among various fields of practice. He soon was immersed in big city law practice.

In early 1961, after he had been practicing almost three years at a demanding level, he was approached by another Chicago lawyer, John K. Edmunds, his stake president (now president of the Salt Lake Temple), who called Dallin on a stake mission. As an accomplished leader of the Mormon community in Chicago, President Edmunds had been a professional and religious example for Dallin and many other young students and professionals. Edmunds's own professional stature and his commitment to the role of the Church in areas outside the West helped Oaks decide to accept the call, even though it meant cutting back in the time commitment he was giving his law firm. The stake mission experience became a significant turning point, not only because of the spiritual rewards he encountered, but also because it gave him a fresh perspective on his law practice, causing a reevaluation of the level of personal satisfaction he was finding there.

About the time of the stake missionary call, Oaks was assigned by the Illinois Supreme Court to represent an indigent Polish youth in a criminal appeal. Although he lost the appeal "on the merits," he found the experience of representing that client more personally satisfying than some experiences he had had representing large corporate clients. This event also caused some reflection about the direction his career should take. In addition, he began wanting to do some writing about matters in which he had taken an interest while at the Supreme Court. That urge to write was part of a desire he had sensed for some time to try to provide intellectual support for some relatively conservative social and political causes whose spokesmen frequently seemed to him to be inarticulate.

An illustration of the kind of writing, as well as the kind of conservatism, that interested him is his 1970 article in the *University of Chicago Law Review* entitled "Studying the Exclusionary Rule in Search and Seizure." This analysis of the law, other studies, and then Professor Oaks's own empirical research on certain law enforcement techniques argues that the exclusionary rule (an important judicially adopted rule making evidence inadmissible in criminal court cases if officers obtain the evidence by means that violate the Constitution and other laws) does not effectively deter illegal searches and seizures by the police. That view is a direct contradiction of the basic justification for having and enforcing the exclusionary rule, as given by the courts and most legal scholars. The article claims that there are other, more effective remedies for illegal police action that would not require the exclusion of illegally obtained evidence and the consequent acquittal of the guilty in criminal trials. Thus, Oaks indirectly supports the premise that the guilty should not be permitted to go free whenever a Constitutional right has been violated, particularly if there are alternative and even more effective ways of protecting against such violations.

Cases presently are pending before the Supreme Court which will require an evaluation and test of Oaks's thesis.

Another illustration is his lecture "The Popular Myth of the Victimless Crime," given as part of the Commissioner's Lecture Series in 1974 at BYU and other Church Education System locations. In that presentation, Oaks analyzes the modern movement favoring the decriminalization of certain offenses involving sex, drugs, and similar subjects. He concludes that such proposals should be studied crime by crime since the principal decriminalization arguments apply to some crimes but not to others. He also gives support for his general view that law should teach and enforce observance of those standards of right and wrong that are generally enough accepted to qualify as an expression of a collective sense of morality. Once again, his views would place him among a minority of philosophers and legal scholars in 1974 America. His scholarship nonetheless offers more sophisticated support for these views than they ordinarily receive.

Returning to the University of Chicago

Dallin was restless enough to think seriously during the summer of 1961 about teaching law, and perhaps practicing, in Utah. He had been approached intermittently about teaching at the University of Utah Law School beginning in 1959, and he received an offer from a Salt Lake City firm in 1960. He had written his mother an explanation of his decision to reject the financially attractive Salt Lake City law firm offer with the offhand comment that, "When and if I return, it won't be just for money."

With these sources of uncertainty on his mind, he was approached that same summer — having rejected a similar approach from the same man the previous fall — by Dean Levi about a teaching position at the University of Chicago Law School. This time he was ready to accept the offer. He began his new academic career that same fall, at the age of twenty-nine. Said his friend Earl Warren of his decision to enter law teaching, "You are made to order for it."

After approximately a year of teaching, the law school appointed Dallin as its associate dean and acting dean during an interim period after Edward Levi was made provost of the university and before a permanent dean was named. Although his role during this eight-month period was essentially that of a caretaker, the experience added a new dimension to his understanding of university life. However, he did not find it as stimulating as full-time teaching and research. Perhaps partly because he was well received in this role, he began soon thereafter to receive feelers regularly from other law schools in search of a new dean. He just as regularly declined any interest in such positions, at least for the time being. In a memo to Phil Neal, Levi's successor as full-time dean at Chicago, he explained the rejection of one such feeler from a Western law school: "I told him that my ties with the West always gave special attraction to any proposal that I move in that direction, but that my recent experience with administrative work made me reluctant to consider any similar proposals for the immediate future. He asked that I call him if my feelings changed." Neal's reply is typical of the reaction of many successful scholars to administrative work: "Why didn't you just tell him you are sane and will let him know of any change in your condition?"

After several years of law teaching, though he was not regarded as the most popular or colorful teacher at Chicago, Oaks acquired the reputation of being a competent classroom instructor. His scholarly and administrative contributions, in combination with his teaching, were such that he was made a full professor in 1964, after three years in rank as an associate professor. By then he had selected trusts and estate and gift taxation as teaching fields, but he still was teaching a variety of other courses in search of a third specialty, including oil and gas, legal research and writing, criminal procedure, and seminars on trial practice, law and poverty, and the U.S. Supreme Court. He published two articles in legal periodicals, edited a book on church and state, and began working with Professor-Emeritus George Bogert on a new edition of Bogert's well-known casebook on trusts. He also expanded his experience with criminal law during the summer of 1964 as a prosecuting attorney in the course of helping the law school establish a suitable clinical training program for its students. This interest continued to grow, resulting in his later coauthorship of a study of the problems of indigent criminals in the Chicago area and his preparation of a 700-page report to the Judicial Conference of the United States on the Criminal Justice Act in the federal district courts.

One of his early publications as a law teacher is illustrative of Dallin Oaks's characteristic attitude of doing what he feels is right and letting the consequences follow. In 1962 and 1963, the Supreme Court handed down its now famous decisions on the unconstitutionality of government-sponsored prayer and Bible-reading in the public schools. Dallin found in a trip to Utah that the decisions were misunderstood by many Latter-day Saints who viewed them as prohibiting prayer and Bible-reading of any kind and for whatever reason. Some people also seemed to favor the compulsory government-authored prayers involved in the cases. Believing the decisions potentially consistent with Mormon doctrine in limiting government interference with religious freedom while encouraging free personal religious expression, he wrote a brief explanation of the meaning and implications of the decisions. As a result of a spontaneous discussion at a Chicago South Stake visit with Henry D. Moyle, counselor to David O. McKay in the First Presidency and an attorney by profession, Dallin gave President Moyle a copy of his comments. President Moyle passed it on to President McKay with his endorsement. President McKay recommended publication of the article in the Church's *Improvement Era* magazine, where it appeared in late 1963.

Probably from the same kind of instincts, Oaks accepted an

invitation in 1966 to join the first editorial board of *Dialogue: A Journal of Mormon Thought* because he thought he might be able to render some service in expressing his judgment about what might be appropriate and constructive for publication in that independent but Church-oriented forum. A 1968 issue of *Dialogue* carried an article he authored on the subject of law and order. The article sets forth his basic view that deliberate defiance of the law — both by citizens and by government leaders — involves unacceptable risks to the well-being of a democratic society. This article, which documents several examples of both kinds of deliberate defiance, was later to have a positive influence on the BYU presidential search committee. More than a year before coming to BYU, Oaks resigned from his position with *Dialogue*.

Dealing with Campus Riots

Professor Oaks was given a clear-cut opportunity to test his views on law and order in 1969 when President Levi appointed him chairman of the University of Chicago disciplinary committee. The main task of the Oaks committee was to conduct hearings for 160 students (105 of whom ultimately were suspended or expelled) who had occupied the university's administration building in a seventeen-day sit-in during a major campus disturbance. Keeping a cool head during several hectic days, amid threats serious enough that he was physically attacked on two occasions and finally given a full-time bodyguard, Oaks maintained his teaching activities while carrying on the required hearings in a brisk but orderly manner. Soon thereafter he shared his priorities on campus unrest in a letter to a friend, stating that universities should be fair first and firm second. Judging from its success, the committee was apparently both.

Gaining More Professional Experience

By late 1969, Dallin desired a leave from his teaching duties and began casting about for some temporary governmental assignment that would enlarge his experience in the fields of his interest. This searching led to his appointment during the first part of 1970 as legal counsel to the Bill of Rights Committee of the Illinois Constitutional Convention, which was to prepare a new state constitution. His work in that capacity evoked an unusually detailed statement of praise from the chairman of the committee, Chicago lawyer Elmer Gertz, in a publication describing the committee's work:

> He . . . was a far more conservative person than myself, but he won my instant and continuous admiration and affection. . . . He would tell me whether he agreed or disagreed with me and why. He had a kind of objectivity that one seldom found. . . .
>
> He was the very best committee counsel at the convention. Although his time was limited and he hoarded it, he seemed to accomplish more in less time than anyone with whom I was acquainted. . . . He had a scrupulous regard for what was right. At the same time, he had an awareness of the psychological aspects of every situation. He seemed to understand the chairman of the committee and every member. Almost without exception, he was able to deal with the diverse personalities without false steps. There was no political maneuvering on his part, no flattery . . . simply diplomatic skill and a desire to establish sufficient territory for successful performance of his duties.[10]

After the completion of his work with the Bill of Rights Committee, Professor Oaks was appointed executive director of the American Bar Foundation (ABF), where he served for a year before his move to BYU. During that time he retained his faculty position at the University of Chicago Law School, which is located next door to the ABF offices. At the Foundation, Oaks headed the legal research organization of the American Bar Association, having an annual budget of about two million dollars and employing between fifteen and twenty lawyers and social scientists. During his year there, he engaged in rebuilding somewhat tattered relations with the American Bar Endowment, the principal funding source for

10. Elmer Gertz, *For the First Hours of Tomorrow: The New Illinois Bill of Rights* (Chicago: University of Illinois Press, 1972), pp. 35-36.

the ABF. In supervising a professional research staff, dealing with a formal board of trustees, evaluating research projects, and maintaining communication between those involved at various levels, Oaks gained further administrative experience.

Both President Oaks and the University were complimented in November 1975 when the name of Dallin Oaks was included with ten others suggested by President Gerald R. Ford as possible candidates to fill the United States Supreme Court seat left vacant by the retirement of Justice William O. Douglas. The vacancy was later filled by the appointment of Federal Judge John Paul Stevens.[11]

Family Life and Church Activity

During his years at Chicago, Dallin and June became the parents of two sons, Lloyd and Dallin D., born in 1957 and 1960. A third daughter, TruAnn, was born in 1962 and a fourth, Jenny June, in 1975. At the time of the BYU presidency announcement in the spring of 1971, Sharmon already had been accepted in the Honors Program at BYU, and Cheri was planning to enroll there the next year.

Because communication and mutual respect have been traditions of long standing in both the Oaks and Dixon families, it is no coincidence that family relationships in Dallin's immediate family have been warm and wholesome. Many of the smallscale public appearances of the president and his wife at BYU have been characterized by fresh and good-natured banter between the two. June has continued her interest in physical activities and probably still prefers a vigorous set of tennis to ceremonial formalities.

Because of well-preserved family ties in Utah and implicit confidence in Dallin, the move to Provo required no great adjustments either for June or the five children. It was a spontaneous acknowledgement of past practice, as well as a knowing expectation for the future, when the new president

11. *New York Times,* 15 November 1975.

Eagle scouts Lloyd Oaks (son of Dallin and June) and Rod Merrell admiring some of the works of sculptor Mahonri Young with President Dallin H. Oaks.

N. Eldon Tanner, Harold B. Lee, Joseph Fielding Smith, and Dallin H. Oaks at the inauguration of Oaks as president of BYU in 1971.

ended his inaugural address with an expression of gratitude for the cooperation and understanding of his family.

The Oaks family always has been heavily involved in Church activity. Reference has been made to Dallin's stake mission, which began in 1961. He thereafter became president of the Chicago Stake mission, and in 1963 he was made a counselor in the new stake presidency when the stake was divided. He continued to serve in the stake presidency until the BYU appointment came. In that capacity, he learned much about the administration of Church programs, the conducting of public meetings, and speaking to Church audiences. This also was a significant period of growth in his loyalty and orthodoxy in following Church leadership.

There were times during these periods of unusual experience and preparation when Dallin wondered where it might all lead. He always has been like his mother in his instinctive feeling that God is close to man. One senses in his most personal correspondence and in his occasional written records of his feelings an unusual degree of confidence in divine Providence that is of the pervasive kind, not limited to matters obviously touching the religious. That confidence also has been tempered by a high sense of personal responsibility. What he told a student body audience in 1974 is an apt description of his own way of working: "You belong to a community of workers and doers, not to a community of dreamers or ascetics, piously and passively waiting for the millennium. We are working to bring it to pass. The Lord's blessings — including inspiration for direction and guidance — come to his children who are on the move." With that philosophy, Dallin has never doubted that his life, as well as the lives of others, was being influenced by divine forces. No fair treatment of his life could omit that fundamental element of his personality. It occurred to him more than once during those few years so packed with intense and varied experience that God might expect to reap a harvest of some kind from that kind of cultivation — and he sensed that such a harvest would not be solely for his personal benefit. He was not self-conscious or ambitious about what might be in store for him, but when the time came, he was not surprised.

46

Decentralization

Replacing Wilkinson

In his recent history of Yale University, Brooks Kelley observed that "All presidencies are, to a greater or lesser degree, personal ones. Even in a university as large as Yale had become, the president was able to set the tone of the entire place. Especially was this so when the president was one of whom it could be said . . . 'When he made a decision it was thoughtful, clear, backed with lawyerlike reasoning, and defended unswervingly.' As a result, [A. Whitney] Griswold's administration was even more personal than most. It is this fact as well that makes his term controversial.[1]" That university presidencies all tend to be more or less personal is also reflected in the title of that excellent volume on the early history of the University of Chicago — *Harper's University*[2] — referring, of course, to William Rainey Harper, the legendary founding president of the University of Chicago.

Brigham Young University was no exception, especially since what was said above about Yale's A. Whitney Griswold might easily have been said about BYU's Ernest L. Wilkinson.

---

1. Brooks M. Kelley, *Yale: A History* (New Haven, Connecticut: Yale University Press, 1974), p. 429.
2. Richard J. Storr, *Harper's University: The Beginnings* (Chicago: The University of Chicago Press, 1966).

Thus, when Dallin Oaks assumed his responsibilities on 1 August 1971 he was, in a sense, the president of Wilkinson's University. This was even more true for Oaks because he retained essentially the same senior administrative officials who had been selected by President Wilkinson and who have (except for natural attrition due to a Board decision that all officers in the Church except General Authorities should retire at age sixty-five) continued to function in those positions. Moreover, Oaks had nothing to do with the making of the University up to that time. It was shaped thoroughly by Ernest L. Wilkinson and his predecessors.

It was a source of both strength and weakness that the Wilkinson presidency had been such an intensely personal one. As indicated in the previous chapters, the strengths spoke for themselves in the tremendous increase in the size of the student body, the improvement in intellectual and spiritual growth, and the building of a magnificent campus which appeared almost to run itself when the new president arrived. On the other hand, even though Wilkinson had unusual support and praise from the Board of Trustees for what he accomplished during his administration, there were faculty members who resented the aggressive, personal style that had shaped and molded the campus for more than twenty years. Although those persons would acknowledge that the University probably still would be struggling around the fringes of community college status had it not been for the remarkable and relentless leadership of Ernest Wilkinson, they did have a point — one that is recognized in the well-established American tradition — that no university president has a life tenure in his position. No matter how personal any presidency may be, it is at least as true at BYU as it is elsewhere that "A university is no man's possession. Physically a school may be the investment of a proprietor, and it may sometimes be identified with its master because it expresses his thought and will; but a university is something more."[3] This was especially true for what many regarded as a school of destiny,

3. Ibid., p. vii.

whose future was wrapped up with the future of a church of destiny.

A giant stage had been set, with actors, props, scenery, technicians, and even a large audience, and after the announcement of Wilkinson's resignation all were waiting with expectant optimism for a new president to assume the role as their leader. He would strike his own kind of balance between a presidency that would inevitably be personal and a University that inevitably belongs to thousands of people, each of whom feels, for his own personal reasons, that he has some stake in the outcome.

In President Oaks's first few days on campus, it became immediately apparent to him that he had assumed the leadership of a huge organization. He quickly sensed that even a one-or two-degree turn in the direction it was already moving would take great planning and great effort. Whether and to what extent he could influence such a turn — or even whether he wanted to — had to remain an open question in the early weeks of his presidency. He was given a whirlwind tour of campus during his first few days that left him literally breathless. In one of his first excursions alone in the Ernest L. Wilkinson Center, he got lost when an elevator door opened unexpectedly on the bottom floor; and neither he nor those who were with him knew quite where they were. That kind of experience gave him a certain empathy with others who were coming to the 30,000-member University community with high expectations and little concrete information.

As impressionistic as it may be, one way of conveying what awaited the new president in 1971 might be to quote from a staggering set of images shared by President Oaks with the faculty in his annual address to them in the fall of 1974:

> I am constantly impressed with the complexity of the University. An annual report to the faculty is a suitable time to share a few measures of the size and varied nature of the institution that supports the efforts of our teachers and scholars.
>
> Some idea of the complexity of the registration process is suggested by the fact that we have 170,000 individual

class registrations in an average semester, and that we are then compelled to process over 26,000 change cards, with an average of three class changes per card, totalling 80,000 changes, or almost half of the original class registrations.

Over in Continuing Education, we serve 250,000 students per year in 183 different locations.[4]

The library checks out an average of 1,100 books for each working day of the school year.

More than a million persons attended activities on campus last year, almost 800,000 in the Marriott Center and almost 300,000 in the Harris Fine Arts Center.

More than one-third of our alumni, about 45,000, change their addresses annually. That comes to an average of 180 address changes that must be obtained and posted during each working day of the year.

Last year we had 9,000 different persons on our payroll, 6,100 part time (including 5,800 students) and 2,900 full time. The latter consisted of 1,060 faculty, 540 administrative employees, and 1,300 staff employees.

The total amount we paid to student employees during the academic year ending 31 August 1973 was $6.4 million. The total amount we received from students in tuition and fees in that same period was $13.5 million. In other words, forty-seven cents out of every dollar we received in tuition and fees was paid out to student employees. I think those figures underline our basic philosophy to keep our tuition as low as possible and to maximize our student employment to assist young men and women in their efforts to work their way through college.

Six out of ten of our alumni have attended BYU since 1961 and therefore have been out of school less than thirteen years. Another way to describe the youthfulness of our alumni is to say that those of us who are older than forty-one years of age are in the oldest one-fifth of the alumni group.

---

4. Since that time, the number of people served annually by Continuing Education has climbed to around 300,000.

> Our campus contains 10 miles of streets and 22 miles of sidewalks, with 200 acres of lawn and 130 acres of floor area in all buildings on the main campus.
>
> An institution of this size and complexity is bound to have serious problems in communicating. One measure of the magnitude of these problems is contained in the following figures:
>
>> Each month our switchboard handles 400,000 telephone calls.
>>
>> The number of pieces of mail received at BYU, mailed at BYU, and circulated within our own campus mail system is one million pieces per month.
>>
>> Each month we use seventy-four tons of paper for all University activities. To make that quantity of paper more vivid, if you divided our yearly paper usage in equal shares among the 28,000 persons comprising our full-time University students and personnel, you would have sixty-four pounds per year for every one of these 28,000 people.[5]

Managing a campus community of this complexity would be difficult enough even under ordinary conditions. However, during the early 1970s the nation was confronted with crises of rare proportions relating to energy shortages and economic inflation. On the subject of inflation, the University administration found the Board of Trustees substantially more sympathetic than many public universities were finding their legislatures on the common and discouraging problem of costs increasing at astonishing rates. The Board rallied to aid construction projects, defray operating expenses, and finance other significant budgetary items in ways that avoided prohibitive tuition increases for individual students. When confronted with what became known as the "energy crisis," the BYU administration acted quickly and firmly to discourage the unnecessary consumption of energy in all forms. Even after the crisis seemed to have passed, the University con-

---

5. Dallin H. Oaks, "Annual Report to the Faculty," *A Wise Steward* (BYU Fall Faculty Workshop Speeches, 1974), BYU Archives, pp. 8-9.

tinued to maintain its complex plans in such a way that its energy consumption has been reduced on what may be a permanent basis. An important factor in that reduction was the installation of a sophisticated device developed at BYU that monitors power availability in low priority areas when campus wide energy demands have reached a predetermined level.

Decentralization

Until the Oaks presidency, administrations at BYU were always authoritarian in nature. Maeser and his assistants exercised strict control over the students. Half a century later, Harris still retained absolute control over all major administrative decisions. Wilkinson was given instructions that he alone was to be responsible for selecting faculty members (subject to approval of the Trustees) and determining their salaries. While he met and consulted each week with the Faculty Advisory Council, consulted with many faculty members both on and off the council, and often followed their recommendations, he made the final determination in all administrative matters. However, with the remarkable growth of the Church and the increasing number of members competent to fill high Church positions, by the time of Oaks's appointment the General Authorities were beginning to delegate more authority, as in the case of Assistants to the Council of the Twelve and Regional Representatives of the Twelve. At the same time, the Board had become more amenable to the decentralization of authority at BYU.

The highly centralized administrative structure was natural for the size of the operations at BYU during the early years of the Wilkinson Administration. However, the burgeoning growth of the school during the later years of Wilkinson's tenure made it difficult for a centralized organization to keep in touch with all the details involved in administering such a large university. As the center of an operation the size of the one described above, the BYU president's office seemed to Dallin Oaks in his early weeks like a great Asian river into which all tributaries, both familiar and unfamiliar, inevitably seemed to flow. He soon perceived that one of his immediate tasks had to be decentralization, not only of administrative tasks, but, more importantly, of authority and responsibility. He also sensed that he must be careful not to tinker prematurely with the huge, well-oiled, and efficient machine that kept things in constant operation at BYU.

In retrospect, because the personal styles and leadership philosophies of Wilkinson and Oaks were different, it is remarkable that the transition occurred so smoothly. This fact seems even more noteworthy when it is remembered that President Wilkinson remained on campus following his retirement from the presidency, thereby risking some personal awkwardness both for himself and for President Oaks. Although invited to remain in the Smoot Administration Building, Wilkinson chose to move to the Faculty Office Building where there would be no suspicion of his attempting to influence the new administration. None of the problems that had been feared were ever realized, due to the professional and personal respect in which each of the two presidents holds the other. As noted by Sam F. Brewster, the widely experienced director of Physical Plant for the University from 1957 to 1974, who himself had served on an interim presidency committee at Alabama Polytechnic Institute (now Auburn University), "I think it's been one of the most enlightening transitions from one administration to another that I have ever seen."[6] Brewster's optimistic assessment is representative of the way the transition was viewed by most, due in large part to the fact that Oaks made virtually no important changes in such highly visible areas as the University's top-level administrative organization and in the much talked-about dress and grooming standards.

A Change of Tenor

It soon became clear that there was to be a change in tenor and emphasis that ultimately would lead to broad-scale or-

6. Transcribed interview of Sam F. Brewster by Bruce T. Reese, May 1974, in the possession of Bruce T. Reese.

ganizational change, as well as differences in attitude that had both organizational and philosophical implications. One early and significant example of a change in tenor was President Oaks's statement in his inaugural address dropping a broad hint about the role that political opinions would play during his administration. It should be noted that Oaks's statement on this subject is not a statement about the merits of any particular political point of view, but about the role of any political viewpoint in university life:

> As an important corollary to our goal of academic excellence, I would like to suggest that Brigham Young University has no political objectives, only intellectual and spiritual ones. The principles we learn and teach here will be translated into political opinions and action. This is appropriate, for many of us have — and all of us should have — strong feelings on these important matters. Nevertheless, in the realm of learning, in the work of the university, our attitude toward matters purely political should be characterized by Thomas Jefferson, whose first inaugural address counseled that, "error of opinion may be tolerated where reason is left free to combat it."
>
> In this connection, I hope we can achieve a moratorium on the use of the words *liberal* and *conservative* on this campus. I am persuaded by observation and experience that the damage caused by the use of these words far exceeds the value of the communication they foster. Among intimate friends, thoroughly familiar with one another's connotations and intent, these words may convey a clear meaning. But when these labels go out into the world to be repeated by others less knowledgeable and intimate, they become the enemies of understanding.[7]

Oaks's concerns were not with just one side of the political spectrum. His views on the role of political attitudes in university life had been influenced by his relationship with University of Chicago President Edward H. Levi, who had been his dean when he was a faculty member at the University of

---

7. Dallin H. Oaks, "Response," *Inaugural Addresses* (Provo, Utah: Brigham Young University Press, 1971), pp. 22-23.

Chicago Law School.[8] President Levi spoke out passionately against the politicization of college and university campuses during the student unrest of the late '60s and early '70s. In 1968, Levi had said, "The house of learning is indeed a place for confrontation, but it is the confrontation of the minds which is called for — a confrontation in which none is vanquished, for the victory will belong to all."[9]

The relaxation of the political climate on the BYU campus under Oaks has been perceived by some administrators and faculty members, particularly in the College of Social Sciences and in the Department of Economics, as one of the most significant implications of the Oaks presidency.[10] The change is thought to be important by these same administrators and faculty members, not only as a means of encouraging the expression of differing political and social views on the campus, but also as making representatives of a wider spectrum of political thought feel welcome on campus. To many outsiders, the broadening of tolerance on this issue under the Oaks Administration would seem relatively modest because of the continued absence from campus dialogue of any true representatives of radical or revolutionary movements and the

---

8. Oaks has publicly commented that Levi's administrative style probably had more influence in the molding of his own attitudes toward university administration than the influence of any other person. Remarks of Dallin Oaks at University Leadership Seminar, BYU Campus, 23 January 1975.
9. David W. Hacker, "A Classy Academic Is Named Attorney General," *The National Observer,* 25 January 1975.
10. Transcribed interview of Martin B. Hickman by Bruce T. Reese, May 1974, in the possession of Bruce T. Reese. To some extent, "depoliticization" at BYU might be indicative of a judgment on the part of the First Presidency during the time of Oaks's appointment that the official expression of strongly held political opinions among Church members should be deemphasized in order to promote maximum harmony. For further indications supporting that view, *see* Harold B. Lee, "The Iron Rod," *Ensign,* June 1971, pp. 5-10; Harold B. Lee, "Choosing to Do Right in an Era of Crisis: A Plea to Those in Public Office," *Ensign,* July 1972, pp. 29-33; Harold B. Lee, "Teach the Gospel of Salvation," *Ensign,* January 1973, pp. 60-63; and Harold B. Lee, "President Harold B. Lee's General Priesthood Address," *Ensign,* January 1974, pp. 96-101.

absence of people overly belligerent toward the University's sponsoring Church. In an internal sense, however, the more relaxed atmosphere is regarded by some as a noteworthy development, both theoretically and practically.

Organizational Changes

President Oaks's attitude toward decentralizing the "Asian river" of administrative flow into his office stemmed from a number of sources. One was his judgment that it was impossible for one man effectively and intelligently to administer the affairs of a university suddenly grown so huge. He sensed a general administrative need to share responsibility, which in his view also entailed a sharing of authority. His willingness to enter into such sharing where it seemed appropriate was in part the result of the openness of his personality and his ultimate willingness to trust other people. He also was influenced once again, not only by President Levi's administrative style, but by Levi's philosophy of the role and functioning of a university. Reflecting that influence as well as his own judgment about it, Oaks believes that an administrator is simply one who facilitates and promotes the really important work of a university — teaching and research.

Some portion of the decentralization process was nonorganizational and quite intangible. During the first few weeks of the Oaks Administration, word began to spread that he was open, approachable, and genuinely interested in people. That feeling seemed shared by cooks in the cafeteria, janitors on the custodial staff, and the players on the football team, as well as by deans, administrators, and faculty members. Students often were taken by surprise to see the new president politely ask if he could join them for lunch at a cafeteria table, where an exchange of ideas and laughter often would take place. Faculty members were delighted to find that he replied, as Wilkinson had attempted to do, within a day or two to their memos. One Sunday afternoon in the fall of 1971, the distraught relative of a student finally telephoned the president's home because he was not otherwise able to deliver an urgent message. Because he was spending that Sunday with his family, the president simply piled the family into the car and drove to the girl's apartment to deliver the message. When the girls living in the apartment saw him coming up the walk to their doorstep, they began scurrying rapidly to whip the apartment into shape. As he approached the door, he heard one of them yell, "You guys, it's the principal!"

The impression of such stories spread quickly throughout the close-knit BYU community, large as it was. These informal sources, together with the warmth, candor, and alertness that came across in President Oaks's early public appearances, all added up to one widespread and spontaneous conclusion: he cared and could be trusted. It was a significant first impression.

Like Wilkinson, who even before his arrival on campus wrote each faculty member asking suggestions for improvement, Oaks let it be known that he would listen to suggestions. When the department chairmen (some seventy leading faculty members across campus) were asked early in Oaks's first academic year what they regarded as the University's most critical problems, their reactions were both frank and practical. They said they were concerned that many University policies were ambiguous and contradictory; they felt they had only limited responsibility and essentially no authority for dealing with such matters as salary and faculty hiring; they thought the faculty lacked effective means for policy input because the Faculty Advisory Council that had existed in the past seemed not to be taken seriously; they felt marked ambiguity about their own roles; and, in general, they were concerned about what some considered distrust between the faculty at large and the University administration.[11]

The Central Administration

On his second day in office, President Oaks advised the ten-member Administrative Council, which had acted pre-

11. The problems identified by the department chairmen are listed in a memo from William R. Siddoway to Dallin Oaks, 13 January 1972, Dallin H. Oaks Presidential Papers, BYU Archives.

viously as the major policy-making body of the University, that it was dissolved immediately. The same statement was given to the Vice-Presidents' Council, which had consisted of seven members of the Administrative Council. Most of these officers, as well as several others, had reported directly to President Wilkinson. Oaks's memo to that group of people was crisp but friendly. In its entirety, it said:

> Effective August 1, 1971, the Administrative Council and the Vice-Presidents' meeting will be dissolved. The functions of deliberation, decision, and correlation performed by these groups will be performed in another manner, which will be defined hereafter. This action in no way affects the assignments, responsibilities, or titles of any of the persons in either of these two groups.[12]

The new president's approach to dealing with his organizational heads drew a distinction between staff and line functions. He established the practice of a weekly meeting with his two primary line officers — Executive Vice-President Ben E. Lewis (who had responsibility for business, physical plant, and most financial functions) and Academic Vice-President Robert K. Thomas (who was responsible for all academic and faculty matters). Dean A. Peterson retained his function as an administrative assistant to the president and acted as an executive secretary for the three-man general policy-making group. The president announced that, in addition to Lewis and Thomas, the only line officers who would report to him directly would be Heber G. Wolsey, his assistant for public relations, and Dean of Student Life J. Elliot Cameron. The staff personnel who would report directly to the president were to be Clyde D. Sandgren, vice-president and general counsel; Dean A. Peterson, administrative assistant; and Bruce C. Hafen, assistant to the president for ad hoc assignments. The other members of the former Administrative Council — Robert J. Smith, associate academic vice-president;

12. Memorandum from Dallin H. Oaks to the Administrative Council and vice-presidents, 2 August 1971, Oaks Presidential Papers, BYU Archives.

Fred A. Schwendiman, assistant vice-president for business; William R. Siddoway, assistant academic vice-president; and Sam F. Brewster, director of physical plant — continued to report through either Lewis or Thomas, depending upon their function. Oaks adopted the style of inviting members of these groups to join his weekly policy and coordination meeting (which came to be called the President's Weekly Meeting) when subjects pertaining to their areas of responsibility were discussed by the president and his two policy-making vice-presidents.

Some natural attrition has taken place among the central administration. Heber G. Wolsey was reassigned to a management position with the Department of Public Communications at Church headquarters in Salt Lake City. He was replaced in 1973 by Bruce L. Olsen, a former assistant dean of Admissions and Records for the University. William R. Siddoway was called on a three-year assignment as a mission president for the Church in 1972, and no one was asked to fill his vacancy as his functions were taken over by other existing administrators. Sam F. Brewster retired in 1974 as Director of Physical Plant, having served intimately since 1957 with President Wilkinson in the planning and construction of most of the campus. His replacement was Fred A. Schwendiman, who now functions as director of Physical Plant under the title "Assistant Vice-President — Physical Plant." Clyde D. Sandgren retired in 1975 and was replaced by H. Hal Visick, whose title became "Assistant to the President — General Counsel." Visick had been employed by Wilkinson early in 1971 as associate general counsel.

Other than this normal attrition, there were no changes in personnel among central administrators during the first four years of the Oaks Administration. That observation is made more noteworthy when it is remembered that all of the original members of Oaks's central administration were, with one exception,[13] appointed to their administrative posts by Ernest

---

13. President Oaks hired Bruce Hafen from outside the University community. Interestingly, however, Hafen first had been approached by

Fred A. Schwendiman, who became Assistant Vice-President — Physical Plant after the retirement of Sam F. Brewster in 1974.

L. Wilkinson. President Oaks has made no secret of his admiration for Ernest Wilkinson's judgment in personnel selections. His leaving people where they were confirms that observation.

During the 1971-75 period, Oaks, with the approval of the Trustees, appointed two new presidential assistants. One was Lorin F. Wheelwright, former dean of the College of Fine Arts, who in 1973 was assigned the task of planning and supervising the University's centennial celebration. The other was BYU English Department faculty member Marilyn Arnold, who in 1975 was appointed as an assistant to the president for special projects. Dr. Arnold has, among other things, played a key role in giving administrative attention to the general needs of women employees of the University.

Three new posts for assistant academic vice-presidents also were created during the 1971-76 period. One was that of Assistant Academic Vice-President — Research, to which former Director of Research Leo P. Vernon was appointed. The second was Assistant Academic Vice-President — Learning Resources, to which Darrel J. Monson, formerly Director of Communications Services, was appointed. The third was Assistant Academic Vice-President — Graduate Studies and Library, to which former dean of the Graduate School Chauncey C. Riddle was appointed.

As indicated later, normal retirement attrition made it necessary for an unusually high percentage of the University's deans to be replaced between 1971 and 1976. In addition, college reorganizations and other changes accounted for the appointment by Oaks of enough other deans that, by mid-1976, his administration had appointed ten of the existing seventeen deans. In view of the new decentralization philosophy, these appointments must be viewed as some of

---

Ernest Wilkinson about coming to assist him (Wilkinson) with the early work on the J. Reuben Clark Law School. Wilkinson recommended him to Oaks. As matters developed, he became Oaks's liason with Wilkinson in the early days of the Law School project.

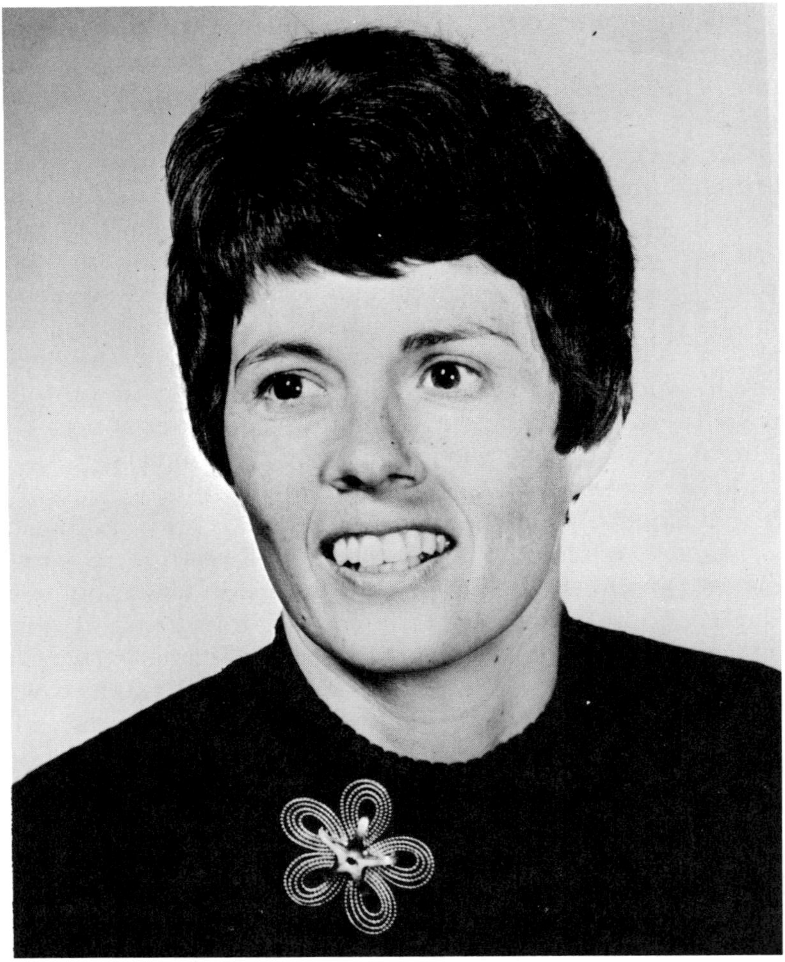

Marilyn Arnold of the English
Department, who was
appointed special assistant
to President Oaks in 1975.

the most significant decisions made by the new president and his advisers. In summary, Oaks's appointments at the dean level include the following:

College or Area	Former Dean(s)	New Dean(s)
Religious Instruction	Daniel H. Ludlow Roy W. Doxey	Roy W. Doxey Jeffrey R. Holland
Law School	(new school) Rex E. Lee (on leave	Rex E. Lee Carl S. Hawkins (acting)
Graduate School of Management	(new school)	Merrill J. Batemen
College of Business	Weldon J. Taylor Bryce B. Orton (acting)	Bryce B. Orton (acting) Merrill J. Bateman
College of Education	Stephen L. Alley	Curtis N. Van Alfen
College of Fine Arts	Lorin F. Wheelwright	Lael J. Woodbury
College of General Studies	Lester B. Whetten C. Terry Warner (on leave)	C. Terry Warner Marion J. Bentley (acting)
College of Physical and Mathematical Sciences	(new college)	Jae R. Ballif
College of Physical Education	Milton F. Hartvigsen	Clayne R. Jensen
Admissions and Records	Frank McKean	Robert W. Spencer
Continuing Education	Harold Glen Clark	Stanley A. Peterson
Library and Information Sciences	(new school)	Maurice P. Marchant

Many new academic departmental chairmen also have been appointed since 1971, along with new heads of other administrative or academic units, including new head coaches in football and basketball.[14]

14. New appointments to key management positions are summarized in tables included in the appendices.

A harmonious relationship has existed from the beginning among Oaks, Lewis, and Thomas. Both Thomas and Lewis had had two decades of experience at BYU, each in various facets of his basic interest — Thomas, the academic side; and Lewis, the business interests of the school. Thus, the two of them gave the new president primary access to the background of virtually every development of the previous decade, whether in personnel, financial matters, or general relations with the Board of Trustees. The relationship of these three has been characterized by Robert K. Thomas as "the only troika I've ever seen that worked." The reason it seems to work, in Thomas's view, is that there is an extremely high trust level among them, in spite of their known differences in background and perspective. Says Thomas, "Each one of us feels very free in expressing himself. We don't worry about how the others are going to react. We put it out, [knowing] we're not going to have to waste time worrying about anyone's feelings. We can count on [an honest] reaction; and that makes the difference."[15] When President Oaks was asked what specific administrative philosophy governed the working of this important "troika," his response was simple:

> I think the most important thing in our decision-making is the prayerful consideration we've given to the problems and the fact that we've had a thorough consultive relationship [with each other] and with others that we brought in; and then a kind of listening and feeling good about [a problem] and then just running.[16]

Of course, this approach has not excluded frequent planning, fact-gathering, evaluation, and analysis.

President Oaks's assumption of faculty leadership and his taking the initiative for academic reforms has resulted in a subtle kind of reordering of the functions of his two primary vice-presidents, who had served under President Wilkinson in

---

15. Transcribed interview of Dallin H. Oaks, Robert K. Thomas, and Ben E. Lewis by Bruce C. Hafen, 2 December 1974, in the possession of Bruce C. Hafen.
16. Ibid.

Leo P. Vernon, Assistant
Vice-President — Research
at BYU.

somewhat different ways than they have served under Oaks. Under Wilkinson, Academic Vice-President Robert K. Thomas was looked upon by the faculty as their spokesman and advocate. The academic deans have continued to report to Thomas and he has exerted a major influence in the Oaks Administration, particularly in the areas of academic reevaluation and the selection of academic deans. His influence has been less visible to the faculty, however, because Thomas and Oaks have agreed that visible leadership by the president on matters of academic innovation and emphasis would provide a stronger basis of support, persuading the faculty that the University's new academic goals were of high priority. However, Thomas's close involvement in academic reforms and key personnel selections since 1971 has been a major factor, not only in the quality of the decisions, but also in reducing the time necessary for the president to understand the problems and in ensuring that the background and implications of existing needs are fully perceived before administrative action is taken.

In the meantime, the president has looked to Executive Vice-President Ben E. Lewis for strong leadership in the administration of support services. Oaks has felt less at home in that area and has developed great confidence in Lewis. Nevertheless, Oaks has learned quickly and also has demonstrated increasing concern that the administrative staff feel that they are fully participating members of the University community. He continues to rely heavily on Lewis's experience and judgment, even though he consciously assumes responsibility for major decisions in nonacademic areas. However, as indicated above, the nature of the relationship between Oaks, Lewis, and Thomas has resulted in better joint decision-making and in better communication and coordination between academic and nonacademic viewpoints than might often be true in universities organized along more compartmentalized lines.

That the functions of top-level administrators at BYU have changed in only modest ways is indicative that President Oaks's approach to decentralization and reorganization has been cautious. Prior organizations, appointments, and approaches that seemed to work well were left untouched unless the evidence indicated a need to proceed otherwise. This freed him to concentrate on those areas that demanded more attention.

Decentralization of Middle Management and Faculty

When Oaks shifted his focus to governance of the University and a careful consideration of the role that should be played by faculty, department chairmen, and deans, a number of changes began to emerge. In September 1971, it was announced that all University-wide committees would be eliminated effective October 15 of that year. In the interim, a "committee on committees" was established under the chairmanship of Jae R. Ballif, then chairman of the Faculty Advisory Council, to review the functions and purpose of all previously existing University committees. The result of that committee's work was a streamlining and reordering of functions aimed at stepping up efficiency while infusing much wider participation on the committees by faculty members and students. When the new committees began to be appointed, most of the appointments were new ones. As time goes on, it has become a typical pattern for the administration to assign the evaluation of some important problem to an existing committee — or a new committee if necessary — with such assignments frequently resulting in recommendations that ultimately have been implemented. A few notable examples, discussed more fully elsewhere, are the General Education Council, the Curriculum Council, and the committees on Patent and Copyright Policies, Conflict of Interest, and Professional Development. In view of the traditional disdain of faculty members for university committee work, an awareness of new latitude, responsibility, and authority has been a generally productive development.

Much of the decentralizing that went on during this period was made possible because of a responsive attitude on the part of the Trustees of the University. The early '70s were a period of extensive reexamination of Church programs, resulting in numerous organizational realignments. This general willingness to evaluate existing structures played a key role in the organizational adjustments at BYU because so many prior centralizing policies had been established by the Trustees and could be altered only with their approval. Historically, the Board had vested absolute power and responsibility in the BYU president, with little room for delegation. Thus, the Faculty Advisory Council that existed under President Wilkinson necessarily had little more that symbolic administrative effect, and its power and interaction with the faculty was limited. As has been noted earlier, however, Neal Maxwell's appointment coincided with the beginning of a new era in the Church Educational System.[17]

New authorizations allowed decentralization of decision-making powers. While final authority still remained with the president, he was permitted to range farther in obtaining advice and data. President Oaks thus delegated important advisory powers to the Faculty Advisory Council. Oaks told Council members that he expected from them a quality work product and that he intended to participate in their deliberations with them. In the words of Howard Barnes, one of the early chairmen of the Faculty Advisory Council under Oaks, "He rolled up his sleeves and argued issues back and forth across the table and was very open. On numbers of occasions, he indicated, 'Well, if this is what you want to do I have some reservations, but we'll go your way.' "[18] Jae R. Ballif, the first

---

17. Editor's Note: Traditionally, presidents of BYU vigorously opposed the appointment of an overall commissioner for the Church Educational System. They feared this would lessen the leadership at BYU and adversely affect its administration. While Wilkinson recognized this danger, he felt that other benefits would more than compensate. As previously noted, he urged the appointment of an overall commissioner, which seems to have been beneficial to BYU, as well as to the Church. Having a commissioner in Salt Lake City who can daily translate to the Trustees the needs of the University instead of being bogged down with administrative details in Provo has been of special help (*see* chapter 45).
18. Transcribed interview with Jae R. Ballif and Howard Barnes, former chairmen of the Faculty Advisory Council, by Bruce T. Reese, May 1974, in the possession of Bruce T. Reese.

Faculty Advisory Council chairman under Oaks and later the dean of a reorganized college, found that the Deans' Council was far less lively as a policy input group than the new Faculty Advisory Council.[19] This is probably because the deans have gradually come to be more autonomous representatives of their colleges than a sounding board for general University policy, although the deans as individuals do have substantial input on policy matters.

One important move that gave vitality to the Faculty Advisory Council was the administration's decision (which also required a change in policy by the Board of Trustees) during 1971-72 that all members of the forty-member council should be nominated by popular election in their various colleges and then be appointed by the president. Spurred on by finding a receptive, if not always acquiescent, ear in administration, the Faculty Advisory Council has generated new proposals and has provided constant review of virtually every new program affecting the faculty before such programs have become official policies of the University. This council at BYU is still not the equivalent of a faculty senate, however, because the University administration retains the right to make its own final decisions. Nevertheless, the Council probably has become the most important policy input group on a University wide basis during the Oaks years. Even though the president always has the right to reject their counsel, he has known it would be unwise to do that except on rare occasions, lest he undermine the seriousness with which the Council members have taken their responsibility.

A parallel organization representing nonfaculty employees, the Administrative Advisory Council, was organized in 1972. That Council has had a somewhat similar function in providing the administration with review of proposals and suggestions for improving University procedures and other matters affecting administrative and staff employees.

It remains to be seen whether the University's faculty and general administrative staff will continue to be enthusiastic

---

19. Ibid.

and productive in their participation in the University's governance. The members of the BYU community were generally hungry for participation at the beginning of the Oaks years, and perhaps as a direct result of that hunger, the general scale and quality of participation seems to have been exceptional. There is some question about how much enthusiasm the faculty can maintain for involvement in Universitywide problems once the new programs initiated in the early 1970s have been adopted. Faculty participation in *departmental* (as distinguished from Universitywide) policy-making is likely to increase on some specific issues to be mentioned below, but the most important fact about already increased Universitywide faculty participation may be simply that the right to participate meaningfully has been acknowledged. In spite of consistently strong and authoritative recommendations that faculties should be given a major role in university governance function,[20] it also has been observed that:

> Most people in a college are most of the time less concerned with the content of a decision than they are with eliciting an acknowledgement of their importance within the community. . . . Faculty members are more insistent on their right to participate in faculty deliberations than they are on exercising that right.
>
> Much of the argument is over the symbols of governance — who has the right to claim power? Since the main symbols of power and status are participation and victory, the university decision-making system is crowded with instruments of participation and claims of victories: committees, faculties, ad hoc groups, reviews, memoranda, votes, meetings, rallies, conferences. The system is typically not crowded with actual participation except where validation of status positions is involved. It

20. *See The Management and Financing of Colleges* by the Committee for Economic Development (1973) of The President's Commission on Campus Unrest (1970) (Washington, D.C.: The Carnegie Commission on Higher Education, 1973).

> is often hard to sustain student and faculty interest in the activities of a committee — even one whose existence they apparently consider a matter of some import — unless some highly symbolic conflict between groups can be arranged.[21]

There has been meaningful participation, as well as an acknowledgement of the right to participate at BYU since 1971.

Permission of the Board of Trustees to delegate governance responsibilities to deans and department chairmen is probably an even more significant form of decentralization than the participation of faculty members in committee work and the Faculty Advisory Council. That greater significance is the result of one single factor — the delegation of financial authority. Previously, the primary role of deans and department chairmen was that of being an advocate for their faculty in dealing with an administration that exercised extensive, and in some cases total, control over such matters as salaries, raises, and budgeting.[22] This practice had been dictated in large part by the policy of the Board of Trustees requiring that individual salary information be kept confidential. That policy remains in effect, even though the circle of those who are privy to the confidential information has necessarily been broadened by the decentralization policies described in the text. In addition, the rule of the Board of Trustees had been that once budgets were established, there was no carryover of unspent funds from one year to the next for any organizational subunit of the University. Further, no transfers between budget categories were permitted, meaning that even if a department had overestimated its needs for supplies or capital equipment, it could not use such excess to cover an underestimate in such areas as computer services or research projects. The rigidity and administrative centralization in that

---

21. Michael D. Cohen and James G. Marsh, *Leadership and Ambiguity: The American College President* (New York: McGraw-Hill, 1974), pp. 121-22.
22. Transcribed interview of Ernest L. Wilkinson by Bruce C. Hafen, 4 March 1975, in the possession of Bruce C. Hafen.

system did not spring primarily from University-level policies, but from the Board of Trustees.

It is symbolic of a major shift in philosophy that since the appointments of Neal Maxwell and Dallin Oaks, deans and department chairmen have not only been given substantial new authority and responsibility for making budget recommendations but, even more important, they have been given responsibility for defending and administering them. This, of course, has not been solely due to the new administrative machinery, but is also an indication of the trust level that has existed between BYU and the office of the Commissioner of Church Education. It likewise reflects the prevailing level of confidence in both BYU and the commissioner on the part of the University's Trustees. Shifts among budget categories within a single college are now permitted, and some amounts of unspent funds may be carried over from one budget year to another. Salary information, which previously was not shared with department chairmen, is not only known to department chairmen, but the size of initial salaries and annual merit increases now is determined largely by the recommendations of deans and department chairmen.

In a related vein, the Professional Development Program (described in more detail below) also has resulted in the shifting of authority to administer research funds and sabbatical leave funds to the hands of deans and department chairmen. Both of these resources had been centralized in the past. Departments and colleges also have greater input into their budget for computer services, which previously came out of a central computer budget.

The thrust of these policies has been to create capacities for flexibility and movement within the continuing budget, giving incentive to deans, department chairmen, and faculty to demonstrate by their use of allocated funds their competence to administer their own affairs. Built into the system is an accountability process by which budgetary and financial decisions of the deans and department chairmen are monitored by the University's Research Division, a central University auditing office, and annual interviews between the deans and the administration. President Oaks and Vice-President Thomas have stated that, although some colleges are catching on to this system faster than others, most of them have received the message that their judgment in the quality of their faculty's work will be scrutinized and, if warranted, rewarded. For example, after the decentralized budgeting and review process had been in effect for about two years, the administration was so impressed with the quality of management in one of the academic colleges that, "We've been inclined to give them program improvements that we would never have given them if they hadn't made such a demonstration of the care with which they've allocated their funds and evaluated the way they [have used them]."[23] Oaks and Thomas have further pointed out that there has been "a spectacular increase in research time allocations" because departments have been told that if they can teach the same number of students effectively with fewer faculty, they are permitted to allocate the freed-up faculty resources in some other way that benefits their program.[24]

The result of all these changes is increased candor, efficiency, and flexibility. The deans seem persuaded that the administration really does want to serve their defensible needs and can do that only if it is fully informed concerning the college's actual problems and expectations.

It is by no means certain, of course, that this kind of decentralization will result in a net improvement in long-run productivity. The arrangement may devolve to a mere diffusion of budget-making authority, but there is reason to hope that it will in fact increase faculty productivity, enable greater correlation between compensation and merit, and stimulate the most significant potential faculty projects. Whether these hopes are realized depends primarily on the quality control exercised by deans and department chairmen and on the

23. Transcribed interview of Dallin H. Oaks, Robert K. Thomas, and Ben E. Lewis by Bruce C. Hafen, 2 December 1974, in the possession of Bruce C. Hafen.
24. Ibid.

actual functioning of the new accountability mechanism. It is still too early to tell how such questions will be answered, but proponents of economic incentives at the lowest feasible level of management are encouraged by these developments.

Delegation of financial authority has increased the power and responsibility of the department chairmen in other ways as well. An ad hoc committee appointed in 1971 to study the problems of the department chairmen, chaired by Martin B. Hickman, dean of the College of Social Sciences, found that department chairmen viewed themseves as essentially powerless. Because they did not know their faculty members' salaries, they were unable to negotiate with new faculty members about salary. The Hickman Committee made what it thought were relatively far-reaching recommendations to remedy these perceived problems; the administration, however, went even further than the committee in giving the department chairmen greater responsibility and authority.[25] The changes gave the department chairmen a greater role in the identification and selection of new faculty. Although names of potential faculty members must still be cleared with the Board of Trustees and the central University administration, and although rank and salary guidelines are normally reviewed with the deans of respective academic colleges, the department chairman has become the responsible negotiator in the hiring process, including the setting of starting salaries. The department chairmen also were given the responsibility of making periodic evaluations of each faculty member for such purposes as salary increases, advancements in rank, research leaves, course assignments, and committee assignments. In summary, as of the fall of 1972, the department chairmen had primary authority and responsibility for all of the activities and professional development of their faculty members.

Accompanying this major shift was an increased measure of responsibility and authority given to the deans as they as-

25. Transcribed interview of Martin B. Hichman by Bruce T. Reese, 16 May 1974, in the possession of Bruce T. Reese.

sumed the role of working with and supervising the new activities of department chairmen. Deans were assigned ultimate accountability for the selection, reward, motivation, and promotion of all college faculty members. In this connection, each college began to adopt explicit guidelines for rank and salary advancements and methods for reviewing departmental decisions.[26]

In late 1974, the Hickman Committee, assisted by Gene Dalton of the Organizational Behavior Department, conducted another evaluation of the role and functioning of the department chairmen to determine whether the policies adopted by the University in 1972 had had any tangible effect. The study showed a clear movement of both authority and responsibility from the central University administration to the deans and department chairmen. The study also showed a high level of satisfaction with that shift on the part of both faculty and department chairmen. The only source of dissatisfaction at the end of 1974 was that many department chairmen felt inundated with administrative responsibilities and thus felt less than ideally effective in stimulating their faculty in research and teaching efforts.[27]

The implications of these role changes for deans and department chairmen are just being realized and thought about. One dean has observed that both he and his faculty perceive his role to be more ambiguous in one sense than it was in the past.[28] Deans and department chairmen now often are viewed as agents of the University — quite different from the advo-

---

26. *See* a University policy statement entitled "The Role of the Department Chairman," dated 28 June 1972, effective 28 August 1972. The policy statement is said to be "responsive to the several recommendations made" by the Hickman Committee on the role of the department chairman. The implications of the new role definition for department chairmen also were explained in the annual address of President Dallin H. Oaks to the 1972 Fall Faculty Workshop (Dallin H. Oaks, "Annual Report to the Faculty," *Together for Greatness,* BYU Fall Faculty Workshop Speeches, 1972, BYU Archives, pp. 26-28).
27. 1974 Department Chairmen Survey.
28. Bruce C. Hafen interview with Lael Woodbury, February 1974.

cate role most frequently played in the past. The role of the dean and department chairman seems to have become dual: assuming responsibility for the administration of financial and personal matters previously reserved for the central administration, while at the same time administering those affairs in a way that maximizes the individual professional development, and commensurate rewards, of each faculty member. Only the future will demonstrate whether the deans and department chairmen can deal with the ambiguities of that dual role in a manner that will increase individual faculty productivity and professional satisfaction while at the same time achieving the larger corporate goals of the University, most of which tend toward such things as efficient utilization of resources.

It already has been mentioned that increasing faculty participation in University decision-making processes has been a recurring theme in the reports of recent studies of American higher education. In addition, studies that have focused exclusively on governance matters have found a tendency among large educational institutions to be overcentralized. A Carnegie Commission report in 1973 noted, in connection with a major recommendation, that "Strong centralization of authority . . . on larger campuses can delay decisions and make them less responsive to specific problems."[29] If some of the studies of higher education are correct, decentralizing and delegating processes should make a university as large as BYU not only more efficient, but they also should increase its ability to handle student concerns and faculty dissatisfaction.

Departmental faculties at BYU still do not have the degree of autonomy and authority that might be typical at other universities. For example, the revised goal definition for department chairmen adopted in 1972 provides simply that faculty with professorial rank will be involved in the process of selecting new faculty on a consultative basis and will have their

---

29. The Carnegie Commission on Higher Education, *Governance of Higher Education* (Washington: U.S. Government Printing Office, 1973), p. 15.

recommendations given careful consideration. The selection process was expected to be characterized by consensus-building rather than by formal voting procedures or by an imposition of the will of the department chairman.[30]

This illustration is given, not to show that further decentralization is likely, but to illustrate the point that BYU is likely to retain some authoritarian characteristics, probably because of its unique relationship to a Church in which hierarchical authority patterns are well-established and, indeed, honored traditions. Enough of that element of governance exists at the University that, for example, the views of the Faculty Advisory Council always will remain "advisory," and the recommendations of deans and department chairmen for budgetary, personnel, curriculum, and other matters still are subject to administrative approval. For the same reason, academic departmental governance is unlikely to become fully democratic. At the same time, however, faculty experience with the Oaks Administration thus far indicates that, while the University administration may retain ultimate authority, it will use that authority sparingly. The administration seems determined to make the governance of the University as much a participative process as possible. Moreover, the faculty as a whole seem happy with the existing blend of participation and exercise of central authority. The process appears to be working, probably more because of mutual trust and good will throughout the University community than because of the winning of hard-fought battles by factions bent on claiming their fair share of authority. If that set of attitudes and that kind of balance can be maintained, the prospects for harmonious and participative University governance in the future must be regarded as bright.

30. Dallin H. Oaks, "Annual Report to the Faculty," in *Together for Greatness,* p. 27.

47

Academic Development under Oaks

In an essay entitled "Universities and Their Function," Alfred North Whitehead wrote, "You can secure certain formal requirements, that lectures are given at stated times and that instructors and students are in attendance. But the heart of the matter lies beyond all regulation."[1] Dallin Oaks has unhesitatingly accepted Whitehead's insight as to the teaching function. In President Oaks's words, "The most important thing that happens on this campus is what goes on between the beginning and the ending of each classroom period."[2] The real potential for positive action, he believes, lies with the faculty — in the nature of things — and cannot be taken away from them.

Perhaps this comment on Oaks's philosophy of university administration helps explain why it was neither casual nor trite for him to tell his faculty in 1973 that

> I cannot acknowledge the importance of this group more authentically than to concede my awareness that the

---

1. Alfred North Whitehead, *The Aims of Education* (New York: Mentor Books, 1929), p. 99.
2. Interview of Dallin H. Oaks by Bruce C. Hafen, 17 June 1974.

> *teacher* is the only worker who is absolutely essential to a teaching institution. . . . All the rest are in support of the teaching function. I hope that concession makes none of you disdainful of the rest of us. . . .
>
> Before coming to this position, I spent ten years as a classroom teacher at the University of Chicago. . . . That ten-year experience was entirely sufficient to give me an acquaintance with the problems and joys of teaching, the demands of scholarship, and the aspirations of the faculty.
>
> The administration of a university is responsible to give leadership by identifying objectives, by structuring incentives, and by exerting encouragement and persuasion. But . . . the critical creative work of the institution is in the hands of the faculty.[3]

Given the truth of what Whitehead and Oaks acknowledge as the life-giving quality in university life, it is a reflection upon the poor tools and talents of historians generally that they are unable better to capture a description of what has been brought to, expressed, felt, and carried away from the classrooms of universities through the centuries. The same should be said of those moments beneath the trees, along the walks, and within the walls of those quiet spots where private and often inspiring conversations have sprinkled the campus. So often that is where the real torches are passed from one generation to another, where the real insight comes, from faculty to student and vice versa. But just as "The heart of the matter lies beyond all regulation," it also lies beyond our power of adequate description and documentation. Nevertheless, intimate, individual stimulation of mind and spirit has always been, and continues to be, the heart of the matter at Brigham Young University. Whatever else may have changed since 1971, that prized characteristic of life at BYU goes on unchanged.

---

3. Dallin H. Oaks, "Annual Report to the Faculty," *Excellence in Learning* (BYU Fall Faculty Workshop, 1973), BYU Archives, pp. 23-24.

Academic Goals of the Oaks Administration

These prized characteristics go on in ways that have a slightly different hue and focus than might be true elsewhere. One apt description of that difference — a view shared by many BYU faculty members — is reflected in the words of Martin B. Hickman, a former University of Southern California teacher who in 1970 became dean of the College of Social Sciences at BYU. In 1971, he told a BYU faculty group:

> Now the Church has never hidden . . . what it considers the mission of BYU to be. One would have to be illiterate or obtuse not to know that BYU exists under a different mandate than most private and all public universities. Hence, I assume that any teacher who gives consideration to teaching at BYU must also weigh the implications of that mandate. The decision to come to BYU . . . reflects ultimately an acceptance of the values on which this university rests and a desire to participate in its mission.
>
> If these are the motives which bring a teacher to BYU, then academic freedom is completely compatible with the open commitment of the university to an explicit value system. Indeed, teaching at BYU may be a means of restoring the wholeness to one's life. Those of us who have taught elsewhere are very much aware that our employment was conditional upon how successfully we camouflaged the sources of our value system — the gospel. Whatever academic freedom we had, it did not include the right to place our classwork explicitly within the overarching concepts of the gospel. Our values had to be smuggled in or deliberately excluded; we lived a dual life as scholar and Mormon, unable in the classroom to unite the two into an integral whole. That division of professional and religious life is overcome at BYU and the opportunity is thus created to restore to our lives an abiding unity. Unless this right to unite our scholarly and religious lives has a significant meaning for us, unless teaching at BYU is a flight to freedom, unless we welcome the values of the gospel with the joy of the returning

> pilgrim, the decision to come to BYU loses the heart of its meaning.[4]

One important fact, then, about student-teacher relationships at BYU is that they touch on matters both educational and religious, often in a way that affects the totality of the lives of both teachers and students. To those who value the strength that comes from that kind of perspective, BYU's uniqueness in this area may always outweigh any of its other limitations.

Understanding and highly valuing this kind of wholeness, the Oaks Administration has nevertheless taken a series of forceful steps toward strengthening the academic productivity of faculty work without losing what already exists. In his inaugural address, the new president stated that he had two primary goals. The first was to reinforce the University's drive for excellence as an academic institution; the second, to preserve the distinctive spiritual character and standards of the University. In his words:

> Our reason for *being* is to be a university. But our reason for *being a university* is to encourage and prepare young men and women to rise to their full spiritual potential as sons and daughters of God. We seek to prepare them to live and serve *in* the world, but we encourage them not to be *of* the world. The enormous resources devoted to this institution could not be justified if we did not provide a unique educational experience. What makes us unique is the spiritual dimension we provide.
>
> . . . [However,] we cannot use success in attaining our spiritual goals . . . as an alibi for failure to enjoy first-class status as a university. We must reinforce our drive for excellence in all areas of the University and persist for superiority in some. We must be conscious of all that this goal requires for distinction in teaching and research and for providing our students with intellectual experiences as challenging as they could receive anywhere.[5]

---

4. Martin B. Hickman, "Academic Freedom at Brigham Young University," address to the Association of American University Professors, BYU Chapter, Spring 1971, in the possession of Martin B. Hickman.
5. Dallin H. Oaks, "Response," *Inaugural Addresses* (Provo, Utah: Brigham Young University Press, 1971), pp. 18-19.

This statement of goals was an appropriate response to the challenge given to the new president by Harold B. Lee of the First Presidency:

> This, then, President Oaks, is your law of instruction and a guide to keep before your faculty and your students — to prepare yourself and them for the work of the ministry as they go out to take their places in worldly affairs.
>
> We pass on to you, also, the divine admonition to have those under your tutelage "study and learn, and become acquainted with all good books, and with languages, tongues, and peoples" (D&C 90:15). Brigham Young University, indeed the whole educational system of this Church, has been established to the end that all pure knowledge must be gained by our people, handed down to our posterity, and given to all men.
>
> We charge you to give constant stimulation to these budding scientists and scholars in all fields and to the urge to push back further and further into the realms of the unknown.[6]

As if responding to this, just as President Wilkinson had responded twenty years earlier to the prophetic prediction that his administration would be an era of great growth for the school,[7] the emphasis during the Oaks Administration has been on academic excellence. Inevitably, the focus of that emphasis has been primarily on the faculty: "We must continue to increase our faculty's qualifications . . . since the faculty is obviously the key to the excellence of a university."[8]

Faculty Profile, 1975

Data on file in the University's personnel records provide the basis for drawing a statistical profile of the typical BYU faculty member in 1975 and a comparison with his counter-

---

6. Harold B. Lee, "Installation of and Charge to the President," *Inaugural Addresses,* pp. 13-14.
7. "Report of Proceedings of the Inauguration of Ernest Leroy Wilkinson," *The Messenger,* November 1951, p. 16.
8. Dallin H. Oaks, "Response," *Inaugural Addresses,* p. 19.

Harold B. Lee, President of
the LDS Church from 1972
to 1973.

part in earlier years. There is obviously no single prototype, and information from earlier years is available only on selected subjects; however, the following generalizations show some recent trends:

BYU's typical teacher in 1975 is male, was born in Utah, attended BYU as a college student, and then obtained a doctoral degree at some university outside his native state. Perhaps having some experience between the completion of his graduate work and his return to Provo, he has been a BYU faculty member for only nine years and is the parent of four children. He is one of 1,182 full-time faculty members, a group six times the size of the full time faculty in 1951.[9] Fifty-six percent of his colleagues have undergraduate degrees from BYU, and seventy-seven percent of his colleagues who hold doctoral degrees (or sixty percent of the faculty) obtained them from universities outside the State of Utah. By comparison, in 1951, eighty-five percent of the faculty had undergraduate degrees from BYU, but closer to ninety-four percent of the faculty who held doctoral degrees had obtained them from universities outside the State of Utah.

The percentage of faculty members who hold doctorate degrees has increased from twenty-six percent of the full-time faculty in 1951 to sixty percent of the full-time faculty in 1975. The typical faculty member in 1975 could hold faculty rank at the assistant professor, associate professor, or full professor levels, since the 1975 faculty is almost equally divided among these three levels, except for the fifteen percent of the full-time faculty who are ranked as instructors. By contrast, in 1951,[10] forty percent of the full-time faculty held the rank of instructor and another thirty percent held the rank of assist-

---

9. Almost forty percent of the 1975 faculty have been at the University less than five years. Some 535 of the 1,182 full-time faculty members are Utah-born, while the remainder represent thirty-eight other states and twelve foreign countries in their places of birth.
10. Information concerning 1962 and prior years is taken from *A Unique Faculty* (Brigham Young University, May 1962), cpm 30b, box 2, BYU Archives. Statistics for 1975 are based on a computer analysis of University personnel records, 27 February 1975.

ant professor. The remaining thirty percent of the faculty in 1951 were divided between associate professors (ten percent) and professors (twenty percent).

The University's typical teacher in 1975 has not changed much in some ways since 1951. The average age is forty-four in 1975, while it was just under forty-two in 1951. The number of faculty who are married has also remained constant at a level just under ninety percent. Among those who are married, the average number of children is 3.8 in 1975, a slight increase over 1951, when the average number was 3.19. The overwhelming majority of faculty members in 1975, as in the past, hold some kind of position in The Church of Jesus Christ of Latter-day Saints. Some 6.5 percent of the faculty serve in general Church positions, either on committee assignments, as Regional Representatives, or on general boards in auxiliary organizations. The remainder hold positions in resident stakes and wards or in the student stakes and branches organized on campus.

This kind of statistical profiling may show some general tendencies, but it probably fails to reflect the rich backgrounds and diverse experiences of a full-time faculty that numbers almost 1,200 people. As stated by President Oaks in his opening remarks to the BYU student body in 1971:

> The world is all about us. You students come from every state in the union and from more than sixty foreign countries. Almost a third of you have had two years' missionary service, living among the peoples of this and foreign lands. Our faculty has been educated in almost every major university in America and in many other great universities of the world. Of course, all of us can benefit from further broadening of our experience, but the remarkable variety of living experiences represented on this cosmopolitan campus does suggest that most of us have had ample opportunity to be exposed to the world and its problems.[11]

---

11. Dallin H. Oaks, "A New President Speaks to BYU," *Speeches of the Year* (Provo, Utah: Brigham Young University Press, 1971), p. 15.

With this philosophy and faculty, the basic thrust of changes in organization of the Oaks Administration was to increase the potential for increased quality in the fulfillment of the faculty's special role. The decentralization of authority and responsibility already mentioned was designed in large part to enable front-line evaluation and stimulation of individual faculty productivity.

Role Clarification and Professional Development

A number of specific additional sources of reinforcement for individual faculty productivity has also emerged. A theme that runs through all of these developments has been clarification of roles and expectations, not only of the administration, the deans, and the department chairmen, but also of individual faculty members. Perhaps the most symbolic indication of this clarification is the formalizing of an annual interview policy during 1973-74, under which a department chairman or dean now has a "stewardship interview" with each faculty member at least annually. Presumably, some kind of informal exchanges have been taking place between teachers and their file leaders for years, but this formalizing policy was intended to force a more specific definition of expectations on the part of each faculty member with the person who would be responsible for evaluating and assisting in the fulfillment of those expectations. One objective of the annual interview is to review each teacher's commitment to the basic goals of the University. In a broader sense, however, the interview typifies a kind of ongoing process that was described in the report of the general University committee on conflicts of interest:

> Each academic department chairman . . . should assume the affirmative responsibility of understanding the complete context of each faculty member's work, including the peculiarities of his family situation; his general and specific professional aspirations; his church and civic commitments and interests; his preferences and his talents for teaching, research, and administrative work; as well as a thorough ongoing awareness of all factors that

> bear on his productivity. As the chairman and the faculty member engage in the continuous sharing process implied by this description of their relationship, each faculty member's employment understanding with the university will be defined and redefined as required by the circumstances. Only when such a relationship exists will it be possible for the faculty member and his chairman to define together the ways in which the faculty member might spend his time most effectively.[12]

Contrary to some assumptions, the purpose of these interviews and the evaluation process which they include has not been mere "publish or perish" jawboning, which has never been the approach taken at BYU. BYU policy has traditionally been that excellence in teaching is more important than research. However, a more flexible approach has emerged, which originated with a statement of policy consensus by the Faculty Advisory Council in early 1973 to the effect that faculty members should concentrate their efforts on teaching or research, according to their interests and talents.[13] As that policy was developed through consultation with the Faculty Advisory Council, the academic deans, and the administration, the idea emerged that faculty members should have some choice about the kind of emphasis they would individually like to establish for themselves. Thus, each faculty member may ultimately work out a different mix of teaching loads, administrative work, research time, and other projects, depending upon his unique circumstances as evaluated mutually by himself and his department chairman. In one college, several models have been suggested among which faculty members might choose — these include the teacher-teacher, the teacher-administrator, and the teacher-research scholar.[14]

---

12. Report of the University Committee on Conflicts of Interest, 6 May 1974, pp. 6-7.
13. Faculty Advisory Council Minutes, 8 March 1973, Dallin H. Oaks Presidential Papers, box 55, folder 9, BYU Archives.
14. Dallin H. Oaks, "Annual Report to the Faculty," *Excellence in Learning,* pp. 25-26.

Professional Development Program

A related set of developments has resulted in the creation of the Professional Development Program. This program grew out of the work of a committee, chaired by Dr. Marion Bennion of the College of Family Living, appointed in the summer of 1973 by the administration and the Faculty Advisory Council for the purpose of evaluating the effectiveness of the University's sabbatical leave program. Under that program, faculty members had generally assumed that virtually every faculty member had the right every seven years to take a one-year leave from his regular teaching duties at half salary (or one-half year at full salary) in order to pursue some project of professional interest. After substantial interaction between that committee and other University faculty members and administrators, the committee submitted a set of recommendations that boiled down to a proposed elimination of the leave program as it had been known so that the financial resources represented by the program could more flexibly and intelligently be administered. Expanding vigorously on the proposals of the committee report, the administration, the Faculty Advisory Council, and the Deans' Council ultimately applied the committee's concept to three major existing areas of financial resources — compensated leaves, research funds, and adjustments in teaching loads. The expanded proposal was submitted by the administration to a general faculty meeting in April of 1974, where it was — to the surprise of many — approved unanimously by a standing vote of the University faculty.[15] It was subsequently approved by the Board of Trustees.

As adopted, the program provides that the professional development of each faculty member is his individual responsibility. Teaching and creative work are thought to be the basic components of what is meant by "professional development." Each faculty member is to design his own plan for such development, including the kind of teaching, research projects,

15. University General Faculty Meeting Minutes, 11 April 1974.

off-campus leaves, and whatever else he believes will best fulfill his professional objectives. The test for the success of that fulfillment is demonstrated by quality rather than mere effort. Individual plans must of course be integrated with departmental and college plans, guidelines, and resources. The program also provides that all funds previously budgeted for sabbatical leaves and all special research funds (previously administered by a central University research office) are now administered by deans and department chairmen. In addition, deans and department chairmen have been given increased flexibility in the assignment of individual teaching loads.

As a result, department chairmen now have significant freedom and responsibility for designing for each faculty member the best possible combination of resources, with a view to maximizing two significant objectives — customized individual professional development and optimum utilization of existing resources. The relatively rigid presumptions that formerly existed regarding teaching loads, compensated leave arrangements, summer research projects, and other such matters are now the tools rather than the masters of the department chairmen and their faculty.

Whether the hoped-for benefits of the Professional Development Program are realized depends significantly upon the ability of individual faculty members and department chairmen to make wise judgments concerning the best use of their primary resources — time and money. Basic to the entire concept is the idea that compensated leaves, released time, and summer research grants are not a reward for past services, but a stimulus for future improvement and development that is beneficial both to the faculty member and the University. The size of the financial resources involved in this combined program is indicated by the University's proposed preliminary budget for the 1975-76 academic year, which allocated an amount in excess of eight percent of aggregate faculty salaries for professional development — leaves, support funds for faculty research programs during the academic year, summer research fellowships, special research funds for interdepartmental programs, and other research salaries.[16]

Salary Increases and Promotions

Another significant trend running through the developments of the kind described above has been the premise that salary increases and promotions for individual faculty members should relate directly to their own productivity, as measured by their qualitative success in achieving the objectives of their own professional development program. Although salaries were always intended to be related to competence, the hope of these policy changes is that the combination of more specific standards, individualized planning, and decentralized salary authority will make rewards even more commensurate with merit. The discretionary administration of merit increase funds by deans and department chairmen is the key method by which greater efficiency, as well as greater individual incentives, are to be made available for the professional academic work of the faculty.

These policies were obviously related to, and to a large extent dependent upon, the decentralization of authority mentioned in the previous chapter. However, it soon became apparent that the accountability standards accompanying the delegation of authority to academic administrators were uncomfortably vague. Moreover, only limited, thorough, ongoing monitoring and evaluation functions were being performed by the central administration. Accordingly, in late 1974, a special task force was appointed under the chairmanship of Assistant Academic Vice-President Leo Vernon to develop guidelines and procedures leading to a comprehensive reporting and evaluation system. The work of the task force is expected to produce practical and specific accountability standards designed to aid the administration, deans, department chairmen, and those with similar duties in their attempts to measure and reward productivity. Evaluation

---

16. Robert J. Smith, associate academic vice-president, to Thomas H. Brown, chairman of the Faculty Advisory Council, 11 December 1974.

standards are likely to focus upon overall college and departmental productivity, as well as upon individual faculty teaching and research.

Retirement Policies

Several other University policies relating to faculty members have been clarified, developed, and formalized. At the time of Oaks's appointment the president already had the authority to retire faculty members at the age of sixty-five, but Oaks's predecessors had not exercised that authority unless they felt the teacher in question was no longer able to perform intellectually, spiritually, or physically. Soon after Oaks's arrival, the Board of Trustees adopted a more fixed retirement policy, under which virtually all employees and administrators are retired from full-time activity at the end of the year in which they reach sixty-five years of age. This basic policy was in the process of being adopted Church-wide prior to President Oaks's appointment, but it fell to him to enforce it at BYU — although this was a much easier rule to enforce than judging the qualifications of each person at the age of sixty-five. Although the relative inflexibility of the retirement policy caused understandable ripples of dissatisfaction when the policy was first being implemented, acceptance of the policy has not posed a major problem. Surprisingly, by the simple application of that retirement policy, it became necessary during the first four years of Dallin Oaks's presidency for him to appoint five new deans, as well as other administrative heads in the University's management, thereby giving him a highly unusual opportunity for appointing people of his own selection to fill key positions in a newly decentralized organization.

At almost the same time as the new retirement policy became operational, the University's retirement plan for its employees came under the supervision of the newly organized Deseret Mutual Benefit Association (DMBA), a Church-owned and operated employee benefit plan for all employees of the LDS Church which has handled the University employee insurance benefits program since 1970. Previously, the University employees' retirement benefits had been administered by a large private retirement plan organization. Although the change in plans seemed to offer greatly improved total benefits, there was substantial dissatisfaction with the originally proposed fifteen-year vesting requirement of the DMBA plan. In early 1975, DMBA announced a reduction in the vesting requirement to ten years of continuous service, which makes the benefits of the plan more advantageous to University employees.

Continuing Faculty Status

After several years of rapid growth, the size of the University's faculty has stabilized, and the administration is developing a set of long-range policies designed to stimulate faculty productivity for people who are likely to remain members of the faculty for many years. The specter of stagnation under such circumstances has haunted other universities, which have recently awakened to the realization that after enjoying several years of the luxury of regularly appointing new people to their growing faculties, expansion is at a standstill. They now face the prospect of seeing those same people "tenured-in" by tenure policies that were originally designed to maximize academic freedom, but which have the practical effect of guaranteeing job security in ways that make it difficult for university administrations to put teeth into their policies for faculty improvement and their competency standards.

At first, the problem of tenure did not seem to portend this negative risk for BYU because there has never been formal tenure here. The Wilkinson Administration had previously evolved an informal procedure in which a faculty member received a new contract annually for the first three years and after that merely a notification of his new salary. This was an indication that the faculty member was doing satisfactory work, but the policy against legal tenure continued. President Oaks, however, felt that the terms of faculty status at BYU should be formalized, and therefore he announced the following policy to the faculty in 1972:

> Members of the faculty are appointed by the Board of Trustees upon the recommendation of the President of the University. Unless otherwise provided hereafter, all faculty appointments are for a period of one year, renewable in successive years with the approval of the President. The initial three years of service of any person when first appointed to professorial rank (Assistant Professor, Associate Professor, or Professor) shall be a probationary period during which the faculty member's performance will be reviewed annually and discussed in an interview with the department chairman, dean, or academic vice-president. At the conclusion of the three-year probationary period, the faculty member will either be advised that his or her appointment will not be renewed, that it will be extended for a period of not more than three years, or that he or she will be given appointment forms that signify the attainment of continuing faculty status. Continuing faculty status signifies that a faculty member has successfully completed the probationary period and that he or she is recognized as a continuing member of the faculty.[17]

At Oaks's suggestion, the Board also adopted the policy that faculty members who have attained continuing faculty status may be terminated only by the Board upon such procedures as the Board should specify. Other faculty members may be terminated by the president. Prior to this time, the president had the authority to terminate the appointments of all faculty, including those having the equivalent of continuing faculty status.

As a practical matter, the tradition had developed at BYU that the most likely reason for the termination of a faculty member was his failure to observe the principles of personal conduct required of all faculty and students at the University. It has been the hope of the Oaks Administration that continu-

17. Dallin H. Oaks, "Annual Report to the Faculty," *Together for Greatness* (Brigham Young University, 1972), pp. 30-31.

ing faculty status would not be granted as a matter of course to those who observe the school's conduct standards, but would be granted only when a dean and department chairman had also made a substantive professional judgment according to rigorous productivity standards. To date, the standards applied in the different colleges have varied to such an extent that it cannot yet be said that the continuing faculty status concept consistently requires the level of performance that might be expected of new faculty members at a university of comparable quality elsewhere.

Thus, in a sense the current BYU approach has most of the disadvantages of a normal tenure system without the concomitant advantages, except in a few colleges. The principal disadvantage lies in the difficulty of terminating an experienced faculty member for reasons relating to his or her competency, whether or not the experienced teacher has established his or her professional standing. At the same time, neither the productivity leverage nor the increased hiring selectivity usually made possible by stiff tenure standards is available when the test for granting continuing faculty status is primarily longevity and personal conduct. Some BYU faculty believe that the brotherhood relationship implied by the common bond of the Church among the faculty appropriately precludes the kind of harsh judgments sometimes made in decisions denying tenure on other campuses. However, the present approach runs the risk of limiting the flexibility of academic departments in improving their personnel during a period of little or no growth. In order to avoid just that dilemma, two leading studies of higher education in the early 1970s have recommended that only a fixed fraction of full-time faculty members be granted tenure or its equivalent.[18] It would appear that with a limit on future growth and a faculty

---

18. The Committee for Economic Development recommends that only about half of the available faculty positions should be tenured, in order to preserve appointment flexibility during low growth periods (The Carnegie Commission on Higher Education, *Governance of Higher Education* [New York: McGraw-Hill, 1973], pp. 57-58).

having an average age of forty-four, BYU's success in promoting professional productivity will depend upon its effectiveness in employing incentives and enforcing standards to stimulate existing personnel without requiring termination for incompetent performance.

Overlaps in University and Faculty Interest

In the process of clarifying roles and expectations for its personnel, the Oaks Administration has pushed hard for the adoption of policies relating to overlapping faculty and University interests in areas such as copyrights, patents, and conflicts of interest. Agreement upon a formalized basic patent policy, whereby employees could participate in the benefits from patented work, was relatively easy to establish because of past informal practice. The copyright policy became more difficult to establish since there were fewer guidelines and assumptions upon which faculty and administrative personnel were able to agree. In the fall of 1971, a Creative Works Committee was appointed, working in conjunction with the Faculty Advisory Council and chaired by Leo Vernon, director of research. After working through more than twenty drafts of a copyright policy, the committee finally agreed on a concept that would depend to a large extent upon individual negotiation between a University employee and his supervisor. The policy recommended by the committee seemed to them to strike a reasonable balance between the need to give incentive to individuals as a means of stimulating creative work while at the same time ensuring that the University's financial interest in the work products of its employees would be protected. The principles involved in the new copyright policy were not formally adopted until 12 April 1973.[19]

In conceptual agreement with the copyright policy, the University has also adopted a "residual rights" policy designed to extend the copyright policy to situations in which

19. Dallin H. Oaks, "Statement Concerning Copyright Policy," Dallin H. Oaks Presidential Papers, 12 April 1973, box 38, folder 11, BYU Archives.

employees create media presentations and other instructional tools that have commercial value. The adoption of this policy grew out of the work of the newly organized Division of Instructional Services.[20]

In the summer of 1973, an ad hoc University committee under the chairmanship of Bruce C. Hafen was appointed to develop a set of University policies dealing with conflicts of interest. That committee likewise found that there were differing general attitudes among University employees, some of whom felt the University should not interfere with attempts by employees to supplement University incomes on their own time. On the other hand, some believed that the apparently long-standing practice of BYU employees earning supplemental income by work outside their University employment seriously undermined the academic mission of the University. This committee's approach also gravitated toward the notion of individual negotiation between University employees and their immediate supervisors. The committee's recommendations emphasized the importance of full disclosure on the part of employees to their supervisors so that an essentially positive attitude might develop toward the working out of problems in which University and personal interests overlap. Awareness throughout the campus of conflict of interest problems has been heightened by the work of this committee, although its specific policies are still in the process of being defined by various colleges and administrative areas.

Research

Increased concern with professional productivity has sharpened the focus on the role of research efforts among University faculty members, even though BYU's role is essentially that of an undergraduate school. Although no fixed ratio of graduate to undergraduate students existed when Oaks came, the administration has since developed a guideline limiting the total number of graduate students to

20. More details on the Division of Instructional Services are given later in this chapter.

approximately 2,000 in a total student body of 25,000. Excluding law students, who might be regarded as professional school students rather than graduate students in the traditional sense, the projected ceiling on graduate student enrollment would be roughly 1,500. These figures, as a proportion of the total student enrollment, give Brigham Young University a very high ratio of undergraduate to graduate students in comparison with other major American universities.

A recent study of certain attitudes at a large number of American universities arrived at three factors for measuring the extent of a university's interest in research output. These three criteria were the volume of contract research in the university, the percentage of graduate students in the student body, and the number of doctoral degrees awarded. On the question of the number of graduate students in the total student body, the universities included in this study ranged from a high of sixty-five percent to a low of ten percent.[21] The target figure of 2,000 at BYU is eight percent of the total enrollment, putting the University at the extreme low end of this scale. It does not fare much better when measured by the other two criteria. The current administration hopes that a reduction in the number of graduate students will enable concentration on quality in those departments capable of conducting superior graduate work. It has been a source of frustration to some faculty members over the years since graduate programs were first established at BYU that the school's best qualified graduates tend to seek their graduate training elsewhere. As a result, there has been some agitation for an increased emphasis on graduate work in order to increase the overall academic quality of the university's programs by attracting those faculty and superior students who would be involved in graduate programs of recognized quality. For the present, however, graduate work will continue on a

21. Edward Gross and Paul V. Grambsch, *Changes in University Organization, 1964-1971* (New York: McGraw-Hill, 1974), pp. 88-89.

relatively small scale and be limited to those departments best able to perform superior graduate work.

One organizational change made to improve the quality of at least three graduate programs was the establishment in May 1975 of a Graduate School of Management under the deanship of Merrill J. Bateman, who had also recently been appointed dean of the College of Business. A former faculty member in the University's Department of Economics, Dr. Bateman was serving as a vice-president of M&M/Mars Corporation at the time of his appointment. The new school will become the third graduate entity at BYU, the other two being the Graduate School and the Law School. Included in its programs are three master's degree programs formerly in the Graduate School — the Master of Business Administration, Master of Public Accountancy, and the Master of Accountancy. Other professional programs that emphasize management skills may be included as the program of the new school develops.

In addition, the master's degree program in library science was given the status of a professional school in 1975, with the creation of a School of Library and Information Sciences. The first acting director of the new school was Maurice P. Marchant, replacing H. Thane Johnson, former director of the master's program, who returned to full-time teaching. The library school will continue to report to the dean of the Graduate School.

The creation of these entities soon after the creation of a Law School indicates a continuing desire by the University administration to give special emphasis in its graduate training programs to professional disciplines that affect policy and management in both the public and private sectors. The University's Graduate School is left with responsibility for the selective administration of programs that are more in the nature of traditional academic training than training for the professions and professional management.[22]

---

22. "Formation Announced of New Graduate School," BYU *Daily Universe,* 20 May 1975.

Merrill J. Bateman, named dean of the new Graduate School of Management in 1975.

Maurice P. Marchant, named dean of the new School of Library and Information Sciences in 1975.

On the whole, Brigham Young University is and will likely remain predominantly an undergraduate university, without the support of graduate work at the scale involved in major research universities. The question might therefore be raised whether a serious premium should be placed on original faculty research. When an education writer for the *Los Angeles Times* put that general question to President Oaks in 1974, the president replied:

> We are predominantly an undergraduate institution. Ninety percent of our students are undergraduates, and it would take a considerable force to move us away from undergraduate education.
>
> But I also believe that in order to have proper teaching, you need to have a lively, creative, creating faculty and that is what we have set out to achieve.[23]

With these qualifications and purposes in mind, creative work has still been an important ingredient in the growing emphasis on professional development as a corollary to good teaching. Once responsibility for the administration of research funds designated for support of faculty research projects was transferred to deans and department chairmen, Leo P. Vernon, former director of the centralized Research Division, was named assistant academic vice-president for research. Under his direction, the Research Division has continued to monitor the use of these funds and determine the budget allocations of each academic college for research purposes on the basis of the quantity and quality of research done during the previous year. All proposals for external funding continue to be relayed through the Research Division in order to provide the kind of control necessary to maintain the administration's policy on its use of research funds. Several indicators show that interest in research has increased markedly during the early 1970s. For example, 157 proposals were submitted through the Research Division for external research funds (those not a part of the University budget) in

---

23. *Los Angeles Times,* 8 August 1974, p. 33.

1973. In 1974, that number increased to 247. The amount of nonfederal external research funds has increased threefold from 1970 to 1974.[24]

In addition to increased activity involving individual and departmental research projects, several interdisciplinary centers have also been established during recent years in response to University and Church interests, as well as national problems. These research units have included a group of faculty members from the Physics and Mathematics Departments engaged in an intensive study of nuclear fusion as a potential energy source. The Center for Health and Environmental Studies, involving faculty members from the departments of Civil Engineering, Botany, Zoology, Microbiology, Sociology, Animal Science, and Geography, has been focusing on such problems as parasite control, pesticide pollution, missionary health, and the environmental impacts of power plants in Utah. Mention has been made elsewhere of the Charles Redd Center for Western Studies, which involves faculty from the History Department and other disciplines related to Western American studies.[25] In addition, working with the benefit of the largest research grant ever awarded to BYU, the Institute for Computer Uses in Education (the TICCIT Project) has developed a nationally recognized program of individualized, computer-assisted courses in English and mathematics.

The University's Language Research Center and the expansion of the Language Training Mission[26] have made Brigham Young a national leader in both teaching and research involving foreign languages. One notable project presently under way is the development of methods for computer-assisted foreign language translation, which has important implications, both for the increasingly internationalized Mormon Church and for other international

---

24. Martha Cummings, "BYU Research Projects Flourish," *Monday Magazine,* 2 December 1974, p. 12.
25. *See* Volume 3, chapter 41.
26. *See* chapter 54.

applications. The interdepartmental Institute of Ancient Studies[27] has given the University increased capability for evaluating a new outpouring of ancient manuscripts having both historical and religious implications. The Center for Business and Economic Research in the College of Business has stepped up its efforts in response to the needs of local and regional planners. The Center for High Pressure Studies was established to extend the pioneering work in this area done by Dr. Tracy Hall. The previously established Thermochemical Center continues to be very active in selected areas of chemistry and biochemistry. And finally, the interdisciplinary Family Research Center organized in 1971-72 has initiated several scholarly projects on the large and important subject of family study, including a major review of moral development and ethical reasoning in children.

One other indicator of increased research and writing efforts by University faculty has been the striking increase in activity at BYU Press, which was publishing only five books per year in 1971; in 1974, the Press published thirty-three titles.[28] The dollar-volume of books sold has increased almost tenfold, and one nonfictional work, *Roughing It Easy,* reached the *New York Times* bestseller list.[29] A large fraction of these books are the results of efforts by University faculty members in their specialties.

The Federal Funds Problem

The University's heightened interest in research efforts has come into conflict with its long-standing policy of remaining independent from the use of federal funds.[30] As President

---

27. *See* chapter 49.
28. Interview of Ernest L. Olson, director of the University Press, April 1975, by George R. Ryskamp. As a further indication of the scholarly emphasis, as well as the overall quality of the work of the University Press, it was approved in May 1975 as one of the sixty-five major university presses which comprise the membership of the Association of American University Presses (BYU *Daily Universe,* 15 May 1975, p. 10).
29. Ernest L. Olson to Bruce C. Hafen, 9 September 1975.
30. *See* Volume 3, chapter 41.

Oaks pointed out to the faculty in April 1973, the sharp increase in the total federal grants and contracts awarded the University faculty is a tribute to their increasing competency, but it also stands as a serious threat to the independence of the institution. As mentioned elsewhere,[31] since the independence of private higher education is essential to the performance of its unique function, any threats that undermine that independence must be taken seriously. At the same time, the availability of government funds for research projects to a faculty that has been stimulated to greater research efforts is also a concern. Nevertheless, the Oaks Administration has formalized a policy of minimizing its reliance on federal research funds.[32] The gist of the University policy, which was announced to the faculty on 12 April 1973, was summarized by President Oaks in one sentence: "We are limiting the amount and duration of federally-financed research at BYU in order to safeguard our independence as a private, Church-related educational institution."[33] After explaining with some care to the faculty all the reasons why federal financing posed a threat to the independence of the University,[34] the president further stated that efforts to obtain private research funds had been substantially increased.[35] In addition, budget support has been obtained

---

31. *See* chapter 52.
32. This policy is a radical departure from the national norm. For example, in 1976 it was reported that the University of California received $245.8 million in federal contract and grant funds (Ralph Kinney Bennett, "Colleges Under the Federal Gun," *Reader's Digest,* May 1976, p. 128).
33. BYU Faculty Meeting Minutes, 12 April 1973.
34. *See* chapter 52.
35. Substantial progress has been made in the area of private funding. Except for the large Institute for Computer Users in Education (TICCIT) grant in 1972, federal funding has remained at an essentially constant level of $1.5 million since 1970. Taking into account the high rate of inflation since 1971, the University's actual reliance on federal monies is declining. In addition, private funding has increased steadily from 1970. In 1974, private funding accounted for $1.61 million, or fifty-one percent of the external research funds from all sources.

from the Trustees of the University to promote faculty research activities. Further, the University has cooperated with independent research organizations, such as the Eyring Research Institute, founded in 1973. This corporate entity, owned and operated independently from the University, makes application for federal grants and fulfills its research commitments through the part-time use of qualified scholars who are currently employed at BYU and other institutions of higher education in the State of Utah. By more ardent pursuit of private funding, increased internal research funding from the Board of Trustees, and work with private research foundations, the University has considerably broadened research opportunities without increasing reliance on potentially dangerous federal programs.

Teaching and Curriculum Revision

All the developments regarding attempts to improve the quality and productivity of the BYU faculty have a singular objective — the improvement of undergraduate as well as graduate teaching. At the same time, the tenor of the early 1970s at BYU seems to bring a pervasive expectation that both the students and the faculty will develop more serious and productive commitments to academic quality. If an evaluation of actual teaching and learning throughout the University community seems missing from these pages, that is because of the difficulty involved in making any kind of reasonably objective measurement rather than because the teaching and learning are thought to be less important than the proliferation of committees and formalized policies. Having acknowledged that limitation, there are nevertheless strong evidences that the Oaks Administration is highly concerned with what happens in the classroom and has taken affirmative steps to improve certain aspects of it, even if the matter is essentially "beyond all regulation."

One of the new president's first initiatives in this area was a request for a Universitywide review of the entire academic offering, including an evaluation of curriculum, majors, general education requirements, and degrees being awarded. In launching an orderly review of the entire curriculum, the University's Curriculum Council was reorganized, under the continued chairmanship of Dr. John H. Gardner, into a smaller body with greater policy-making powers. The previous Curriculum Council had consisted of one representative from each college, and the primary function of the committee was to review requests for new courses. Under the new organization, powers were vested in a seven-person council, assisted by an adviser appointed from each academic college. In addition to evaluating new curriculum proposals, the council took on the further task of encouraging a revision of the entire University curriculum. The administration directed each academic department to examine its departmental course offerings with a view to decreasing the offering by twenty-five percent. While the Curriculum Council was to encourage that action, implementation responsibility was given directly to the deans and department chairmen so that they and their faculties would be forced to evaluate those items in the existing course offerings that could not be justified under objective criteria to be adopted by each department. The rationale for this approach to curriculum review was set forth in the summary of Curriculum Council actions dated 21 November 1972:

> With the indication from the administration that our overall budget is not to increase (in constant dollars) in future years, if we are to continue to build toward ... greatness ... we must do so by thoroughly scrutinizing what we are doing, cutting out that part which we feel is dispensible and putting the money saved into other things which ... can move us more effectively in the direction we should be going. The best judgment of the departments and the [Curriculum Council] must be brought to bear on these matters. It is the Council's desire that proposals for change be initiated at the grass roots rather than being imposed from above.[36]

36. "Summary of Curriculum Council Actions, July 1972-December 1972," p. 14.

As the curriculum revision process continued, the requirements for departmental majors were also reexamined, as were all two-year associate degree programs. It has been the president's view that available majors, as well as requirements for majors, should have some clear relationship to career opportunities or graduate study, insofar as judgments of that kind are possible. Indicative of that view was the administration's decision in 1972 to terminate the major in genealogy, on the grounds that there was simply insufficient employment demand for persons with that kind of training. Genealogy courses continued to be offered in order to give that instruction a broader impact that is not necessarily vocational.[37] Another illustration of this attitude was the University's decision in 1972 to place a quota on the number of persons who could become degree-seeking candidates in the undergraduate College of Education, due to the unusual oversupply of elementary and secondary teachers.[38]

Upon the retirement of Dean Ernest C. Jeppsen in the fall of 1972, the colleges of Industrial and Technical Education and Physical and Engineering Sciences were reorganized. The Technical Institute was discontinued, and its various two-year programs were transferred to closely related colleges. The four engineering departments, along with the Department of Technology and the Department of Industrial Education, became the new College of Engineering Sciences and Technology, with Armin J. Hill as dean. The remaining science departments — Chemistry, Geology, and Physics — and the departments of Mathematics and Statistics, in addition to the Department of Computer Science (which previously had not belonged to an academic college), formed the new College of Physical and Mathematical Science, with physics professor Jae R. Ballif as dean.

Four-year programs in electronics technology, design and

37. *See* Dallin H. Oaks, "Annual Report to the Faculty," *Together for Greatness,* p. 25.

38. "Cuts Imposed on Education Majors," BYU *Daily Universe,* 8 August 1972.

Armin J. Hill, named dean
of the new College of
Engineering Sciences and
Technology in 1972.

Jae R. Ballif, named dean of the new College of Physical and Mathematical Sciences in 1972.

graphics technology, and manufacturing technology had been developed in the College of Industrial and Technical Education under the direction of Dean Jeppsen. The reorganization placed these engineering-related technical programs in the same college as the traditionally more theoretical engineering disciplines. The growth of four-year technical degree programs in other colleges since 1967 reflects the increasing overlapping between what had traditionally been thought of as "technology" as distinguished from "engineering." A blending of the practical and theoretical underpinnings of the two fields at BYU has been facilitated by these department and major realignments.

The new College of Engineering Sciences and Technology moved into the University's new engineering building (authorized by the Board in 1969) in the fall of 1973. While the building had been designed prior to the combination of the two programs, last minute modifications made possible a joint use of the building. The larger lab needs of the technology department have resulted in some overcrowding in the new building; however, research in the engineering fields has been increased substantially by the use of the new facility.

Over the years, several of the two-year programs leading to an associate degree within the College of Industrial and Technical Education had become increasingly similar to academic programs in other colleges, thus necessitating other changes during the reorganization. In the area of nursing, a student could pursue a two-year terminal degree (sufficient to qualify one to become a Registered Nurse) in the College of Industrial and Technical Education and then find it necessary to start from the beginning of the four-year nursing program in the College of Nursing if advanced studies were desired. After the reorganization of the colleges, the two-year nursing program was integrated into the four-year program, both within the College of Nursing, so that a student could terminate with an associate degree after two years or continue without loss of progress toward a baccalaureate degree in nursing. Similar integration of related training programs took place in such areas as business (secretarial) education. At the same time, the president reemphasized the need for regular academic departments to design two-year associate degree programs "as a recognition of skills gained and as an honorable exit point for a student who, for one reason or another, finds it inadvisable or unnecessary to continue to a full baccalaureate program."[39] The emphasis on associate degree programs was an appropriate way of dealing with the traditionally high dropout rate of BYU undergraduates.[40] By the summer of 1974 the total number of associate degrees awarded by the various colleges had doubled, from 229 in 1971 to 455 in 1974.[41]

Some faculty members were concerned that developments such as these indicated the emergence of priorities for the University that were too vocation-oriented, thus raising the long-standing debate about how much a university should concern itself with the specific vocational transferability of what it provides to its students.[42] However, concern on that

---

39. Dallin H. Oaks, "Annual Report to the Faculty," *Together for Greatness,* p. 24.
40. *See* the discussion concerning this problem in volume 3, chapter 37. Even as recently as 1974 it was reported that more than one thousand students leave the University after two years and never return to any college or university (Dallin H. Oaks, "Annual Report to the Faculty," *A Wise Steward* [Brigham Young University Press, 1974], p. 10).
41. Dallin H. Oaks, "Outline of Administrative Instructions," BYU Administrators Leadership Seminar, 9 July 1974, Exhibit 15.
42. Some students of higher education, including education at Brigham Young University, have been concerned with what they perceive to be an overemphasis on vocational training at the expense of the intellectual development that emphasizes understanding, creativity, and sensitivity without regard to occupational interests. BYU scholar Hugh Nibley, for example, has felt that "the authorities have tended to delegate the business of learning to . . . those others (who) have been only too glad to settle for the outward show, the easy and flattering forms, trappings, and ceremonies of education. Worse still, they have chosen business-oriented, career-minded . . . programs in preference to the strenuous, critical . . . mind-stretching exercises that Brigham Young recommended. . . . As a result, whenever we move out of our tiny, busy orbits of administration and display, we find ourselves in a terrifying intellectual vacuum" (High Nibley, "Educating the Saints: A Brigham Young Mosaic," *BYU Studies,* Autumn 1970, p. 86).

point has not yet developed to a material degree.

College of General Studies and the General Education Revision

The development of a new program for general education has been given high priority because of "grave concerns about the overall quality of our existing general education effort."[43] The foundations for an extensive reevaluation of the University's general education offering were laid in June 1972, when the General College was reorganized and its name was changed to the "College of General Studies." Retiring Dean Lester Whetten was replaced by C. Terry Warner, former chairman of the Philosophy Department and director of the Honors Program. In addition to retaining its departments of American Indian Education, Career Education, and General Education, the reorganized college was given responsibility for administering the Honors Program (formerly a separate entity that reported directly to the academic vice-president), the Philosophy Department (formerly in the College of Religious Instruction), and the two ROTC units at BYU. The administration gave Dean Warner a specific charge to develop a new concept of general education. A General Education Council representing a cross-section of the academic colleges was appointed to begin working toward the adoption of a totally revised general education program.

In the meantime, all of the University's diverse efforts in vocational and career counseling (as distinguished from academic counseling of students who had selected a major field, which was treated as "college advisement") were brought under the supervision of a central committee to coordinate them with the Career Education programs within the College of General Studies. The Career Education arm of the reorganized college beefed up its career counseling strength and began offering each student with an open major a greater variety of counseling opportunities, as well as a

---

43. Dallin H. Oaks to the BYU Faculty, 6 May 1974.

C. Terry Warner, named dean of General Studies in 1972. This administrative unit was formerly known as the General College.

course in career education. In 1973, Richard Heaps of the Personal Development Center staff became Director of Career Education in the College of General Studies and chairman of the Career Education Coordinating Committee on campus. This committee included representatives from college advisement centers, preadmissions counseling, the Personal Development Center, and the Department of Career Education.[44]

A Department of University Studies was also organized within this college in September 1972, with Spencer J. Condie of the sociology faculty as its first chairman. This department created for the first time at BYU the possibility for a student to design his own major. The assumption was that a majority of students utilizing the new department would adopt a flexible interdepartmental program to obtain what is essentially a liberal arts degree. The department also authorized the creation of student-initiated courses in which students and a faculty member whom they might select could initiate a course tailor-made to their mutual needs and interests. Obviously, the stress in this department is upon flexibility in meeting student needs. By Winter Semester 1975, there were 250 students seeking a four-year degree majoring in University Studies. The high degree of customized curriculum planning inherent in this new department's approach allayed some of the fears of those who believed that the University administration was tending toward excessive vocational rigidity in the undergraduate preparation it would authorize, as in the development of associate degree programs and the discontinuance of the genealogy major. The introduction of the University Studies major, together with the vocation-oriented efforts, suggested that the University was seriously concerned with serving a variety of student needs.

The Honors Program and Department of American Indian Education continued to serve their specialized constituents without major organizational or philosophical changes. Dean

---

44. C. Terry Warner to Bruce C. Hafen, 3 January 1975.

Terry Warner was succeeded as director of the Honors Program in 1974 by Thomas F. Rogers from the Department of Asian and Slavic Languages. Evidence continued to be forthcoming that the University's Indian Education Program, which is administered almost entirely by Indians, is among the nation's most successful.[45] Indian leadership has been prominent in the success of the programs. John Maestas, a Pueblo-Mexican American, was made chairman of the Indian Education program in 1973. Other Indians taking key positions include John Rainer, a Taos-Pueblo Indian, and Dr. Thomas E. Sawyer, a Cherokee Indian who coordinates all Indian Student Services on campus.

Improving Basic Education Skills

As these functions of the College of General Studies were continuing, the General Education Council, under the chairmanship of Dean Warner, began to organize subcommittees and to initiate a broad-based dialogue on the subject of general education for undergraduate students. There seemed to be a general consensus among both faculty and students that the existing general education program was not all that it should be. Among the reasons advanced for that feeling were the low priority given general education classes by some departments that gave highest priority to training students majoring in their disciplines. Another problem was that of offering the same course as both an introduction to a discipline for majors and as a general education exposure to the field for nonmajors — two different purposes for a course usually calling for two different perspectives. Another source of apparent dissatisfaction was that the existing general education courses were heavily information-oriented rather than skill-oriented. The Council and its subcommittees therefore took on the monumental and yet fundamental task of evaluating what a general college education ought to entail.

After a long and involved series of large- and small-scale

45. For further details on the success of the Indian program at BYU, *see* Volume 3, chapter 40.

meetings, feedback sessions, interim reports, and reevaluations, the General Education Council proposed its first actual recommendation in a general faculty meeting on 30 January 1975. The recommendations proposed an interdisciplinary approach to the teaching of basic skills and competencies. Though taught within the framework of some traditional academic area, the student — and thus the teacher — would be evaluated for the development of certain skills. The evaluation process would be separated from the classroom experience. The program was broken down into two categories. In Category I, the students would be required to demonstrate such competencies as writing, reading, and mathematical skill which are basic to a university education. It was assumed that the average student would complete this category during his first year of college. Category II was divided into five broad substantive areas, but its evaluations and instruction were to reinforce Category I competencies and encourage critical thinking, creativity, and individually designed integration of curriculum. The total general education program was expected to involve around forty semester hours, about sixteen of which would be intensive in-depth study outside a student's major field, which might be interdepartmental in nature. Proposed "evaluations" would be approved by standing committees of the General Education Council, who would also render assistance in developing and perfecting proposed evaluations.[46] It is indicative of the creativity and promise shown by the Council's proposals that a national committee working on general education, the Project on Change in Liberal Education, has designated BYU as one of twenty-one colleges and universities selected from more than 180 applying schools to share in the development of general education concepts nationally.[47]

---

46. *See* "An Invitation from the General Education Council to the Faculty," 20 January 1975.
47. The national project is cosponsored by several associations of colleges and universities. Its initial funding came from a $595,000 Carnegie Corporation grant ("BYU To Participate In Special Project," Provo *Daily Herald,* 16 April 1975).

After the January report, the Council returned to examine the translation of this conceptual scheme into a program capable of being administered to more than 5,000 new students each year. The council proposed that the colleges be charged with implementation of the programs and that evaluation of each college's success would be part of the dean's annual stewardship interview. The administration endorsed this proposal and issued a set of procedures for initial implementation of the program.

It is much too early to evaluate the merits of the proposed general education plan. Its proposals are modest in the sense of leaving the initiative for designing the courses within existing departmental frameworks, but they are sufficiently innovative that they have posed something of a threat to teachers and departments accustomed to being assured of a "captive audience" of students who were required to take specific courses offered by their departments as part of their general education requirements. The program will also offer a challenge to the students of BYU. The flexible approach to general education will require a great deal of individual student motivation and self-discipline. The new program seems to assume that the gradual improvement in student attitudes toward academic pursuits over the past decades will continue to a significant level. The first courses offered under the plan involved freshmen entering the University in Winter Semester 1976. Implementation of the plan will proceed under the general supervision of Marion J. Bentley, assistant dean of the College of General Studies.

The University administration judged the Council's proposal to be promising for several reasons:

> It relies on the efforts of human beings rather than the structure of a program. It works through, rather than against, our academic departments, who will continue to control their own general education courses and budget. Nevertheless, it makes these departments accountable for the productivity of their general education courses — a necessary feature of any program able to promote university-wide dedication to excellence in general edu-

> cation. Instead of favoring some subjects and methods and excluding others, the administrative framework invites all quality approaches to general education teaching from all colleges, departments, and faculty members. Further, it brings faculty members together as respondents to one another's work or as co-workers in the development of evaluation methods and instruction. The mutual education that will result seems a sound approach to encourage continuing improvement of participating faculty. And because the proposed framework builds upon the present one, we will be able to avoid convulsive shifts of resources or procedures in adopting it.[48]

As with several other important developments that have been initiated since 1971, the approach to general education is responsive to a need that seems to exist in most universities. General education has been pointed out as a notable example of the way in which student needs and interests have been traditionally sacrificed to the "necessities of organizational life in a university."[49] One of the more pessimistic comments on the subject of general education, although touched with a ring of realism, came from a member of the Committee for Economic Development in a leading study of higher educational problems in 1973:

> University and college departments are organized by subject matter. The generally useful skills and abilities that students need to acquire are not the main interest of these departments. Most college teachers are specialists, and many of them do not have a good general education. As a result, much of what students are required to learn has little relevance or significance to their present or future lives. Only incidentally, if at all, the students acquire facility in the intellectual processes they will need in their careers and other activities. The vested interests, the reward structure, and the traditions of the faculty make it almost impossible to develop appropriate programs of

48. Dallin H. Oaks to the BYU Faculty, 20 January 1975.
49. Michael D. Cohen and James G. March, *Leadership and Ambiguity: The American College President* (New York: McGraw-Hill, 1974), p. 107.

> general liberal education. If the public does not rally to the support of general education, university and college faculties might do well to ask whether they deserve such support.[50]

Thus, the general education need identified at BYU is hardly a unique problem. That the problem has been addressed with such a large commitment of creative resources as those brought to bear by BYU's General Education Council is indicative of the willingness of the administration to take a fresh look at large-scale educational questions, even though doing so may be threatening to the faculty at large. If these innovations are successful, BYU stands to make a contribution, not only to its own educational methods, but to the present needs of higher education generally. There seems to be little question about the need for innovation leading to improvement if American colleges are to be worthy of the financial support, as well as the prestige, that once were freely given but which have come under close and skeptical scrutiny.

The development of the new general education program is an example of President Oaks's approach to academic changes at the University. Almost four years elapsed from the time the Council was formed until the plan was first implemented in January 1976. The change was largely faculty motivated and designed. Initial proposals came from a group of faculty members representative of many colleges at the University, but before the proposal was adopted by the administration it had received widespread scrutiny and a broad base of support from the faculty as a whole. Programs such as general education thus become the property of the whole University community; each member shares responsibility for its successes and its failures.

Recruiting Senior Faculty Members from Other Institutions

A significant demonstration of the growing prestige of Brigham Young University during the last few years is the

---

50. Committee for Economic Development, *The Management and Financing of Colleges* (Committee for Economic Development, 1973), p. 86.

increasing number of prominent faculty members from other institutions who have joined the BYU faculty. Two full professors were hired in 1967-68, two in 1968-69, seven in 1969-70, and five in 1970-71, the last year of the Wilkinson Administration. These were succeeded by groups of five in the 1972-73 and 1973-74 school years. While introducing a number of notable professional teachers who had transferred to BYU in 1972, President Oaks stated:

> I am sure it is true that the prestige of an institution is due in greater measure to the votes of knowledgeable faculty members than to any other factor. Faculty members vote with their feet. When a faculty member leaves one institution and moves to another, that is a judgment about the prestige and potential of the institution. It is, therefore, particularly heartening to see individuals of this stature choosing to join us at Brigham Young University. These examples could be multiplied many times over.[51]

Some of the men to whom he was referring, who had recently joined the faculty, included Allen Bergin, professor of psychology at Columbia; Arthur Henry King, professor of English in Iran and Pakistan, and for many years assistant director general of the British Council for Cultural Relations; Gene Dalton, professor of organizational behavior from Harvard; Peter Crawley, professor of mathematics from the California Institute of Technology; Carl S. Hawkins, professor of law from the University of Michigan; and Edward L. Kimball, professor of law from the University of Wisconsin.

Harold B. Lee Library Addition

The other highly visible example of academic emphasis was the ground-breaking in the summer of 1974 for a new addition to the main University library that will more than double current library facilities. When combined with existing facilities, the total library space will include 430,000 gross

51. Dallin H. Oaks, "Annual Report to the Faculty," *Together for Greatness*, p. 29.

Removal of a large tree south
of the Harold B. Lee Library
at the beginning of
construction of the addition
to the library.

square feet (225,000 of which will be in the new addition), with study stations for 5,000 students, a total volume capacity of two million books, and an enlarged technical services area designed to process and catalogue a projected 90,000 volumes annually. The new building will also house a learning laboratory containing sophisticated electronic and media information retrieval systems. The library will also include television lecture sets, video cassettes, computer-assisted instruction, and a wide variety of microform materials.[52] The need for an addition to the library facility had become obvious by the fall of 1971, when the University celebrated the addition of the one millionth volume to its library. The library had been constructed in 1961 when there were 11,000 students enrolled. With a current new book acquisition rate of about 100,000 volumes annually, space for student seating in the library had been disappearing at the rate of about 300 seats per year.[53] Along with progress on the Harold B. Lee Library addition, groundbreaking ceremonies were held on 13 February 1976 in Laie, Hawaii, for an addition that will triple the floor space at the BYU — Hawaii campus library.

Instructional Services

The concern with instructional resources demonstrated in the library decision was also reflected in the creation of Instructional Services in 1972, which had the effect of combining all instructional and learning resource units under a single head. Darrel J. Monson, former director of the Division of Instructional Services, was appointed to administer the new organization under the title "Assistant Academic Vice-President for Learning Resources." The guiding concept of the new organization was to pull into a common area all University units, including the library, that dealt with the design, production, distribution, or evaluation of learning

52. *Request,* a publication of the BYU Student Development Association, 1974.
53. "Library, Fund Campaign Meet Approval," BYU *Daily Universe,* 26 October 1971.

resources. With this change, several areas previously a part of Instructional Services were transferred to the library. This included Educational Media, which distributed an extensive supply of audiovisual equipment, and all the learning resource centers, some of which had been located in the various colleges. The reorganization was further refined in the spring of 1975 when the departmental organizations within the production arm of Instructional Services, including Instructional Television, which had been separated from the general Broadcast Services arm of the university in 1971, were merged with Instructional Photographics Production and the Motion Picture Studio into a single large Division of Media Development and Production in order to integrate their existing resources and personnel. This change reflected the recent modification of traditional lines among the areas of media production. In addition, the Division of Instructional Research, Development, and Evaluation, with its departments of Instructional Development Services, Instructional Evaluation and Testing, some instructional psychology and design programs, and the Institute for Computer Uses in Education, became part of the Learning Resources umbrella. With these changes, the respective roles and functions of each component of the Learning Resources area were intended to be more clearly defined and directed toward the academic upgrading of the school's instructional support systems.[54]

Participation in Fund-raising

Students and University employees have played key roles in both soliciting and donating funds for the library addition. In 1972, a "Together for Greatness" program was inaugurated among faculty and staff members, encouraging their own participation as donors to the school's development program. By 1974, sixty percent of the employees were participating in a direct cash contribution program that provided the Univer-

---

54. The unification reflected in the developments described here began in 1965 and developed through several intermediate stages that are traced in Volume 3, chapter 42.

sity with $125,000 each year in unrestricted donations. This amounted to more than twenty-five percent of BYU's annual unrestricted cash contributions since many of the gifts made to the Church Educational System are in the form of tangible property and deferred gifts.[55] Donald T. Nelson, director of the Development Office, which serves the entire Church Educational System, has reported that "Together for Greatness" is having a significant positive impact in off-campus fund-raising efforts in its demonstration of support for the proposition that "charity begins at home." Foundations and industry officials view the large-scale participation of a university's own employees in its development program as encouraging.[56]

Enlargement of the Bookstore

Early in 1973, the administration was authorized by the Trustees to expand the existing bookstore space to nearly twice its original size in order to accommodate increased demand for bookstore services and merchandise. An ad hoc committee of the Faculty Advisory Council had given special consideration to various aspects of the bookstore operation and participated in a review of plans for the space addition, as well as evaluating its academic service functions. As an outgrowth of the committee's work and a related study by the administration, Neal Lambert, a member of the English Department faculty and former chairman of the Faculty Advisory Council, was given a part-time appointment in the bookstore with the title "Academic Adviser to the Bookstore." In that capacity, Lambert solicits and conveys faculty recommendations concerning general, as well as scholarly, reading materials. He has also assisted the bookstore manager, Roger Utley, in designing a faculty reading area in the new addition and in promoting increased awareness of academic quality in the reading and book selection of students and faculty.

This long and varied list of developments in the last few

55. Interview of Donald T. Nelson, April 1975, by George R. Ryskamp.
56. Ibid.

A view of the foundation for
the addition to the Bookstore
that was completed in 1975.

years at BYU, with its hints about the direction of the University, has not gone unnoticed. A feature story in the *Los Angeles Times* in August 1974 described at some length the emphasis on academic upgrading under the Oaks Administration, which the article suggested was setting BYU on a new course.[57] The *Times* seemed impressed primarily by the recent hiring of scholars from other prestigious universities and the strong encouragement being given to research and the quality of graduate work, in spite of the University's continued intent to remain predominantly an undergraduate school.

It should be noted, however, that reactions to the apparent commitment to upgrade academic quality have not been uniformly enthusiastic. Some unsettling effects, for example, have been created among the faculty members themselves, particularly among those who believe that their strength lies in teaching and who are unsure of their research or other creative scholarly abilities. The flexibility of the approaches to faculty evaluation may help to minimize fears of that kind. Some who have been members of the University community for many years do not share the view that the academic emphasis of recent years is in fact a new development since the Church and the University have always sought that kind of excellence.[58] Some faculty members who were significantly engaged in research prior to the advent of the Professional Development Program have noted with some irony that the program, including paperwork and evaluation, has cut into their research time. Some alumni of the University were dismayed by the reprinting of the *Times* article in the September 1974 issue of the alumni magazine, *BYU Today*. The theme of their concern (one alumnus characterized himself and other

---

57. William Trombley, "BYU Sets Its Sights High — Seeks Top Academic Reputation," *Los Angeles Times*, 8 August 1974.
58. *See*, for example, Wayne B. Hales, professor emeritus of physics, "Reappraisal: Indeed, There Is Another View of the Mormon University," *BYU Today*, November 1974, p. 14. In this article Hales takes issue with the implication of the *Times* story that recent developments at the University represent a sharp break with past traditions and efforts.

alumni as "the unlettered peasants who attended BYU before the [academic] 'Golden Age' ") is a fear that an overemphasis on research will diminish the quality of teaching and tend to isolate the faculty from the University's students.[59] They realize that every teacher now has a greater opportunity to influence more students than Karl G. Maeser, who began with only twenty-nine students. They wish the reputation of the school for superior teaching to continue and not be dominated, as it is in many universities, by research.

The size of any shifts in attitudes or productivity toward the academic side has not yet been substantial enough to warrant either high praise from those who would like to see it or grave concern from those who fear it. There has been a renewed emphasis on faculty productivity of all kinds, supported by a number of administrative policies that are intended to encourage evaluative processes. But the caution expressed throughout this treatment of the 1971-75 period must be emphasized here perhaps more than on other subjects — it is still too early to tell what all of the pump-priming and stage-setting will mean in the long run. Once again, not only what goes on in the classroom, but the quality of so much that goes on in the laboratories and the libraries is "beyond all regulation," leaving the final judgment about the faculty's academic aspirations and the place of teaching and research among those aspirations to the cumulative day-by-day decisions and accomplishments of individual faculty members and students. What all that may mean cannot be measured with any degree of certainty for some time to come.

1976 Accreditation

As this volume goes to press, the University has received a copy of the report of the evaluation committee assigned to review BYU's ten-year accreditation for the Northwest Association of Schools and Colleges. The evaluation team visited the campus on 23-25 March 1976.

---

59. *See* "Letters/Comments," *BYU Today*, November 1974, p. 15.

The approach of the accreditation team, composed of fifteen distinguished educators from fourteen different universities and colleges, along with the executive director of the Commission on Colleges of the Northwest Association of Schools and Colleges, was strikingly different from that of the accreditation team which evaluated the University in 1966. The earlier committee gave the University a draft report of its reporters' comments relating to different areas of the University which was not reviewed by the chairman. The University then, by invitation, responded to this draft report, pointing out some serious mistakes and challenging certain observations. However, the Committee did not answer the challenges and did not issue a final report.

In its draft report, the 1966 Committee measured the University largely on the basis of criteria applicable to a secular institution. The report was accordingly very critical of the College of Religious Instruction and certain programs and philosophies of the institution. Some members of the Committee even orally stated that BYU should have some persons on its faculty who are violently opposed to Mormonism. While the Committee members (there were two of them) assigned to the area of religious instruction were amazed at the number of students taking courses in religion (practically the entire student body), they thought the professors who taught Old Testament and New Testament needed more training, presumably in some divinity school, a procedure which had once been attempted and abandoned at BYU. The Committee members commented that religion courses appeared to be "designed largely to inspire toward better living rather than toward a better understanding of man and his relation to God and the rest of the cosmos." They recommended that the college should establish "some kind of a 'rational plank' on which their fellow educators in other institutions can move back and forth between BYU uniqueness and common intellectual sharing." They also felt that some effort was needed to promote sharper "intellectual encounters."

The evaluator of the College of Social Sciences in 1966 spent his entire energies investigating and reporting what he perceived to be a lack of free inquiry at Brigham Young University. He made no evaluation of the curriculum of the college; the number, demeanor, or quality of the students; or the competence of the faculty. Expressing his impression of the school based on his narrow review, he said, "It is essential that unrestricted freedom of inquiry exist and be actively encouraged at all levels of the institutional organization. Since this goes to the heart of what constitutes a great university, it is basic to this report to find that *such freedom does not exist at Brigham Young University.*" In support of this thesis he cited several supposed restrictions on free speech which, in its reply to the draft report, the University categorically denied. These denials were not answered by the Committee.

The 1976 Committee, on the other hand, adopted a different approach, as explained in the introduction to its report:

> Institutional evaluation, as practiced by the Commission on Colleges, begins with an institution's definition of its own nature and purposes; and a declaration of its goals and objectives pursuant upon that definition. The institution is then evaluated, essentially in its own terms, from the point of view of how well it appears to be living up to its own self-definition; and how well its goals and objectives fit that definition, as well as the extent to which they appear to be carried out and achieved in practice.[60]

With this approach the 1976 Committee, instead of taking issue with the programs and philosophies of BYU, expressed the view that BYU's

> goals, educational philosophy, and ideals are solidly grounded in the strong religious tradition and commitment of the Mormon Church. The Committee hereby expresses its admiration of the integrity of the institution in living by those ideals. The general objectives and purposes of the institution as described in its report were

60. Dr. Arthur Kreisman, chairman, "Report to the Commission on Colleges of the Northwest Association of Schools and Colleges," Evaluation Committee Report, Brigham Young University, Provo, Utah, 23-25 March 1976, Dallin H. Oaks Presidential Papers, BYU Archives, p. 1.

> found to be real, and to be implemented in fact throughout the spectrum of institutional practice.[61]

The overall thrust of the 1976 Evaluation Committee's report was highly favorable, finding BYU "to be a vibrant and vital institution of genuine university calibre."[62]

Because the entire Committee report is unusually informative and sympathetic to the objectives of the University, as well as accurate and complete in its analysis of the school's present status, the report will be reviewed in some detail, with emphasis on suggested cautions and recommendations for improvement.

At the outset, the Committee was high in its praise of the self-study report which had been prepared by an institutional self-study committee, with Dr. Keith Warner of BYU's Sociology Department as chairman.

College of General Studies

The Committee recorded that this college "is composed of departments or programs for Aerospace Studies, American Indian Education, Career Education, General Education, Honors, Military Science, Philosophy, and University Studies," and that "The Program for American Indian Education is dealt with separately elsewhere in this report."[63] It concluded that

> The educational programs encompassed . . . are innovative, worthwhile, well thought out, and thoroughly deserving of support. They add important dimensions of strength and service to the University and its students. The central administration of General Studies and its several programs is intelligent, alert, and well-informed. This is a high powered cadre of enthusiastic, energetic, and knowledgeable people who are dedicated to the causes they serve and doing a very good job with the materials at hand. Compliments are due to all involved,

61. Ibid., p. 2.
62. Ibid.
63. Ibid., p. 5.

> and to the University administration for having the vision to initiate and support this enterprise.[64]

Nevertheless, because of the varied nature of the programs encompassed in the College of General Studies, the committee thought its effectiveness would be enhanced by having it directed by an assistant vice-president who could command the support needed.[65]

Continuing Education

The large Continuing Education program at BYU was the subject of two divisions of the report. The Committee noted that "The Continuing Education program at Brigham Young University is recognized as one of the largest programs in the country. It also has the reputation of offering quality programs of instruction in keeping with the goals and objectives of both the Church and the University."[66] The report further stated that "Continuing Education has two major functions: (a) the noncredit religious instruction conducted for and under the supervision of the Church, and (b) credit and noncredit programs of continuing education conducted under the supervision of the University."[67] As to the noncredit courses the committee observed:

> These programs are designed to help fulfill the educational mission of the Church as it relates to religious instruction. The programs are conducted on a self-support basis and the majority of instruction is provided by regular Brigham Young University faculty. . . . They are quite economical when compared to equivalent noncredit programs of other institutions. The economy results from a combination of dedicated service from the faculty, large numbers of participants, and administrative planning which groups the programs by geographic areas.[68]

---

64. Ibid., p. 8.
65. Ibid., p. 11.
66. Ibid., p. 12.
67. Ibid.
68. Ibid., p. 13.

As to credit programs, the Committee commented favorably on evening classes, special courses and conferences (noncredit), and home study. Speaking of evening classes, the report concludes: "This is a unique structure and is one way of developing a strong evening program so that working students can take part of their program during the evening. The need for this type of program on campus is quite obvious — enrollment increases each year."[69]

The Committee pointed out that nonuniformity of courses and trouble with the transferability of credit are problems with nondegree credit courses. The team strongly recommended "*that Brigham Young University exert the leadership within the state to obtain from all professions, including education, recognition of the CEU* [*Continuing Education Unit*] *as the professional inservice measurement of credit leading to professional growth and development.* Use of this measurement would eliminate the need for nondegree credit numbers and the use of pre- and post-conference assignments."[70]

The Committee concluded that home study courses are "well prepared, precautions are taken to avoid compromise of examinations, and periodic evaluation and reviews of all courses are conducted."[71] The evaluation team noted that off-campus centers are located in Salt Lake City, Ogden, Idaho, and California and that "The degree programs [these centers conduct nondegree programs as well] include an intern doctoral program, master of public administration (MPA), masters degrees in library science and in a variety of areas of education, baccalaureate degree in nursing, and a number of associate arts degrees." It observed that "These programs are conducted with the same high standards that prevail on the Brigham Young University campus."[72]

Concerning the Bachelor of Independent Studies, the Committee commented: "This unique program is providing degree opportunities to students unable to participate in a

69. Ibid.
70. Ibid., p. 19.
71. Ibid., p. 14.
72. Ibid., p. 15.

campus degree program. It is not designed as a career development baccalaureate program but provides a strong liberal education. Approximately 200 students are currently registered in the program."[73]

Viewing the program of Continuing Education as a whole, the Committee noted that it obviously has the support of the administration and faculty, as demonstrated by the fact that over ninety percent of the regular faculty are involved in instruction within the program.[74] It concluded: "Credit and noncredit offerings of Continuing Education appear to be of exceptionally high quality. This high quality is the result of an approval system for both faculty and courses which directly involves the academic department of the course being offered."[75] It paid high tribute to the organization of the Continuing Education program by stating, "A Continuing Education program which serves 300,000 students annually must be well organized if the students are to be served efficiently. The accreditation committee found the organization excellent with all personnel understanding and meeting the responsibilities assigned to them."[76]

As to its recommendations, the Committee urged (1) "more administrative space" for proper performance, (2) that "*Continuing Education salaries should be increased to more adequately reflect payment for the time and effort of the faculty members*,"[77] (3) that libraries in the off-campus centers be improved, (4) that there be follow-up evaluations of students educated at the off-campus centers, and (5) that "*an appropriate system be established for awarding academic rank to adjunct faculty teaching in continuing education*."[78]

Physical Education

The College of Physical Education was given praise in the

73. Ibid., pp. 15-16.
74. Ibid., p. 16.
75. Ibid., p. 17.
76. Ibid.
77. Ibid., pp. 17-18.
78. Ibid., pp. 19-20.

following areas: (1) accomplishments of its objectives and purposes in all six academic areas, (2) sound financial support, (3) excellent faculties and equipment, (4) immaculate appearance, (5) adequate library, (6) two self-evaluations in last three years, (6) excellent communication, (7) high morale, (8) regular student evaluations, (9) clear policy statements, and (10) the publication within the last ten years of thirty-four books authored or coauthored by the faculty. In what may have been a surprise to the University president, and certainly to the Trustees, the report stated, "Construction contemplated within the next five to ten years includes an intramural activity building, and the enlargement of the stadium to a seating capacity of 45,000 to 50,000 with accompanying construction of football offices, training room and dressing facilities."[79]

Student Services

The Accreditation Report devotes ten full pages to student services. It begins its evaluation of this division by stating:

> A visitor to Brigham Young University is overwhelmed by the beauty of the setting and the hospitality of the staff, students, and faculty. The attractive buildings, grounds, and friendly students quickly convey a feeling of being a part of a well-organized and caring community.
>
> Students are heavily involved in at least three levels of activity. First, they are enrolled in what appears to be a quality academic program. Second, they participate in a multifaceted activity and recreational program which runs from early morning to late at night six days a week. Third, since over 95% are LDS, they are members of a local religious "branch" which provides a personal attachment to a basic group from which they derive personal and spiritual guidance and support. These "branches" have their own programs and activities which demand the commitment of the members.[80]

---

79. Ibid., p. 26. At BYU, Intercollegiate Athletics are under the auspices of the College of Physical Education in order to avoid athletic abuses.
80. Ibid., p. 29.

The report then makes a point which has concerned the last two University administrations: "Due to the high level of involvement attention to the academic may be slighted."[81]

As to the financial program, the report notes: "In contrast to the financial aid program which existed at the time of the previous review, financial aid is now centralized in one office with six full-time professional staff members. The amount and nature of financial aid available has been increased significantly."[82] In addition, "Long and short term loan funds provided by the church now total over two million dollars and [are] on roughly the same terms as the federal National Direct Student Loan program."[83]

Also in the realm of student services, the report notes that "One of the most creative developments has been the establishment of academic advisement centers in all of the colleges. . . . The advising system is closely related to the Personal and Career Assistance program. . . . These services are coordinated with the Placement Office through the council of directors described under administration."[84]

Reporting on the Honor Code administered through the Office of University Studies, the Committee observed that this office handles

> approximately 3500 cases a year, about 2000 dealing with violations of the campus dress code. The counselors in the Standards Office attempt to utilize various campus resources in changing the behavior of students. Direct confrontation in counseling is always involved, but there is a heavy reliance upon the student's campus religious group or "branch" for support.
>
> If the student does not respond, other sanctions can be utilized. Students have the right of appeal of any deci-

---

81. Ibid.
82. Ibid., p. 31. Whether collections on these loans match the extraordinary record of the previous administration is not known, for no information has been made available as to losses on loans. *See* Volume 3, chapter 41, for the prior record.
83. Ibid., p. 32.
84. Ibid., p. 33. The council referred to is apparently the Faculty Advisory Council (BYU's substitute for an Academic Senate).

> sions of the Standards Office to a faculty-student Code of Honor Committee.[85]

Noting that extracurricular activities are centered in the Wilkinson Center, the report comments that actual use of the facility "often tops 33,000 persons per day. The Center provides the major food service for the 80% of the students who commute. The food service is exceptional in quality, low in cost, and easily accessible."[86] The report also notes that

> The Associated Students of Brigham Young University is extremely well organized and effective. It serves as the activity programming board for the University and is involved in every type of activity from assisting with new student orientation to surveying off-campus housing. The officers and elected council are extremely mature, well trained and effective in their leadership roles.... Student involvement must be among the highest in the United States and contributes to the obvious high level of student morale.[87]

As to the residential life of the students, the Committee reported that

> The University is unique in that it not only manages the residence halls for approximately 20%of the students, but cooperates with off-campus landlords in a program of management, supervision, training of staff, and inspection of facilities for the mutual benefit of the landlords and the University. Students are expected to observe the same standards of conduct in off-campus residence units as they do on campus. The University provides a landlord-tenant agreement which sets forth these understandings. The University in turn assists in the training of off-campus residence staff and arbitrates disputes which arise.... The residence halls appear to be effectively managed and are conducting an extensive program of educational, social, and cultural activities.[88]

---

85. Ibid., p. 35.
86. Ibid.
87. Ibid., p. 36.
88. Ibid., pp. 36-37.

In concluding its discussion of student services the report states:

> One cannot help but be impressed with the high level of morale which pervades the campus. Much credit must be given to the new leadership of the institution and the creativity of the staff. . . . Above all one is impressed with the commitment of students, faculty and staff to the goals of Brigham Young University and to the motivating Spirit which makes this a truly unique institution.[89]

Humanities

In reporting on the College of Humanities the Committee stated that "By any relevant standard the faculty in the College of Humanities is excellent. They have been recruited from the finest graduate schools."[90] It commended the college explicitly for decentralization of power, appropriate teaching loads, and increasing faculty salaries. Even so, the Committee suggested that consideration be given to the following measures:

1. "Placing [the departments of] Philosophy and Journalism in the College of Humanities at some future appropriate time."[91]
2. Better salaries for faculty and graduate student instructors.
3. Improve next physical facilities.[92]
4. Improvement of the language lab.
5. The hiring of more full-time faculty so as to cut down on a heavy reliance on graduate students.

The Committee commended the Language Research Center in the College of Humanities for its "valuable research especially aimed at serving the Church and its needs. The research into the possibilities of machine translation of languages is exciting and promising. In addition, other research and scholarly projects of traditional concern to language de-

89. Ibid., p. 37.
90. Ibid., p. 39.
91. Ibid., p. 38.
92. Ibid.

partments are fostered by the Center in language analysis, teaching methodology, and language proficiency evaluation."[93] Based on its observation, the Committee recommended that

> Since various departments are experiencing a decline in enrollments, careful planning must prevail in formulating new programs so that no programs are established at the expense of other departments. The new general education program, for example, might contribute to the already declining enrollments in various departments. This factor as well as the job market for majors in the college to a large extent should determine the emphasis given to specific programs.[94]

The committee further recommended that

> Perhaps BYU should consider implementing the foreign language house program, one which has been very successful at many universities. Under this program students would live in language groups supervised by native speakers of the respective languages. This would provide inexpensive, extensive conversational experience available to those not fortunate enough to have participated in missions or the Study Abroad programs.[95]

The extensive Language Training Mission, which has just started operation, will more than fulfill this recommendation. The respective departments of foreign languages will fully cooperate with this mission (*see* chapter 54).

Social Sciences

While no evaluation was made of the faculty as a whole in the College of Social Sciences, as in other areas the report did state that the faculty expressed their "admiration for the prevailing conditions of intellectual work, the quality of colleagues, and of students, and with the encouragement

---

93. Ibid., p. 40.
94. Ibid., pp. 40-41.
95. Ibid., p. 41.

provided by the University for their personal and professional growth."[96] The report was largely confined to matters of concern arising from (1) "the absence of a notion of collective objectives for the college,"[97] (2) "the tendency to reward publication and research more highly than teaching competence,"[98] (3) "insufficient attention given the quality of the work undertaken in the name of research,"[99] (4) a need to "coordinate and oversee individual faculty research interests more closely . . . to determine that the time released for research purposes is compensated by the fruits of those efforts,"[100] (5) "ambivalence about teaching":[101] "No faculty interviewed . . . identified himself as primarily an able teacher or a scientist or scholar devoted to teaching with a faculty now largely recruited for research promise,"[102] (6) a lack of "satisfactory ways of determining the effectiveness of departmental programs,"[103]and (7) a lack of guidelines for those not seeking careers in their major field.

The Committee noted that "The college as a whole has expressed concern for its dispersion. . . . Psychology, Geography, and History contain within them interests that exceed the normal limits of social science inquiry whilst Economics, central to some conceptions of the social sciences, rests outside, in the School of Business."[104] It further stated that the faculty desire a single specialized building,[105] that "The problem of lack of adequate space is felt acutely by some departments, notably anthropology and geography."[106] Finally, the report stated that "The ceiling on enrollments in the university presents special problems to the College of Social Sciences

---

96. Ibid., p. 42.
97. Ibid.
98. Ibid., p. 43.
99. Ibid., p. 44.
100. Ibid.
101. Ibid.
102. Ibid., p. 45.
103. Ibid., p. 46.
104. Ibid., p. 47.
105. Ibid.
106. Ibid., p. 48.

where it is coupled with an internal decline in enrollment by reason of changed student interest."[107]

Graduate School

The accreditation report asserted that "The stated objectives of the institution and of the Graduate School are quite clear and concise, and are presently compatible,"[108] but that while "The level of financial assistance for graduate students has increased" it "still is not at a level to compete for the top graduate students."[109]

As to the graduate faculty, the reporters observed: "It is noteworthy that some 95 percent of the graduate faculty hold the terminal degree in their field. There would appear to be a need to make it more stringent to become a member of the Graduate faculty."[110] The evaluation also recommended that "Efforts should continue to employ non-LDS faculty who meet the high standards of quality and training. . . . Freedom of inquiry is an essential aspect of all education and institutions of higher learning have a special commitment to it. The private, church-related institution very often bears the burden of Caesar's wife and must be scrupulous in the defense and advocacy of open and free inquiry."[111] The Committee observed that

> Decentralization of the graduate program to the colleges and academic departments reflects the general administrative thrust of the institution. It is entirely too early to tell what implications will result from this structure; but certainly it will require close scrutiny from the administration to insure that the individual units function effectively. Decentralization will generally put stress on standards of quality, financial support, and will cradle a more sharpened sense of competition for resources between academic units.[112]

---

107. Ibid.
108. Ibid., p. 49.
109. Ibid.
110. Ibid., p. 50.
111. Ibid.
112. Ibid., pp. 50-51.

Concluding its report on the Graduate School, the Committee wrote that "Brigham Young University has the potential and capabilities to develop a truly outstanding Graduate School. There are outstanding members of the faculty, excellent facilities, dedicated administrators and capable students; these are the ingredients of a quality program."

Among other recommendations, the report urged:

> "The need for strengthening the intellectual curiosity of and students to create an atmosphere of enthusiastic learning is very real." The excitement of learning for teacher and student comes from the pursuit of knowledge in an open marketplace of ideas and it is this excitement that should mark graduate study.[113]

Research

Noting that the University obtains some forty-eight percent of its research fund from private sources,[114] the report observes:

> There is a firm commitment to research, but the institution has exercised its option in terms of maintaining control over institutional facilities and programs by not accepting certain types of federal funds. One precaution is that certain private funds do come with many restrictions and limitations and should be evaluated in those lights.[115]

Admitting that "There are never sufficient funds to cover all research endeavors," the report stated that the administration is making "major efforts to make money available for research projects. One of the avenues is the Professional Development Funds. These monies are available for program development, international travel, research equipment and other special projects that need support not available from other sources."[116]

---

113. Ibid., pp. 51-52.
114. Ibid., p. 53.
115. Ibid.
116. Ibid.

As to administration of the Research Division, the Committee reported: "The administration . . . is extremely well organized and efficient. It is a pleasure to see an operation of growing dimensions perform in such an outstanding manner."[117]

Biology

Speaking of the biological sciences, the report concludes that "The goals and objectives outlined in the self-study reports are being met or in time will be met."[118] The Committee recommended

> that the departments continue to examine their programs to determine their strengths and weaknesses. They should then decide the areas of their respective disciplines in which they wish to excel and try to funnel their resources into these areas. This has been initiated in two areas and they should be commended. The departments cannot be all things to all people but must develop expertise in selected areas, especially at the doctoral level of training.[119]

The Committee was pleased with the physical facilities, which were described as "far beyond the minimum needed to carry out the programs in the departments. The teaching and research laboratories are well designed and equipped. Support facilities are well staffed and equipped. The facilities are well utilized. Since little growth in the university is planned, the facility will probably be adequate for some time."[120] The library holdings in the biology area were pronounced outstanding.[121] As to the college's educational program, the report stated that "Acceptance of graduates from these departments into medical schools, dental schools, and graduate schools indicates the effectiveness of the programs."[122] The

117. Ibid., p. 55.
118. Ibid., p. 56.
119. Ibid., pp. 56-57.
120. Ibid., pp. 57-58.
121. Ibid., p. 58.
122. Ibid.

Committee noted that "Most of the faculty in the Biology Division have the terminal degree. Numerous universities are represented. Relatively few faculty have their doctorate from Brigham Young University although many have received one of their degrees here."[123]

The reporter found "Essentially unanimous satisfaction was expressed for the administration in the college for both the department chairmen and dean. Satisfaction was expressed for the increased responsibility and control relegated to the dean and departments. . . . However, the growth of higher administrative positions, i.e., vice presidents, assistants to vice presidents, etc., seems to be occurring in spite of the shifting of responsibilities to the colleges and departments."[124]

Concluding its report on biology, the Committee observed:

> The College of Biological and Agricultural Sciences is one at which the university can point with pride. It is well staffed, well equipped, has outstanding facilities and significant numbers of well-qualified students. The university should avoid at all cost eroding this sound program. Continued support is essential to its well being. A major concern of this reviewer is stated in the following observation.
>
> Academic Freedom is the cornerstone of our academic community; without it there is no university. There have been comments by faculty from this and other colleges relative to the subtle pressure exerted to discourage research, discussions and forums by students and faculty on certain controversial areas, e.g., human population problems, birth control, behavioral patterns of humans and other topics of natural science and social science. Although there seems to be few or no explicit statements indicating restrictions on faculty and student activity there are implicit acts that result in the suppression of thoughts and ideas.
>
> If the President wishes to develop, as he is so quoted in

123. Ibid.
124. Ibid., p. 59.

the self-study report, a "Great University," freedom to investigate and discuss ideas should be jealously protected and administrators prohibited from imposing any infringement on academic freedom.[125]

Physical and Mathematical Sciences

The Committee began its review of this area by stating:

> The College of Physical and Mathematical Sciences has impressed the reviewer with its ability to adequately carry out the tasks which it has set for itself, viz., to offer competitive undergraduate majors in the several fields of physical science, mathematics, statistics, and computer science, to serve a significant role in the General Education program of the university, to offer a medium sized but respectable graduate program, to perform teaching service functions for disciplines outside its own college, and to participate actively in research programs that span several other colleges. The administration at all levels in the College appears to be vigorous, innovative, and concerned. It generally impressed the reviewer with its awareness and openness with respect to the College's weaknesses and needs, as well as being justifiably proud of its strengths and accomplishments.[126]

It reported that "Policies on the acceptance of Federal funds do not seem, on the whole, to be an impediment to the operation of most graduate level research programs."[127]

As to the makeup of the faculty, the report states:

> The fact that such a high percentage of faculty and students are LDS presents some dangers, but also accords some advantages. At this point it would seem that the balance falls on the positive side, but this should not be used to justify efforts at restricting non-LDS representation at BYU. . . . Because of a built-in loyalty of the student body to BYU, the faculty appears to have been able

125. Ibid., pp. 60-61.
126. Ibid., p. 62.
127. Ibid.

> to resist the trend toward grade-inflation so prevalent elsewhere. The inclusion of the Computer Science department in the college along with mathematics and statistics accrues to the benefit of all three departments. . . . On the whole the College of Physical and Mathematical Sciences is performing well.[128]

American Indian Services

An entire section of the report is directed to the BYU program entitled "American Indian Services." The report begins by stating that "The Indian Education Department is the largest on campus and is the major thrust toward Indian education." While this statement is inaccurate, for many departments are larger than this one, still BYU has a larger Indian education department than any other university in the country.

The report describes the physical facilities (in one building) as excellent. The department has twenty full-time faculty members. Each faculty member teaches twelve hours and has a counseling load of twenty-two students:[129]

> Financial assistance for Indian students, as with counseling, is housed with the Indian Education Department. The staff is very knowledgeable and competent in handling the special and unique way Indian students are funded (Tribe and BIA). . . .
>
> The library holdings on or about Indians is stated to be approximately 40,000. However, access to these holdings is very difficult. No effort has been made to tag or identify these books by area or Tribe. Secondly, the book collection appears to be well worn and somewhat outdated.
>
> Minor effort could make the library more useful if the collection were arranged with Indian student interest in mind. Some effort should be made to make the collection accessible to the Navajo students as they are the largest Tribe on campus (approx. 50%).[130]

---

128. Ibid., pp. 63-65.
129. Ibid., p. 66.
130. Ibid., p. 67.

The Committee summarized its report as follows:

The American Indian Education Department is a very unique education effort and experience. Although it is a rapidly growing department, this growth has been very orderly and well administered. Its major strong points are as follows:

1. The department is separated from the rest of the University so as to provide an identity for the Indian students yet closely integrated with the University to be an integral part of the total educational experience.

2. Specialized counseling and financial assistance is readily available and on a personal basis with faculty members who have the same academic interests.

3. [There are] Adequate space and facilities for all the Indian students' educational and social activities. This includes space for student governmental programs.

4. Salaries and operating expenses are adequate and should be considered a strong point relative to other Indian programs.

5. [There is] A significant commitment to Indian educational excellence by the University Administration and especially the faculty of the Indian Educational Department.[131]

Libraries and Learning Resources

Under this subject the Committee reported:

As of this evaluation, the Brigham Young University Library and its media services receives a very high rating. Its self-evaluation was thorough, with strengths and weaknesses presented frankly and honestly. For all of its basic functions, the Library appears to be adequately funded, well staffed, and approximately up-to-date with its technical work. Although somewhat crowded for space at this time, the new wing, to be occupied sometime this fall, effectively doubles the present available space. This new wing has been well planned, and appears to be carefully constructed by the contractor.[132]

---

131. Ibid., p. 68.
132. Ibid., p. 70.

Even so, the committee recommended "a special appropriation of approximately $500,000, to be expended over a five year period, be made to the library for the purchase of retrospective resources, particularly for back files of journals and other serials. This should be in addition to the regular appropriation of around $1,000,000 per year for the acquisition of current publications and nonprint resources."[133] Speaking to the controversial subject of "Library Automation," the report recommended "that the BYU Library NOT undertake automation projects at this time. With the large networks [such as those at Stanford and the University of Washington] approaching operational status, I can see little valid justification for 'reinventing the wheel.' "[134] Instead, the reviewer recommended that a group of professional and nonprofessional librarians be charged to study the best plans for the future. He also recommended "against undertaking to reclassify the Library collections into the Library of Congress Classification system."[135]

As to Media Services, the Committee reported:

> The University is to be commended for dividing the activities in the media field into a Development and Production unit on the one hand, and a services group on the other. The Library's media services correspond directly with its book services: the Library does not produce books, it does not develop or write the books. It does provide an all-campus access to books. Likewise, in its present configuration, the Library does not develop or produce films, television programs, etc., but it does provide a campus-wide service of these materials. The division makes for a much cleaner and better operation than is usual.
>
> The BYU Library today is in very good condition overall. The Library Staff, the University Administration, and the governing board are to be congratulated.[136]

133. Ibid.
134. Ibid., pp. 71-72.
135. Ibid., p. 72.
136. Ibid., p. 73.

Family Living

The Committee report on the College of Family Living was most laudatory, although it contains specific suggestions for improvement. It said, "The College of Family Living is a strong College and one that the University can point to with great pride."[137] The reporter concluded that

> The goals of the departments are in tune with the goals of the college which are in harmony with the goals of the University and The Church of Jesus Christ of Latter-day Saints, as identified by the self-study. The goals are living in the actions of the faculty, the students, and the supportive staff as they carry out the curriculum within the learning environment. Witnessing the idealism, the dedication and the quality of learning was most refreshing and reassuring. With the growing awareness on the part of the total faculty for research and/or creative endeavors the departments and the college will need to build in due recognition for quality teaching so that teaching is not sacrificed for research and/or creative endeavors.[138]

The reporter added that

> The department of CDFR has developed outstanding graduate programs, some of which have achieved national recognition. . . .
>
> Of particular noteworthiness is the involvement of undergraduates and graduates in practicums of field experiences, and internships. . . .
>
> Administration within the college seems very much on top of what is going on within the college and displays concern for needs of the total college. . . .
>
> Students do feel an important part of the college and that faculty are accessible to them. . . .
>
> Research is and has been an integral part of job definitions in the department of CDFR.[139]

---

137. Ibid., p. 78.
138. Ibid., p. 74.
139. Ibid., pp. 76-77.

As to criticisms and suggestions, the report states that "Housing appears to be somewhat lost in the curriculum of the College."[140] The evaluator also felt that there should be an (1) "increasing [of] the interdisciplinary, interdepartmental approach to curriculum and to research within the College of Family Living," (2) a greater utilization of "the expertise, understanding and skills of the home economics education faculty within the total college," (3) "a climate conducive to quality research," and (4) a capitalization on the "interdisciplinary aspects of the College."[141]

Physical Plant

As to the Physical Plant, the Committee reported:

> The Physical Plant is in excellent condition. Most of the buildings are of recent construction and have been exceptionally well maintained. The grounds are immaculate. It is almost impossible to believe that some 25,000 people are using these facilities. The Maintenance Department and staff deserve special commendation.
>
> To carry out this maintenance program a large number of part-time student workers are employed. Naturally with student labor there is frequent turnover, and the need for continuing retraining. Efficiency and neatness of operation would suggest hiring permanent employees. It was refreshing to hear from the vice president in charge of the physical plant that his division recognized a role in the total educational process of the University and that training students for work was an integral part of that process.[142]

Instructional Staff

The Committee reported that

> The faculty are involved in the formulation of funda-

140. Ibid., p. 76.
141. Ibid., pp. 78-80.
142. Ibid., p. 83. This suggestion for having permanent employees instead of using students would run contrary to the policy of the institution to provide work for students.

> mental policies through the Faculty Advisory Council (BYU's equivalent of an Academic Senate). The FAC appears to be functioning well after its few years of operation. . . .
>
> The salary schedule at Brigham Young University has improved significantly over the past five years. . . .
>
> Although by Board policy, salary information at Brigham Young University is confidential, the Administration has made a careful study of salary schedules at nine different institutions (University of Colorado, University of Utah, San Jose State, University of Washington, Washington State University, University of Oregon, University of Arizona, Arizona State and Utah State). . . . This compilation of data will provide a guide to the future salary goals of Brigham Young University.[143]

As to freedom of speech, the report states:

> Within the parameters outlined in the statement on the nature of the institution and what is expected of its members, there appeared to be no other established limits on freedom of teaching, investigation or learning. The Committee did find some ambiguity on the part of a few faculty members as to what would constitute unacceptable areas of teaching and/or research. Some sort of advising system for these kinds of issues would seem to be desirable.[144]

Administration

The report is very commendatory of the University's administration:

> The relationship between the sponsoring Church, the Board of Trustees of Brigham Young University and the University, while somewhat unique is sufficiently delineated at present to allow for a smooth operation. The governing board is composed of very able and dedicated individuals with various professional backgrounds. They are deeply interested in the University and committed

143. Ibid., pp. 83-84.
144. Ibid., p. 85.

through their Church relationships to its future growth and development. . . .

The executive administration of the University is particularly able and dynamic. It is making a serious and determined effort to develop a climate within which learning can take place, and the University community appears generally appreciative of the administration's commitment. There seems to be satisfaction with the delegation of authority and responsibility — although as might be expected some members of the faculty find the new process more time consuming than they might like — while others find the administrative officers "slow" in making decisions — which of course the administrative officers hope will be made at the lower level.[145]

The report notes that

The University has recently changed its sabbatical leave program to a "development leave" program. The difference is not merely nominal. In the new program a faculty member will be granted support for study, research, etc., for self-improvement. He may not take an unrelated position while on leave. Not everyone will be automatically given a development leave. This new policy remains to be tested in practice.[146]

The committee enthusiastically supported BYU's position against "federal intrusion and intervention into the internal affairs of colleges and universities,"[147] which is discussed in chapter 52.

Conclusion

The conclusion of the report, presumably concurred in by the fifteen members of the Committee, gave "special citation" to the following:

1. The overall excellence and organization of the self-study report.

145. Ibid., pp. 85-86.
146. Ibid., p. 85.
147. Ibid., p. 86.

2. The splendid response made by the institution to the recommendations in the 1966 evaluation report. There is ample evidence of the great progress that has been made.
3. The high level of morale among faculty and students.
4. The definition of institutional goals and objectives, and their general implementation in practice.
5. The effective and efficient manner in which institutional administration has been decentralized, so as to place key operational decisions as close as possible to the faculty, and allow for faculty input.
6. The excellence of the physical facilities.
7. The excellence of the general advisement of students throughout the institution.
8. The high standards which were found to be prevailing in all areas.[148]

In addition to the specific recommendations concerning individual colleges, the committee observed:

1. It appeared to us that there might be too many graduate — and, in some cases, even undergraduate — students instructing class sections. . . .
2. There appeared to be a strong emphasis on research throughout the institution. While this is understandable in a university, the Committee wondered whether it was being overdone. . . . Research certainly ought not to be promoted at the expense of teaching. We think that, while promoting research, the University ought also to make it clear that teaching is important and that good teaching is a valid item of reward. Nor should assignment to teaching duties ever be allowed to appear to be a punishment for inept research.
3. The University has devised an interesting format for the continued professional development of faculty. We recommend that some sort of parallel format be devised for the continued professional development of administrators.
4. As noted earlier, the University has carried out an admirable program of administrative decentralization.

---

148. Ibid., p. 87.

Aerial view of the BYU campus in 1975.

There seems to be a question among some faculty whether that has now gone too far. A number of comments were received by Committee members indicating that it was more and more difficult to get clear-cut and rapid decisions. Without criticizing the general process, which we think is good, the Committee recommends that a watchful eye be kept on the line dividing an unhealthy authoritarianism from an unresponsive delegation of authority.

5. Some members of the faculty appear to have genuine problems of conscience in attempting to determine valid matters of research, writing, and discussion within the context of Church doctrine. There is much uncertainty in some quarters and a real hesitancy to even broach the subject. Most of this, we think, is unnecessary and could be corrected and clarified by a statement on the subject of academic freedom within the context of Church doctrine by the President. Indeed, we recommend that consideration be given to the development of some process or format whereby faculty with such qualms could submit their topics, projects, etc., for an official opinion with reasons given, and without prejudice to the submitter.[149]

---

149. Ibid., pp. 87-89.

48

Campus Life in the Seventies

During the period since 1971 there has been little evidence of fundamental changes in student body composition or in the roles played by BYU students. There have been a few refreshing developments in the University's student service areas and some attempts to improve student attitudes toward academics. Most students have also experienced a healthy rapport with the administration, characterized by open, two-way communication and mutual respect.

The number of students enrolled during the regular academic year has remained relatively constant since 1971. Further, there have been no significant changes in the academic credentials or personal statistics describing the classes that have entered each year. The male-female ratio has remained roughly constant at 6:5,[1] although women have constituted a slightly increasing percentage among freshmen

---

1. For Winter Semester 1975 the figures were 13,471 men and 11, 656 women. The ratio of *single* men to *single* women, however, is 5:6, with 9,106 single men and 10,802 single women enrolled in the Winter Semester 1975 (Brigham Young University Office of Institutional Research, *Enrollment and Composition of the Student Body Winter Semester 1974-75,* 17 January 1975, BYU Archives, pp. 1, 44-45).

and a slightly decreasing percentage among seniors. Graduate student enrollment accounted for about ten percent of the student body in 1971 (2,384 students), but it has gradually declined, moving closer to the eight percent target projected by the administration.[2]

It appears probable that the University's enrollment ceiling, set by the Trustees, will continue indefinitely at a level of approximately 25,000 students. During 1972-73, the administration, with the assistance of economists from the faculty, conducted a study on the likely economic effects on the University community and the surrounding area of various hypothetical reductions in total enrollment. The study showed conclusively that any such reductions would result in major disruptions with very little savings, given the established financial commitment to overhead expense. Based upon these findings, there is little likelihood that the Board of Trustees will change the present ceiling.

As mentioned elsewhere,[3] BYU's basic role has emerged as that of a large, essentially undergraduate institution that attracts an overwhelming percentage of its students from committed members of The Church of Jesus Christ of Latter-day Saints, while welcoming others who desire to study in the environment its standard create.[4] That role is likely to continue.

---

2. Brigham Young University Office of Institutional Research, *Enrollment and Composition of the Student Body Winter Semester 1973-74*, 15 January 1974, BYU Archives, p. 95.
3. *See* chapter 47.
4. The University's attitude toward the two to three percent of the student body who are non-Mormon was expressed by President Oaks in his 6 September 1973 address to the student body: "This year, as always, our student body includes hundreds of students who are not members of The Church of Jesus Christ of Latter-day Saints. We welcome you and anticipate that your presence here will enrich our education as well as yours. We invite you to take part in the active religious life of our campus branches and stakes. If you choose not to, we urge you to affiliate with the church of your choice in this community. We urge upon you our conviction that each of us should have an active religious life along with our university studies."

Student Services

One of the developments in student services in the early 1970s is illustrated by *Ice Cream and Elevators,* a movie produced on campus in 1970. The movie opened with a scene familiar to students throughout the 1960s — the interminable waiting lines involved in the three-day registration process at the beginning of each semester. Students enrolling after 1974 are not likely to appreciate the dramatic change in registration that has been gradually replacing those long lines with computer forms. Preregistration had been talked about prior to 1971, but the first step toward actual change came in the fall of 1972 with the introduction of a new preregistration process which has become increasingly automated. A student registering in Winter Semester 1972 received a computer-prepared packet of class cards that he had previously requested; he then took them through a streamlined registration process to pay tuition and to make any necessary changes. By Winter Semester 1975 students could skip registration altogether. Some 18,500 students paid their tuition for the upcoming semester before going home for Christmas and then received computer confirmation of their requested class schedules by mail. Changes were made during the first few days of classes by traditional add and drop procedures. A total mailing system was instituted for Winter Semester 1976.[5]

The creation of an automated registration process has placed enormous demands on many of the administrative offices and on the Computer Center. During the period of transition, two systems were required, that of the newly developed program and the former backup program in case something should go wrong with the new programs.[6]

Changes in registration were just one way in which the administration was trying to serve the students better. Robert W. Spencer, who was appointed dean of Admissions and

---

5. "Winter Enrollment Nears 25,000 Limit," BYU *Daily Universe,* 6 January 1975.
6. Bruce C. Hafen interview with Ben E. Lewis, 2 April 1975.

Records in 1971, believes that significant changes in attitude have been established in the University's entire approach to student-oriented records and financial services.[7]

Related to increasing automation of the registration process has been the development of an increasingly automated records and student information system that monitors a student's progress through the University. The new system, placed into operation during the winter of 1976, serves two major functions. First, it provides administrative personnel with comparative data on requirements in the various majors and areas of emphasis. It also enables a determination of department and major demands for individual classes. Second, the system monitors student progress toward graduation by identifying at the end of each semester those classes completed and those requirements yet remaining for graduation. This information is provided for both general education and major requirements.

Financial Aid and Student Counseling

In the fall of 1971, the offices of Student Loans and Undergraduate Scholarships were combined into the Office of Student Financial Aids. The result was a new administrative procedure to assist students with their financial needs. After a student's needs are evaluated, assistance may be given from one of several alternative plans or combination of alternative plans, including BYU short-term loans, BYU long-term loans, federally insured loans, Basic Educational Opportunity Grants, BYU grants-in-aid, BYU scholarships and awards, and private scholarships and awards. Whether this office or succeeding administrators will have the same success with respect to advising students and making and collecting loans as Wendle Nielsen during his long tenure in the Wilkinson Administration remains to be seen (*see* Volume 3, chapter 41). The Office of Student Financial Aids also works closely with the Student Employment Office in assisting students to find

7. Bruce T. Reese, transcribed interview with Robert W. Spencer, May 1974, in the possession of Bruce T. Reese.

work while they are attending the University.

Another development significantly affecting student life has been the academic advisement program. Prior to 1969 there were several elaborate but cumbersome advisement programs that imposed heavily on faculty time. Both students and faculty complained about the ineffectiveness of advisement. In the fall of 1969, the responsibility for advisement was assigned to the Division of Admissions and Records. After a complete study of the advisement problem, it was recommended that a student advisement center be established on a pilot basis in the College of Fine Arts and Communications. Two years later, extensive evaluations indicated the success of the college advisement center concept, and the program was extended to all of the colleges by fall 1973.

College advisement centers provide academic counseling on a walk-in basis. Faculty remain an integral part of the advisement program, but "first-line" advisement and clerical responsibility have been shifted to the centers. The centers are designed to be both uncomplicated for the students and relatively inexpensive to operate.

In terms of specific practices, each college advisement center is organized to counsel students on graduation requirements and the student's standing in relation to them; to offer materials on all majors within the college; to make appointments for students who need specific faculty advisement; and to assist in the evaluation of transfer credit for departmental and major requirements. The centers also coordinate graduation with the University Graduation Office and notify students of deficiencies in their standing. One measure of the success of the college advisement center program is indicated by the report that in the spring of 1973 only forty prospective graduates had not been cleared for graduation three weeks prior to their graduation date; in previous years, as many as 900 seniors had not been cleared at that same point in time prior to graduation.[8]

---

8. Erlend D. Peterson, "College Advisement Center Summary Report," 22 May 1973, box cpm 23C, BYU Archives, p. 3.

The centers have also been instrumental in a substantial decrease in the average number of credit hours taken by graduating seniors. In 1972, students had taken an average of 148 hours, or 9.5 semesters, before graduating; by 1975, those figures had fallen to 139 hours, or 8.8 semesters. This resulted not only in financial savings to students, but also in the freeing-up of almost 32,000 credit hours, which allows 1,000 students to attend the University who would have otherwise been barred by the enrollment ceiling.[9]

Simultaneously with the establishment of the college advisement centers, the responsibility for career counseling of new students was shifted to the reorganized College of General Studies,[10] which gave depth and objectivity to career counseling that had been lacking when it was mixed with specific curriculum advisement.

In addition to these organizational adjustments, the University administration publicly counseled students and faculty against pressuring new students into premature selections of major fields.[11] Students with an undeclared major were assigned to the College of General Studies, which was developing plans for systematic vocational counseling and exposure to various academic fields in order to help students make more informed career decisions.

An organizational development that also symbolically reflected the administration's desire to serve real student needs more completely occurred in January 1972 when J. Elliot

---

9. Address by Dallin H. Oaks at Annual University Conference, August 1975.
10. *See* chapter 47. Some vocational counseling functions, such as testing and highly personal individual counseling, remained with the Personal Development Center under the direction of the dean of Student Life.
11. "New students need not declare their major on entering the University. If they are committed to a particular subject area. such as the sciences, they can enroll in the appropriate college without declaring a specific major in that college, or they can join most other freshmen in enrolling in the College of General Studies from which they can transfer readily to another college when they have chosen a major" (Dallin H. Oaks to entering freshmen, fall 1974).

Cameron, who had served for several years as dean of students at the University, was given the title "Dean of Student Life." The services directed by Cameron were also reorganized to shift the focus of his office from student discipline to student service. Suggestive of this shift in philosophy was another name change that identified the former student counseling center as the "Personal Development Center." This change, which was initiated by the personnel of the counseling center, was part of an attempt to change the image of the University's professional counselors from those who deal only with maladjusted students to those who help all students learn to cope with typical college problems, such as loneliness, lack of social adjustment, and other problems.[12]

The New "4-4-2-2" Calendar

On 4 November 1971 the *Daily Universe* headline "Semester Change Approved: Out Before Christmas" announced an innovative new calendar that would become effective in the fall of 1972. Referred to as both "4-4-2-2" (expressed in terms of months of study) and a "year-round modular calendar," the new calendar was composed of three full sixteen-week semesters in each academic year, the last of which would be divided into two eight-week terms in which classes would meet twice as frequently, allowing full credit as in a regular sixteen-week semester.[13]

It was Dallin Oaks's view that the new calendar would be one of the most significant developments of his administration, at least in terms of long-range effects.[14]

Prior to this announcement, the traditional two-semester calendar plus a ten-week summer session had been in effect at BYU since 1960, when the University had abandoned its four-quarter calendar. The Fall Semester had ordinarily

12. "Dean of Students Gets New 'Student Life' Title," BYU *Daily Universe,* 6 January 1972.
13. "Semester Change Approved," BYU *Daily Universe,* 4 November 1971.
14. Bruce C. Hafen, interview with Dallin H. Oaks, April 1974.

begun in late September and had ended in late January. Students found that the Christmas holiday period was less than a real holiday under this system. The post-Christmas dangling semester fragment was uncomfortable for both students and faculty, and the break between fall and winter semesters within only a few weeks after the Christmas vacation seemed redundant and multiplied winter travel. From a long-range standpoint, the old two-semester calendar was making a less efficient use of the physical and personnel resources of the University. An increase in the efficient use of those resources not only would make economic sense, but it would also offer a way of giving more students the opportunity of attending the University without affecting the enrollment ceiling of 25,000.

The need for some kind of change had been recognized and studied during the last years of the Wilkinson Administration. In the spring of 1971 the Board of Trustees approved a calendar change that would end Fall Semester before Christmas — if the University could work out the mechanics.[15] By the time Dallin H. Oaks assumed his presidential duties in August of that year, a number of alternatives had been proposed by administrators assigned to evaluate the problem. For a variety of reasons, one of which was the unsuccessful history of trimester calendars at other universities, the problem of working out the mechanics proved to be a vexing one. Under considerable pressure for an early decision, President Oaks ultimately recommended the 4-4-2-2 concept, a system largely of his own creation, although there were a few schools using a somewhat similar program.

When first proposed, the new idea raised several questions. The schedule would be much more intensive, compressing work that faculty and students had been accustomed to performing in nine months into two four-month semesters. Spring sports would extend beyond Winter Semester, forcing some athletes to be enrolled for Spring Term. Some physical

15. Ernest L. Wilkinson to Neal A. Maxwell, 5 May 1971, box 578, folder 3, Wilkinson Presidential Papers, BYU Archives.

education and botany classes would be hindered by the lack of appropriate weather during Winter Semester. Maintenance crews would be hard-pressed to find time for repairs and renovations. Finally, the leisurely pace of Summer School and the three-week time lapse between the end of Summer School and the beginning of Fall Semester would be replaced by a business-like around-the-clock pace.

Even so, the more Oaks and his vice-presidents considered the advantages of the new proposal, the more enthusiastic they became. On the point of resource utilization, they were impressed that under the new calendar, school would be in session forty-nine weeks of the year, as compared with forty-four weeks under the former system. The "2-2" portion of the new proposal offered flexible modular opportunities. For example, courses designed for a sixteen-week semester could be taught in an eight-week half-semester simply by doubling class time; no extensive modifications of existing course materials would be required. Further, the same half-semester-length courses could be offered during the regular semesters for the convenience of missionaries, servicemen, and others who were returning at midpoints during the semester. The five-week, six-week, and ten-week summer sessions and the eight-week "block plan" arrangements offered previously had suffered from a lack of selection of courses to persons entering school at times other than the beginning of regular semesters, largely because such courses required extensive modifications to fit the various time periods.

One of the most difficult implementation problems for the new calendar was the arrangement of class schedules for the first Spring-Summer semester (Spring Term and Summer Term). Students needed to be sold early on the advantages of the new program in order to permit academic departments to balance course offerings for those who did attend. Under the direction of Dean Spencer and a former Summer School dean, Dean A. Peterson, an intense publicity campaign, together with provisions for preliminary registration and early tuition deposits, was organized soon after the new plan was announced, not only on campus but through feeder high schools and admissions advisers. The new plan offered several advantages to students. For example, the summer vacation (the time between the end of Winter Semester and the beginning of Fall Semester) had been increased by three or four weeks. Thus, students desiring to work in the summer could become available for jobs sooner. Since the semesters would be essentially interchangeable, students would also have the freedom to take the traditional "summer vacation" in the autumn or winter, according to seasonal employment or other personal preference. Finally, since students could take two and one-half semesters of classes per year and still enjoy a two-month vacation, they could complete their college program, if desired, in three calendar years.

For faculty members, the new calendar increased the time pressure on those who taught in successive semesters, but the flexibility offered by scheduling sabbatical leaves, teaching, and research at the time of year best suited to a faculty member's needs has largely offset that disadvantage. Faculty members are able to fill a two-semester teaching commitment in a shorter time, thereby offering some faculty the possibility of an eighteen percent increase in salary for teaching a two-month Spring or Summer Term, while still having a two-month vacation during the remaining half-semester.

During the first two years under the new calendar, the response toward treating the spring and summer terms as the equivalent of fall and winter semesters was less than overwhelming. However, the anticipated dislocations that would be caused by disruptions of traditional scheduling proved to be surmountable. The administration viewed the new calendar as moving in the right direction, though its gains were gradual and modest by the end of the 1975 Summer Term. Initial registration for the first spring and summer terms in 1973 was 8,332 and 6,726 students respectively, numbers substantially lower than the announced goal of 10,000 students for each of the two terms. Both figures were an improvement over the total number of students who had enrolled in the two five-week terms during the Summer School of 1972, however, and noticeable increases by 1974 permitted the most significant statistical testimony to the emerging success of the new calendar — the total number of student credit hours taught nearly doubled between Summer School of 1972 and Spring-Summer Semester of 1974.[16]

The success of such a calendar change is largely dependent upon the willingness of faculty members and the interest of students in making the idea work. If large numbers of either faculty or students had not believed the idea would or should work, it probably would have failed, simply from absence of sufficient participation to give the Spring-Summer Semester the depth and quality of course offerings upon which many of the anticipated advantages of the calendar depended. The apparent success of "4-4-2-2" may be attributable not only to the University's leadership, but also to its student and faculty community who, in the words of Commissioner Neal A. Maxwell, have a unique and deeply felt commitment to "making things work out."[17] Thus, the commissioner told the faculty at its Fall Workshop in 1972 that he expected BYU to succeed with its new calendar even though other universities had been unsuccessful in implementing similar schedules.[18]

---

16. Total student credit hours for 1972 Summer School were 54,049.5. In the 1974 Spring-Summer Semester, student credit hours totalled 96,478.5. The number of daytime student enrollments since the new calendar became effective have been

	Spring (8 weeks)	**Summer (8 weeks)**
1972	7,104*	6,558*
1973	8,332	6,714
1974	8,828	7,318
1975	9,057	7,720

*5-week sessions

(Source: Office of Institutional Research, *Brigham Young University Enrollment Résumé, 1974-75*, August 1975, cpm box 20h, folder 1, BYU Archives, pp. 7-8.)

17. Neal A. Maxwell, Speech to BYU Administrators Workshop, Summer 1974.

18. Neal A. Maxwell in *Together for Greatness* (Brigham Young University, 1972), BYU Archives, p. 12.

The Code of Honor

From the beginning of the Oaks years there has been increasing recognition of the concept of student rights. Some of that concern must have been sparked by growing national recognition of the rights of college students in such matters as due process, privacy, and confidentiality. During the closing months of the Wilkinson Administration a review of the entire approach to student discipline had begun, and completing that task held high priority for Dallin Oaks, who had himself served as chairman of a disciplinary committee during a period of serious student strife at the University of Chicago.[19] Following some study of the subject, the University adopted a revised statement of the Student Code of Honor. The Code of Honor was drafted in consultation with administrative and staff employees, faculty, student body officers, and the commissioner of the Church Educational System. It was adopted by the Church Board of Education and the BYU Board of Trustees for Ricks College, LDS Business College, and Brigham Young University on 5 January 1972. It reads as follows:

> The Church of Jesus Christ of Latter-day Saints sponsors colleges and a university in order to provide an education in an atmosphere consistent with the ideals and principles of the Church. The maintenance of high standards of personal behavior and appearance is essential to the preservation of that atmosphere and to the development of men and women who personify these ideals and principles. By enrolling or accepting employment at a Church college or university a person signifies his willingness to live in accordance with the following principles, whether on or off campus:
>
> 1. Abide by the standards of Christian living taught by The Church of Jesus Christ of Latter-day Saints. This includes graciousness and consideration for others and the observance of high principles of honor, integrity, and morality.

---

19. *See* chapter 45.

2. Be honest in all behavior. This includes not cheating, plagiarizing, or knowingly giving false information.

3. Respect personal rights. This includes —

(a) not physically or verbally abusing any person and not engaging in conduct that threatens or endangers the health or safety of others; and

(b) not obstructing or disrupting the study of others; the performance of official duties by college or University personnel; the teaching, research, disciplinary, administrative, or other functions of the college or University; or other authorized activities on college or University premises.

4. Respect property rights. This includes refraining from theft, concealment, damage, or misuse of the property of others.

5. Obey, honor, and sustain the law.

6. Avoid drug abuse. This includes refraining from the possession, use, or distribution of any narcotic or dangerous drug (as defined by applicable law), except as prescribed by a licensed medical practitioner.

7. Comply with all college and University regulations. This includes compliance with rules relating to campus organizations and to the use of on- or off-campus housing or other facilities.

8. Observe the Word of Wisdom. This includes abstinence from alcoholic beverages, tobacco, tea, and coffee.

9. Live the law of chastity. This includes abstinence from all sexual relations outside the bonds of marriage.

10. Observe high standards of taste and decency. This includes refraining from disorderly, lewd, indecent, or obscene conduct and expression.

11. Observe prescribed standards of dress and grooming.

12. Help others fulfill their responsibilities under this code.[20]

In addition to the Code of Honor, a sophisticated code was adopted which includes procedures for the initiation of charges against students for alleged violations of the behavior

20. *Code of Honor,* cpm box 45d, BYU Archives.

code, a statement of student rights to notice and hearing, and appellate procedures in cases involving allegations of serious misconduct.

Although serious student misconduct had never been a major problem at BYU, the University's clarifications of its substantive and procedural expectations in disciplinary matters, as well as its concern for fairness with students involved in charges of misconduct, was a step recommended by the President's Commission on Campus Unrest to enable universities to cope intelligently and fairly with the problems that had disrupted campuses throughout the country during the 1960s.[21]

All of these changes in student services, from a student's first registration experience to his graduation, have had the individual student in mind. These improvements in services seek "to provide each individual [student] with an opportunity for experience . . . to achieve socially, academically, and spiritually, and if there are factors in the background that tend to impede progress, to identify and modify so as to eliminate those factors."[22]

One Code of Honor subject — dress and grooming standards — has claimed more attention than most other student life matters. In 1971, the year of Dallin Oaks's appointment, dress styles — particularly men's hair length and women's clothing — were changing enough to cause speculation that the standards might change under a new president. One relaxation of prior standards came during the Wilkinson Administration in early 1971, when female students were given permission to wear slacks and pantsuits (though not blue jeans and the like) on campus. However, following consultation with the Board of Trustees, President Oaks spoke with unmistakable clarity on the remainder of the standards in his first address to the student body in the fall of 1971:

---

21. Commission on Campus Unrest, *Report of The President's Commission on Campus Unrest* (Avon, 1971), p. 14.
22. Bruce T. Reese, transcribed interview with J. Elliot Cameron, May 1974, in the possession of Bruce T. Reese.

> I have received many inquiries during the past few months about whether the standards of Brigham Young University will be maintained. The answer is yes. There are three major areas in which we have high standards for all members of the university community: academic, conduct, and appearance.[23]

The new president then explained and illustrated the standards he had in mind in each of these three areas. Regarding the standards of conduct that govern performances on campus, Oaks said, among other things:

> This university is a home for ideas; for growth, for expansion of intellectual horizons; and for challenge to the mind, the body, and the spirit. But we will not welcome onto this campus — any more than thoughtful Latter-day Saint parents will welcome into their home — the blasphemous, the sordid, the crude, or the vulgar. Those characterizations are not self-defining, and there may be differences from time to time in the application of the principle. But the principle itself is clear. We will continue to be selective about what we tolerate on this campus and even more selective about what we sponsor.[24]

He then spoke at some length about the standards for dress and grooming and the reasons for their existence, noting that the standards are specified by the Board of Trustees of the University rather than by the president or some other University official:

> I regret having to devote so much time to this subject. I do so under the compulsion of necessity. I am conscious that you cannot make a great university by lowering hemlines and shaving chins. I have no desire to make the razor and the tapemeasure symbols of my administration. Along with the overwhelming majority of students and faculty at this institution, I want all of us to be about the business of learning. Let us observe these standards

---

23. Dallin H. Oaks, "A New President Speaks to BYU," *Speeches of the Year* (Provo, Utah: Brigham Young University Press, 1971), p. 8.
24. Ibid., pp. 9-10.

> of appearance, not neglecting the weightier matters that bring us here.
>
> Before leaving this subject, however, I need to address myself to any person who . . . cannot observe our standards of dress and grooming. If you intend to ignore or subvert these rules or use them as an occasion for protest, please go somewhere else. This is a university seriously concerned about the pursuit of education. . . . If you choose to ignore the rules you have agreed to observe, demonstrate the sincerity of your protest by leaving. Let us part peacefully and without injury to one another. Sample the environment at some other institution. If you find it to your liking, carry on your studies there. If not, we invite you to return and participate with us here on the same basis as others.
>
> Some may complain that our standards of conduct and appearance make Brigham Young University a controlled environment. That is true. Since we are an institution that promotes learning "by study, and also by faith," it should not be surprising that we are concerned to exclude some forces and influences of the world. A worshipping assembly that desires to enjoy the influence of the Spirit of the Lord does not meet on a busy thoroughfare after the manner of the world. Our standards are responsive to our mission and to our approach to learning.[25]

Despite that optimistic beginning, however, enforcement of the standards — both those dealing with hair length and those dealing with short skirts — continued to be a vexing problem. That minority of students who would not voluntarily comply with the standards had a high degree of visibility on campus, but it was difficult for the handful of people in the Office of University Standards to deal with them. Checks of hair length and short skirts were established in connection with registration at the beginning of each semester, but the president found it necessary to make more than one formal request of faculty members to assist in counseling violators of the stan-

25. Ibid., pp. 13-14.

dards who were in their classes. Oaks tried hard to strike the delicate balance of obtaining consistent and fair enforcement without becoming offensive or seeming to give the problem more priority than it deserved. Not all faculty members shared the president's view that they had a responsibility for dealing with these problems, although but few of these expressed their viewpoint publicly.

Because of resulting national publicity, the problem of making a mountain out of what the president preferred to regard as a molehill was compounded each time new public statements were made on the subject. Illustrative of that publicity was a feature article in the *Los Angeles Times* in August 1974. The paper ran two articles about BYU, one dealing with its increasing concern with academic quality and the other with its code of conduct. The second article began with the statement that "Though academic life at Brigham Young University is changing, BYU's traditionally stern attitude toward student discipline and dress is not."[26] Once their attention had been drawn to campus standards by the visibility and novelty of the long hair problem, outside observers such as the *Times* writer usually found it quite novel that the University administration continued to take a hardline stance toward the disciplining of those who smoked cigarettes, drank intoxicating beverages, used illegal drugs, or even took a fling at "streaking," that brief nationwide campus fad of 1973-74 involving quick dashes by naked students.

The University's handling of such problems predictably drew either applause or ridicule from various sectors, both on campus and off. Some faculty members thought President Oaks's handling of the hair and dress problems brought him closer to breaching his solid rapport with the University community than any other issue during the early years of his administration. Even those who held to this view, however, were unable to offer any realistic alternatives to strict enforcement of the code, in view of the two-sided pressure of

26. "BYU Changing but Not Its Discipline," *Los Angeles Times,* 8 August 1974.

publicly known standards and highly obvious noncompliance. Sensing both the risks and the delicacy of the situation, Oaks made only one off-hand comment to the faculty in his annual faculty message at the Fall 1974 Workshop:

> I feel obliged to say a word about dress and grooming standards, since this subject is so prominent that if I were to omit any mention some would think I had signalled a weakening of commitment. [Some faculty members] have counseled me against making frequent public mention of the dress and grooming standards, and I have tried to follow that counsel. But the success of that strategy depends on the faculty doing its part. If I am sparing in what I *say,* the faculty must be vigorous in what they *do*.[27]

Student Involvement and Activities

Generally speaking, the rapport between the Oaks Administration and its students has been remarkably cordial. Some of the changes already discussed have helped to persuade students that the University does have their interests at heart.

One measure of the administration's willingness to listen to students and involve them on a modest scale in University governance has been the appointment of students to roughly fifty institutional committees.[28] In September 1972, President Oaks publicly acknowledged that student initiative had led to the major addition to the existing library, for which ground was broken in late 1974. Moreover, student involvement in University fund raising was formally approved for the first time in connection with the establishment of the Student Development Association, which was responsible for raising cash and pledges toward the new library addition exceeding $200,000 during its first year of organization. The fund solicitation was conducted among BYU students, as well as in a

27. Dallin H. Oaks, "Annual Report to the Faculty," *A Wise Steward,* BYU Archives, p. 18.
28. Bruce T. Reese, transcribed interview of J. Elliot Cameron, May 1974.

coast-to-coast campaign among friends and alumni of the University.[29] The director of Development for the Church Educational System has noted that both the success and the style of the Student Development Association have attracted national attention. Conscious of that national attention, the student fund-raisers adopted the theme "Building, Not Burning," suggesting a more reverent attitude toward university buildings than had been displayed on some campuses in the past.

Student involvement generally, as always at BYU, continued over an immense variety of activities. Participation by large numbers of students came from functions within the academic colleges, the athletic programs, clubs, ASBYU, and the campus branches and stakes of the Church. In December 1972, a new constitution for the ASBYU was written and approved by special election. With only thirteen percent of the student body voting, some murmurs of student apathy were heard.[30] In the spring of 1974, however, thirty-six percent of the student body voted in the final elections for ASBYU officers, a figure that is relatively high at a time when size and other factors have been contributing to the depersonalization of student involvement on large college campuses generally. While an attempt has been made by the administration to limit the continual proliferation of nonacademic activities (as discussed later in this section), student life since 1971 has not been characterized by much change, but rather by a constant — if somewhat reduced — pulse of activity, variation, and improvement.

With a student body of 25,000 it is not possible even to summarize all the student activities of a four-year period. As illustrative samples, however, mention might be made of activities within the College of Fine Arts and Communications,

---

29. Dallin H. Oaks, "Address to the BYU Student Body," 5 September 1972.
30. "Small Vote Approves ASBYU Constitution," BYU *Daily Universe*, 4 December 1972.

the ASBYU, the Program Bureau, the athletic department, and the student stakes of the Church.

The College of Fine Arts and Communications, administered by Dean Lael J. Woodbury, who succeeded retiring Dean Lorin F. Wheelwright in 1973, provides students, faculty, and community with a wide variety of cultural programs for both spectators and performers. During the 1973-74 school year, for example, 294 concerts were performed in the Harris Fine Arts Center, attended by an aggregate audience of more than 250,000. During that same year, there were sixteen faculty-directed stage productions, two television productions, and more than 200 student productions. The quality of these productions is suggested by their reception outside the University community. The BYU Philharmonic Orchestra (a student orchestra) performed in March 1974 before the national convention of the Music Educators National Conference in California, and their performance "received an electrifying standing ovation" from that critical audience.[31] The A Cappella Choir toured the Scandinavian countries in the summer of 1974. The Drama Department represented the state of Utah in 1972 and again in 1974 at the Region IV American College Theatre Festival. BYU performing groups are heard throughout the nation on "Speaking of Music," a weekly thirty-minute program produced by the Music Department and broadcast by the ABC radio network.

One highlight during each of the past several years has been the Mormon Arts Festival,[32] an effort directed toward bringing together the best in the performing and visual arts from throughout the LDS community. A highlight of the 1974 festival was the premier performance of BYU composer-in-residence Merrill Bradshaw's oratorio *The Restoration* by the BYU Philharmonic Orchestra and the Oratorio and A Cappella Choirs, with the University Chorale. In March 1972 the first Mormon Arts Ball was held in conjunction with the

---

31. Dr. James A. Mason, president, Western Division, Music Educators National Conference, to Dallin H. Oaks, 27 March 1974.
32. *See* chapter 54.

Couples dancing in the Harris
Fine Arts Center during the
Mormon Arts Ball in 1972.

Festival. The Ball is now an annual formal affair held in the Fine Arts Center, planned and sponsored by the ASBYU Culture Office and the College of Fine Arts and Communications. The 2,500 people who attend each year view a wide selection of student and professional talent performing simultaneously in the many theatres and rooms of the Fine Arts Center while a Music Department orchestra and jazz ensemble play for those who wish to dance on the main floor or the galleries of the central exhibition area.

BYU students continue to perform in faraway places. Three groups from the University's Program Bureau are now internationally known. The Young Ambassadors travelled to Japan (1970), Europe (1971), the Eastern United States (1972), and Central and South America (1973). Sounds of Freedom was the first BYU group to perform in Africa with their tour of Rhodesia and South Africa. In 1971 the Lamanite Generation was organized by BYU's director of student productions, Janie Thompson. Its members came entirely from Indian students on campus. Their first tour was to Indian reservations across the nation. In 1974 they toured the Eastern United States, and in 1975 they went to Central and South America.

On campus, there has been a wide variety of musical concerts. The 1974 Homecoming Week performance of the popular singing group "The Carpenters" attracted the largest college concert audience ever when 23,000 BYU students filled the Marriott Center. At the other end of the spectrum, weekly "Concerts Impromptu" are held in a small, informal location in the Wilkinson Center where any student can participate by either performing or listening. The nearby ELWC Art Gallery features weekly student shows and some outstanding outside exhibits. Overall involvement of students is difficult to measure, but the trend in the last few years, paralleling a nationwide trend, has been toward small group activities with a particular emphasis on small group branch and stake Church activities. Nevertheless, in the 1973-74 school year the ASBYU Social Office reported that there were more than 143,000 admissions to the concerts and dances it sponsored.

That same year, 29,000 used the expanded hobby center (as compared to 3,500 ten years before).

The well-established tradition of competitive intercollegiate debating continued under the coaching of Jed Richardson of the Speech and Dramatic Arts Department. During 1974-75, the undergraduate debate team compiled a 390 to 103 win-loss record in various debate tournaments sponsored by the national conference of the Educational Debate Association.

Statistics tell only part of the story. While most traditional activities have been carried on with only slight changes, the Oaks years have seen a marked emphasis on service with the development of two new offices, Student Community Services (SCS), organized in 1971, and the student Ombudsman service, organized in 1970. Students wishing to render community service could work in programs which involved rest homes, the American Fork Training School, or the State Mental Hospital. Involvement with youth was encouraged through the "You've Got a Friend" and "Sub for Santa" programs. In response to environmental concerns, SCS accelerated a beautification and conservation program. Often working in conjunction with the BYU student branches of the Church, SCS provided tools, coordination, and in some cases funds for the repair and renovation of homes and public areas.

The Office of Ombudsman or "citizen's protector" was created to assist students with problems in three categories — difficulties with University administrative or service departments on campus, legal assistance through the help of volunteer attorneys, and consumer services. Typically, the student Ombudsman and his staff investigate the complaint and then either seek redress for the student or help him to understand why no redress is available. In all these activities the emphasis is on serving the "student complainant in a manner which provides the opportunity for his own personal development in understanding, dealing with, and solving his own problems."[33]

---

33. "Description of the Office of Ombudsman," 1973, p. 7.

Another project, sponsored jointly by ASBYU and Admissions and Records, is one of the best examples of frankness in administration-student communications. In the spring of 1973, several students approached Erlend Peterson, assistant dean of Admissions and Records, about the possibility of a student-written orientation book. They argued that a student product would carry more credibility with incoming students. Inherent, however, in that argument was a lack of administrative control over the substance of the handbook. Peterson convinced the administration of the book's potential. Three students wrote the book during May 1973, and, with considerable cooperation from the *Universe* and the *Banyan* and herculean efforts by the University Press, the book was mailed to incoming freshmen in August. Either in spite of or because of the book's candor and humorous touch, the response to *Beginning BYU* was enthusiastic, and a student-written orientation book has since been an annual exercise for three or four superior students. Administration enthusiasm for *Beginning BYU* was certainly heightened by its receipt of a national award as the best student orientation publication of 1973.

The Centennial Celebration

One unique series of campuswide events began in April 1975 as the University initiated its year-long observance of the one hundredth anniversary of its founding. The first event was the opening of the cornerstone of the Karl G. Maeser Building. The cornerstone had been laid on 16 October 1909 by Joseph F. Smith, then President of the Church. Opened at the ceremony with an old-fashioned can opener when an electric saw blade broke in attempting to cut the pure metal of its exterior, the box contained a copy of the original Deed of Trust for BYU, volumes of scripture, copies of the school paper, diplomas, photographs, a telephone directory, and other memorabilia. The annual spring graduation exercises the following day were billed as the Centennial Commencement. The graduation address, focusing on the school's history and entitled "Seven Steps to Greatness," was delivered by

Church Historian and BYU faculty member Leonard J. Arrington. Also at the Commencement exercises, President Oaks noted that in the school's one-hundred-year history, 82,500 degrees had been awarded. Of that number, 3,485 (4.2 percent of the 82,500) were awarded at the Centennial Commencement.

Remaining Centennial events, including guided tours, displays, sculpture unveilings, activities sponsored by individual colleges, and musical productions depicting the history of the school, were carried on under the leadership of Centennial director Lorin F. Wheelwright, dean emeritus of the College of Fine Arts and Communications and production manager for the Arts Division of the 1947 Utah State Centennial Commission. The theme adopted for the Centennial was "BYU: Dedicated to love of God, pursuit of truth, service to mankind." The "fruitful tree" of the Centennial logo, already familiar to residents of the campus community by the beginning of the Centennial observance, was used extensively during the celebration.

The beginning of the Centennial celebration was also the occasion for the inauguration by the University of a major new fund-raising effort, the "Second Century Campaign," the objective of which was to raise $20 million in donations during the Centennial year. The drive was designed to finance major projects in construction; endow scholarly institutes, chairs, centers, and scholarships; and provide funds for numerous other specific projects.[34] By April 1976 more than fifteen million dollars had been contributed. Since the Second Century Campaign was to conclude on 31 August 1976, it is likely that the twenty-million-dollar goal will be reached by that time.[35]

The Centennial events also included the construction of a new carillon, a gift to the University from its students, alumni, employees, and friends, and the erection of two modernistic

34. BYU *Daily Universe,* 29 April 1975.
35. Glenn V. Bird, untranscribed interview with Barry B. Preator, 8 June 1976.

A view of activities at the opening of the Maeser Memorial cornerstone in April 1975. This event launched BYU's year-long centennial celebration.

Leonard J. Arrington, LDS Church historian and speaker at BYU's centennial commencement exercises in 1975. Dr. Arrington also served as coeditor of volumes 3 and 4 of this history.

sculptures, including "The Tree of Wisdom" by Frank Nackos, placed north of the Harold B. Lee Library, and "Windows of Heaven" by Frank Riggs, placed east of the Widtsoe Building. Announcement of the plans for the bell tower and the sculptures brought negative reactions from some within the University community who felt that the expense involved in the relatively elaborate celebration was not justified.[36] Whether those critics prove to be correct in their assessment will probably depend upon the effect of the celebration on the attitudes of both the public and the members of the campus community. Certainly the intent of the entire Centennial celebration was not to be just another extravaganza, but to serve the purpose that any worthwhile study of history serves — learning the lessons of the past to create a more memorable and meaningful future.

Sale of Lower Campus

Soon after the beginning of the Centennial year, the University signed an agreement that ended a historical era.[37] The city block near downtown Provo that was for many years known as "lower campus" was sold to a development group headed by BYU graduates who plan to renovate the old buildings in creating a specialty shopping and entertainment center called "Academy Square." The agreement specified that the exteriors of the buildings would not be substantially changed.

For more than a year prior to the decision to make this disposition of the property, the administration had been considering alternative proposals for making the best long-range use of lower campus. It had become clear that indefinite use of the time-worn buildings for University educational purposes was not economically feasible, especially since virtually all University activities were based on upper campus. At the same

---

36. Without any intended irreverence, but with characteristic student humor, the "fruitful tree" of the Centennial logo was dubbed "Lorin's Lollipop," and "The Tree of Wisdom" was called "Dallin's Oak."
37. "Lower Campus Is Sold," BYU *Daily Universe*, 15 May 1975.

time, both the Board of Trustees and the University administration were seeking some means of preserving the historical flavor and the heritage represented by the grand old buildings and grounds that were the BYU of an earlier time. The Academy Square concept seems to promise wholesome reverence for the past, while at the same time making the renovated former campus an attractive new addition to the community.

Athletics

BYU's long-standing reputation for consistently fine athletic teams and excellent athletic facilities has been sustained during the 1970s. The appointment of a thorough-going academician like Dallin Oaks from the University of Chicago, which eliminated collegiate football from its athletic program, raised some fears among the faithful followers of the "BYU Cougars" that the school's athletic programs might be downplayed as more academically oriented programs began to receive serious attention. Some thought it quite possible in concentrating on academic upgrading for the new president to adopt a theme such as that of the "bold president of the University of Oklahoma who hoped to develop a university of which the football team could be proud."[38]

Oaks, however, soon reassured the Cougar faithful that they had nothing to fear from his attitudes:

> All of us here recognize the fact that this area has a long-established appetite for basketball. . . . Football is also a chief focal point of alumni interest. Our fans are very anxious for BYU to produce a strong, respected football program, and we intend to do so. . . . Major cutbacks are not anticipated at this time. It is our intention to continue with as strong, and as well-balanced a program as possible.[39]

The new president's view on the University's athletic programs was not a matter of mere acquiescence to alumni or

38. Richard Hofstadter, *Anti-intellectualism in American Life* (New York: Alfred A. Knopf, 1964), p. 301.
39. Dallin H. Oaks, Speech to BYU Cougar Club, 19 April 1972.

A partial view of the crowd in the Marriott Center during a BYU basketball game.

student demands. After living with the problems of maintaining the broad and expensive range of BYU programs for a few years, he told an audience of Southern California alumni in 1974 that he was more convinced than ever of the value of the school's support of athletics.[40] He began to realize that nationally publicized success in sports-minded America is a key to the country's positive attention; that it has value, not only for the University's reputation, but more importantly for the reputation of the Church as an institution that fosters a healthy philosophy of the balanced life and builds young men and women of high standards and self-discipline. Oaks has also realized the principle involved in his favorite Knute Rockne saying: "Prayers work best when players are big." He has become a vigorous supporter of high-quality recruiting and standards of skill and competency, while not compromising the school's standards of personal conduct where athletes are involved.

Symbolic of the historical fact that big-time intercollegiate athletics are here to stay at BYU was the opening in December 1971 of the Marriott Center.[41] With a seating capacity of 23,000, the cavernous arena is the largest indoor university facility of its kind in the United States. The Marriott Center might also be a symbol of the size and variety of student activities that are well-established traditions at the University. The center was designed not only for spectator use at athletic contests but also for regular use for student body assemblies, popular and classical concerts, and Church gatherings.[42] In-

40. Dallin H. Oaks, Speech to Southern California area alumni, 31 March 1974.

41. The Marriott Center was dedicated on 4 February 1973. For a more detailed description of the building and its facilities, *see* chapter 36.

42. During 1972-73, the first full year of its use, the Marriott Center seated 272,943 basketball fans at BYU games; 20,000 at a state high school basketball tournament; 161,274 at Forum and Devotional Assemblies, including the dedication of the building; 91,753 for concerts, lyceums, and commencement exercises; and 212,376 at student stake firesides, stake conferences, and televised general Church priesthood meetings. Thus, about two-thirds of the attendance was for activities other than basketball (Marriott Center Records).

deed, the largest crowd on record since the center opened has been for a student body devotional talk by President Spencer W. Kimball.

During the first year of the center's use, BYU basketball fans set a national home attendance record, averaging 21,818 per game. The attendance was undoubtedly helped that year by the basketball team's winning more Western Athletic Conference (WAC) games than ever before on its way to becoming the first team to win the WAC basketball championship two years in a row. Of help both to the fans' attitude and the team's success was the play of Kresimir Cosic, a native Yugoslavian who won national recognition in his homeland and in the United States. At the end of that year, Stan Watts retired as head basketball coach after twenty-three years, during which time he compiled an impressive win-loss record of 431 wins and 260 losses. In 1970 he was appointed chairman of the Department of Intercollegiate Athletics. Assistant Coach Glenn Potter was named to replace him. During Potter's tenure as head coach from 1972 to 1975, the BYU team improved defensively. However, he was never able to field a consistently winning team (his win-loss record was 42-36). After resigning as head basketball coach, Potter continued at BYU as a doctoral student, graduating in 1976. He was replaced by former UCLA Assistant Coach Frank Arnold. Arnold's first team had a 12-14 record in 1975-76.

Another major coaching position became vacant when football coach Tom Hudspeth resigned after the 1971 season. He was replaced by Assistant Coach LaVell Edwards, who gradually built his own brand of BYU football into enough strength to win the WAC championship in 1974. Having started the season with three straight losses to nonconference foes and a tie with Colorado State, Edwards's team showed enough determination to attract national attention by winning seven straight games, the conference title, and the right to represent the WAC in the University's first post-season game at the 1974 Fiesta Bowl in Tempe. Losing star quarterback Gary Sheide in the first quarter because of a shoulder separation, the Cougars fell to Oklahoma State, 16-6.

Frank Arnold, who was named
head basketball coach at
BYU in 1975.

The early 1970s witnessed the retirement of Dean Milton Hartvigsen, who presided over almost twenty years of expansion in the University's athletic programs as dean of the College of Physical Education. He was replaced by Assistant Dean Clayne Jensen in 1974. Hartvigsen's comments to a *Los Angeles Times* writer in 1974 illustrate something of both the success and the philosophy of the University's athletic programs:

> We feel an interest in athletics is very much a part of our educational program. But there's no reason to treat them differently than the academic program. The coach's assignment is viewed just as a class assignment. We're trying to give athletics some educational dignity.
>
> We've been conference all-around champion 11 of the last 12 years. One year [1970] we were fourth nationally. . . .
>
> But we've tried meticulously, too, to conform to the rules of the WAC and the NCAA. We've had no problems. Because of our continual attention to an educational point of view, we have excellent faculty and student support.[43]

As indicated by Hartvigsen's statement, the University's successes have included a wide range of sports beyond the most popular ones, ranging from baseball and track to swimming, wrestling, gymnastics, and golf. BYU's consistently successful golf program, as an example of involvement in sports that do not have mass spectator appeal on the college level, has produced several All-Americans during Coach Karl Tucker's tenure. The best-known alumnus of Tucker's program is Johnny Miller, who captured the nation's imagination in 1974 by breaking the all-time money-winning record in professional golf. After Miller had won his first four tournaments in 1975, a long-time pro golfer made a comment which, while facetious, suggests in a subtle way something about the underlying reasons why BYU and its sponsoring Church are not likely to play down the potential of their sports program: "Seeing him play so well makes me want to join his church."

43. "Y Sports Program Unique," BYU *Daily Universe*, 30 January 1975, reprinting an earlier article featured in the *Los Angeles Times*.

LaVell Edwards, head football coach at BYU since 1972.

The Daily Universe

As discussed in a previous chapter,[44] campus events, as well as local and international news, have long been reported in the pages of the student newspaper, the *Daily Universe.* In 1972, the *Daily Universe* was reorganized to align it more fully with the University's Communications Department as explained in chapter 38.

Although the change appeared to offer better potential experience for journalism majors, some students, along with some members of the off-campus media community, viewed the move as a "faculty take-over," which they thought would result in a repression of student rights of free speech. They had been hoping that the freshness of a new administration might tend to expand both the range and depth of student commentary in the campus community. In one of the last editorials[45] by the completely student-edited campus newspaper, the *Universe* editor expressed some cautious optimism, noting that the change was long overdue. He saw hopes in the new approach for greater student involvement in the paper, as well as increased professionalism. He recognized, however, that some risks of excessive control were involved. After one semester under the new arrangement, an unsolicited letter from twenty-one students on the paper's staff (including most of the student editors) acknowledged their "conversion" to the wisdom of the change.[46] Daily readers of the paper also seem to feel that the new approach has produced an effect quite the opposite of what had been feared. One objective indication of the paper's quality is that it was judged to be the "best all-around collegiate newspaper in Utah, Wyoming, Colorado, and New Mexico" in both 1974 and 1975 by Sigma Delta Chi, the society of professional journalists. Involvement

---

44. *See* Volume 3, chapter 38.
45. "Student Editors View New *Universe* Policy," BYU *Daily Universe,* 17 May 1972.
46. For a detailed account and evaluation of the *Universe* changes, *see* Edwin O. Haroldsen, "Realism Grows for Students after J-profs Take Over Paper," *Journalism Educator* (April 1973), p. 6.

of faculty members who have had professional experience in the public media field seems to have created more respect, not less, for the free speech concept. In addition, educational experience for participating students has improved markedly. Increases in sophistication, maturity, and social consciousness have all been shown to such an extent that the student newspaper is much less frequently referred to with that student-coined phrase that had become well known on the campus in earlier years — "The Daily Unifarce."

Academics in Student Life

It is difficult to know whether there have been actual increases in student concern for academic and professional excellence since Dallin Oaks came to BYU, but there has been a clear rhetorical emphasis. The effect of that emphasis on the faculty has been dealt with elsewhere,[47] but many student leaders and those who have spoken to and with students have also picked up the theme. In his fall 1972 address to the students, Oaks quoted a statement made by President Harold B. Lee at Oaks's inauguration a year earlier, President Lee said, "It was never intended that the leaders of this Church be an ignorant ministry in the learning of the world" and that the Lord expects Church members "to keep pace with scientists and scholars and the development of modern knowledge."[48] The following year Oaks was even more direct. He described a casual conversation he had with a student who just transferred to BYU from another college:

> I asked him to tell me about his experience at BYU. "Well, I don't know much about the studies yet," he responded, "but the social life is sure great, and that's what it's all about here at the Y, isn't it?" I ground my teeth at that answer. What I wanted to reply was: "No, you feather-headed, indolent child, *social life isn't* what it's all about. This is a university. *Learning* is what it's all about. You are here to get an education." Instead, I

47. *See* chapter 47.
48. Dallin H. Oaks, "Reject the Mediocre," BYU *Daily Universe,* 6 September 1972.

> managed a gentler suggestion that he ought to discover some other purpose for his enrollment or his stay would be frustrating and short. Now, this young man meant no harm. He was suffering from a misapprehension whose victims are all too common among our students, alumni, and supporters. It concerns the purposes and functions of this University.
>
> Let us banish forever the illusion that Brigham Young University exists for any purpose other than to provide a university education. Social life, physical exercise, Church activity, cultural development, good times — all these are here. . . . But none of these ingredients is sufficient in itself or in combination to justify the enormous capital investment and annual financial support appropriated to Brigham Young University.[49]

There was no fear in the president's mind that in making such a statement he would not be warmly endorsed by the Board of Trustees. From time to time throughout his administration, members of the Executive Committee and the Board of Trustees had pointedly asked him to make clear to the members of the BYU community that achieving sound educational goals has a higher priority than anything else that takes place on the campus — including certain kinds of Church activity. As recently as May 1973, some of the Trustees stated their concern that some students appeared to view the University as "too much of a playground."[50]

That concern on the part of the Trustees expressed itself in the spring of 1974 when the presidents of the ten campus stakes of the Church[51] were invited to an informal conference

49. Dallin H. Oaks, *Challenges for the Year Ahead* (Brigham Young University, 1973), Dallin H.Oaks biographical file, BYU Archives, pp. 11-12.
50. Dallin H. Oaks memorandum to file, 4 June 1973.
51. On 13 April 1975 the number of student stakes was increased to twelve in a joint stake conference session in the Marriott Center. In connection with that reorganization, the boundaries of the stakes were adjusted and facilities realigned. Three of the twelve stakes were designated as exclusively married students stakes, while the other nine stakes were designated for single students only. Previously, only one of the stakes had been exclusively for married students.

with some of the Trustees. The "playground" problem was discussed at some length, along with other matters relating to student attitudes at BYU, and the ecclesiastical leaders were invited to make suggestions on how the Church program in the campus stakes and branches could be modified to give greater encouragement and emphasis to serious academic pursuits. The outcome of this and subsequent meetings was a statement issued by the First Presidency of the Church during the summer of 1974 directing the leaders in the BYU campus stakes to limit the weeknight Church activity of their members. One specific concern of that letter was the extent of the activity that had been engaged in by the "family home evening groups" within student branches. These mixed groups of between ten and twenty single students evolved over several years into very successful subunits of the single student branches. Their very success, making students eager to participate in everything from "family home evenings" on Monday to nightly "family prayer" in some groups and frequent other impromptu get-togethers, was the cause of their conflict with the academic goals of the University. Cutting back on that activity has been a mildly frustrating task for campus Church leaders because of the enthusiasm of the single students for the former program. Another result of the First Presidency directive was the decision by the University administration and the BYU stake presidents to free Tuesday evenings, which had been the night of branch MIA activities, for campuswide scheduling of academic programs.

Some experienced faculty members believe that the change in academic emphasis has not yet resulted in any perceptible differences, either in student practices or attitudes.[52] On the other hand, student participation has increased in academically oriented lecture series, films, and student publications.[53]

---

52. Bruce T. Reese, transcribed interview of Martin B. Hickman, Jae R. Ballif, Howard W. Barnes, and Marion J. Bentley, May 1974, in the possession of Bruce T. Reese.
53. Indicative of this trend is a comparison of the programs listed in the 1966-67 ASBYU Academics Office History with those of 1971-72 and 1972-73 (BYU Archives).

Another mild inference might be drawn from the observation that four of the five ASBYU presidents between 1971 and 1975 served the year prior to their being elected student body president as ASBYU academic vice-president, with a natural emphasis on academically oriented programs. Moreover, the campus library has reported an overall increase of book circulation of twelve percent during regular semesters between 1969 and 1974, with student enrollment figures remaining relatively constant. During that same period the number of books checked out for outside-the-library use increased by twenty-four percent. The use of nonbook library materials increased by fifty-two percent, while the use of micromaterial and interlibrary loans, usually indicators of primary research, increased by forty-two percent and fifty percent respectively.[54]

As another indication of increased academic emphasis, there has been an enrollment increase of twenty percent (from 858 to 1,050 students) in the undergraduate Honors Program since 1971. Established in 1961,[55] the Honors Program became a major attraction to BYU for gifted Mormon high school graduates from across the nation by offering access to superior teachers, small classes, highly flexible curriculum planning, and stimulating intellectual cross-fertilization among the students themselves. In a sense, the growth of this program during a period of stable overall enrollment indicates increasing acceptance throughout the Church of the concept that BYU indeed can prepare talented students for graduate and professional study by maturing both their educational skills and their spiritual moorings in ways that are reciprocally strengthening. By 1975, the founder of the program, Robert K. Thomas, had become academic vice-president of the University, and the second full-time director, C. Terry Warner, had become dean of the reorganized College of General Studies with the charge to revitalize and revise the entire concept of general education at

---

54. Reports to BYU library director, 1968-69 and 1973-74.
55. *See* Volume 3, chapter 37.

the University.[56] As a result, the Honors Program experience may have a significant influence in the future, with a general spreading of the program's established ability to provide a high-quality liberal arts education while stimulating both fresher and deeper religious convictions among students. It remains to be seen, however, whether the general student body has sufficient initiative and motivation to benefit from increased freedom in defining and pursuing their own educational aspirations. This will certainly be tested in the new general education approach.

Only the future will show whether students will generally take academic preparation — both vocational and nonvocational — as seriously as the Trustees, the administration, and the faculty would hope. One BYU dean believes that the increase of serious discussion of the matter during the Oaks years may at least make students begin to feel that they are failing in the performance of their religious duties if they are not successful in excelling in their educational pursuits.[57] He also thinks that little substantive change will take place until Church members generally, from whose homes BYU students predominantly come, develop greater concern for the values of education — as distinguished from mere vocational training.

There may be nothing very new in the emphasis of the early 1970s on this subject. BYU teachers and leaders have always talked about the pursuit of academic excellence, in one form or another. However, the increased capacities and commitments of the present faculty, who are themselves largely the products of the labors of a much smaller band of scholars from earlier BYU generations, will give future historians an opportunity to determine the extent of the growth of pervasive intellectual quality at a Mormon university.

---

56. *See* chapter 47 for a discussion of the University's new general education program.
57. Bruce T. Reese, transcribed interview of Jae R. Ballif, May 1974, in the possession of Bruce T. Reese.

49

Religious Instruction at BYU: An Ongoing Challenge

It was probably too much to expect that there would never be intellectual tension between BYU religion instructors and teachers trained in and confined to the teaching of traditional secular disciplines. Minor disturbances in this area during the Cluff Administration gave way to a thoroughgoing academic crisis in the days of George Brimhall. Under Harris there were also some controversies. During the Wilkinson Administration, the Board made a number of administrative changes and established policies designed to reduce friction.

Nevertheless, shortly after Dallin Oaks came to the campus he sensed that some further changes might be in order. To get at the heart of the problem, he assigned his staff to solicit written responses from some 200 faculty members and to interview selected persons in depth. The questions ranged from a reconsideration of the basic religion requirement in the University curriculum (two hours of religion credit were required for each semester in residence) to the roles of the full-time religion faculty and other faculty in the teaching of religion on the campus. This information, together with that from other available sources, gave him needed perspective on many topics under the broad heading of "Religious Instruction."

Historical Background

The necessity for spiritual and religious training was the primary reason for the establishment of Brigham Young Academy in the first place. Brigham Young's one-sentence mandate to Karl G. Maeser that not even the alphabet or the multiplication tables should be taught without the Spirit of God[1] has remained the classic statement of BYU's educational philosophy for generations of students and teachers. Even the Articles of Incorporation of Brigham Young Academy, dated 18 July 1896, provide in Article IV that, "In addition to the usual education given in an institution of like character, the Old and New Testament, the Book of Mormon, and the Doctrine and Covenants should be read and their doctrines inculcated in such college." When the school became a university the same emphasis was reiterated. In 1913 the faculty adopted a resolution that "all students be expected to take theology."[2] During the 1920s and 1930s some Church leaders feared that Mormon religious concepts were not being properly taught at BYU. This could have been the reason why some General Authorities favored the curtailment of certain classes, the abandonment of BYU, or making it a feeder to the University of Utah and other secular institutions.

To meet this problem, in the early 1930s a number of professional teachers obtained advanced degrees in theology at non-Mormon theological seminaries, hoping to provide greater academic credibility in religious instruction at Church institutions. Such training emphasized scholarly research in speculative or philosophical theology, which at times suggested conclusions incompatible with the established doctrines of the LDS Church. Moreover, the abstract and secular

---

1. Reinhard Maeser, *Karl G. Maeser* (Provo, Utah: Brigham Young University, 1928), p. 79.
2. Most of the information for this section is taken from Boyd K. Packer, *Seek Learning, Even by Study and Also by Faith* (Brigham Young University Religious Instruction, 1974), Boyd K. Packer biographical file, BYU Archives; and a memorandum from Bruce C. Hafen to Dallin H. Oaks, 23 February 1972.

analysis of theological precepts sometimes proved to have little relationship to spiritual enrichment and improved behavior. Formal theological training, and the academic flavor that often accompanied it, generally introduced an unwelcome dimension to a church that had been both taught and led by a lay ministry. Church members had always believed in the concept of continuous revelation to the Church through its leaders, who were sustained by the membership as prophets in the full scriptural sense. Therefore, it has been fundamental to Mormons that "It is not to a university . . . that the world must turn for ultimate authority in the field of religion. . . . By direction of him whose Church this is, that authority is held by a group of ordinary men called from many walks of life . . . who are ordained as apostles, sustained as prophets, seers, and revelators, and presided over by one authorized to exercise all the keys of scriptural authority existing upon the earth."[3] Accordingly, the acquisition of advanced degrees in abstract theology from non-Mormon seminaries was discouraged.

Regardless of where teachers were trained, the objective of scholarly research in theology — the interpretation, and often the discovery, of new doctrine — always posed a conflict for trained theologians in a church that looked to lay leaders for doctrinal interpretations. At the same time, the need for full-time religion teachers throughout the Church Educational System grew steadily and rapidly. That growth had the clear support of the General Authorities, a few of whom were themselves former professional religion teachers in the Church Educational System. The growing demand, however, did not diminish the dimensions of the conflict.

To ensure proper religious teaching the Board of Trustees in 1940 adopted a policy requiring each student to take a two-credit-hour religion class each semester as a prerequisite to graduation. The Board also decided upon changes in the curriculum to ensure that it expressed Mormon religious

---

3. Boyd K. Packer, *Seek Learning, Even by Study and Also by Faith,* pp. 8-9.

concepts. In that same year the Division of Religion was organized on campus with five professional religion teachers who previously had been involved in teaching nonreligious subjects.

President Wilkinson, with the consent of the Board of Trustees, authorized the University to grant master's and doctor's degrees reflecting the Mormon view of religion as a way of life rather than as a study of abstract precepts. To strengthen this program the Division of Religion in 1959 was named the College of Religious Instruction. Proponents of the graduate programs in religion explained that individuals receiving these degrees would be better prepared to teach at LDS institutes than if they relied on purely secular training and their own private study of religion. In practice, however, it was found that some of the most effective teachers in the College of Religious Instruction were those who had received their advanced degrees in areas other than religion but had applied the same scholarly discipline in their personal study of the gospel.

Some leaders of the Church, including President David O. McKay, were uneasy about the establishment of graduate degrees in religion from the day the decision was made. This concern stemmed in part from the source-of-doctrinal-authority conflict identified above, and in part from the realization that persons with graduate degrees in Mormon theology had no place to turn for employment other than the Church Educational System.

Although religion credit had been required since 1940, in 1961 the question arose whether a specific course should be required for all students, particularly entering freshmen. The faculty of the College of Religious Instruction was sharply divided over the issue, with some favoring the Book of Mormon and others favoring a study of Mormon theology as the basic required course. Some of the longstanding concerns about an overemphasis on academic theology were both implicit and explicit in that discussion. The Board's decision that the required course be the Book of Mormon restated a priority historically given to "religious" as distinguished from academically oriented "theological" instruction. A distinction between those two terms — religion and theology — was drawn by President David O. McKay in speaking at the University in 1937:

> The Brigham Young University is primarily a religious institution. It was established for the sole purpose of associating with facts of science, art, literature, and philosophy the truths of the Gospel of Jesus Christ.
>
> In making religion its paramount objective, the University touches the very heart of all true progress. . . .
>
> I emphasize *religion* because the Church University offers more than mere theological instruction. Theology as a science . . . may consist merely of intellectual study. Religion is subjective, and denotes the influences and motives to human conduct and duty which are found in the character and will of God. One may study theology without being religious.[4]

The University's original objectives in teaching religion courses had been characterized by the religious — as distinguished from the theological — function. The 1912 catalog, for example, stated that "As far as possible, practical religion is emphasized in order that students may have faith in God and develop a religious character." But with the introduction of professional religion teachers, some desire to teach doctrinal subjects with a more theological or academic emphasis had been only natural. Thus, the philosophical differences expressed in the 1961 controversy were reflective of an understandably ambivalent commitment to academic objectives in the College of Religious Instruction.

In the meantime, some serious academic work was being produced in the college that was not so much theological in nature as it was historical. Since he came to BYU in 1946, Hugh Nibley's well-known work with ancient languages and manuscripts has been both illustrative and symbolic of that

---

4. David O. McKay, "The Church University," *Messenger* 11 (October 1937):3-4, BYU Archives.

kind of scholarship.[5] This and the work of some other Church history specialists added what might be termed a historical-academic function to the work of the College of Religious Instruction.

An unconscious overlapping of these three functions — the religious, the theological, and the historical — accompanied by differences in basic assumptions among those whose work found an emphasis in one of the three areas, over the years produced strong differences of opinion about the extent to which the College of Religious Instruction was achieving its intended purposes. Thus, the student-oriented, faith-building type of religion teacher was confused about whether he should be doing serious research and writing; the scholarly theologians were concerned about reassuring Church leaders that their research efforts were intended to be supportive; and the serious historical scholars in the college wondered why the teaching of gospel principles should not be left to the Sunday Schools so that the College of Religious Instruction could devote its resources to the study of ancient documents and to Mormon history.

Another problem was the phenomenon that might be called "integration" — the active and forthright blending of gospel teachings with instruction in standard academic disciplines. Many persons both inside and outside the University have believed that such integration is the basis for BYU's uniqueness and, indeed, much integration has taken place throughout the school's history. Even apart from the existence of a separate religion faculty, however, there has been a gradual tendency toward decreased academic integration. Some faculty members in the nonreligious disciplines have assumed that religious instruction is the responsibility of the college bearing that name, that students will do their own integrating, and that excessive discussion of religious principles might impair the professional and academic quality that they think

---

5. For a sketch of the work and personality of Hugh Nibley, *see* "Hugh Nibley: If He's Got It All Together, Why Does He Stand All Alone?" *BYU Today* 28, (May 1974):12-13.

their courses should have.

The ideal — and for many faculty members the common practice — has been that outlined by President Spencer W. Kimball:

> It is proper that every professor and teacher in this institution would keep his subject matter bathed in the light and color of the restored gospel, and have all his subject matter perfumed lightly with the spirit of the gospel. Always, there would be an essence and the student would feel the presence.[6]

Many of the university's most able scholars have always involved Church values and insights in research within their academic disciplines, and this kind of integration is probably increasing. Some disciplines lend themselves to such integration more than others. The colleges of Social Sciences and Family Living, for example, are two areas in which "integration" could take place with great frequency in research and writing efforts.[7]

Beginning in the 1950s and continuing through the 1960s, a fairly aggressive form of integration took place in classrooms within the College of Religion, where some teachers took what were essentially religious stands against specific tenets, if not at times against the entire value of some academic disciplines in the physical and social sciences. This became a source of serious conflict when the religion teacher was thought by other faculty members to have no special

---

6. Spencer W. Kimball, *Education for Eternity* (Provo, Utah: Brigham Young University Press, 1967), p. 11.
7. For a specific illustration of this kind of integration, *see* the BYU Forum Address of psychology professor Allen E. Bergin, 3 June 1975. In that lecture, Bergin, who came to BYU in 1972 from the faculty at Teachers College, Columbia University, and who served during 1974-75 as president of the Society for Psychotherapy Research, an international multidisciplinary organization, engaged in some introspective self-criticism of his own professional field and concluded that Mormon psychologists could contribute significantly to a better understanding of psychotherapy and the processes of psychological counseling by finding ways to articulate gospel concepts within the framework of their discipline.

expertise in the discipline he was attempting to integrate with his religious studies. Conversely, when some faculty members in the regular academic disciplines either did not spend much time with active integration of religious and academic subjects or disputed some religious stands on what they viewed as academic questions, a few students and teachers wondered — sometimes aloud — whether this meant that the academic faculty were teaching views incompatible with the gospel. Thus, differing assumptions about the propriety and most desirable manner of achieving integration became another source of strain on the campus.

Another historical factor of some significance in the development of BYU's religious training function has been the student wards and stakes. Until the first stake was organized during the 1950s the Division of Religion assumed responsibility for all religious activity, as well as all religious instruction, on campus. The student wards (called student "branches" since 1972), 120 in number by 1975, have since taken over a large share of the practical and informal religious instruction, leaving only formal religious courses for the University. The branches have also provided intimate contact between students and faculty members from all academic disciplines who are called to serve in ecclesiastical assignments through Church organizational channels. These associations may have brought the University community as close to a real fulfillment of its traditional religious function as any other single development. Still, because much of the teaching of religion within the student branches has been done by students, an important place has remained for the religious approach in the University religion classroom.

One highly visible form of religious instruction on campus has been the devotional assemblies, at which General Authorities spoke weekly during the Wilkinson Administration. Students could register for and obtain one hour of religion credit by attending devotional and forum assemblies. This was not sufficient, however, to relieve them from taking a theology class. Still there was uneasiness because of the absence of any satisfactory means of ensuring that attendance was accurately reported and because not all teachers included the substance of the devotional addresses in their examinations, even though they were permitted to do so.

Changes during the Oaks Administration

With this background, the Oaks Administration concluded that some adjustments were essential. One of the first steps was the decision, approved by the Board of Trustees in May 1972, that except for those already enrolled in these programs, no future master's or doctor's degrees would be awarded by the College of Religious Instruction. Students expecting to teach in institutes or seminaries or expecting to teach religion at Church schools were encouraged to take heavy course loads in religious subjects, but to major in some other field. In this way they benefited from a standardized degree, which gave them job opportunities elsewhere and also made them well prepared to teach religious subjects in accordance with LDS Church doctrine.

Another change was the removal of academic credit for attendance at devotional assemblies. At the same time, the number of weekday devotional assemblies was cut in half. The traditional Thursday morning forum assembly[8] was discontinued, and forum and devotional assemblies were held on alternate Tuesdays. One of the most significant features of the former devotionals was the policy, adopted during the Wilkinson Administration, of having a General Authority speak to a multistake fireside once a month. This practice was continued and reemphasized during the Oaks Administration and the firesides are now attended by students from twelve stakes. Attendance has averaged around 18,000 (about sixty-nine percent of the student body and faculty) during 1975-76, and the crowds could be accommodated only in the Marriott Center. Average attendance at the Tuesday devotional assemblies approximated thirty-three percent of the

8. Academic credit for attendance at forum assemblies was also discontinued.

student body and faculty for the 1974-75 school year when fifteen assemblies were held, compared with thirty-seven percent of the student body and faculty as an average during the entire Wilkinson Administration when twenty-five to thirty assemblies were held each year. The average attendance at forum assemblies has declined substantially — from an average of thirty-two percent of the student body and faculty during the entire Wilkinson Administration, when twenty-five to thirty assemblies were held each year, to less than fourteen percent of the student body and faculty for the 1974-75 school year, when twelve assemblies were held (*see* Volume 3, chapter 37).

The religion requirement in the curriculum was also changed in the spring of 1972. Greater flexibility was allowed in transferring credit for religion courses taken in institutes of religion at other campuses, and the previously informal policy of not requiring religion courses for graduate students was formalized. The primary change in the requirement was the shift from a "credit-hour" requirement to a "religion course" requirement, which enabled seniors to fulfill their requirement by taking one-hour courses for credit, in contrast to the typical two-credit-hour courses comprising the bulk of the religion curriculum. The one-hour courses offered to seniors and graduate students have included lecture series, seminars, and departmental or college colloquiums designed to achieve an active integration of religious and academic subjects. Many of these courses for seniors are now being taught by the faculty in academic departments throughout the University.

The Board of Trustees gave President Oaks the right to select teachers for the Book of Mormon classes from any of the colleges of the University, a right that was also given to President Wilkinson but to which deans and department chairmen objected because it permitted the taking of their best professors for this purpose. Nevertheless, during his administration Wilkinson had used thirty teachers for that purpose. The new authority given to Oaks, with added instructions from the Board of Trustees, gave new emphasis to Religious Instruction. Budgets were arranged to compensate academic departments for the time their personnel spent teaching religion courses. Between 1972 and 1975, sixty-four teachers, representing most departments on campus, taught a Book of Mormon class. Among the benefits of this arrangement is the fact that teachers have acquired fresh perspectives on their regular academic work and have had reawakened in themselves a sensitivity to the underlying purpose of the University.

Institute of Ancient Studies

Within a year of these initial changes the University established the Institute for Ancient Studies, an interdisciplinary organization designed to promote the development and dissemination of information relating to ancient manuscripts of religious significance. The first director of the Institute was Hugh Nibley, and the members of the Institute were appointed from the College of Religious Instruction and the Department of Classical Languages in the College of Humanities. The administration also gave increasing encouragement to cooperation between the History Department and the College of Religious Instruction in pursuing research and teaching projects involving academically oriented Church history subjects.

In 1972, distinguished Utah State University historian Leonard J. Arrington was appointed LDS Church historian. He was also appointed to the Lemuel H. Redd Chair of Western history at BYU. At the same time a center for the study of Western American history was created in the BYU History Department. Arrington's appointment as Church historian was a significant change from the pattern of having a General Authority fill this position. It was a clear signal from Church leaders that they recognized the legitimacy and necessity of serious professional research and writing in the field of LDS Church history.

These developments indicated a desire on the part of the Trustees and the University to encourage serious scholarly work in the historical subfields of religion that best lend them-

Dr. Hugh Nibley, first director
of the Institute of Ancient
Studies at BYU.

selves to academic treatment without conflicting with the concerns about excessively academic approaches to practical religion or doctrinal matters.

Designation of the College of Religious Instruction Changed

The next step came in the summer of 1973 when the name of the College of Religious Instruction was changed to Religious Instruction. Some of the reasons for this were given in a memorandum of 3 April 1973 which President Oaks discussed with the faculty:

1. Everywhere else in the University the term "college" identifies a degree-granting entity. Thus, degrees are conferred in the "college" convocations. But the College of Religious Instruction grants no degrees — graduate or undergraduate.
2. Having a "College of Religious Instruction" listed in our catalog parallel with the Colleges of Physical Education, Social Sciences, Engineering Sciences and Technology, etc., may convey to non-LDS readers the idea that BYU has a "ministerial school."
3. Discontinuing the "college" entity for religious instruction would emphasize the idea that *all* University faculty are involved in the teaching of religion, either in formal religion classes or through the permeation of religious values into the teaching of their respective disciplines. There are important legal reasons for emphasizing this point.
4. Discontinuing the "college" entity for religious instruction would tend to reduce the sensitivity about a "paid ministry," since the existence of a "college" emphasizes the concentration of specialists in the field of religion.
5. The number of faculty in the College of Religious Instruction is comparatively small.

In connection with this reorganization, the Philosophy Department was transferred from Religious Instruction to the College of General Studies. Immediately, many faculty members, particularly those in the former College of Religious

Instruction, became concerned that this change signalled the beginning of a move toward eliminating full-time religion teachers from the University. However, Elder Boyd K. Packer of the Council of the Twelve explained in a meeting with the BYU religion faculty that there was no such intent. Elder Packer, himself a former teacher and administrator in the Department of Seminaries and Institutes of Religion in the Church Educational System, said:

> Your work is not to be isolated as the other disciplines may well be. . . . Hereafter religious education will not be limited to one college. It will be an influence contributing to, and drawing from, every segment of the University. . . .
>
> Once again, the acceptance of the decision was a remarkable thing. It could not have been achieved with an assembly of brethren less than you are. I hope you can understand how this decision is a significant vote of confidence in you. Perhaps we needed the experience of having a college of religion. Certainly that experience will serve us for generations to come.[9]

Not long after the announcement of the college reorganization, Dean Roy W. Doxey retired and Jeffrey R. Holland was appointed dean of Religious Instruction. Dean Doxey had administered the college since 1971, replacing Daniel H. Ludlow, who had been appointed to a full-time position with the Church Correlation Committee. Dean Holland, a BYU graduate who taught in the Department of Seminaries and Institutes before receiving a Ph.D. in American Studies at Yale, was thought to be a man of sufficient academic training and ability to command the respect of and to communicate with faculty throughout the campus community; at the same time, he had established a reputation of being a superior teacher of "practical religion" with special appeal to a broad spectrum of college-age minds.

The effect of these developments is likely to be the increasing identification of a core group of religion teachers whose

---

9. Boyd K. Packer, *Seek Learning, Even by Study and Also by Faith,* p. 9.

teaching styles will follow the "religious" motivational approach more than the theologically analytical approach, although there is still a place for careful thought and analysis of doctrine. Full-time religion teachers who are really Church historians (ancient and modern) or language specialists (particularly, specialists in ancient languages) are likely to do their scholarly work in association with some other regular academic discipline. Those whose specialty has been academically oriented theology (as distinguished from historians and language scholars) are likely to decline in both number and impact as time goes on now that the graduate programs in religion have been phased out.

A few unresolved questions remain as the practical implications of a more fluid relationship between the full-time religion teachers and the other University faculty members are worked out. For one thing, the inherent risks of the "captive audience" in required religion classes continues to be something of a question mark, but the advantages outweigh the disadvantages and the policy is not likely to change. Elder Packer has also expressed his concerns about the possible tendency of BYU religion teachers to be diverted excessively from teaching to research and writing. He is also concerned about those who may adopt "pedagogical hobbies," such as an overemphasis on "economics or politics" and "certain patterns of Church government." However, the mutual skepticism that has prevailed over the past few decades between the religion teachers and teachers in other disciplines is likely to decline as the faculty enters a period of increased cooperation and reciprocal communication.

With the beginning of the 1975-76 school year the role of various forms of religious instruction on the campus seemed more clearly defined, thus creating an improved climate and attitude of optimism on this subject among religious instruction faculty and the University generally.

The Richard L. Evans Chair of Christian Understanding

In November 1972, approximately one year following the death of Elder Richard L. Evans, a member of the Council of

Dr. Truman G. Madsen, first incumbent of the Richard L. Evans Chair of Christian Understanding.

the Twelve and a Trustee of the University, BYU announced the creation of the Richard L. Evans Chair of Christian Understanding. Truman G. Madsen of the faculty of Religious Instruction was named its first incumbent. The stimulus for this professorship came from Lowell Berry, a nonmember of the Church from Northern California who was a long-time friend and fellow Rotarian of Elder Evans. Berry's donation of $250,000 was matched by the contributions of others. The stated purpose of the professorship, one that had been well served by the philosophy and activity of Elder Evans during his lifetime, was the "promotion of understanding among people of differing religious faiths through teachings and other activities centered in Jesus Christ and his teachings."

With that purpose as a guide, Dr. Madsen, an experienced scholar in the field of philosophy and a popular author and lecturer on religious subjects, has initiated a series of approaches that have brought the University's and the Church's world view into closer communication with the American intellectual community. His lecturing took him to sixty different college campuses during the first year of the chair's existence. In addition, he has initiated a "commuting professorship" in Mormon studies at the Graduate Theological Union at the University of California at Berkeley. With this kind of beginning, the Evans Chair promises reciprocal communication at a sophisticated level between Mormonism and leaders of thought within other Christian communities.

50

BYU, the Church, and the Church Educational System

A recent study of university governance made the following comment on university boards of trustees:

> The Board of Trustees once governed the institution in detail. It represented the denominational church that originated the campus, or a well-defined model of "Western civilization," or both. It knew what it wanted in the socialization of students to moral beliefs and/or cultural behaviors. . . . The first delegation of authority by the Board to the President in the history of the University of California came in 1891 when the President was permitted to hire a janitor, provided he reported his action promptly to the Board. Much has happened to Board control since that day.[1]

The role of the Board of Trustees of Brigham Young University has also varied from one period to another, but contrary to the growing pattern of large-scale delegation at other universities, the BYU Board has maintained full responsibility for a kind of general environmental control that continues to make Brigham Young unique among the large

1. Carnegie Commission on Higher Education, *Governance of Higher Education* (New York: McGraw-Hill, 1973), p. 31.

universities of America. The BYU Board has been able to fill that role in spite of the increasing size and complexity of the University, without involving itself unnecessarily in operational details.

This pervasive and positive influence has not changed in recent years because there has been no change in either the principles or the organizational facts affecting the relationship between the University and its Trustees. The underlying principle governing the Board's role was reiterated by Marion G. Romney of the Council of the Twelve in his remarks to the first faculty meeting held under the Oaks Administration in the fall of 1971:

> Since BYU is a Church institution it must of necessity be administered in the same way the Church is administered — that is, by the priesthood. The Lord established this order, and we cannot rightly change it. This means, of course, that the major policies and administration procedures at Brigham Young University are and must continue to be determined by its Board of Trustees, which is composed, in the main, of General Authorities.
>
> We are aware that there are universities in which the administration, in large measure, determines policies. There are other universities in which faculties have a major voice in determining policies. In some universities the students themselves dictate. Whatever justification there is in such universities for this type of government does not exist here. . . .
>
> Not only is the board charged with the responsibility of determining general policies with respect to physical plant and personnel matters, but it is also responsible for the academic courses offered and, insofar as it can be predetermined, for the content of forum lectures.
>
> The trustees of BYU are deeply interested in academic excellence; they desire that scholastically BYU be unexcelled. . . . In all its efforts to promote such excellence, however, the . . . saving of souls always takes precedence over the urge to compete with other universities in academic offerings and worldly honors.[2]

---

2. Marion G. Romney, "Responsibilities of the LDS Teacher," *Horizons*

This basic view, taken seriously by those who administer the affairs of BYU, suggests that this is one board of trustees that has not relinquished much authority over the years. However, having chosen trusted individuals for important stewardship positions within the Church Educational System, the Board allows a great deal of latitude, manifesting great respect for the power of its position by exercising restraint in the use of that power.

As mentioned previously,[3] the reorganization of the First Presidency in 1970 initiated some new attitudes toward Church education. Reference has already been made to the roles of President Harold B. Lee and Commissioner of Education Neal A. Maxwell in the formulation of policies for an expanded educational system. The top-level appointments throughout the Church Educational System under Maxwell continued to reflect a combination of proven academic competence and loyalty to the Church. People who were both competent and orthodox were also appointed to administer the affairs of the newly established Historical Department of the Church.[4] A group of trained Mormon historians was assigned to write an updated history of the Church; a select committee on Church education was appointed by Commissioner Maxwell to take a fresh look at many educational issues. Similarly fundamental new looks were concurrently being taken at the organizational philosophies and effectiveness of other arms of the Church, ranging from an overall correlation program and internal communications and public relations to youth activity programs. In all of these things, the Church began to draw heavily upon persons who had established expertise in the private professional sector. What was happening at BYU, then, was part of a general pattern of reevaluation in many of the Church's subunits.

Unlimited (Brigham Young University, 1971), pp. 1-2. For a similar statement, *see* Boyd K. Packer, "Set Your Hands to Lift Them," *Excellence in Learning* (Brigham Young University, 1973), pp. 3-13.

3. *See* chapter 45.
4. *See* chapter 47.

Even though there has been no change in the basic role and authority of the Board of Trustees since 1971, there has been a redefinition of the role of the University in the context of the Church Educational System, a regularization of communication channels, and a two-way attitude shift that has been both productive and expansive.

The Maxwell-Oaks Relationship

Neal A. Maxwell's appointment as commissioner of Church Education became effective exactly one year prior to the date on which Dallin Oaks assumed office at BYU. The revival of the commissioner's office portended a different role for BYU than had existed when the leadership of the Church Educational System and the leadership of the University rested in essentially the same hands. President Marion G. Romney has indicated that the Trustees of the University, who also form the Board of Education for all other units of the Church Educational System, recognized the need to place greater stress on educational programs that could extend the unique influence of the Church Educational System to much larger numbers of people through means other than the traditional university approach. Though BYU was to remain in many respects the keystone of the system, the Board's view of the educational needs of its people required that BYU not dominate the educational system. Thus, one of the first actions taken by the officers of the Board after Oaks had accepted his appointment (but before the appointment had been made public) was a meeting at Chicago's O'Hare Airport, to which President Romney flew from Salt Lake City and Neal Maxwell flew from his extended assignment in England. This was the first meeting between Maxwell and Oaks, although Maxwell had been intimately involved with the decision leading to his appointment.[5] While a number of matters were discussed at that meeting, President Romney stated later that its main — though unexpressed — purpose was to impress upon BYU's

5. *See* chapter 45.

new president that he would be reporting to the commissioner and would be part of an educational system that had a much broader scope than BYU, in spite of the University's disproportionate physical size in the Church Educational System. President Romney came away from that meeting satisfied that Oaks understood the concept and that Oaks and Maxwell would be able to develop a harmonious relationship.[6] Experience since that time has proven that his instincts were correct.

BYU's role in the educational system has undergone gradual definition as Oaks, Maxwell, and others have tried to feel their way into the most appropriate working relationship — one that would take full advantage of the University's resources, while at the same time responding to the educational needs of all Church members. At the inauguration of President Oaks, Commissioner Maxwell set forth his views on that subject as follows:

> As the only university [in the Church Educational System], we are confident that under your presidency Brigham Young University will see itself not as an isolated, self-sufficient, austere academic Everest, but rather as a living university . . . that leans into the fray of fellowship with its impressive human and spiritual resources to serve the entire Church Educational System and men and women everywhere, and as a rapprochement of theology and university in the best of that tradition.[7]

In retrospect, it is difficult to imagine how more harmonious relationships and mutual expectations could have been developed between BYU and the remainder of the Church Educational System. The development has been an evolving one, as will be illustrated by several examples mentioned below. An essential ingredient in that evolution has been the personal rapport between Oaks and Maxwell. Both of them

---

6. Bruce C. Hafen, untranscribed interview with Marion G. Romney, 12 July 1974.
7. Neal A. Maxwell, "Greetings to the President," *Inaugural Addresses* (Provo, Utah: Brigham Young University Press, 1971), p. 1.

brought to their jobs certain assumptions that have avoided many potential sources of misunderstanding. Of basic importance, for example, is the unreserved personal acceptance by both men of the concepts permeating Marion G. Romney's description of the Board of Trustees. In addition, both men come from academic backgrounds and share many of the same assumptions about the role and purpose of teaching, research, and the overall objectives of universities. They also share an instinctive commitment to candor and full disclosure in personal as well as professional relationships. Their conferences and correspondence lack pretense, maneuvering, and second-guessing. Another important characteristic common to both men is the instinct to resolve a problem or make a decision as quickly as possible, provided there is a secure factual basis for any decision and all its implications have been thought through. In a relatively informal setting in the fall of 1974, President Oaks introduced Neal Maxwell as the speaker at a small gathering of BYU faculty and administrators. The comments made by President Oaks about the commissioner in his introduction and the commissioner's comments in his response offer some insight into the reasons for the personal and professional respect between the two men. Said the president in introducing the commissioner:

> It is a thrill to work with Neal Maxwell, because he has mastered as well as any person I have ever associated with the very delicate balance between directing and bossing, between creating a total state of anarchy within which people could run willy-nilly and on the other hand creating a feeling of openness within which one is free to make all of the right choices and really has some very valuable though skillfully guarded counsel on what those choices are. I have never felt that the Commissioner has directed us in specific things and yet the power of his leadership and the force of his example and the influence of his direction has never been absent from the scene while I've been there. And, it's something that needs to be felt. It can't be explained very well. I must have at least demonstrated that in what I've said already. But I'm trying to say

that we love Neal Maxwell very much.[8]

In reply, the commissioner said:

> No one, I am sure, has ever had any deeper or more consistent support from the Board of Trustees than President Oaks has. The level of confidence couldn't be higher. . . . Dallin never comes unprepared nor is he ever inarticulate. Nor indeed is there any effort ever to fail to give disclosure to the board, and I want you to know that esteem for Dallin exists not only with me but at the board level also.[9]

BYU and the Commissioner's Office

With those personal feelings paving the way, Maxwell and Oaks began to establish a relationship between the University and the educational system on a relatively inductive basis. Rather than creating in advance some comprehensive guidelines about their respective roles, they have proceeded from the general principles given them by the Board about the kind of relationship that ought to exist and then have worked out each question as it has arisen. Thus, the initiative on most matters has been taken at the University level, with the administration identifying a need and then taking it to the commissioner if further guidance or approval seems desirable or necessary. The commissioner decides whether to take the matter to the Executive Committee of the Board of Trustees, with which the commissioner and President Oaks meet monthly. Then, in consultation with the Executive Committee, they determine what matters need to be taken to the Board for disclosure or approval.

Commissioner Maxwell and President Oaks agreed very early in their relationship that they should solve problems at the lowest level possible and should avoid circumventing normal channels by going directly to the First Presidency.

8. Dallin H. Oaks, introduction of Neal A. Maxwell at deans and administrators workshop, Brigham Young University, 9 July 1974.
9. Neal A. Maxwell, talk at deans and administrators workshop, Brigham Young University, 9 July 1974.

That decision has probably required more planning and lead time in order to move smoothly through established channels, but it seems to have been fruitful in view of the broad-based support and trust that have been generated. One indication of the value of this decision is that between 1971 and 1975, both the commissioner and the president have served under three different Presidents of the Church, and yet no discernible change in policy or relationship with the Board of Trustees has been caused by any of those changes in the presidency of the Board of Trustees.

The commissioner's closeness to the Board of Trustees (Neal A. Maxwell was sustained as an Assistant to the Council of the Twelve in April 1974, in addition to retaining his duties as commissioner of education), has enabled President Oaks and the commissioner to make unusually accurate advance assessments of what matters needed to be taken to the Board, how the Board might react, and what kinds of questions or problems would be raised by the Board so that their concerns could be anticipated and responded to, insofar as possible, in initial proposals.

President Oaks and his staff have frequently prepared graphs, charts, and summaries of studies pointing out why a particular need existed and why it needed to be dealt with in the way proposed by the University and the commissioner's office. The sight of President Oaks entering a Board meeting with a whole armload of visual aids is reminiscent of the Wilkinson Administration. The Board has been given candid explanations about the need for an addition to the new library, changes in the religion requirement, personnel matters, and numerous other subjects. On matters for which the president has direct authority to act, a brief report is made to the Executive Committee or the Board in order to keep them fully informed. In this way, a healthy balance has been struck between the Board's philosophy of maintaining responsibility for operational policies and the practical necessity of letting the president have considerable latitude in operational decisions.

In the University's dealings with the Board, the

commissioner's role has been more that of a counselor than that of a hurdle. The BYU administration has learned to trust Commissioner Maxwell's instincts to such an extent that it has been reluctant to approach the Board about matters for which the commissioner has little enthusiasm. At the same time, the commissioner's independence and objectivity have put him in a position to be an advocate for the University in ways that have been much to its advantage. As a result, when he has been persuaded that some BYU need is legitimate and worthy of Board consideration, he has been listened to by the Trustees as an objective evaluator who has no stake in the outcome. The reverse of that process has also been true when the commissioner has felt it inappropriate or untimely to advance a particular proposal or idea.

One example of the fruit borne by this relationship has been the degree of confidence manifested in the commissioner's office and in the University in permitting decentralization of financial authority, consistent with other decentralization going on in the Church.[10] That fiscal flexibility, and hence the kind of decentralization of authority and responsibility needed at BYU, would probably not have been possible without the high level of mutual trust existing among the various policy-making levels.

Another example cited by Commissioner Maxwell was the Church's decision to enlarge the Language Training Mission at BYU and construct a large language training complex adjoining the BYU campus.[11] Commissioner Maxwell has said that,

> Given the amount of money involved, the complexity of that task and what it implies, it probably could not have been ventured at all if there weren't the feeling that

10. *See* chapter 46.
11. The Language Training Mission was originally established by the Church at BYU in 1961. In 1969, additional missions were established at Ricks College in Idaho and at the Church College of Hawaii. The new BYU complex will consolidate the other two missions into a single mission in Provo.

> locating the facility here [in Provo] would put it near the expertise and the changing technology that are obviously going to be so much in evidence in the years ahead. . . . That building will probably have more influence on this planet than anything else I can think of, with the possible exception of a temple. And I really believe that the thousands of young men and women who are going to learn languages there, some of which [languages] we aren't even teaching now, will be a tremendous source of leaven to the world. Well, that's here. That ought to tell you something. It's not on North Main Street [in Salt Lake City], and that is symbolic of part of what I'm trying to say here.[12]

Assistance of BYU to Church Educational System

During the 1970s a number of new ways have been established in which BYU could work cooperatively with and assist the Church Educational System that extend far beyond the Provo campus. Neal Maxwell has referred to this as an "ecumenical spirit" that makes the system one of cooperating rather than competing entities. In one of the very few initiatives taken by the commissioner's office toward BYU, in early 1972 the commissioner asked the University to establish a five-year plan, partly for budgetary purposes and partly for "clearer identification of those academic areas in which you feel we should build excellence. These ought to be areas where we have the human resources to program them and areas in which there could be a happy coincidence between BYU's prospects for excellence and the Church's needs."[13] Several examples of that kind of happy coincidence between BYU's prospects and Church needs have developed, some of which have involved the sharing of BYU administrative expertise and some the sharing of academic expertise.

---

12. Neal A. Maxwell, talk at deans and administrators workshop, Brigham Young University, 9 July 1974.
13. Neal A. Maxwell to Dallin H. Oaks, 23 February 1972.

Sharing BYU Expertise in Building Construction

One illustration of this kind of sharing of BYU's expertise has to do with the construction of facilities. The new Language Training Mission, one of the larger construction projects ever initiated by the Church, has drawn heavily upon BYU's extensive experience in planning and overseeing the construction of educational facilities. With that project, which is not a part of the University, added to the construction of the new Law School Building,[14] the addition to the main University library,[15] the addition to the bookstore,[16] the carillon bell tower,[17] and an addition to the school's motion picture studio, there was greater dollar volume of new construction in process on or near the campus in early 1975 than at any other specific time in the school's history.[18] In addition to these local projects, the commissioner's office has designated BYU building planners as the planners for all necessary major construction and maintenance matters within the Church Educational System. During the early 1970s, construction projects involving the BYU planning staff have been underway at Ricks College, at the Church's Hawaii campus, and in Fiji, Tonga, and Mexico.[19]

Division of Responsibility for Continuing Education

Another early example of cooperation was the decision in 1972 to expand availability of resources in BYU's Division of Continuing Education by treating that Division as the continuing education arm of the Church Educational System. This decision came shortly after the retirement of Harold Glen Clark as dean of the Division of Continuing Education and his appointment as president of the Provo Temple.[20] Dean

14. *See* chapter 51. The Law School had been authorized during the Wilkinson Administration.
15. *See* chapter 47.
16. Ibid.
17. *See* chapter 48.
18. Ben E. Lewis to Bruce C. Hafen, 17 March 1975.
19. Ibid.
20. *See* chapter 49.

Clark's successor, Stanley A. Peterson, has since reported both to the BYU administration and to Commissioner Maxwell as the Division's resources have been utilized in areas of need identified from the perspective of the commissioner's office. BYU has retained jurisdiction over the Continuing Education programs for which academic credit is granted, but such noncredit programs as Education Weeks, Know Your Religion Series, and special programs such as those for the development of increased literacy among Church members in Latin America have come under the direct supervision of the commissioner's office.

Project Mexico

As outlined in Volume 3, chapter 43, "The World Becomes Our Campus," Continuing Education has long been in the process of extending its impact throughout the world in a variety of programs designed primarily for Church members but including many other participants. One new program is "Project Mexico." Approved in March 1972 by the Board of Trustees on a one-year trial basis, the program grew until, by 1974, 120 college students were working in Mexico City's Universidad Ibero-Americana and participating in service projects requested by the Presiding Bishopric of the Church and by local Church leaders. The students offered instruction and practical aid in such diverse subjects as nutrition; food and home management; field testing of selected field crops, vegetables, fruits, and berries; genealogical training; housing construction; and improved craft skills. This program was directed by BYU faculty member Lyman S. Shreeve.

Literacy Project for Bolivia, El Salvador, Colombia, Peru, and Ecuador

Another service program initiated under the commissioner's office in 1972 was the Bolivian Literacy Project. Under the direction of BYU's Grant Von Harrison, Spanish language tutorial training and evaluation materials were developed and field tested in La Paz, Bolivia. By September

Stanley A. Peterson, dean of
Continuing Education at BYU
since 1971.

1973, a total of 188 local adult students were being taught to read by 115 tutors, including LDS missionaries, as well as educated Bolivians. By the spring of 1975, approximately 200 persons were completing the Bolivian program each month. The literacy project was extended to Guatemala in 1973 and was taken to El Salvador, Colombia, Peru, and Ecuador in 1975. In addition, a new companion program to the reading program has been introduced to teach the people in all of the same countries how to write and do mathematics on the same tutorial basis as the Bolivian Literacy Program. Participants in these projects have had high praise for the value of Church-sponsored educational programs of such fundamental practical value.

Master's Program in Samoa

Also in 1972, upon the request of the Department of Education of American Samoa, BYU established a two-year master's degree program in Samoa offering advanced training in Education Administration. Instruction was provided by visits from BYU faculty members. After master's degrees had been earned by seventeen people in May 1974, a new contract was requested by the American Samoa Department of Education for the University to conduct another program in education involving both the curriculum and administration fields. The new two-year program commenced in June 1974, with twenty-seven students enrolled.

Bachelor of Independent Studies

One other significant Continuing Education innovation begun during the Wilkinson years and coming to fruition in more recent times is the Bachelor of Independent Studies program.[21] This program enables adult students, studying at home, to participate in an organized collegiate program of study in the sciences, humanities, and other University disciplines. The first six graduates of this adult college study

---

21. *See* Volume 3, chapter 43.

project received their bachelor's degrees in August 1974. By 1975, a total of 150 students was enrolled in the program, ranging in age from twenty-one to seventy-five.

Integration of "Semesters Abroad" Programs

Involving the commissioner's office in Continuing Education also enabled a sharper focus in evaluating the role of the University's study abroad programs, which had been a mixture of sightseeing tours and serious study programs. The study abroad program has been reorganized so that BYU "semesters abroad" in Salzburg, Paris, Madrid, Jerusalem, and London (added in 1975) are closely integrated with campus departments and have a prearranged, rigorous curriculum particularly suited to the location involved. The permanency of the University's commitment to the study abroad concept may be inferred from its decision in 1974 to purchase the facilities previously rented in Madrid. Travel study programs, which have not been characterized by an academic emphasis, have remained available as adult educational programs in which no academic credit is granted.

Scope of Continuing Education

The size and scope of Continuing Education ranks BYU as a leader in that field. In 1973-74 the University's total enrollment in this area (247, 523) was the largest in the country, and its enrollment in individual programs was equally impressive. By 1974-75, enrollment had increased to 301, 179.[22] The establishment of this kind of foundation for adult education may put the University in a position to innovate and set standards that are of growing interest to students of higher education. The Carnegie Commission on Higher Education and HEW's 1971 report on higher education have both stressed the need for abolishing traditional thinking about a "college age" and encouraging continuing access to college campuses. There is increasing support for the idea that for-

22. "BYU Receives Plaudits in Continuing Education," Provo *Daily Herald,* 30 April 1975.

mal learning should be a lifelong process and that universities should make whatever adjustments are necessary to offer their services across a broader age spectrum in a variety of new ways.[23] BYU seems to be doing some of those things, even though a substantial fraction of the total Continuing Education enrollment is accounted for by courses having a clear religious emphasis.

University Development Program Becomes Educational System Development Program

In the fund-raising area, the Church has also taken advantage of the University's expertise, thereby avoiding the need to duplicate such expertise elsewhere. In early 1971 the University Development Program became the Church Educational System Development Program, with Ben E. Lewis as chairman of the entire program and former BYU Development Deputy Director Donald T. Nelson as director.[24] At the same time, broader-based and more conservative guidelines were established for accepting donations, particularly those deferred gifts that obligated the University to make cash payments while awaiting the fruition of principal gift proceeds. During the first year of the new operation, the endowment fund for Ricks College more than tripled. By 1974 the fund-raising needs for the Church Social Services Program were integrated into the Development operation. Even as it has assumed these more extensive responsibilities, Development has continued to increase the funds raised expressly for BYU purposes. By 1975 the Development Office was annually raising about six times as much as it had raised in 1970, with the greater part of this amount designated for BYU.

---

23. *See* Frank Newman, *Report on Higher Education* (Cambridge, Massachusetts: MIT Press, 1971); and Carnegie Commission on Higher Education, *The Purposes and the Performance of Higher Education in the United States: Approaching the Year 2000* (New York: McGraw-Hill, 1973).
24. For historical background on the BYU Development Program, *see* Volume 3, chapter 41.

Donald T. Nelson, director of
the Development Office at
BYU since 1971.

Included in the educational funds raised by the Development Office between 1971 and 1975 were gifts of cash or property ranging from $500,000 to approximately $1,000,000 from Robert and Adell Hild, Sidney M. and Veoma L. Horman, Wayne Kees, J. Willard and Alice Marriott, the Charles Mott Foundation, D. Jordan Rust, and Ernest L. and Alice L. Wilkinson. Both the scope and the sophistication of the fund-raising organization have increased materially since 1971; as a result, the university's prospects for establishing a substantial permanent endowment are now relatively bright.[25]

BYU Admissions Adviser Program Becomes Church Educational System Admissions Adviser Program

In 1966, under the Wilkinson Administration, a BYU Admissions Adviser Program was set up under the direction of William R. Siddoway. At that time some uncertainty existed among Church members regarding which students should attend BYU and which students should be encouraged to attend classes near their homes where there were institutes available.

By 1968 the function of this adviser program was broadened so that students were advised with respect to all Church educational institutions. Lynn Johnson was appointed coordinator, William R. Siddoway represented BYU, Dan Hess represented Ricks College, and Alma P. Burton represented the institutes and seminaries. Under the leadership of this committee, conferences were held at high schools throughout the Church, and students were advised as to which of the Church educational institutions would be best for their individual needs.

In 1970 a letter sent out by the First Presidency encouraged

25. Bruce C. Hafen, untranscribed interview with Donald T. Nelson, May 1975. For other references to Development projects since 1971, *see* chapter 46 on the BYU employees' "Together for Greatness" program; chapter 48 on the student development effort; chapter 49 on the endowed chair in Religious Instruction; Volume 3, chapter 41 on the endowed chair in history; and chapter 51 on the law student loan fund.

students to remain at home for the first few years of college if they could live at home and attend a suitable institution served by an LDS institute of religion.[26] At the same time, however, BYU was authorized to conduct a recruiting program among promising high school graduates throughout the country, and under this program a BYU alumnus in each stake of the Church was appointed to provide information and assistance to college-bound students who might be interested in BYU.

In 1974 the concept of extending information to all in the Church Educational System was formalized so that students received further information about the variety of programs available throughout the Church Educational System, including BYU, BYU — Hawaii, LDS Business College, Ricks, and various institute programs. The BYU Admissions Adviser Program became the Church Educational System Admissions Adviser Program.

The program now receives overall policy guidance from an executive committee chaired by Dan Workman of the commissioner's office. The associate chairman of that group is BYU's dean of Admissions and Records, Robert Spencer; other Church Educational System units also have representatives on the committee. The operational management of the program belongs to D. Mark Barton, former chairman of the BYU Admissions Adviser Program, who receives instructions from a coordinating committee of other representatives from Church Educational System units. The coordinating committee is chaired by Fred A. Rowe, assistant dean of Admissions and Records at BYU. Once again, the emphasis is on serving the educational needs of individual Church members rather than merely serving the educational interests of one institution within the system.

Church College of Hawaii Becomes Branch Campus of BYU

In April 1974 the commissioner's office announced that the

---

26. "BYU Enrollment Closed Off at 25,000 Says President Smith," BYU *Daily Universe,* 18 February 1970.

Church College of Hawaii, a four-year college which had previously reported directly to Kenneth Beesley, associate commissioner of Church Education, would become a branch campus of Brigham Young University. Commissioner Maxwell has indicated that there were several reasons for the decision to make the Hawaii campus a branch of BYU. One reason was to give the Hawaii campus the name and the prestige of the University in order to reflect more accurately the function, as well as the Church affiliation, of the Hawaii campus. Another factor on which Commissioner Maxwell placed some importance was the idea of giving the Hawaii campus access to the expertise represented at BYU which could not be replicated at other points within the Church Educational System. The commissioner also foresaw the possibility of permitting some better reciprocal flow of personnel and ideas between the two campuses, although the personnel and the corporate identity of the Hawaii campus were to remain autonomous as a subsidiary of BYU rather than a fully merged organization.[27] The first dean of the Hawaii campus was Dan W. Andersen, who had been acting as academic dean at the Church College of Hawaii prior to the change. Stephen L. Brower, former president of the Hawaii campus, joined the faculty in Provo as a professor of sociology.

Academic Cooperation

In an area that might be regarded as academic cooperation, by the beginning of 1971 several BYU faculty members were already involved in significant Church Educational System projects, including the literacy project in Bolivia and other American countries already mentioned and an economic survey of the Pacific Basin which the commissioner believed would profoundly affect decisions regarding curriculum at the Hawaii campus and the Church's elementary and secondary schools in the Pacific. In addition, research projects on family matters and population attitudes were being stimu-

---

27. Neal A. Maxwell, "BYU Can Do It Better," *Brigham Young University Intercom,* Summer 1974, BYU Archives, p. 5.

lated by the commissioner's office.[28]

Another example of participation by BYU through the Church Educational System in projects of interest to the Church at large is the work of the University's Language Research Center, discussed hereafter, which is conducting research on a variety of projects designed to aid the Church in its new role as a world organization. The center is preparing an intercultural data bank that will eventually provide information to translate not just words but also ideas and concepts which change from one culture to another. Materials are also being prepared that might be useful in the opening of new mission fields in countries where Church missionary work has not yet been initiated.[29] There is also potential significance for the Church's increasingly internationalized role in BYU's research work on direct computer translation of languages. As mentioned by President Harold B. Lee at the inauguration of Dallin Oaks:

> Brigham Young University, indeed the whole educational system of this Church, has been established to the end that all pure knowledge must be gained by our people, handed down to our posterity, and given to all men.
>
> We charge you to give constant stimulation to these budding scientists and scholars in all fields and to the urge to push back further and further into the realms of the unknown. . . .
>
> With our responsibility to teach the people of the world in fifty nations and in seventeen different languages, as we are now doing, think what it would mean to our missionary and teaching efforts if some scholars from this institution were to contribute to this possibility.[30]

The Educational System and BYU have also been given

---

28. Neal A. Maxwell, "The Entering of a New Era," *Horizons Unlimited,* p. 14.
29. George Ryskamp, untranscribed interview of James Taylor, February 1975.
30. Harold B. Lee, "Installation of and Charge to the President," *Inaugural Addresses* (Provo, Utah: Brigham Young University Press, 1971), Dallin H. Oaks biographical file, BYU Archives, p. 14.

cooperative responsibilities for the production of audiovisual material for the Church. In August 1974 a Church Audiovisual Committee was created under the chairmanship of Elder J. Thomas Fyans, with Elder Neal A. Maxwell and Elder O. Leslie Stone as assistant cochairmen and Darrell J. Monson, BYU assistant academic vice-president for Learning Resources, as secretary. Members of the committee included BYU's Ben E. Lewis and Church staff professionals Heber Wolsey, Dean Larsen, Daniel Ludlow, and Verl Scott. The committee was to oversee the production and use of audiovisual materials, not only in the Educational System, but throughout the entire Church.

Smaller but typical examples of the increasing "ecumenical spirit" characterizing BYU's role in the Church Educational System include the special consideration given to transferability of institute courses and scholarships for students entering BYU from other units of the Church Educational System. The University has also shared its work on conflicts of interest, general education, and other matters that have been freshly and intensely evaluated with other units in the system. Further, BYU's Religious Instruction faculty has cooperated with the seminaries and institutes in curriculum planning and the sharing of course materials. Mormon scholars from many locations have also participated in "The Commissioner's Lecture Series" at the invitation of Commissioner Maxwell, by presenting serious academic lectures having religious implications at various locations throughout the Educational System. This program has symbolized and facilitated cooperative interchange among LDS scholars and students.

The 1970s have thus far been a period of great harmony with the Church Educational System and the Board of Trustees. BYU has probably benefited from that harmony commensurate with its efforts to be cooperative and to share both its administrative and academic expertise. The trust generated by this harmonious relationship has also had significant intangible benefits, such as the many small ways in which educators throughout the Church have been reassured about the willingness of the Church's academic community to bring its expertise to bear in directly serving Church needs. BYU's role as a significant resource to the Educational System emerges as a fact that is likely to have far-reaching implications in the years to come. Although BYU is now only one unit of the Church Educational System, it is clear that the University can and will provide both leadership and support for the entire system. This picture of harmony may well be part of an overall harmonious picture of life in the Church in the 1970s.

As this book goes to press a change is being made in the administration of the Church Educational System. Neal A. Maxwell has been released from his position as commissioner of education in order to devote his full time as an Assistant to the Council of the Twelve, and Jeffrey R. Holland, after serving only two years as BYU dean of Religious Instruction, has been appointed the new commissioner of education.

Direct Assistance of BYU to the Church

Although every program and function of BYU is designed to be of assistance to the Church and its members (*see* chapter 54), there are two very important and vital facilities and programs which are not a part of BYU but which are closely allied with and strongly supported by the institution. They are the Provo Temple and the Language Training Mission.

The Provo Temple

The construction of the Provo Temple was an event long anticipated by the local community. Since pioneer times, the large plateau on which the present campus stands was known to the residents of Utah Valley as "Temple Hill" — an expression of the residents' dream one day to have their own temple as promised by Brigham Young. A temple of learning gradually came to take the place of that hope, with the construction of the Maeser Memorial and the entire upper campus. Many interpreted this as a fulfillment of President Young's prophecy. It therefore came as a pleasant surprise when in 1967, the Church announced plans to build a Church temple east of BYU near the mouth of Rock Canyon. With one-third of the thirty stakes comprising the new Provo Temple District consisting of the ten BYU student stakes, and with members of the University community sprinkled liberally throughout the remaining resident stakes, BYU people had a strong feeling for the temple project and played major roles in its development. Executive Vice-President Ben E. Lewis was called as chairman of the site selection and fund-raising committees; Fred A. Schwendiman, then assistant vice-president for business at the University and a stake president, acted as chairman of the Temple Advisory Committee; and Harold Glen Clark was released as BYU's dean of Continuing Education to accept a call to be president of the new temple. One of President Clark's counselors, O. Wendle Nielsen, also left a BYU administrative position to accept the call to full-time temple service. The other counselor was Joseph Y. Toronto, who was a strong supporter of BYU and president of the Spanish Fork Stake, where he had presided for sixteen years. The BYU stakes participated wholeheartedly in the fund raising for the local share of the temple's cost, and the University's Physical Plant Department was given the role of helping to design and to maintain the temple grounds. The director of BYU Food Services, Wells Cloward, assisted in the designing and furnishing of the cafeteria.

The architect for the temple was Emil Fetzer of the Church Building Committee. The general contractors were Hogan and Tingey of Centerville, Utah. Groundbreaking ceremonies were conducted by President Hugh B. Brown on 15 September 1969, and the cornerstone was laid on 21 May 1971, under the direction of President Joseph Fielding Smith. The temple was completed in January 1972 and opened for tours of the public from 10 to 29 January 1972.

Significant in its impact on the University community, as well as the surrounding Utah Valley, was the dedication of the temple on 9 February 1972. Arrangements were made for the proceedings of the dedicatory services, held in the temple itself and under the direction of President Joseph Fielding Smith, to be shown on closed-circuit television in the Marriott Center, the George Albert Smith Fieldhouse, and the de Jong

Concert Hall. Admission to the dedication ceremonies required a worthiness interview similar to a temple recommend interview, further adding to the special feeling of the occasion. As part of the dedicatory services, the congregation in all four buildings participated simultaneously in the singing of "The Spirit of God Like a Fire Is Burning," a hymn which had been composed for the occasion of the dedication of the Kirtland Temple in 1836. In addition to several talks by selected General Authorities during each of the two dedication sessions, the dedicatory prayer offered by President Joseph Fielding Smith was read at each session by a member of the First Presidency. That prayer included the following petition on behalf of Brigham Young University, not only making it unique as a dedicatory prayer, but also making the occasion of the temple's dedication especially meaningful for the University and its future:

> Let that great temple of learning — the Brigham Young University, and all that is associated with it — be prospered to the full. Let thy enlightening power rest upon those who teach and those who are taught, that they may "seek learning, even by study and also by faith." . . .
>
> May those who teach and study in all academic fields have their souls enlightened with spiritual knowledge so they will turn to thy house for blessings and knowledge and learning that surpass all that may be found elsewhere.[31]

Truman Madsen said perhaps all that needs to be said of an event so significant for Utah Valley — a temple of learning was now crowned with a "temple of glory": "This valley will never be the same now that that Building stands there day and night as a witness to Jesus Christ."[32]

During the administration of President Clark and his counselors the Provo Temple became the busiest and most produc-

31. "House of the Lord," BYU *Daily Universe,* 10 February 1972.
32. Truman G. Madsen, "House of Glory," ten-stake fireside address, 5 March 1972, Truman G. Madsen biographical file, BYU Archives, p. 9.

tive temple in the Church. Some 6,389,082 temple ordinances were performed during their tenure, consisting of 2,201,651 baptisms for the dead,[33] 2,136,416 endowments,[34] and 2,501,015 sealings.[35]

From the beginning, students of BYU were encouraged to give priority to their schoolwork since this was the primary purpose in their coming to the University. This, however, did not preclude their participation in the temple, and over ten

---

33. Baptism for the dead is a water baptism performed in a font by a living proxy for and in behalf of dead relatives or others. It is a cardinal belief of the LDS Church that baptism, such as the baptism of Jesus Christ by John the Baptist, is one of the requisites for exaltation in the next life. Since many never had the opportunity to embrace the gospel of Jesus Christ while in mortality and were therefore not baptized, this ordinance is performed in their behalf by living individuals called proxies. LDS people believe that the deceased will then, in the next life, have an opportunity to accept the gospel of Jesus Christ and the baptism that has been performed in the deceased's behalf (*see* James E. Talmage, *The House of the Lord* [Salt Lake City, Utah: Deseret Book Company, 1969]), pp. 75-79.
34. An endowment is an ordinance in which the individual is given promises and blessings of the highest order of the Church, based on specific covenants which he takes with God to live righteously (*see* James E. Talmage, *The House of the Lord,* pp. 79-84). The LDS Church believes that this same endowment was promised to the Apostles by Jesus Christ when he said, "Tarry ye in the City of Jerusalem until ye be endued with power from on high" (Luke 24:49), and that the endowment was given in full to Peter, James, and John on the Mount of Transfiguration (Matt. 17:1-9). This endowment was not given in the temple at Jerusalem since Christ indicated that the Jews had made it a "den of thieves" (Matt. 21:13).
35. Sealings are rituals authoritatively uniting husband and wife in a marriage that is designed to last forever, and children are sealed to parents as a perpetual, never-ending family unit. One of the distinctive beliefs of the LDS Church is that individuals may be married in an LDS temple for time and all eternity. Children born of such a marriage are said to be "born in the covenant," thus automatically becoming a part of the eternal family unit. Children not born in the covenant may be sealed to parents who have been married for time and eternity (*see* James E. Talmage, *The House of the Lord,* pp. 84-91). The power to seal or bind, both on earth and in the heavens, was given to Peter by Christ (Matt. 16:19), was lost during the Dark Ages of apostasy, and was restored on 3 April 1836 to Joseph Smith, according to the Prophet's account (D&C 110:13-16; Malachi 4:5-6).

Provo Temple of The Church of Jesus Christ of Latter-day Saints, dedicated in 1972.

percent of the ordinances were performed by members of the BYU stakes. Students were permitted to go through the temple for their own endowments or to perform work for the dead or to be married for time and eternity, and thousands availed themselves of this opportunity.

President Clark and his counselors were released as the temple presidency in March 1976, after having served for a period of five years.[36] They were succeeded by Orville Gunther of American Fork as President, Joseph T. Bentley of Provo as first counselor, and Harold H. Holley of American Fork as second counselor. Gunther had held many Church positions and at the time of his appointment was a Regional Representative of the Council of the Twelve. Bentley was born in Juarez, Mexico, and had a long record of Church and school service. He had been assistant to the president of BYU, general superintendent of the Young Men's Mutual Improvement Association, assistant administrator of Church Schools, a stake president at BYU, and president of two missions, the Northern Mexican Mission and the Argentine-East Mission. Holley had been a bishop and high councilor in American Fork for a number of years. Under their administration the work of the Provo Temple continues with the same devotion as during the administration of President Clark and his counselors.

Language Training Mission

The Language Training Mission centered at BYU has played and will continue to play a significant role in the international LDS Church missionary effort.[37] While this sub-

36. Ernest L. Wilkinson, untranscribed interview with Harold Glen Clark, 14 June 1976.

37. For many years the Church has operated a "Mission Home" in Salt Lake City for all beginning missionaries to attend for a few days of intensive doctrinal training. All missionaries, whether assigned to English-speaking countries or elsewhere, have participated in this initial training. Recently, the policy was changed so that those assigned to the Language Training Mission at BYU spend only a few hours at the Mission Home.

Harold B. Lee, Joseph Fielding Smith, Nathan Eldon Tanner, and Harold Glen Clark at the dedication of the Provo Temple in February 1972.

ject is treated as a part of the Oaks Administration, some of the General Authorities first considered the creation of a Language Training Mission during the McDonald Administration, and the program began during the Wilkinson Administration. Great progress and growth were made during that period, but the full flowering of the program has occurred during the Oaks Administration.

The idea of establishing a center, school, or institute where missionaries could learn the language of the country to which they were assigned had long been considered. Since the Church believed it had a divine mandate to go "into all the world and preach the gospel to every creature" (Mark 16:15), the mastery of foreign languages was an obvious requirement. The First Council of Seventy gave serious consideration to a language training program as early as 1947,[38] and the BYU Speech and Language departments repeatedly urged the formation of such a center. On the eve of Wilkinson's arrival on campus in 1951, Speech Department faculty members made the following recommendation:

> Inasmuch as the missionary activities are the most intense they have ever been in the Church history, we should have a dormitory on our campus on the nature of an International House wherein students live on one floor and speak nothing but Spanish; on another floor, French and Portuguese; on another floor, Germanic languages, and possibly the fourth and fifth floors where students could have contact with returned missionaries from any country of the world and could live one year at the BYU in preparation for their mission. In such a place the students could study the mores, history, language, and anything pertinent to the success of their mission while they receive university credit. This would weed out the nonlingual assignees and Church authorities could be put over such a house for the pertinent training to augment our "Y" faculty in its Mormon philosophy and

---

38. James S. Taylor, "History of the BYU Language Training Mission," 1975, unpublished typescript in Centennial History files, BYU Archives, p. 1.

> theology. This building would be self-liquidating and would be similar to the several dormitories we so desperately need on the campus, all of them self-liquidating.[39]

In a five-page letter to the First Presidency in August 1952, President Wilkinson focused attention on some obvious advantages of combining the Salt Lake Mission Home with a language training facility at BYU. He urged a professional staff of religious instructors "of tried faith and tested ability . . . familiar with the missionary program." Furthermore, he emphasized that BYU had "personnel prepared to teach nearly every language." He argued that, as the ranks of missionaries grew, it "would be more economical" to use adequate existing facilities at Provo than build a new center in Salt Lake City. And in many other ways he tried to overcome objections which had been made to such a program.[40]

The General Authorities, however, thought it desirable at that time that missionaries be trained in Salt Lake City, near Church headquarters, so that the General Authorities could easily visit and participate in their instruction. Moreover, most missionaries obtained their temple endowments immediately before their departure into the mission field, so it was more convenient to train missionaries near the temple in Salt Lake City. Further, at that time BYU did not have the necessary housing and classroom facilities to accommodate this kind of missionary program.[41]

In 1958, Wilkinson appointed a committee to investigate the role that the University might play in the training of missionaries in foreign languages. That committee, together with the BYU Department of Foreign Languages, prepared a proposal which Elder Henry D. Moyle presented to the General Authorities in 1960. In September 1961, visa problems

---

39. T. Earl Pardoe to Ernest L. Wilkinson, 17 January 1951, Wilkinson Presidential Papers.
40. Ernest L. Wilkinson to the First Presidency, 7 August 1952, Wilkinson Presidential Papers.
41. Ibid. *See also* Ernest J. Wilkins to Earl C. Crockett, 13 July 1964, Wilkinson Presidential Papers.

encountered by missionaries assigned to Mexico prompted definite action. Arrangements had been made with the Mexican government to permit missionaries to enter that country on a special visa which would no longer require disruptive periodic exits from the country, as did tourist visas. Since it took between two and three months for this special visa to be issued, the BYU committee proposed that freshly called missionaries could profitably use that waiting period by attending a special school at BYU to learn Spanish. The proposal was approved by the First Presidency in October 1961. This "pilot" program, organized originally for missionaries going to Mexico, was expanded to include missionaries assigned to Argentina who were having similar visa difficulties. On 8 November 1961, Ernest J. Wilkins, professor of Spanish in the BYU Language Department, was named director of the new program, which was given the name "Missionary Language Institute." That same week, missionaries began arriving and were housed in the Hotel Roberts in downtown Provo. By December 4 there were twenty-four missionaries in residence, nineteen assigned to Argentina and five to Mexico. On that day an excited Wilkinson predicted in a letter to the First Presidency:

> Eighty-five years ago Brother Karl G. Maeser held his first class of 29 students at Brigham Young University. This year before the second semester ends we will have had over 12,000 students on the campus.
>
> This morning I had the pleasure of meeting with the first 19 missionaries who have been sent to the campus to receive training in the Spanish language preparatory to their serving the balance of their missions either in Mexico or Argentina. With the remarkable growth of the Church, which I venture to predict will greatly accelerate in the future, it is not at all unlikely that 85 years from now we will have at the BYU or in other parts of the Church School System as many as 12,000 missionaries being trained to carry the gospel to every kindred, tongue, and people.[42]

---

42. Ernest L. Wilkinson to President David O. McKay and counselors, 4 December 1961, Wilkinson Presidential Papers.

Ernest J. Wilkins, first
president of the Language
Training Mission at BYU.

At the time many thought President Wilkinson was overly exuberant, but the fact is that he greatly underestimated the future of missionary training for which BYU would be responsible. Already, just fifteen years later, there are 23,000 missionaries in the field.

Dr. Wilkinson immediately immersed himself in the task of preparing materials and training teachers. The practice of hiring BYU students who were natives or who had served in Spanish-speaking missions to teach the missionaries was begun at that time. Classrooms were set up in the Alumni House to provide the necessary teaching space.[43]

Although still a pilot project, the value of the program became increasingly evident. Not only did the twelve-week waiting period for visas afford missionaries an excellent opportunity to learn the fundamentals of the language and culture of foreign nations, but it also gave the missionaries time and opportunity to discipline their lives and settle into the serious role of "ambassadors of the Lord." Because of their rigorous daily schedule, missionaries learned entire series of missionary discussions in the foreign language in less than half the time it normally took while in the foreign land itself. Most mission presidents applauded the new program.

The Missionary Language Institute continued to grow as permanent materials were produced and an efficient administrative and teaching staff was developed. By June 1962, because of the increased number of missionaries, Allen Hall, one of the BYU residence housing units, became the first permanent home for the institute. The fact that BYU, simultaneously struggling to accommodate its rising enrollment in proper housing quarters, was nevertheless eager to surrender this facility is a witness to the school's ongoing commitment to missionary work.

In 1962 the teaching of Portuguese was added to the program; during that year, 590 Spanish- and 145 Portuguese-

---

43. James S. Taylor, "History of the BYU Language Training Mission," p. 2.

speaking missionaries went through the Institute. By April 1963 the Brethren had "approved, in theory, the idea of sending all foreign language missionaries to Brigham Young University for training." Other languages were to be added as facilities dictated.[44]

In 1963 the program was transformed from an experimental institute into a permanent mission. Wrote the First Presidency to Ernest Wilkins in April 1963:

> At a recent meeting of the Council of the First Presidency and Quorum of the Twelve, consideration was given to the wonderful work that you are accomplishing as Director of the Missionary Language Institute at the Brigham Young University. . . . It was the sentiment of the Council that under all the circumstances, and considering the nature of the work you are performing, it would be advisable to give this Language Institute the status of a mission . . . [and] that you be appointed president of this mission.[45]

In September 1964, after a 9 July decision to include German-speaking missionaries, more badly needed space was made available through the assignment of the Amanda Knight residence hall to the Language Training Mission (or "LTM," as it came to be called). Obtaining sufficient space was a continuous problem for the mission. Missionaries would come in alternating waves. One month there would be no problem with accommodations, while the next month would bring too many for existing facilities. During that period there never was a constant, predictable flow; immediate and long-range planning was difficult.[46]

During the summer and fall of 1964 "There was considerable discussion regarding the possibility of moving the Lan-

---

44. Ernest J. Wilkins to Ernest L. Wilkinson, 15 April 1963, Wilkinson Presidential Papers.
45. First Presidency to Ernest J. Wilkinson, 30 April 1963, Wilkinson Presidential Papers.
46. Ernest L. Wilkinson to Spencer W. Kimball, 25 November 1963, Wilkinson Presidential Papers.

guage Training Mission to Salt Lake." Some of the old reservations to having this facility in Provo were again voiced. Some Church leaders suggested that the mission should be housed in the proposed Church Office Building which now stands east of Temple Square in Salt Lake City. However, nothing came of these deliberations.[47]

In the meantime the LTM amplified its capabilities, offering Navajo in March 1967 and French in October of the same year. Training in the LTM was extremely demanding. All were required to follow missionary rules of rising and retiring early, having private and group prayers, spending long hours in intensive language training and learning scriptures, and in other ways living as if already in the mission field. Visits with parents or friends were severely restricted and dating was strictly prohibited. No one was permitted to go anywhere without his or her companion.

Sensing the need for proper physical exercise for the young men and the much smaller number of young ladies entrusted to their care, LTM officials worked with the BYU administration to procure proper recreational facilities. A separate cafeteria operated by BYU Food Services in Knight-Mangum Hall provided for most of the dining needs of the mission. In times of overflow, other cafeterias on campus were made available. It was also common to see hundreds of white-shirted missionaries sitting en masse at BYU football or basketball games and at firesides. On almost any given day, clusters of young missionaries could be seen on campus purchasing supplies at the bookstore or running back from the Richards Physical Education Building. Invariably, as part of their training these young people would speak in the language in which they were being trained.

For a few years in which academic credit was given at the end of the three-month period, LTM students were legally students of BYU. This was made possible by the fact that the LTM operated under the BYU budget, even though it was

---

47. Ernest J. Wilkinson to Earl C. Crockett, 13 July 1964.

Language training missionaries studying in one of the language laboratories at BYU early in the 1960s.

responsible directly to the Church Missionary Committee.[48] This practice of giving academic credit (sixteen credit hours) met with objections from the 1966 Accreditation Committee and subsequently was terminated. Today, a returning missionary may obtain sixteen hours of foreign language credit by successfully passing a special examination and an advanced language course after his two years in the mission field.

The relationship between BYU and the Language Training Mission has been somewhat akin to the relationship of Brigham Young Academy to the Church before it became incorporated as a part of the Church in 1896. In that case the Church paid most of the expenses and the school furnished the services, even though Brigham Young Academy was not owned by the Church. The difference here is that the Church owns the Language Training Mission, but all the services, including the housing facilities (outside of the new Language Training Mission buildings), the feeding of the missionaries, the sharing of athletic facilities, and the faculty, are all furnished by Brigham Young University. The Language Training Mission is an arm of the Church, and as such it is responsible directly to the General Authorities. Even though its annual budget has been channeled through the BYU budget, the LTM does not answer to the University. However, the two administrations have worked in close cooperation and with cordial understanding. In one sense the LTM is a voluntary step-child of BYU, but BYU showers on its missionaries all the love and affection it bestows on its own students.

In the spring of 1968, Church leaders decided that all missionaries bound for a foreign land were to be trained at an LTM prior to their departure.[49] However, in order to strengthen other Church schools it was decided "that all languages should not be taught here in Provo." For this reason

48. Ernest L. Wilkinson to Clyde Sandgren, 22 November 1966, Wilkinson Presidential Papers.
49. James S. Taylor, "History of the BYU Language Training Mission," p. 4.

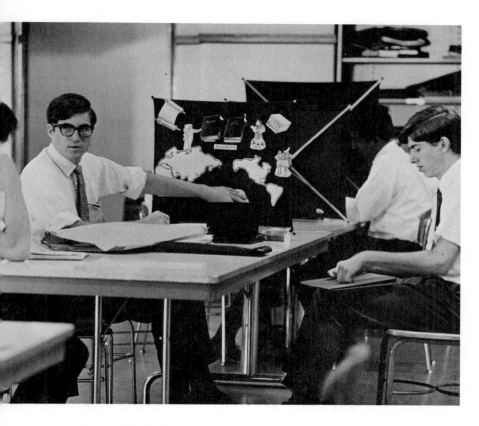

Language training missionaries practicing the missionary discussions in Spanish at the Language Training Mission at BYU.

Dr. Ermel Morton was called as president of a new LTM at Ricks College, where the Scandinavian languages would be taught. At the same time, Kenneth Orton was similarly called as president of the LTM at the Church College of Hawaii, where various Oriental languages would be emphasized.[50] In February 1969 these new missions were organized following the model at BYU and were aided in their establishment and development by the Language Training Mission at BYU.

Meanwhile, it was decided to reduce the customary twelve-week curriculum to eight weeks, beginning in January 1969. This would assure proper selective service status for missionaries. That same year, Italian was added to the BYU Language Training Mission, and Afrikaans was taught beginning in March 1970.

In September 1970, after almost nine years of service, Ernest J. Wilkins and his counselors, James S. Taylor and Derrold D. Harris, were released.[51] Dr. Terrance L. Hansen was named the new president, with Derrold D. Harris and Allen C. Ostergar, Jr., as his counselors. In November 1973, during Hansen's administration, the Church Missionary Committee decided to reunite all of the LTMs at BYU. The sentiment for centralization had never diminished, and when in 1973 the Church announced construction plans for a large, single, self-contained complex of facilities on the north end of the BYU campus, it was decided to bring all the LTMs back under one administrative umbrella where the rapidly growing foreign missionary program could be best accommodated. Keith Wilcox of Ogden and Hal Beecher and John Fetzer of Salt Lake City were chosen as architects for the new buildings, and Paulsen Construction Company of Salt Lake City was awarded the contract.

Unfortunately, Dr. Hansen, just fifty-three years of age,

---

50. Derrold Dee Harris to Fred Schwendiman, 9 January 1969, BYU Centennial History files, BYU Archives.
51. Other men who had served as counselors and assistants were Lewis Bastian, Ross Broadbent, Ben Martinez, Allen L. Litster, Steve Covington, and Allen C. Ostergar, Jr.

died suddenly in May 1974. Shortly after his death, Max Pinegar was appointed president of the Language Training Mission. By that time plans had been completed for the new facilities, and groundbreaking occurred on 18 July 1974. The buildings were completed in July 1976, and classes began on 3 August 1976. From its beginning in December 1961 until May 1975, the LTM trained more than 27,000 missionaries.[52]

The new language training facilities will provide housing accommodations and training facilities for 1,304 missionaries. Other facilities on campus, including the St. Francis School, which is being leased from the Catholic Church,[53] will house 914 other missionaries, for a total of 2,218 missionaries who can be accommodated at one time. Since the term of training in a new language for each missionary is eight weeks, this means that there could be nearly seven terms each year, or a potential total in excess of 15,000 missionaries to be trained each year, all for missions where people speak foreign tongues. In all, the Language Training Mission will be teaching twenty-three foreign languages by the time this volume is published.[54] Undoubtedly, in the years ahead many more languages than these will be taught. Indeed, in May 1976 the Church announced plans to construct a large addition to the facility. This construction actually got underway in June 1976 and will be finished in May 1978. It is contemplated that when the second phase of construction is completed, the Language Training Mission will be able to train 3,000 missionaries at one time, for a total of approximately 18,000 per year. Teaching

---

52. James S. Taylor, "History of the BYU Language Training Mission," p. 5.

53. This facility was formerly maintained as a parochial school by the Catholic Church, but like hundreds of other parochial schools throughout the nation, it closed for lack of operating funds.

54. The twenty-three languages which will be taught when the new facilities open in 1976 are Afrikaans, Cantonese Chinese, Danish, Dutch, Finnish, French, German, Icelandic, Indonesian, italian, Japanese, Korean, Mandarin Chinese, Navajo, Norwegian, Surbo-Croatian, Portuguese, Samoan, Persian, Spanish, Swedish, Tahitian, and Thai. Others are being planned for the future.

Max L. Pinegar, president of the Language Training Mission at BYU since 1974.

this large number is expected to start in the summer of 1978.[55] Consideration is now being given to a plan that will train 24,000 missionaries a year. If this plan is adopted, the Language Training Mission will train approximately as many missionaries in one year as there are students on the BYU campus. In this way the Church, with the help of BYU, will be preparing to fulfill its stated goal of carrying the gospel to every "nation, kindred, tongue and people" (Mosiah 3:20). And, except for those missionaries called to serve in their native lands, this will all be begun at BYU by young men and women, the young men serving as missionaries for two years and the young women for eighteen months, at their own expense.

At the conclusion of their eight-week foreign language training, young missionaries then serve in one of the foreign language missions of the LDS Church (now sixty-two in number and increasing each year). In addition to missions in foreign-speaking countries, the Church now has forty-three missions in the United States and seven in Great Britain, where English is spoken, for a total of 50 other missions. This makes a total of 112 missions.

Before he became President of the LDS Church, Elder Spencer W. Kimball stated that the Church should set the goal of "all young men of missionary age who are worthy" being "called on a mission." After becoming President, he stated he thought the Church could sustain thirty to forty thousand missionaries in the field at one time. Under his leadership there are already approximately twenty-three thousand missionaries in the field, and their numbers are increasing rapidly.[56] With the growth of the Church it may not be too much to say that many living today will witness fifty thousand missionaries in the field at a given time.

With these ramifications in mind, President Harold B. Lee

---

55. Ernest L. Wilkinson, untranscribed interview of Max L. Pinegar, 13 June 1976.
56. Ernest L. Wilkinson, untranscribed interview of Ned Winder, 19 August 1975.

The Language Training
Mission under construction.

described the significance of the new Language Training Mission facilities in these words: "The approval of this new project will have the effect of making Provo the language capital of the world, with Brigham Young University the focal point, and I would just like to observe the approval of this project is not the end — it is just the beginning."

51

The J. Reuben Clark Law School

The idea of a law school at Brigham Young Academy was first proposed in 1897 in a letter to President Benjamin Cluff from J. Whitely, a teacher of civics and public law at the University of Utah, who had successfully prepared a number of students for law schools in the East. Blocked in his attempt to establish a law school at the University of Utah, he wished to organize a law school as "a branch of the Academy."[1] Two years later a proposal to teach law came from A. Alfred Saxey of Spanish Fork, who said that for a salary of $600 per year he would donate a law library of 200 volumes and undertake to get his students admitted to the bar in two years.[2] It does not appear that either of these proposals was brought to the attention of the Board of Trustees.

At a Board meeting on 16 October 1901, Acting President George Brimhall reported that a law school and possibly a medical school could be instituted at once at the Academy

---

1. J. Whitely to Benjamin Cluff, Jr., 12 April 1897, Cluff Presidential Papers.
2. A. Alfred Saxey to Benjamin Cluff, Jr., 1899, Cluff Presidential Papers.

without any charge to the students because local lawyers and doctors volunteered to provide their services. On motion of Reed Smoot, the president was authorized to institute these professional schools. President Brimhall felt so encouraged by the action of the Board that he wrote Cluff, who was in Central America, "I explained to the Board that [the two professional schools] would cause the school to 'bristle like a university,' whereupon Pres. Jos. F. Smith immediately said, 'Well, why not?' "[3] Obviously, however, neither a law nor a medical school was established at that time, probably indicating that the leaders of the financially troubled Academy found that such schools could not be operated free of charge. They also apparently perceived that adding the two professional schools at a time when the college division itself was barely on its feet would be premature.

In 1949, half a century later, Clyde Sandgren, future general counsel for BYU who was then practicing law in New York City, suggested in a letter to Ernest L. Wilkinson, then practicing law in Washington, D.C., that they both should give serious consideration to urging the establishment of a law school at BYU. At that time Wilkinson had no idea that within two years he would be president of the institution. Furthermore, following his appointment as president he felt that the establishment of other colleges should have priority over a law school; indeed, that BYU was not ready for a graduate school of law.

It was not until near the end of President Wilkinson's administration that the idea was revived. Wilkinson himself is partly responsible for the revival by suggesting the same to Elder Marion Romney who, under provisions of President J. Reuben Clark's will, had been made custodian of all his papers. Romney was enthusiastic about the proposal and persuaded President Harold B. Lee, who was then serving as a counselor to President Joseph Fielding Smith in the First Presidency, to endorse the proposal. The persuasion of the

3. George H. Brimhall to Benjamin Cluff, Jr., 16 October 1901, Cluff Presidential Papers.

Board then fell largely upon Elder Romney and President Lee. Both were great admirers of President J. Reuben Clark and advocated strongly not only the establishment of a law school at BYU, but also the naming of the school after President Clark. On 18 June 1970, Romney recommended the establishment of the J. Reuben Clark School of Law to the Executive Committee of the BYU Board of Trustees. The proposal was taken under advisement, pending the results of a feasibility study.

Initial Feasibility Study

The feasibility study, conducted under the direction of President Wilkinson in late 1970, included an extensive behind-the-scenes investigation of such questions as the number of experienced Mormon law teachers who might qualify for consideration as a beginning faculty, the accreditation standards of the American Bar Association and accreditation obstacles that might be encountered, the costs of the physical facilities, including a library, an evaluation of the optimum size and philosophy for a law school at Brigham Young University, and a consideration of supply and demand factors for both legal education and the legal profession. Jay Butler, assistant to President Wilkinson, materially assisted in this study.

One legal educator selected by President Wilkinson for consultation about the feasibility of the project was Dallin H. Oaks, who had only recently assumed his position as executive director of the American Bar Foundation. Oaks warned that BYU should not establish a law school unless it was first class and that such a law school would be very expensive. Later, when being interviewed in connection with his appointment as president, Oaks again made it clear that it would be an expensive mistake to build a mediocre law school and that it would be even more expensive to build an excellent school. Oaks also advised the committee that concern was beginning to grow in the profession and among the law schools about the increasing number of law school graduates, which threatened to saturate the employment market for lawyers.[4]

Included in the feasibility study was a confidential inquiry to the appropriate committee of the American Bar Association concerning whether any obstacles to accreditation might be posed by the peculiarities of Mormon doctrine, assuming that other accreditation standards were met. An encouraging response to that question was received by the University.

After all the facts were in, and despite doubts on the part of some and keeping in mind the realistic facts presented by Dallin Oaks, the First Presidency and Trustees approved the establishment of a law school.[5] The official announcement of the decision was made on 9 March 1971 by President Harold B. Lee at the time of the public announcement of President Wilkinson's resignation:

> At our meeting this morning we announced plans, which have been previously approved by the Brigham Young University Board of Trustees, to establish at this University the J. Reuben Clark College of Law. This college will probably open in the fall of 1973, or thereafter as circumstances may dictate.
>
> The college will bear great significance on this campus. First, because of the name it will bear. President J. Reuben Clark, Jr., was one of the greatest lawyers of our time, internationally known, a student of international law and constitutional law. Perhaps there has not been a more ardent student of the Constitution than President

4. *See The Chronicle of Higher Education,* 14 January 1974, p. 9.
5. There were many who doubted whether the State of Utah could sustain another law school. The Utah State Bar Association made Wilkinson chairman of a committee to survey the question in February 1972. Dean Samuel Thurman, of the University of Utah, and Robert Van Sciver were the other members of the committee. The committee decided that in view of the increasing complexity of our society and the need of more citizens for legal advice another law school could be sustained in the state, especially since many of those trained in Utah would practice elsewhere. The report of the committee, Samuel D. Thurman, Robert Van Sciver, and Ernest L. Wilkinson, "Forecast of Lawyer Placement in Utah," is found in the *Utah Bar Journal,* October-December 1973. This report confirmed the wisdom of the decision made by the Board of Trustees.

Clark; but by his side is President Wilkinson. It is a fact that this Church has looked upon the Constitution, as the Lord has revealed, as having been framed by men whom God raised up for this very purpose. Where else but on this campus should we be concerned about having a school of law where we can train lawyers who will defend the Constitution of the United States, keeping in mind that the Prophet Joseph Smith is quoted as having said that the time would come when the Constitution may hang as by a thread and the elders of the Church may have to step forth to help save it. If we can train lawyers who are soundly based in the Constitution, we will have made a great step forward in helping to send out into the world men who will uphold, defend, and protect the basis of the foundation of the great United States of America.[6]

Reasons for Founding a Law School at BYU

There has been considerable speculation as to the purpose of the Church in founding a law school at Brigham Young University. The thinking of Church leaders is reflected in the emphatic statement of President Lee quoted above. President Wilkinson underscored this same theme in his prayer at the opening ceremony of the school on 27 August 1973:

> While we shall teach at this school all the various theories of law underlying the decisions of our respective legislatures and courts, we must ever recognize that it owes its existence to the profound belief of its Trustees that the Constitution of our country is a divine instrument and that its concepts need expression in a law school.[7]

A similar and more extended view was later expressed by Marion G. Romney, an attorney by profession and by then a member of the First Presidency. He stated that the school was established so that there might be an institution in which

---

6. Harold B. Lee, "Decades of Distinction: 1951-1971," *Speeches of the Year* (Provo, Utah: Brigham Young University Press, 1971), p. 3.
7. Ernest L. Wilkinson, "Opening Prayer at Beginning of J. Reuben Clark School of Law," 27 August 1973, Ernest L. Wilkinson speech file.

Marion G. Romney of the
First Presidency of the LDS
Church. Elder Romney was
one of the prime movers in
the establishment of the
J. Reuben Clark Law School.

students can obtain a knowledge of the laws of man in light of the laws of God.[8]

At the dedicatory services for the law school building which took place on 5 September 1975, President Romney spoke on the subject "Why the J. Reuben Clark Law School?" He stated:

> To begin with, I have long felt that no branch of learning is more important to an individual or to society than law. I further felt that the educational base at Brigham Young University — the flagship of our Church educational system — would be and should be broadened by the establishment of a law school. I likewise felt that the atmosphere of honor, integrity, patriotism, and benevolence prevailing at Brigham Young University would be a good influence upon a law school and its student body. I also desired to have perpetuated on this campus the memory and influence of President J. Reuben Clark, Jr. — a great lawyer, patriot, statesman, and church leader. It's my hope that all faculty and student body members will familiarize themselves with and emulate his virtues and accomplishments.

He then pointed out that

> President Clark . . . believed, as do all Latter-day Saints, that the law which "proceedeth forth from the presence of God" is binding upon this earth and its inhabitants; that "there is a law, irrevocably decreed in heaven before the foundations of this world, upon which all blessings are predicated, and when we obtain any blessing from God, it is by obedience to that law upon which it is predicated" (D&C 88:45-47).

Linking the rationale for the establishment of the Law School to Old Testament and New Testament scriptures, he continued:

> Laws on which a peaceful, progressive, prosperous, and happy society must be built are prescribed in the Ten Commandments and the Sermon on the Mount. Our

---

8. Marion G. Romney, in *Addresses at the Ceremony Opening the J. Reuben Clark Law School,* 27 August 1973, BYU Archives, p. 20.

> knowledge that the origin, scope, and universality of law is thus revealed in the scriptures enhances rather than demeans or diminishes our appreciation and respect for the law of the land.

Then, quoting modern-day scriptures, he continued:

> We believe that governments were instituted of God for the benefit of man; and that he holds men accountable for their acts in relation to them, both in making laws and administering them, for the good and safety of society (D&C 134:1).

Commenting further on Latter-day Saint belief, President Romney pointed out that the Lord himself had revealed that He "established the Constitution of this land, by the hands of wise men whom I raised up unto this very purpose" (D&C 101:77-80). Finally, he quoted the Prophet Joseph Smith's tribute to the Constitution:

> The Constitution of the United States is a glorious standard; it is founded in the wisdom of God. It is a heavenly banner; it is to all those who are privileged with the sweets of its liberty, like the cooling shades and refreshing waters of a great rock in a thirsty and weary land. It is like a great tree under whose branches men from every clime can be shielded from the burning rays of the sun (*DHC* 3:304).

President Romney concluded: "Our background increases our love for the Constitution, deepens our respect for the bar and the judiciary, and urges us, individually, to be law-abiding."[9]

Following the dedication of the Law School Building, Ezra Taft Benson, president of the Council of the Twelve, wrote to President Wilkinson:

> It is my hope that in your history you will give a full treatment as to [the purpose and mission of the law

9. Marion G. Romney, "Why the J. Reuben Clark Law School?" *Proceedings at the Convocation and Dedication of the J. Reuben Clark College of Law*, 5 September 1975, pp. 43-46.

> school] that will be forthright in defending the Constitution of the United States as our Constitutional Fathers intended. I hope the law school will also emphasize the spiritual foundation of this country and its prophetic history . . . as forecast in the *Book of Mormon*. That, I know, was in the minds of the Board when the law school was authorized and, except for that purpose, there would have been no purpose for its creation.

Biographical Sketch of J. Reuben Clark, Jr.

From the beginning of the consideration of the establishment of a law school it was intended that the school be named after J. Reuben Clark, Jr., a 1906 graduate of Columbia Law School. President Clark achieved international distinction in a variety of State Department positions and finally became undersecretary of State and ambassador to Mexico. Secretary of State Philander C. Knox expressed the esteem in which President Clark was held: "I am doing him but justice in saying that for natural ability, integrity, loyalty, and industry, I have not in a long professional and public service met his superior and rarely his equal." He left his professional career in 1933 to become a counselor to President Heber J. Grant and continued to serve in the First Presidency of the LDS Church under George Albert Smith and David O. McKay until his death in 1961. He was the author of numerous scholarly books on religious subjects, including *Harmony of the Four Gospels, Why the King James Version, Our Lord of the Gospels, On the Way to Immortality and Eternal Life, To Them of the Last Wagon,* and *Wist Ye Not That I Must Be About My Father's Business?* He also wrote and spoke extensively on legal and governmental matters, and some of these writings were published in book form under the title *Stand Fast by the Constitution*. Representative of his high standards are the thoughts he expressed in an address to the Los Angeles Bar Association on 24 February 1944:

> Upon the bench and the bar of the country rests the great responsibility of seeing that our liberties and free institutions are preserved. Legislators may be incompetent, ex-

J. Reuben Clark, Jr.,
prominent lawyer,
statesman, and Church
leader for whom the law
school at BYU was named.

> ecutives may be dishonest, but if the bench and the bar be honest and filled with integrity, then under the Constitution, the people are secure, and free institutions will still live with us. But security and liberty both take flight where the [bar and/or] the judiciary [are] corrupt.[10]

Because of President Clark's great reputation the BYU Library had been given his name. Therefore, for a short time both the library and the law school honored his memory. However, to avoid confusion, following the death of President Harold B. Lee in December 1973, the library was renamed in Lee's honor, and President Clark's name remained associated with the law school and the new building which it occupies. That change seemed especially fitting in view of the intimate tutorial relationship that President Lee had enjoyed with President Clark during their years of association together as General Authorities.

Choosing a Founding Dean

Immediately after the announcement that a law school would be established, President Wilkinson was directed to undertake preliminary studies for the planning of a law school building. Also, when Oaks was appointed president of BYU he was requested by the First Presidency to exert his best efforts to see that an outstanding law school of the highest caliber be established at BYU. President Oaks accepted that charge, and work on the Law School project continued along three fronts during the summer of 1971. First, it was necessary to find a competent dean who could handle the difficult task of assembling a high-quality faculty. A competent law librarian was also needed to acquire and supervise an appropriate library. Finally, there was the task of completing estimates and making final recommendations for the preparation of architectural plans for the new law school building.

The search committee for a dean consisted of Marion G. Romney, Howard W. Hunter, Boyd K. Packer, Marion D.

10. J. Reuben Clark, Jr., to the Los Angeles County Bar Association, 24 February 1944.

Rex E. Lee, founding dean
of the BYU Law School.

Hanks, Neal A. Maxwell, Dallin H. Oaks, and Ernest L. Wilkinson. The committee interviewed a number of Mormon law teachers and lawyers over a period of three months. The committee discovered early that the list of qualified Mormon law teachers was not a long one and that if the school were to achieve its objective of high quality, a relatively high percentage of the available candidates would need to be persuaded that the BYU project was worthy of their commitment. That high percentage was ultimately realized. On 9 November 1971, President Oaks announced that the search committee had unanimously recommended, and the Board of Trustees had approved, Rex E. Lee, thirty-six-year-old lawyer from Phoenix, Arizona, as the founding dean of the J. Reuben Clark Law School. Lee had been the top scholar in his class at the University of Chicago Law School and had served as a clerk with U.S. Supreme Court Justice Byron R. White. His record was such that the law school from which he graduated would have been interested in having him on the faculty had he expressed any interest in teaching. He then practiced for eight years with Jennings, Strauss, & Salmon, the largest law firm in Phoenix, Arizona. He also taught an antitrust law class at the University of Arizona Law School. Lee's selection was representative of the blend of practitioner and scholar that the search committee felt was needed in a dean who would be responsible for establishing a new law school.

After the selection of Lee, Ernest L. Wilkinson, who had assisted in the selection but by that time was in the hospital recovering from heart surgery, was not called upon to perform any further assignments in the creation or operation of the Law School, except for minor assistance in planning the Law School Building, on which he had already worked, and the raising of funds. Thus, the establishment, organization, and operation of the Law School became the function of the Oaks Administration.

Selecting the Law School Faculty

Sensing the need for academic experience and believing the faculty to be the key component in the Law School's success,

Dean Lee immediately set about the task of recruiting an initial core of faculty members who were already teaching at nationally known law schools. In addition, to provide the right balance of theory and practice, the new dean hoped to entice to the campus some outstanding practicing lawyers of proven academic ability. By the time the school opened its doors in the fall of 1973, nine faculty members had been employed, more than half of whom had law teaching experience at a number of America's leading law schools. By the fall of 1974, there were fifteen teachers on permanent appointment, representing an aggregate law teaching experience of sixty-five years (an average of 4.3 years per teacher) and an aggregate law practice experience of ninety years (an average of six years per teacher).[11] Virtually all of the faculty members had graduated in the upper five percent of their graduating classes in a total of six different well-established law schools. Three of the fifteen had been clerks to justices of the United States Supreme Court, and all had published scholarly work, either as law students or as law teachers, in legal periodicals. In addition, three of the faculty were coauthors of leading law school textbooks.

A turning point in the faculty recruitment process was a set of decisions to join the faculty during the winter of 1972-73 by Carl S. Hawkins, Edward L. Kimball, and Dale A. Whitman, who were teachers of national reputation at the University of Michigan, the University of Wisconsin, and the University of North Carolina (Whitman had also taught at the University of California at Los Angeles and at the time was on the staff of the Department of Housing and Urban Development in Washington, D.C.). Of similar significance to the practitioners' segment of the legal community were the faculty appointments during the same winter of Woodruff J. Deem, district attorney in Ventura County, California, who had thirty-two lawyers on his staff and who had been president of the District Attorneys Association of California; and C. Keith

11. Rex E. Lee, "The J. Reuben Clark Law School — The Second Year," *Utah Bar Journal*, 1974.

Rooker, a member of the firm of Van Cott, Bagley, Cornwall, & McCarthy, the largest law firm in Salt Lake City. Both men were highly respected and seasoned veterans of the courtroom who would probably never have left their successful practices to enter law teaching but for the exceptional opportunity of helping to found the Law School at BYU. All five of these men had outstanding qualifications, including the fact that Carl S. Hawkins, Woodruff J. Deem, and Edward L. Kimball were all first in their respective classes at Northwestern, Georgetown, and the University of Utah. The early affirmative decisions of these five were instrumental in attracting other faculty and a charter class of students.

Selection of a Law Librarian

Meanwhile, a full-time law librarian was hired early in 1972, together with an experienced law library consultant. David Lloyd, the librarian, and Roy M. Mersky of the University of Texas, the consultant, were so successful in their initial efforts at acquiring a basic collection of legal materials that the volume count in the law library by the time the school opened easily exceeded both the accreditation requirements and the most optimistic early estimates of the Law School planners. By the end of 1974 the library's 150,000 volumes made it the largest law school library between California on the west and Minnesota and Texas on the east. Additionally, this size placed the library in the largest twenty percent of all law school libraries.

Construction and Fund Raising

By the time of Dean Lee's appointment, a team of BYU building planners, pursuant to instructions given by President Wilkinson, had already visited a number of newly constructed law buildings and had made a series of recommendations to the University administration respecting the Law School Building. That team's recommendations were studied by several legal educators, whose advice led to various changes, the most notable of which was to increase the library capacity

St. Francis School in Provo, first home of the J. Reuben Clark Law School. BYU leased the facility from the Catholic Church.

from 100,000 to 200,000 volumes. Construction on the building commenced on 1 May 1973, and the building was occupied during the summer of 1975. In the interim, the first two academic years of the new professional school were conducted in a rented former Catholic high school building located not far from the BYU campus.

In the area of fund raising, the efforts of Dean Lee and former President Wilkinson began to meet with remarkable success. The largest early gift, in the amount of $500,000, was made in early 1973 by Roland Rich Woolley, prominent Los Angeles attorney, for the purpose of creating a revolving law student loan fund. Substantial gifts of real property and other assets were also made by Guy Anderson, Ray and Nellie Reeves, Ernest L. and Alice L. Wilkinson, and Lou Meitus. These donations, together with numerous other contributions from Mormon lawyers and others, had given the school a start toward a substantial endowment by the end of the University's centennial year.

The Doors Open

The fall of 1973, when the J. Reuben Clark Law School opened, was coincidentally the first time in the history of legal education that no American law school had an unfilled place in its entering class.[12] Between 1963 and 1973, enrollment doubled in law schools approved by the American Bar Association. The number of college graduates seeking places in law schools increased even more dramatically, though a lower percentage of applicants was able to find places in law school. This development will inevitably have a significant influence on the number of lawyers in the United States. The executive director of the Association of American Law Schools estimated that there were 375,000 lawyers at the end of 1973 and that law schools would graduate an average of 30,000 new prospective lawyers per year between 1973 and 1976.[13]

---

12. *The Chronicle of Higher Education,* 14 January 1974, p. 9.
13. Ibid.

This national burst of interest in law school combined with the excitement of being a part of the Church's first professional school to make the initial admissions process at the new school highly competitive. From some 400 to 500 applications, most of them from returned Mormon missionaries, 157 students comprised the entering class. Of this group, 12 were women, and 145 were men. Over half were BYU graduates. The average score of the entering class on the nationally administered Law School Admissions Test was 610 (of a possible 800). This initial number of students (150-60) was typical of the class size then anticipated for future years.

During the late fall of 1973, officials of the American Bar Association (ABA) made their initial accreditation visit to the new law school. Based on their favorable report, the House of Delegates of the ABA unanimously voted in February 1974 to give provisional accreditation to the J. Reuben Clark Law School.[14]

In the fall of 1974 the second group of the new law students entered the school with a median Law School Admissions Test score of 628. The median score for the third-year class was also 628, which increased to 636 for the class entering in 1976, placing this class in the estimated ninety-second percentile of all students applying for admission to law schools in the country.

By the time the third-year class was admitted the J. Reuben Clark Law School had become the largest law school in the state. The admissions requirements were so high that many students who were qualified to enter top law schools had to be turned down. Acting Dean Hawkins commented that his greatest disappointment as dean was the necessity of turning down so many students who were qualified to be lawyers, but who did not come within the highest 150 applicants. Hawkins

14. Technically, this approval amounted to "provisional" accreditation since ABA rules do not permit the granting of final accreditation until a school has graduated at least one class of law students. That graduation took place for the Law School at BYU in the spring of 1976. Full accreditation has been recommended by the appropriate committee of the American Bar Association and is forthcoming in 1976.

was acting dean because Rex E. Lee, the founding dean, at the specific request of the attorney general of the United States, had been given a leave of absence to serve as the assistant attorney general in charge of the Civil Division, a distinct honor for Lee and the school. The Law School was fortunate in persuading Hawkins, by urgent request of President Oaks and the unanimous vote of the law faculty, to function as dean in Lee's absence. Hawkins had great status in legal education, having served for sixteen years as a professor at the University of Michigan. He was for several years executive secretary of the Michigan Law Review Commission.

Activities of the Law School

The faculty and administration of the J. Reuben Clark Law School have been occupied largely by starting-up functions during the first three years of the school's existence. No time has been wasted, however, in launching research projects at both the student and the faculty level. A cocurricular program involving forty percent of the second-year class was established at the beginning of the 1974-75 school year for the purpose of initiating student research, writing, and publication efforts of various kinds. This program included the founding of the *BYU Law Review,* a scholarly journal that will include student work and will become largely student-edited, even though it will also publish the work of prominent legal scholars outside the BYU community. In addition, the faculty has initiated two interdisciplinary empirical studies, one dealing with jury behavior and the other with negotiating techniques used by practicing lawyers. Moreover, the research arm of the American Bar Association conducted a year-long study of legal education objectives and techniques during 1974-75 at the Law School, involving both students and faculty.

Moving to Campus

During the summer of 1975, the Law School left its temporary home at the St. Francis High School, some ten blocks

Beginning of construction
on the J. Reuben Clark Law
School Building.

south of campus, and moved into its spacious new facility on the east side of Campus Drive across from the Wilkinson Center and the Harris Fine Arts Center. The move had been eagerly anticipated since the temporary facility had provided barely adequate classroom facilities. The 165,000 volumes in the library were beginning to crowd students and faculty. The new building provided plentiful and excellent classrooms, a library with a 200,000-volume capacity, ample faculty offices, and individual carrels for almost the entire student body. Still, the informality and personal warmth between students and faculty that had been encouraged by the space limitations of St. Francis would be remembered by those involved as a special characteristic of the first two years of the Law School's history.

The Law School Building and Its Dedication

On 5 September 1975 the new J. Reuben Clark Law School Building was dedicated. This was undoubtedly the most nationally heralded dedicatory service in the history of the University. Dignitaries in attendance included Chief Justice Warren Burger and Justice Lewis Powell of the United States Supreme Court, as well as judges of the Ninth and Tenth Circuit Courts of Appeals, the Utah Supreme Court, other state supreme courts, and many lower courts, as well as other public officials from several neighboring states. A special University convocation service was held in the morning, and the dedicatory services convened in the afternoon. All members of the First Presidency and other General Authorities of The Church of Jesus Christ of Latter-day Saints were also in attendance.

Chief Justice Burger had been in the state for several days and had acquainted himself with both the University and the Law School, and especially the faculty. He gave the formal address at the convocation. After admitting that the law profession had not always measured up to its noblest potential and that a critical analysis of it was a real value, he noted that on the other side

> we should remember . . . the countless examples of courageous lawyers supporting the claims of people who were subject to operation or abuse of governmental power. Mr. Justice Jackson once commented that in every vindication of the rights of individuals and in every advance of human liberty in our history, key figures were lawyers who were willing to risk their professional reputations and their futures in pursuit of an ideal.

He then congratulated the University on its new Law School and its great opportunity for meeting the highest professional standards:

> Here at Provo you have carried on the work of a great university for a century, and it is good that you have now added a school of law to carry on the training of lawyers in keeping with the standards that made this institution one of the great centers of learning in America, privately sustained and conducted in conformity with Christian teaching. A school of law with such inspiration and sponsorship fills a significant need in the legal education of this country — a need not met by all law schools today. Guided by these standards, it is safe to predict that this law school will become one of the foremost in the country. . . .
>
> A new law school such as yours has a rare opportunity available to few others. It can engage in a reexamination of the basic assumptions on which our system of justice functions, always remembering that some are fundamental and immutable and some are open to change. We begin, of course, with the Constitution that implemented the ideals of the Declaration of Independence, and few better foundations could be conceived. In this two hundredth year of independence we will do well to look again at both those documents. We see that in the Declaration itself not less than four times the authors expressed direct reliance on God as "the supreme judge," as "the creator," and in the closing sentence the Declaration calls for the protection of divine providence. The uniqueness of this law school is, in part, that your basic charter exemplifies these concepts of the Declaration of 1776. . . . This is indeed a large mission for any school or university, but

> the background of one hundred years of Brigham Young University assures that it will be accomplished.[15]

At the conclusion of the chief justice's address, President Spencer W. Kimball responded with brief comments in which he thanked the chief justice for the high ethical standards he had enumerated, expressed his gratefulness for the opportunities guaranteed by the independence of the Law School, and promised that one of the main purposes of the school was to have graduates measure up to the moral and professional obligations outlined by the chief justice.

President Kimball reiterated the theme of the chief justice: "Here at this college of law we hope to develop an institution where those who attend will become superior in the legal aspects for which they come and also in the ethical part which is so greatly needed in our land." At the convocation, the law school conferred its first honorary Juris Doctor degrees upon Chief Justice Burger, Justice Powell, and President Romney.

At a luncheon, Justice Lewis F. Powell, Jr., told of a moot court hearing he had witnessed at the Law School the day before. Although the participating law students had received only two years of law school training, Justice Powell commented:

> The moot court yesterday afternoon was an unprecedented one. It was composed of the entire active bench of the Tenth Circuit Court of Appeals, together with Judge Wallace of the Ninth Circuit and me — a full panel of nine judges. The participants had the benefit of only two years of law school training. I agree, nevertheless, with the view of Chief Judge David Lewis that he had never heard better moot court presentations.
>
> In passing even tentative judgment on a law school, one must consider the university of which it is a part. Central to my confidence in the quality of your law school is its relationship to Brigham Young University, described this morning by the Chief Justice as one of the finest centers

15. Warren E. Burger, "The Role of the Lawyer in Modern Society," *Proceedings of the Convocation and Dedication of the J. Reuben Clark School of Law,* pp. 2-3.

> of learning in the western world. With these assets one may predict with confidence that the J. Reuben Clark Law School will not merely be a good one: in due time it will rank as a great one.[16]

The dedicatory services in the afternoon were given over to an address by President Dallin H. Oaks on "Ethics, Morality, and Professional Responsibility," to President Romney's dedicatory address on the reasons for the founding of the Law School, and to the dedicatory prayer for the Law School Building. President Oaks gave a serious address on defects both in our law schools and in the practice of the law. He urged that one of the most serious defects in the curriculum of most law schools is the inadequate emphasis on ethics and morality in the practice of law. He quoted retired Supreme Court Justice Tom C. Clark as declaring that "Law schools must consciously undertake the one task that they have universally rejected: instilling normative values in their students." It was Justice Clark's opinion that the need for teaching morality and ethics was never greater because the influences of the church and the family, which formerly developed these virtues, "have drastically diminished in importance in this country, and no other force has arisen to take their place."[17]

Despite this need, President Oaks noted that many law professors feel that law schools will not meet the moral challenge because students' morals are formed before they reach law school, and law teachers have no clear sense of how to teach legal ethics. Others insist that teaching ethics is the responsibility of the bar, which has been lax in both disciplinary standards and their enforcement. Oaks congratulated the chief justice and Justice Powell for their efforts in trying to improve the ethical standards of the bar, both in law schools and in legal practice. He then quoted Professor Harold J. Berman of Harvard Law School as saying that Western society

16. Lewis F. Powell, Jr., "In Defense of the Langdell Tradition," *Proceedings of the Convocation and Dedication,* pp. 14-15.
17. Tom C. Clark, "Teaching Professional Ethics," *San Diego Law Review* 12 (1975):249, 252-53.

Panoramic view of
dedicatory services for the
J. Reuben Clark Law
School Building in
September 1975.

is reaching an "integrity crisis" which threatens the whole Western culture with the "possibility of a kind of nervous breakdown."[18] Berman pointed out that the law has largely lost its former underpinning of strong religious conviction which gave life and emotional attachment to the institutes of the law. He made the point that secularists and rationalists who rely on an intellectual commitment to the law have drained it of the essential emotional vitality needed to provide a deep sense of its ultimate "rightness." Because the moral equation which distinguishes the difference between right and wrong has its roots in religion, Professor Berman concluded that

> Law and religion stand or fall together; and if we wish law to stand, we shall have to give new life to the essential religious commitments that give [the law] its ritual, its tradition, and its authority.[19]

President Oaks then pointed out how the retreat from the moral and ethical aspects of the law, brought about by a disregard for its essential role in the divine plan of structuring social justice, has led to a preoccupation with technical legal procedures rather than the primary goal of determining guilt or innocence. He referred to his published report criticizing the "exclusionary rule," which allows a defendant who is known to be guilty to escape the consequences of his crime simply because law enforcement officers followed an improper procedure in gathering evidence against him.[20] Oaks pointed out that such deficiencies led Justice Walter V. Schaefer of the Illinois Supreme Court to say:

> Almost never do we have a genuine issue of guilt or innocence today. The system has so changed that what we

18. Harold J. Berman, *The Interaction of Law and Religion,* p. 21.
19. Ibid., pp. 24-25, 36-37.
20. "Studying the Exclusionary Rule in Search and Seizure," *The University of Chicago Law Review* 37 (Summer 1970): 665. Since President Oaks's address, the U.S. Supreme Court (U.S. v. James, 96 S. Ct. 3021, 6 July 1976) has largely adopted his viewpoint. As a result, the present spectacle of guilty criminals being released because of the technical mistakes of police officers will be substantially reduced.

> are doing in the courtroom is trying the conduct of the police and that of the prosecutor all along the line. Has there been a misstep at this point? at that point? You know very well that the man is guilty; there is no doubt about the proof. But you must ask, for example: Was there something technically wrong with the arrest? You're always trying something irrelevant. The case is determined on something that really hasn't anything to do with guilt or innocence.[21]

Oaks also emphasized that the legal profession must raise its sights, restructure its priorities, and strive to elevate its professional profile:

> Truth and justice are ultimate values, so understood by our people, and the law and the legal profession will not be worthy of public respect and loyalty if we allow our attention to be diverted from these goals.[22]

He pointed out the inescapable responsibility of the legal profession to develop better procedures for achieving genuine justice, establishing the truth, determining guilt or innocence, and restoring public confidence. He noted that in the final analysis the whole problem revolves around the issue of whether or not the practitioner of the law has been girded in the armor of a strong and abiding sense of moral values and has identified himself with the highest standards of ethical procedures. To achieve this, he asserted the church-related law school has a unique advantage if it will exercise that advantage. He quoted Dean Thomas L. Shaffer of Notre Dame, who said: "Christianity has had too little to do with what is hopeful in the American legal profession. . . . Too many candles are under too many bushels."[23]

President Oaks assured his listeners that the candles of

---

21. Walter V. Schaefer, "A Center Report/Criminal Justice," *The Center Magazine* 69 (November 1968): 76.
22. *Proceedings of the Convocation and Dedication,* p. 33.
23. Thomas L. Shaffer, "Christian Theories of Professional Responsibility," *Southern California Law Review,* no. 48, p. 722.

enlightened Christian morality would not be left under a bushel at BYU:

> We have no diffidence in talking about religious commitment at Brigham Young University, and we will have none in the J. Reuben Clark Law School. Religious commitment, religious values, and concern with ethics and morality are part of the reason for this school's existence, and will be in the atmosphere of its study. As President Marion G. Romney . . . noted in our opening ceremonies, this law school was established to provide an institution in which students could "obtain a knowledge of the laws of man in the light of the laws of God," and the Trustees would like this school to reflect the aura of President J. Reuben Clark: "faith, virtue, integrity, industry, scholarship, and patriotism."[24]

Distinctive Qualities of the BYU Law School

One month before these dedicatory exercises, Acting Dean Carl S. Hawkins circulated to the law faculty a memorandum outlining some of "The Distinctive Qualities of the J. Reuben Clark Law School." Among its aspirations and projected goals he highlighted the following:

> We should be distinguished by the degree of our commitment to the development of our individual students, based upon our revealed knowledge as to the unique worth and dignity of each individual as a child of God.
>
> The Law School should be distinguished by its efforts to research, publish, and teach the Judeo-Christian value assumptions underlying the development of our legal system.
>
> The Law School should be distinguished by its efforts to discover and articulate:
>
> The ultimate spiritual values underlying our Constitutional system and how they may be adapted to different cultures,
>
> The ultimate spiritual values underlying our Common

24. *Proceedings of the Convocation and Dedication*, p. 35.

> Law legal system, and
> The moral and spiritual values underlying professional responsibility.
>
> The Law School should be distinguished by its efforts to research, publish, teach, and work for legal reform in support of family institutions.
>
> The Law School should be distinguished by its efforts to develop lawyering skills as tools to serve the needs of people in the light of their unique worth and dignity as spirit children of God.[25]

The feelings of Acting Dean Hawkins forecasted the conclusion to President Romney's address at the dedication of the Law School Building:

> In establishing this J. Reuben Clark School of Law, we hoped to attract a student body capable of being trained, and assemble a faculty competent to teach, train, and inspire such students to be top flight lawyers and superior judges — men who in their private and professional lives will, by precept and example, implement the high ideals and standards which we have been talking about.
>
> Although we have been in operation but two years, operating in makeshift quarters, we feel that we have made creditable progress. With this new building, we shall move rapidly toward our goals.[26]

Every step taken by the Law School so far indicates that this ideal will be achieved. The faculty continues to grow, and its list of scholarly accomplishments continues to expand. Graduating students are finding jobs, including prestigious judicial clerkships, government employment, and positions with important law firms. In addition, the school has taken vigorous steps toward the establishment of professional respectability with the organized bar, particularly among those pockets of Mormon practitioners located primarily in the Western United States. Many people, both within and outside the legal profession, anticipate that some unique contribution

25. Carl S. Hawkins to the Law School faculty, 23 July 1975, pp. 4-5.
26. *Proceedings of the Convocation and Dedication,* p. 47.

J. Reuben Clark Law
School Building.

can be expected from a law school whose faculty and students believe as a matter of religious principle that the United States Constitution was divinely inspired. A clear moral and ethical concern may be expected to permeate the work of lawyers trained in the BYU environment, and other effects of the Mormon value system will certainly emerge. There is already a sufficient collection of both spiritual and professional resources accumulated at the school to justify more than ordinary hope for the future. As President Oaks said at the Law School's opening ceremony, "The special mission of this law school and its graduates will unfold in time."[27]

---

27. Dallin H. Oaks, "Address at the Ceremony Opening the J. Reuben Clark Law School, 27 August 1973," Dallin H. Oaks biographical file, BYU Archives, p. 2.

52

Toward Leadership in Independent Higher Education

Evolution of Leadership at BYU

During the first three-quarters of a century of its existence, the influence of BYU was confined largely to the Rocky Mountain area, with its affinity to Mormon culture as its dominant characteristic. During its first seventeen years, under the leadership of Karl G. Maeser, the school even shunned the educational training and leadership afforded its faculty by other instutions. During the next twenty-nine years it acquired a reputation as the leading institution for the training of teachers in the State of Utah — a reputation which it has continued to enjoy. This fame spread from Utah to other Western states, and on one occasion one of the larger school systems in California offered to employ without interview all BYU graduates that year who majored in education.[1]

1. The school's present reputation is in sharp contrast with some of the lingering prejudices that operated against Mormons during the second quarter of BYU's existence. Then, Thomas L. Martin, a graduate of Cornell who was recommended for a position on the Cornell faculty by his dean, was refused an appointment by the president because he was a Mormon. He later became a member of the faculty of BYU, and in 1950, he was honored by the American Society of Agronomy as the most outstanding teacher of agriculture in America (*see* Volume 3, chapter 32).

While it still retains Mormon culture as its dominant characteristic, and undoubtedly always will, during the last half-century the University has demonstrated no reluctance to profit from the educational advantages of other institutions. Almost all of the BYU faculty have received their graduate training at universities other than BYU; both BYU faculty and students have shared the mobility of modern America by moving in and out of various campuses with increasing fluidity; and American members of the Mormon Church — including college teachers — were far more committed in 1975 than they had been in 1875 to participation in American institutions, professional associations, and cultural activities.

During the last twenty-five years, BYU's influence has begun to extend throughout the nation, and it has enjoyed the privilege of educating students from 106 foreign countries. With its growth, BYU has begun to assert itself in the formation of national education policy. In the early 1960s, BYU was one of the most outspoken educational opponents to federal aid to education. In the late 1960s it gained a reputation for preserving law and order on its campus, as compared with the riots and anarchy on other campuses. In 1968-69, President Wilkinson served as president of the American Association of Presidents of Independent Colleges and Universities. In that position he was able, under the leadership of Senator Wallace F. Bennett, to block proposed legislation which would have curtailed, in large part, tax exemptions for gifts to educational institutions. If passed, this legislation might have proved fatal to the continuance of many private institutions of learning in the United States.

While BYU gained some prominence as a result of these activities, the most dramatic evidence of its national leadership in independent higher education has occurred during the administration of President Dallin H. Oaks. On 16 October 1975 — the one hundredth anniversary of the founding of Brigham Young University — President Oaks announced that BYU, along with other postsecondary institutions in the Church Educational System, would refuse to comply with certain portions of a regulation promulgated by the U.S.

OF NON-DISCRIMINATION ON THE BASIS OF SEX

Brigham Young University is committed to equal opportunity for men and women in education and employment. Its Board of Trustees has adopted a policy forbidding sex discrimination.

The University is already in compliance with many of the regulations issued under Title IX of the Education Amendments Act of 1972 by the United States Department of Health, Education and Welfare. Any past policy or practice of the University which may have implied discrimination on the basis of sex has been corrected.

While affirming the goal of equal opportunity, Brigham Young University challenges the legality and constitutionality of certain Title IX regulations because they exceed the statutory authority of the Department and infringe on religious freedom.

BYU's opposition to parts of 6 of the 43 designated regulations issued by an executive agency should not be taken as defiance of the law or of the Federal Government. The University believes its position is authorized by the Constitution and laws of the United States. BYU will comply with any regulations which the courts ultimately sustain as lawful.

This notification also states the position of Brigham Young University-Hawaii Campus, LDS Business College, and Ricks College.

REQUIREMENT FOR NOTICE

On July 21, 1975 the United States Department of Health, Education and Welfare published extensive regulations purporting to enforce Title IX of the Education Amendments of 1972, which prohibits sex discrimination in federally assisted educational programs. Section 86.9 of the regulations gives each educational institution 90 days to publish a notice that it does not discriminate among applicants for admission or employment or among students or employees on the basis of sex. Educational institutions are also required to state their policies for compliance with the Title IX Regulations.

POLICY FORBIDDING SEX DISCRIMINATION

The Board of Trustees of Brigham Young University endorses the goal of equal opportunity for men and women in education and employment. Brigham Young University does not discriminate on the basis of sex among its students or employees, or among applicants for admission or employment. We support the nondiscrimination laws and have modified various University policies or procedures which in the past may have been interpreted as discrimination on the basis of sex.

POSITIVE ACTIONS TAKEN

The University has taken major steps to insure equal opportunities for men and women. University scholarships are now awarded without discrimination. Women's athletic programs have received increased financial support, and women's access to facilities and their opportunities for participation have increased significantly. Housing regulations for women are no longer more restrictive than those for men. Salaries of women faculty and staff members are regularly reviewed to insure that women are receiving equal pay for equal work. Policies are in effect which guarantee nondiscrimination in hiring and promotion, and any inequities are being identified and corrected. University departments and colleges have been challenged to avoid sex stereotyping in textbooks, curriculum, and student advisement. University leaders are urging women students to pursue their educational interests with seriousness and vigor.

REFUSAL TO FOLLOW CERTAIN REGULATIONS

Title IX (the statutory law) forbids sex discrimination in every "education program or activity receiving federal financial assistance." However, the regulations issued by the Department purport to dictate policies and activities in many areas of the University, whether or not such policies or activities involve "education" and whether or not they concern a "program or activity receiving federal financial assistance." The regulations effectively ignore these important qualifying words in the statute. They extend government powers well beyond those granted by the statute by insisting that if any part or area of an institution receives direct or indirect federal financial assistance (such as by enrolling students who receive federal aid), then the entire institution is subject to federal regulation. We reject this all-inclusive interpretation, believing that many of the regulations are unlawful because they exceed the Department's statutory authority under Title IX.

BYU has traditionally refused all federal grants. We have limited our receipt of federal funds to a few programs in which the government receives a service equal in value to its payments. While some of our students receive federal assistance (such as veteran's benefits), the statute does not suggest that payments to students should be a basis for regulating every educational policy and activity of the institution. We therefore believe that most of our activities are not subject to the regulations.

We also believe that some of the regulations are unconstitutional because they violate the due process clause or the constitutional guarantee of the freedom of religion.

Nevertheless, we voluntarily choose to follow many of the regulations because we believe them to embody policies which are fair and just. But where we believe the regulations are unconstitutional or illegal and where they prohibit or interfere with the teaching or practice of high moral principles, we will not follow them.

UNLAWFUL REGULATIONS

H.E.W. regulations the University will not follow are:

1. §86.2(g) and (h): Contrary to the broad definitions in this regulation, a university program or activity not receiving federal financial assistance is not subject to the regulations. However, the University will not discriminate on the basis of sex in any university program or activity regardless of the applicability of the regulations.

2. §86.12: The University will notify the Department that it is exempt from certain regulations on the ground of religious belief. However, the Constitution forbids the Department from making any judgment as to the content or sincerity of religious belief. We will resist any attempt by the Department to rule on the validity of our constitutional claim.

3. §§86.21(c), 86.40, and 86.57(b): Brigham Young University will not follow the provisions of these regulations to the extent that they prohibit certain inquiries into or actions based upon the marital or parental status or the pregnancy or termination of pregnancy of present or prospective students or employees. BYU teaches and enforces strict adherence to the highest Christian standards of sexual morality. Our standards of behavior and our admissions, hiring and dismissal policies related to sexual behavior are identical for both sexes. Where an inquiry or action prohibited by the regulations may be necessary to create or enforce the moral climate we desire at BYU, we will disregard the contrary requirements of the regulations.

4. §86:31(b)(5): BYU will continue to enforce rules of appearance which differ for men and women because we believe that differences in dress and grooming of men and women are proper expressions of God-given differences in the sexes. We will resist the imposition of a unisex standard of appearance.

5. §§86.31(c) and 86.37(b): BYU will not discriminate in any federally financed student aid programs or in the University's own financial aid. BYU will also endeavor to persuade private donors to refrain from discrimination on the grounds of sex. Because this regulation would require us to breach agreements with previous donors, the University will continue to administer existing privately financed student aid according to the conditions imposed by the donors. We believe the regulations' requirement that universities not administer financial aid restricted to one sex deprives private donors of property without due process of law. Congress must not have intended that a statute forbidding misuse of federal aid serve as the basis for depriving private donors of their right to use their property as they see fit.

6. §§86.37(c) and 86.41: The sections of the regulations dealing with athletics are not clear. They have been the subject of widespread controversy over their meaning and coverage. We do not concede that these regulations apply to our athletic program, which is not an "education program or activity receiving federal financial assistance." Our women's athletic program is among the best in the nation. We are confident that our voluntary efforts to improve athletic opportunities for women will meet or exceed the requirements of the regulations within the three-year implementation period.

OUR POSITION IS LAWFUL

Our stand in opposition to these regulations should not be taken as defiance of the law or the federal government. We believe our position is lawful—that it is the Department of Health, Education and Welfare that is violating the constitutional and statutory law. Our Church teaches the necessity of "obeying, honoring and sustaining the law" (Articles of Faith 12) and of "befriending that law which is the constitutional law of the land" (Doc. & Cov. 98:6). Therefore, we will comply with any regulation ultimately sustained as lawful by the courts of the United States. In the interim we will follow the policies outlined above, which represent our best judgment on the meaning of the constitution and laws that govern us.

While we have based our refusal to comply with certain regulations on the grounds that they exceed statutory authority and violate our constitutional rights relating to religion, we also oppose such regulations on moral grounds. The teaching of honesty, integrity and chastity must not become exclusively the province of religion. If our government not only abandons the advocacy of moral standards but positively prohibits the practice of such values at teaching institutions, as these regulations appear to do, the destruction of America as a great nation will be both imminent and inevitable.

BRIGHAM YOUNG UNIVERSITY
October 16, 1975

Department of Health, Education, and Welfare (HEW) to enforce Title IX of the Education Amendments Act of 1972 (Public Law 92-318). Title IX prohibits sex "discrimination under any educational program or activity receiving Federal financial assistance."

The refusal to comply was not issued because BYU favored discrimination but because, in its opinion, the regulations went far beyond the statute by including programs not receiving "Federal financial assistance," thus usurping the independence of the University. The University also insisted that certain parts of the regulations pertaining to Title IX constituted unconstitutional interference with religious beliefs and tenets taught by and practiced at the University.[2] The announcement, approved by the Board of Trustees, resulted in as much, if not more, national comment about BYU than previously had been generated by any of the University's notable achievements or peculiar characteristics.

Less than a week earlier, on October 10, members of the Board of Trustees, faculty, student body, and administration had celebrated BYU's centennial with an old-fashioned Founders Day procession from the simple and quiet lower campus — the source of most long-standing BYU traditions — to the University's well-planned and modern "new" home on Temple Hill. That procession witnessed the culmination of a century-long maturation process — from a small elementary school whose continued existence was often questioned even by its founding Church to a position of prominence and respect throughout the country.

Thus, the announcement of BYU's opposition to the Title IX regulation demonstrated BYU's strength and maturity in a sense that transcended local and regional boundaries; in making this announcement, the University acted as a spokesman for American private higher education in its mounting battle

---

2. "Notification of Brigham Young University Policy of Non-Discrimination on the Basis of Sex," statement issued by Brigham Young University, 16 October 1975, Dallin H. Oaks biographical file, BYU Archives.

to maintain a certain degree of independence from federal and state governments. In informal remarks to the faculty prior to the official announcement, President Oaks expressed the hope that other private colleges would join actively in the fight, but he concluded, "It's pretty clear that nobody is going to come out of the trenches until they see our hindparts disappear over the parapets; it is surely true that no one else has the resolve or the resources to speak out for private, independent higher education that Brigham Young University has."[3]

In order to understand BYU's emergence from obscurity to the center stage of private higher education, it will be useful to look briefly at the background of United States higher education generally and private higher education specifically.

The Pre-1960 Period: Religious Origins, New Academic Efforts, and the Growth Boom

From the earliest beginnings in the colonial period until

---

3. In a survey taken by the American Association of Presidents of Independent Colleges and Universities in January and February 1976, of eighty-five responses, representing seventy-five percent of the institutions involved, all but two of the presidents indicated that their students accepted support from some federally funded program, such as a Guaranteed Student Loan, Basic Education Opportunity Grants, or the G.I. Bill. None of the eighty-five institutions considered receipt of government aid by students as being the receipt of government aid by the institution. And even as to aid to the institutions, twenty-six percent reported that they had no governmental grants, contracts, or other direct financial assistance of any kind. Twenty-nine percent reported that they had accepted some government aid, but it amounted to less than two percent of their total institutional expenditures. Twenty-five percent reported that they had received more than two percent but less than ten percent of their institutional expenditures. Fifteen percent reported that governmental help amounted to more than ten percent of their total expenditures. Of the eighty-five institutions, thirty-one had an enrollment of less than 1,000, thirty had an enrollment of between 1,000 and 2,000, eighteen had an enrollment of between 2,000 and 5,000, and only six had an enrollment of over 5,000; namely, Brigham Young University, with an enrollment of approximately 25,000; Howard University, 9,445; Pepperdine University, 9,410; Villanova, 9,130; Roosevelt, 7,628; and Ricks College, 5,800.

about the time of the Civil War, religious influence was clearly dominant in the founding of American colleges and universities. Some variety among the institutions existed, of course, but most of the schools were created to perpetuate both religious and classical education.[4] After the Civil War, government and private interests entered into the field to establish Negro colleges and nonsectarian vocational training schools. The latter category included teachers colleges. As a religious educational institution which, shortly after its founding, became especially concerned with the preparation of teachers, Brigham Young Academy was at that time in the mainstream of American higher education.

In 1900 a scant 238,000 students were enrolled in colleges and universities nationwide, representing 2.3 percent of the population aged eighteen to twenty-four. However, enrollment increased dramatically in later years, as evidenced by the following figures:[5]

Year	Number (in Thousands)	Percentage of Population Aged 18 to 24
1920	598	4.7
1940	1,494	9.1
1950	2,659	16.5
1960	3,583	22.2
1970	7,760	31.7

Enrollment increases between 1960 and 1970 showed a per-

4. Alexander W. Astin and Calvin B. T. Lee, *The Invisible Colleges* (New York: McGraw-Hill Book Company, 1974), pp. 13-15. *See also* Manning M. Patillo, Jr., and Donald M. MacKenzie, *Church-Sponsored Higher Education in the United States: Report of the Danforth Commission* (Washington, D.C.: American Council on Education, 1966), pp. 1-17.
5. The Carnegie Commission on Higher Education, *New Students and New Places* (New York: McGraw-Hill Book Company, 1971), p. 128. In the winter of 1974 an Associated Press account reported a record national enrollment of 10.1 million, together with an estimate that a high of 10.8 million would be reached by 1980. After that time, total enrollment is expected to decline (BYU *Daily Universe,* 16 December 1974).

centage increase in terms of student numbers of 117 percent. Clearly, the growth of higher education in the twentieth century linked college with the American dream of a good life. A 1968 Gallup poll revealed that ninety-seven percent of all parents questioned in a nationwide sample wanted their children to enter college.[6]

As dramatic as the growth surge in higher education was, the shifts in the sponsorship and attitudes about the place of higher learning in the twentieth century were even more dramatic. A large number of nonsectarian vocational schools founded in the second half of the nineteenth century gradually came to include liberal arts offerings in their curricula, thereby invading what had been historically the domain of the church-related college. In addition, of the estimated 2,000 colleges founded during the nineteenth century, only twenty percent of them survived the hazards of poor locations, internal dissent, natural disasters, lack of finances, and insufficient enrollment amid increasing competition. Among those that survived, including church schools, an overwhelming shift toward a nonsectarian emphasis occurred. Thus, the trend is now deeply established toward a homogeneous, secular, universal higher education.[7] One implication of this trend, heavily influenced by changing social attitudes, was the general acceptance of the attitudinal heritage of the vocational college, which, "Unlike the church-related college . . . was not concerned with the student's soul or his morals."[8]

Students of the subject have suggested several reasons for the post-World War II higher education boom.[9] One early impetus was the financial incentive of the GI Bill. In addition, in the early 1960s the postwar baby boom had its impact on the college market. Furthermore, the Russian launching of Sput-

---

6. Terry Sanford, "Who Should Pay the Bill?" *Change,* May-June 1971, p. 6.
7. Alexander W. Astin and Calvin B.T. Lee, *The Invisible Colleges,* p. 23.
8. Ibid., p. 21.
9. *See* generally, David A. Shannon, *Twentieth Century America,* 2nd ed. (Chicago: Rand McNally & Company, 1969), pp. 596-599.

nik in the fall of 1957 awakened many Americans to the relationship between advanced technology and national defense.

Much of the increased interest in college education may also be attributed to growing American affluence and a perceived relationship between material success and education. Since the advent of the adding machine in the mid-1800s, America has become increasingly self-conscious about its own statistics.[10] When the statistical have-nots discovered — through surveys, newspapers, periodicals, and other sources — that a substantial amount of America's wealth was being held by those who attended college, the children of the have-nots were increasingly pointed toward college. And as American society became more literate, a college education came to be viewed as the key that unlocked the door to the opportunities of the age. The notion that a college diploma was a passport to real participation in the country's economy influenced not only the expectations of college students but the curricula of the colleges themselves.

In terms of relative causes, the growth of the college-age population since 1950 accounted for about forty-five percent of the total enrollment increase, while the rest is thought to be attributable to other factors.[11]

As pointed out in chapter 44, during the period from 1950 to 1971 there was a 500 percent growth in public institutions, as compared with a 75 percent growth in church-related private institutions. Yet, at the same time BYU had a 450 percent growth in enrollment. Although this phenomenal growth of the school during the '50s and '60s was influenced by national and Churchwide developments, the main cause for the expansion at BYU was the campaign for enrollment waged by BYU itself[12] and its increasing popularity among members of

---

10. Daniel J. Boorstin, *The Americans: The Democratic Experience* (New York: Random House, 1973), pp. 167-244, provides a delightful account of the statistical mentality in America.
11. The Carnegie Commission on Higher Education, *New Students and New Places,* p. 11.
12. *See* Volume 2, chapter 28, pp. 601-15.

the Church, which itself tripled in membership between 1950 and 1970.

Nationally, the great increase in both round numbers and the percentage of the college-age population who came to college changed the emphasis in higher education away from a system designed for a small and relatively elite group to one providing broad and almost universal access. There were not only many more students, but the students were also more diverse in their interests and in their abilities to cope with the traditional expectations of college life.[13] There were few well-formulated plans for dealing with either the numbers or the variety of college students who seemed to spring full-grown from the cities and suburbs of America. It has been observed that the boom came so fast that "Higher education and its administrators and priests could have had little time or opportunity to develop a philosophy or even a practical analysis of the situation after the boom; they were able to do little more than meet public demand."[14]

Campus Unrest

Toward the end of the 1960s, other phenomena largely foreign to higher education appeared widely on campuses across the nation. Among the most important of these was a complex set of events that came to be characterized either as "campus unrest" or "campus anarchy." Initial involvement of college students in protest movements began in the late 1950s as students began demonstrating their support for the black civil rights movement. This development was significant chiefly because of its breadth; the involvement of students in peaceful protest had actually been rather common on American campuses since the turn of the century.

What began to happen in the '60s, however, was a new

13. The Carnegie Commission on Higher Education, *Governance of Higher Education* (New York: McGraw-Hill Book Company, 1973), p. 8.
14. Tom Wicker, "America and Its Colleges: End of an Affair," *Change*, September 1971, pp. 22-23.

phenomenon in student culture — the introduction of violent protest — which is treated more fully in Volume 3, chapter 39.[15] The primary subjects of such protests were the black civil rights movement, the escalation of the war in Southeast Asia, and, eventually, the university itself. These issues brought forth a variety of actions and reactions from a developing youth subculture that had the manifestations of a revolutionary movement.[16]

While many of the criticisms of the student movement were directed at American society and its materialistic values, as well as at the government and its unpopular war, the protest movement also focused on the limitations of the universities and their ambiguous assumptions, questioning the very nature and purposes of higher education. One of the serious sources of criticism was the increasing professionalization of the faculty. Teaching and research, traditionally the primary functions of universities, had been joined by a public service function (which was seen as a means of supporting or condemning the escalating war), and emphasis seemed to shift away from teaching to the other two areas of endeavor.[17]

As students increased their cry for instruction on topics of social interest and in other areas, the universities responded only haltingly. They found themselves caught between often legitimate student concerns on one side and the competing legitimate concerns of the public and governmental sector on the other side. Unfortunately, the public sector was paying an increasing share of the cost of education. The cost of public higher education rose — from an average per capita cost of $957 in 1950 and $1,620 in 1960 to $2,676 in 1970.[18] Tuition

---

15. *See also* the President's Commission on Campus Unrest, *Campus Unrest* (Washington, D.C.: U.S. Government Printing Office, 1970), pp. 51-89.
16. For a passionate description of what is predicted as the "coming American revolution," its causes and its nature, *see* Charles A. Reich, *The Greening of America* (New York: Random House, 1970).
17. The President's Commission on Campus Unrest, *Campus Unrest,* pp. 187-201.
18. The Carnegie Commission on Higher Education, *Higher Education: Who Pays? Who Benefits? Who Should Pay?* (New York: McGraw-Hill Book Company, 1973), p. 50.

covered about one-third of that cost, while public funding and private donors provided the other two-thirds of the cost.[19] In the decade of the 1960s, while combined private and public higher education expenditures grew from $7.6 billion dollars to $24.9 billion,[20] governmental expenditures in higher education pyramided from 1.1 billion dollars in 1950 to 2.6 billion dollars in 1960 and 10.8 billion dollars in 1970.[21] In part because of their continued acceptance of and reliance on federal support, the universities were viewed as part of "the system" and became the continuing object of student protests.[22]

A Financial Crisis: The Burden of Support Shifts to the Federal Government

For many reasons, some of which are difficult to isolate, the student protest movement began to lose its visible and violent momentum during the early '70s. Of considerable importance must have been the public reaction against it and the realization that many of the ends of the civil rights movement had been achieved, both in terms of major legislation and national attitudes.[23] It gradually became a certainty that America would withdraw from the war in Vietnam, even though actual withdrawal did not come until January 1975. One other factor in the slackening of hostilities may have been economic inflation, in both the nation as a whole and in higher education. With rising costs and changing attitudes, funding difficulties for many universities often made response to even legitimate student demands extremely difficult.

The financial crisis threatened particularly the survival of private institutions. Simply expressed, the problem was one of

---

19. Ibid., p. 1.
20. The Carnegie Commission on Higher Education, *The More Effective Use of Resources* (New York: McGraw-Hill Book Company, 1972), p. 8.
21. The Carnegie Commission on Higher Education, *Higher Education: Who Pays? Who Benefits? Who Should Pay?*, p. 20.
22. The President's Commission on Campus Unrest, *Campus Unrest*, p. 31.
23. Indeed, the country's commitment to civil rights legislation would become a substantial burden upon higher education.

increasing costs and diminishing sources of revenue. Higher costs were attributable to the heavy increases in expenditures caused in large part by the increase in student enrollment, sharp decreases in teaching loads, expanded responsibilities for research and public service, and unanticipated and mounting rates of inflation. On the other side of the ledger, private institutions had not been able to raise tuition levels high enough to cover rising costs because of competition from public institutions which offered low tuition at the expense of the taxpayers. Tuition sources for private schools were also becoming relatively less available as many students began to choose vocational or career training in preference to the traditional liberal arts approach. Many also simply decided to postpone college since the draft pressure had eased.[24]

A related cause of concern was that public confidence in higher education was badly shaken by the events of the 1970s. State legislatures, not without reason, became reluctant to increase appropriations for state-supported institutions.[25] Public institutions, however, were able to overcome the lack of state support by the enormous increase in federal support. This support was not available to church-related institutions. Concern also was growing among the college-trained, as well as the college-bound, due to developing employment attitudes that questioned the assumption that college is a ticket to higher income, higher status, and great security.[26] This

---

24. "Now It's Colleges Seeking Students," *U.S. News & World Report,* 6 September 1971, p. 42.
25. Tom Wicker, "America and Its Colleges: End of an Affair," *Change,* September 1971, p. 25.
26. *See* Caroline Bird, *The Case Against College* (New York: David McKay Company, Inc., 1975). In Bird's view, "in strictly financial terms, college is the dumbest investment a young man can make" (p. 63). In general, however, statistics do not bear this out, as the following summary indicates:

Years of School Completed	**1968 Lifetime Income for Men Age 18 to Death**
Elementary: Less than 8 years	$213,505
8 years	276,755

particular disillusionment might have been predictable in view of the ambiguous and even paradoxical attitudes and preparation brought by American students from their homes to college campuses during the boom years. The widespread, albeit diverse, belief in the value of a college education that was so prevalent ten years earlier was paradoxical in view of the general suspicion with which Americans have traditionally viewed the "intellectuals" at whose feet their youth would be taught in the colleges and universities.[27] The inconsistency of these attitudes is heightened by the fact that "At great effort and expense, they [Americans] send an extraordinary proportion of their young to colleges and universities; but their young, when they get there, do not seem to care even to *read.*"[28]

The effect of these problems on private schools was, for some of the reasons indicated above, particularly acute. Virtually every prominent study of higher education during the late 1960s and early 1970s pointed to the indispensable value of educational diversity in the type and character of colleges and universities.[29] There has been, however, a historical and

---

High School: 1 to 3 years	308,094
4 years	371,094
College: 1 to 3 years	424,280
4 years	584,062
4 years or more	607,921
5 years or more	636,119

Source: Bureau of the Census, *Current Population Reports,* "Consumer Income," Series P-60, No. 74, 30 October 1970, p. 14. Notwithstanding these statistics, records maintained by the BYU Placement Center lend support to the view that college graduates were having more difficulty locating jobs in 1974 than in 1969. Those difficulties reflected the general economic troubles of the early '70s, making it more difficult to know just how much difference college diplomas made in a complex period of economic slowdown.

27. *See* generally, Richard Hofstadter, *Anti-Intellectualism in American Life* (New York: Alfred A. Knopf, 1964).
28. Ibid., p. 301.
29. The Research and Policy Committee of the Committee for Economic Development, *The Management and Financing of Colleges* (New York: Committee for Economic Development, 1973), p. 17; Russell Kirk,

increasing tendency toward homogenization and similarity in the kind of education being made available by both public and private institutions. The dominant theme of the remarks of University of Chicago President Edward Levi at the inauguration of President Dallin H. Oaks at BYU in November 1971 was his concern that our "system of higher education as a whole is now strikingly uniform," such that students do not have "a choice between institutions which offer different modes of learning, but between institutions which differ in the extent to which they conform to the model of the prestige university."[30] If this observation is correct, the major justification for continued support of private education, which is more costly to individual students, is disappearing. Many observers feel that the future of private colleges depends upon their ability to maintain some kind of educational uniqueness and to persuade their patrons of the justifiability of that uniqueness.

In many cases, the uniqueness of private colleges is thought to be in their freedom to take positions of value orientation seldom, if ever, taken by public institutions. John A. Howard, then president of the American Association of Presidents of Independent Colleges and Universities, said in 1971 that the principal uniqueness of many private colleges lies in offering an education that teaches the value of accepting restraints and obligations as being essential to the maintenance of an ordered society.[31]

The last of the true church-related colleges face the most serious financial crisis of all. Contrary to the experience of

---

"How May the Independent College Survive?" *National Review,* 21 January 1972, p. 47; "Any Future For Private Colleges?" *U.S. News and World Report,* 6 September 1971, p. 43; Frank Newman, chairman, *Report on Higher Education* (Cambridge, Massachusetts: MIT Press, 1971), chapter 4; and the Carnegie Commission on Higher Education, *Higher Education: Who Pays? Who Benefits? Who Should Pay?,* pp. 7ff.

30. Edward H. Levi, "Inaugural Address," *Inaugural Addresses* (Provo, Utah: Brigham Young University Press, 1971), p. 6.

31. "Any Future For Private Colleges?" *U.S. News and World Report,* 6 September 1971, p. 45.

Brigham Young University, churches have historically played a minor role in the financial support of the colleges they sponsor.[32] As a result, "The churches no longer pay the bills, and so the school nominally related to churches have had independence thrust upon them, whether or not it has been passionately sought by someone calling the signals. Headquarters [of the churches] continue to list great and near-great universities as part of the empire. [However,] the real decisions are made locally, with the help of Washington."[33] This kind of independence has forced church schools to look almost exclusively for private assistance from those who are persuaded that a true Christian college is worthy of their financial support. At the same time, the tendency has been for Christian colleges, once support from the founding church has subsided, to accommodate "the world." Thus, church-related colleges have faced, in addition to a financial crisis, an identity crisis: Can they justify the financial support of that group of private patrons who might be interested in the unique contribution of a true church college while operating what tends to be a secularized college? The answer seems to be that with the widespread secularization of American society, many still support these schools, but those true church-related institutions who have largely avoided secularization have more devoted support. In 1972, *Christianity Today* editorialized:

> An institution with a clear, unambiguous creedal commitment will attract the sympathy and merit and support of people of like mind, especially since the image of secular educational institutions has been greatly debased in the public as well as the Christian mind. And when a Christian school has gone beyond creedal commitment to integrate faith and learning and to advance a com-

---

32. Alexander W. Astin and Calvin B.T. Lee, *The Invisible Colleges,* p. 19. *See* Volume 3, chapter 41 for a discussion of the small amount contributed to colleges by their founding churches.
33. Julian N. Hartt, *Theology and the Church in the University* (Philadelphia: The Westminster Press, 1969), pp. 17-18.

> prehensive life- and world-view consonant with Scripture, it will enlist the support of innumerable Christians.[34]

Even so, it has proved challenging for private schools of all kinds to find someone to pay for their independence. The number of private, accredited four-year colleges and universities running current fund deficits (i.e., annual expenditures exceeding annual income) increased from about one-third of all such institutions in 1968 to nearly sixty percent in 1971.[35] A more recent study, sponsored by the Association of American Colleges, indicates that private colleges have survived the recent economic crisis by a considerable amount of belt-tightening, but that twenty-seven percent of the schools surveyed remained in serious financial trouble. The study commented that "the odds against their survival are formidable" if no corrective action is taken.[36]

Federal Intervention in Higher Education

In 1952 the Commission on Financing Higher Education declared that the strength of higher education was "founded upon its freedom," which "must be protected at all costs." The Commission predicted that dependence on federal financing would bring government controls that would destroy cherished originality and diversity and "would in the end produce uniformity, mediocrity, and compliance."[37]

Speaking before a committee of Congress in 1961 in behalf of the Board of Trustees of BYU in opposition to an extensive program of federal aid to education, President Wilkinson, supported by outstanding educators, urged that the adoption

---

34. "Christian Colleges Search for Survival," *Christianity Today*, 26 May 1972, pp. 26-27.
35. The Research and Policy Committee of the Committee for Economic Development, *The Management and Financing of Colleges*, p. 14.
36. "Bowen-Minter Report on Higher Education," *The Chronicle of Higher Education*, 8 December 1975, pp. 6-7.
37. The Commission on Financing Higher Education, *Nature and Needs of Higher Education* (New York: Columbia University Press, 1952), pp. 158, 162.

of a substantial program of federal aid to schools could easily result in federal control of education. He also warned that a small program of federal aid would soon blossom into an unwieldy colossus.[38]

Despite warnings from leading educators, whose views were shared and propounded by BYU, Congress passed a federal aid program which began with appropriations of about $2,200,000 in 1951 and grew to almost $21,000,000,000 in 1972.[39] As predicted by Dr. Wilkinson and others, this tremendous increase in federal funding of higher education has resulted in substantial federal interventions in the administration of higher education, particularly in the formulation of educational policies of institutions receiving federal aid.

Public and private universities have, of course, previously participated in the economic community as employers, contractors, and otherwise. Beginning in the 1930s they became subject to state and federal laws in such well-known areas as labor regulation, social security measures, unemployment taxes, and health and safety codes. Their special role as educational institutions exempted them from certain taxes and regulatory measures, but the general need for compliance with federal regulations was not an altogether strange idea to many college administrators. Nevertheless, despite earlier warnings, many administrators have been shocked by massive new regulations over their practices. Indeed, it has now become common practice for the government to promote certain legislative policies by requiring direct recipients of federal money to conform to those policies.

38. *See also* Volume 3 chapter 41 for statements of leading American educators (including Cary Croneis, president of Beloit College; Nicholas Murray Butler, President of Columbia University; and Ray L. Wilbur, President of Stanford University) on the danger of an extensive program of federal aid to education.
39. Figures for 1951 are from Seymour E. Harris, *A Statistical Portrait of Higher Education* (New York: McGraw-Hill, 1972), pp. 619, 640; 1972 figures are from U.S. Bureau of the Census, 95th ed., *Statistical Abstract of the United States: 1974* (Washington, D.C.: U.S. Government Printing Office, 1974), p. 247. More recent figures are unavailable.

For many private educational institutions the growing financial crisis has seemed to mean that the only realistic alternative to accepting federal support (and controls) would be to cease operations. It is fair to assume that most schools did not want federal controls, but they were unrealistic in thinking that they could have federal aid, which they favored and lobbied to obtain, without some kind of controls.

Before 1960 the federal controls that existed in the educational field did not seem particularly onerous. During the 1950s the federal presence had indirectly influenced educational policy in making substantial research funds and other incentives available in the physical and biological sciences, but only a limited number of persons in government or education anticipated what would be spawned by regulations reflecting the depth of policy commitment created by the civil rights movement and its culminating legislation in the 1960s. Several important limitations on government intervention were pushed back as policymakers responded in unprecedented ways to what had become an appeal to the national conscience: the need to end racial discrimination. The traditional distinction between public and private institutions became blurred as means were sought to prohibit private discrimination. The traditional notion that government regulation is negatively restraining (telling a citizen what he should not do) rather than affirmatively compelling (telling a citizen what he shall do) was also changed with the introduction of affirmative action programs. Whereas prior concepts had typically required subject institutions to refrain from overt discriminatory acts, these new regulatory programs required those subject to the regulations to initiate, at their own expense, policies and practices to eradicate discrimination within their own scope of activity. The required nexus between governmental subsidy and private action was also expanded so that indirect federal aid began producing some of the same consequences that had previously flowed only from direct grants or contracts.

In this atmosphere the federal government began to enter fully into the inner councils of academic decision-making. As stated by Kingman Brewster, president of Yale University:

> My fear is that there is a growing tendency for the central government to use the spending power to prescribe educational policies. These are matters which they could not regulate were it not for our dependence on their largesse. I am worried that maybe we do not have any obvious constitutional basis on which to resist this encroachment. It will always be asserted that the government as grantor, lender, or contractor, has a legitimate interest in all aspects of our behavior, once they have financed any part of our activity.[40]

In a series of public remarks beginning in 1972, President Dallin Oaks expressed similar fears about the unfortunate coincidence that financial stress in higher education came at a time when powerful interest groups were seeking to correct long-standing discriminations that have adversely affected their opportunities for education and employment. Because government officials have accepted the goals of such groups, Oaks said, pressure is applied to private educational institutions that seems to give the elusive goal of social justice priority over purely educational goals. In the process, governmental authorities have become involved in the management of higher education. While affirming his strong support for providing equal opportunity in higher education without regard to race, creed, or sex, Oaks echoed the sentiments of other presidents of private colleges and universities that "The disappearing differentiation in higher education is the direct result of federal controls on higher education. The inevitable effect of centralized standards to which all must adhere is to restrict the latitude for institutional management and thus eradicate differences between institutions relating to employment policy, admissions policy, scholarship and other financial aids, housing, and use of buildings. I have also sug-

---

40. Kingman Brewster, Jr., in an address to the American Bar Foundation, February 1975, quoted in John Walsh, "Higher Education and Regulation: Counting the Costs of Compliance," *Science,* 31 October 1975, p. 445.

gested that we are on the threshold of additional federal controls restricting the content of courses and the manner of teaching."[41] He also expressed concern that "If America's institutions of higher learning lose control of . . . who attends, who teaches, and what standards are enforced — private, independent higher education will no longer exist."[42]

The prediction of the Commission on Financing Higher Education that dependence on federal financing would bring governmental controls that would destroy cherished originality and diversity and the fears expressed by Wilkinson, Oaks, and other educational leaders have unfortunately come to pass. In the words of President Oaks in an address given before the National Association of College and University Attorneys at Dallas, Texas, on 18 June 1976,

> The last twenty years have seen increasing federal financing and increasing federal controls. Today there are no national commissions or national educational organizations speaking out for the freedom of higher education, and relatively few making the case for diversity. Along with federal financing, we have accepted federal controls, and higher education is well on its way to becoming a regulated industry. Heavily dependent on federal financing, higher education — like a business in financial peril — is in danger of a receivership in which its management would pass to an absentee creditor in Washington. The 20-year pattern of finance and control has created a regulatory mood in which institutions without direct federal financial support are nevertheless in danger of colonization by ambitious government regulators. The sovereign authority to make and execute educational policy is being taken away from the trustees, administration, and faculty of our universities and col-

41. Dallin H. Oaks, "Threats to the Independence of Private Higher Education," speech before the Salt Lake City Rotary Club, 23 January 1973, Dallin H. Oaks Personal Papers.
42. Testimony of Dallin H. Oaks before the Postsecondary Education Subcommittee of the Education and Labor Committee of the U.S. House of Representatives, 24 June 1975, Dallin H. Oaks biographical file, BYU Archives, p. 19.

> leges. On more and more important questions, the policy-making authority is being claimed and exercised by remote government rule-makers.[43]

Examples of federal rule-making are not hard to find. In an article appearing in *Reader's Digest* for May 1976, Ralph Kinney Bennett tells of HEW bureaucrats ordering Columbia to prepare a detailed report on the race, sex, and ethnic background of its faculty and administration, despite the fact that such a report was a violation of New York state law: "Rather than be cut off from federal funds, which then composed half its $175-million annual budget, Columbia, in the early 1970s, resorted to a ludicrous, time-consuming exercise in snooping. 'Census reporters' were told to uncover the required personal information by noting physical characteristics and analyzing last names." Based on the result of this study, Columbia "vowed to exercise 'affirmative action.' " That is, "Columbia will hire faculty and staff not just on the basis of academic achievement or qualification but also upon whether applicants are female, have dark skin or Spanish surnames. 'No one likes to be in the position of negotiating with Uncle Sam for his survival,' says Columbia president William McGill. 'Our instincts were to promise almost anything to get the government off Columbia's back.' "[44]

HEW has also imposed quotas on colleges receiving federal aid. These quotas require that faculties and student bodies must contain a certain percentage of minority groups. In the words of Bennett, "Department bureaucrats have used this authority to influence admissions, hiring, administration of scholarships, the most vital affairs of colleges and universities." He then quotes Russell Kirk, editor of *The University Bookman*, as saying, "Washington is using the force of law to

---

43. Dallin H. Oaks, "A Private University Looks at Government Regulation," an address delivered before the National Association of College and University Attorneys, Dallas, Texas, 18 June 1976, Dallin H. Oaks Personal Papers.
44. Ralph Kinney Bennett, "Colleges under the Federal Gun," *Reader's Digest*, May 1976, pp. 126-127.

compel colleges to hire underqualified and unqualified persons as professors merely because they are members of one 'minority' or another." Bennett also points out that

> More than 70 leading educators, including three Nobel laureates, have joined to protest "the relentless continuation of unjust and discriminatory quota programs which are imposed on every college in America having federal contracts. That these programs have been established in the name of affirmative action in no way mitigates the evil they accomplish.[45]

Bennett continues:

> The academic community has become so hooked on the federal dollar (from $10,000 annual grants to small colleges, to $245.8 million in federal contract and grant funds to the University of California) that it cannot afford to stand and fight. For 2500 of the nation's 3000 colleges, federal money is simply built into their budgets. Thus, Brooklyn College sought to meet HEW requirements by circulating a detailed questionnaire to its faculty seeking racial and ethnic information. Urging faculty members to disregard their personal feelings, the college's president reminded them that "considerable sums which the university receives from the federal government are in jeopardy" and "we have no choice but to perform this task as quickly as possible."[46]

The Women's Movement and Higher Education

One of the facets of federal intervention in the educational policy of American universities has been the government's insistence on equality of treatment for men and women.[47] In the 1960s there occurred a resurgence of the women's movement in America, and this included political and legal efforts

45. Ibid., p. 127.
46. Ibid., p. 128.
47. Much of the information in this section is taken from Monte Stewart, "HEW's Regulation under Title IX of the Education Amendments of 1972: Ultra Vires Challenges," *Brigham Young University Law Review*, June 1976, pp. 133-87.

to eradicate sex discrimination in American education. This was especially true of women's leaders in education. They were interested, not so much in the rights and advancement of women in general, but rather in the rights and status of women within the field of education. Legislation destined to help their cause was, however, slow in maturing. Title VII of the Civil Rights Act of 1964 prohibited sex discrimination in employment, but it exempted educational institutions from the coverage of the title.[48]

The Equal Pay Act of 1963, which was aimed at eliminating the discriminatory practice of paying women less than men for the same work, likewise excluded academic women from its coverage.[49] This statute was, however, amended in 1966 to include within its orbit "any employee employed in the capacity of academic administrative personnel or teacher in elementary or secondary schools."[50]

Nonetheless, prior to 1972, academic women's groups had only one effective tool against sex discrimination in higher education — Executive Order No. 11,246. The order prohibited colleges and universities holding contracts with the federal government from discriminating against women. Under this order, the most prominent of the academic women's groups, Women's Equity Action League (WEAL), filed with the Department of Labor a class action suit against every university and college in the United States.[51]

---

48. The original section 702 of the Civil Rights Act of 1964, 78 Stat. 255, provided that "This title shall not apply to . . . an educational institution with respect to the employment of individuals to perform work connected with the educational activities of such institution."
49. When Congress enacted the Equal Pay Act of 1963, the Fair Labor Standards Act of 1938 provided in pertinent part that "The provisions of sections [206] and [207] of this title shall not apply with respect to (1) any employee employed in a bona fide executive, administrative, or professional capacity" (*Fair Labor Standards Amendments of 1961,* Pub. L. No. 87-30, section 9 [a] [1], 75 Stat. 71, as amended, 29 USC section 213 [a] [Supp. IV, 1974]).
50. Stewart, "Ultra Vires Challenges," p. 138.
51. WEAL broke off from the National Organization of Women (NOW) in the fall of 1968. The split was prompted by a disagreement over the

This and other actions and investigations by federal agencies aroused Congress. As early as 1970, Congressional hearings revealed a clear pattern of discrimination against women students in admission to higher education,[52] particularly with respect to elite private universities.[53]

In 1971, several proposals were introduced in Congress to eliminate sex discrimination, but these were not enacted. That same year, Representative Edith Green introduced a measure (H.R. 7248) to prohibit sex discrimination in education which was adopted by the House. This measure provided that no person "shall, on the basis of sex, be excluded from participation in, be denied the benefits of, or be subjected to discrimination of any educational program or activity receiving federal financial assistance." In February 1972, Senator Bayh introduced a bill in almost the exact language of Representative Green, but including other provisions as well. Both bills were passed by the respective houses of Congress and were therefore sent to conference.

On 8 June 1972, Congress adopted a conference version of the Green and Bayh antidiscrimination measures, including Title IX of the 1972 Education Amendments. The language of Title IX was new. It was signed into law by President Nixon on 23 June 1972 and was designated The Education Amendments of 1972.[54]

Title IX Controversy: What Constitutes Federal Aid to a University

The Department of Health, Education, and Welfare was authorized to promulgate regulations to effectuate the provisions of Title IX. The statute provided that when the regulations were originally issued in their proposed form, the public

---

abortion issue. WEAL focuses its "energies on legal and economic discrimination in education and employment and makes a special effort to recruit women who already occupy positions of power" (Stewart, "Ultra Vires Challenges," p. 139).

52. Stewart, "Ultra Vires Challenges," footnote 24, p. 140.
53, Ibid., footnote 25, p. 140.
54. Public Law 92-318, *U.S. Statutes at Large,* 86:235.

had 120 days to comment; then, when the regulations were issued in their final form, Congress had 45 days in which to reject the regulations.

In 1974, two years to the month after passage of the original legislation, HEW published its proposed Title IX regulation. The regulation generated such a heated debate both in Congress and among the public that nearly 10,000 formal responses were received during the 120-day comment period. On 4 June 1975, HEW published its final Title IX regulation. From this date Congress had forty-five days in which to reject the regulation by concurrent resolution or permit the regulation to become effective. The Subcommittee on Postsecondary Education of the House of Representatives Committee on Education and Labor held hearings on the regulation for six different days. Dallin H. Oaks testified in opposition to the HEW proposal before the subcommittee on June 24 as president of BYU and as secretary of the American Association of Presidents of Independent Colleges and Universities. The House Postsecondary Education Subcommittee expressed disapproval of several aspects of the regulation, but its resolution of disapproval was never voted on by the full House before the forty-five-day period ended. Although other attempts were made to disapprove the regulation, these attempts were unsuccessful, and the regulation became effective on 21 July 1975.

While the 1972 Educational Amendments (of which Title IX was a part) amended certain other statutes, Title IX contained some entirely new provisions not a part of any prior statue. The operative language of this title, in its entirety, reads:

> No person in the United States shall, on the basis of sex, be excluded from participation in, be denied the benefits of, or be subjected to discrimination under any educational program or activity receiving Federal financial assistance.[55]

55. Testimony of Dallin H. Oaks before the Postsecondary Education Subcommittee of the Education and Labor Committee of the U.S. House of Representatives, 24 June 1975, p. 4.

A lay interpretation of the statute would seem to mean that any educational or other institution operating a program or activity receiving federal assistance cannot discriminate in the operation of that particular program or activity on the basis of sex. This was undoubtedly the general interpretation made throughout the country. But the regulations devised by HEW by educators have, in the opinion of BYU administrators, gone far beyond the language and meaning of the statute itself.

The regulation provided that the phrase "federal financial assistance" included not only direct grants or loans to entities such as a university, but also "other funds extended to any entity for payment to or on behalf of students admitted to that entity, or extended directly to students for payment to that entity." The regulation defined "recipient" as any entity to whom financial federal assistance is extended, directly or through another recipient, and which operates an education program or activity which receives or benefits from such assistance.[56]

The regulation further stated that Title IX applies to every recipient and to each educational program or activity operated by such recipient which receives or benefits from federal financial assistance.[57] Although it is not expressly stated in the regulation, Health, Education, and Welfare takes the position that all educational programs and activities of a "recipient" benefit from federal financial assistance. Stated differently, if any single educational program of an institution receives federal assistance, all of the programs and activities of that institution are subject to the regulation. Indeed, HEW stated this view in a memorandum released simultaneously with the final regulation.[58]

HEW Secretary Weinberger repeated this interpretation when testifying on the Title IX regulation before a House subcommittee:

---

56. Stewart, "Ultra Vires Challenges," p. 148.
57. Ibid.
58. Ibid., p. 150.

> The regulation, briefly, provides as follows: Except for certain limited exemptions, the final regulation applies to all aspects of all educational programs or activities of a school district, institution of higher education, or other entity which receives Federal funds for any of those programs.[59]

Were the interpretation of HEW to the effect that the receipt of federal aid in any one educational program applied to all educational programs and that the receipt by a student of federal aid is imputed to the institution so as to make it a recipient of federal aid, interpreted literally, this would mean that BYU could no longer accept veterans as students. Nor could it accept those who obtained a federally insured loan or educational grant and still assert that it does not receive federal aid. However, it is likely that if BYU should be held to be in violation of Title IX, HEW will not terminate federal aid to students already receiving such and already enrolled at BYU. More probably, any termination of funds would be prospective only, applying to students who have not yet matriculated at BYU. Whether retroactive or prospective, despite the continuing refusal of BYU to accept its share of the millions in government aid tendered to and accepted by other universities, under this interpretation BYU would still be classified as a recipient of federal aid as long as even one BYU student received federal assistance. As to HEW's interpretation, President Roche of Hillsdale College (1,000 students), which had refused to accept any federal aid for the school, but ten percent of whose students received some kind of federal aid, exclaimed that it was "as if the government were to nationalize a supermarket because someone had bought groceries there with a Social Security check."[60]

---

59. *Hearings on Sex Discrimination Regulations Before the Sub-Committee on Postsecondary Education of the House Committee on Education and Labor,* 94th Congress, 1st Session (Washington, D.C.: U.S. Government Printing Office, 1976).
60. Ralph Kinney Bennett, "Colleges under the Federal Gun," *Reader's Digest,* May 1976, p. 129.

Viewing this and other parts of the regulation as being beyond the scope of the statute,

> Former Congresswoman Edith Green (D., Ore.), the author of Title IX, has said: "If I or others in the House had argued that this legislation was designed to do some of the things which HEW now says it was designed to do, I believe the legislation would have been defeated. I myself would not have voted for it, even though I feel very strongly about ending discrimination on the basis of sex."[61]

Viewing certain of the regulations as unjustifiable encroachments upon the rights of BYU to operate as an independent institution, Brigham Young University decided to speak out on the issue. Accordingly, President Oaks, supported by the Board of Trustees, objected to certain of the regulations, primarily on four general grounds: (1) that the receipt by one program of an institution (of which BYU has over 100) of federal aid cannot in fact or law be ascribed to all programs of the institution, (2) that the receipt by a student of some kind of federal aid cannot be held to be receipt of federal aid by the institution, (3) that the federal government has no constitutional right to deny an institution the right to prescribe moral standards or to deny the enforcement of moral standards for its own university students, and (4) that the government has no constitutional right to examine and judge the validity of any religious tenet of the University, for these tenets are protected by the First Amendment to the Constitution.

The statement of President Oaks follows:

Policy Forbidding Sex Discrimination

The Board of Trustees of Brigham Young University endorses the goal of equal opportunity for men and women in education and employment. Brigham Young

61. Ibid., p. 130.

University does not discriminate on the basis of sex among its students or employees, or among applicants for admission or employment. We support the nondiscrimination laws and have modified various University policies or procedures which in the past may have been interpreted as discrimination on the basis of sex.

Positive Actions Taken

The University has taken major steps to insure equal opportunities for men and women. University scholarships are now awarded without discrimination. Women's athletic programs have received increased financial support, and women's access to facilities and their opportunities for participation have increased significantly. Housing regulations for women are no longer more restrictive than those for men. Salaries of women faculty and staff members are regularly reviewed to insure that women are receiving equal pay for equal work. Policies are in effect which guarantee nondiscrimination in hiring and promotion, and any inequities are being identified and corrected. University departments and colleges have been challenged to avoid sex stereotyping in textbooks, curriculum, and student advisement. University leaders are urging women students to pursue their educational interests with seriousness and vigor.

Refusal to Follow Certain Regulations

Title IX (the statutory law) forbids sex discrimination in every "education program or activity receiving federal financial assistance." However, the regulations issued by the Department purport to dictate policies and activities in many areas of the University, whether or not such policies or activities involve "education" and whether or not they concern a "program or activity receiving federal financial assistance." The regulations effectively ignore these important qualifying words in the statute. They extend government powers well beyond those granted by the statute by insisting that if any part or area of an

> institution receives direct or indirect federal financial assistance (such as by enrolling students who receive federal aid), then the entire institution is subject to federal regulation. We reject this all-inclusive interpretation, believing that many of the regulations are unlawful because they exceed the Department's statutory authority under Title IX.
>
> BYU has traditionally refused all federal grants. We have limited our receipt of federal funds to a few programs in which the government receives a service equal in value to its payments. While some of our students receive federal assistance (such as veteran's benefits), the statute does not suggest that payments to students should be a basis for regulating every educational policy and activity of the institution. We therefore believe that most of our activities are not subject to the regulations.
>
> We also believe that some of the regulations are unconstitutional because they violate the due process clause or the constitutional guarantee of the freedom of religion.
>
> Nevertheless, we voluntarily choose to follow many of the regulations because we believe them to embody policies which are fair and just. But where we believe the regulations are unconstitutional or illegal and where they prohibit or interfere with the teaching or practice of high moral principles, we will not follow them.[62]

President Oaks then took specific exception to certain provisions of the regulation which he considered contrary to the underlying statute and which he said the school would not follow, most of which have been enumerated previously. In addition, he opposed the provision which prohibited any person from giving a scholarship to either a man or woman on the ground that this was a violation of due process rights — "the right of the donor to select whether he wants the scholarship to go to a man or a woman." One of his final specific objections was to provisions which some interpreted as requiring

---

62. *Notification of Brigham Young University Policy of Non-Discrimination on the Basis of Sex,* Brigham Young University, 16 October 1975, Dallin H. Oaks biographical file, BYU Archives.

equality in athletic programs.[63]

These provisions have generated great controversy among U.S. colleges and are the subject of the only legal action resulting from the Title IX regulation thus far, a suit by the National Collegiate Athletic Association against HEW, filed in the latter part of February 1976.

In concluding the official statement of the University, President Oaks made it plain that the University took its stand because it believes it is lawful:

> We will comply with any regulation ultimately sustained as lawful by the courts of the United States. In the interim we will follow the policies outlined above, which represent our best judgment on the meaning of the constitution and laws that govern us.
>
> While we have based our refusal to comply with certain regulations on the grounds that they exceed statutory authority and violate our constitutional rights relating to religion, we also oppose such regulations on moral grounds. The teaching of honesty, integrity and chastity must not become exclusively the province of religion. If our government not only abandons the advocacy of moral standards but positively prohibits the practice of such values at teaching institutions, as these regulations appear to do, the destruction of America as a great nation will be both imminent and inevitable.[64]

The Title IX regulation required universities to publish in local newspapers within ninety days of their adoption notice that they do "not discriminate on the basis of sex in the educational programs or activities" which they operate. Only

---

63. This interpretation seemed contrary to the testimony of Health, Education, and Welfare Secretary Casper W. Weinberger himself, who testified before the House Subcommittee on Postsecondary Education that this act "does not require equal expenditures for male and female teams, does not require women to play football with men, and does not require two separate, equal facilities for every or any sport" (*Higher Education and National Affairs,* 27 June 1975, p. 4).

64. *Notification of Brigham Young University Policy of Non-Discrimination on the Basis of Sex,* Brigham Young University, 16 October 1975, Dallin H. Oaks biographical file, BYU Archives.

two institutions of higher learning chose to publicly challenge the regulations — BYU and Hillsdale College, a small, prestigious college in Hillsdale, Michigan. A pioneer in independent education since its founding in 1844, Hillsdale routinely admitted blacks before the Civil War and was among the first to award bachelor's degrees to women. "We've been dedicated to equal opportunity throughout our existence," said its president, George Roche. "And we've sought to measure faculty and students by one yardstick — individual ability and performance."[65]

Commenting on the failure of other universities to join BYU and Hillsdale in publicly proclaiming their refusal to follow the regulations, the *Wall Street Journal* exclaimed, "The major disappointment is that few of the larger prestigious private universities have joined in condemnation of the bureaucratic power play." The reason, as previously emphasized, is apparent — they are afraid they may lose their federal aid.

HEW's first response to BYU's announcement was a simple acknowledgment of receipt of the notification. But in March 1976, Secretary of HEW David Mathews announced that no legal action was then planned against BYU or Hillsdale College.

Secretary Mathews's announcement may have been due to the merits of the legal position of BYU and Hillsdale or to the public clamor against the Title IX regulation. Although criticism of the regulations was based on a wide variety of grounds — with all of which BYU officials would not necessarily agree — statements of support for the position taken by BYU and Hillsdale College have appeared in the *Wall Street Journal*, the *National Observer*, *Change*, *Science*, and the *National Review*. The University's stand was also publicized in two Associated Press articles and in *The Chronicle of Higher Education*, *Science*, *Higher Education and National Affairs*, and the *New York Times*.[66]

---

65. Ralph Kinney Bennett, "Colleges under the Federal Gun," *Reader's Digest*, May 1976, p. 129.
66. "Private Colleges at Bay," *Wall Street Journal*, 4 December 1975; *National Observer*, 6 December 1975, p. 7; George W. Bonham, "Will

HEW's decision not to take action may also reflect the attitude of its new secretary, David Mathews, who was appointed in 1975. Writing in *Science,* John Walsh commented:

> In his former post as president of the University of Alabama, he [Mathews] characterized federal regulations as threatening "to bind the body of higher education in a Lilliputian nightmare of forms and formulas. The constraints emanate from various accrediting agencies, Federal bureaucracies, and state boards, but their effects are the same: a diminishing sense of able leadership on the campuses, a loss of institutional autonomy, and a serious threat to diversity, creativity, and reform. Most seriously, that injection of more regulations may even work against the accountability it seeks to foster, because it so dangerously diffuses responsibility."[67]

After Secretary Mathews's announcement there was an exchange of correspondence between Martin H. Gerry, acting director of the Office of Civil Rights, and President Oaks, which, on 12 April 1976, was followed by a visit of four representatives of HEW and a representative of the Office of Civil Rights to President Oaks and some of his associates. A friendly and congenial discussion followed in which both sides openly and frankly expressed their views. On 16 August 1976 the University received a letter from the director of the Office of Civil Rights of the Department of Health, Education, and

---

Government Patronage Kill the Universities?" *Change,* Winter 1975-76, p. 10; John Walsh, "Higher Education and Regulation: Counting the Costs of Compliance," *Science,* 31 October 1975, p. 445; "Calling the Tune," *National Review,* 19 December 1975, p. 1458; R.C. Roberg, 18 October 1975, and George W. Cornell, 24 November 1975; *The Chronicle of Higher Education,* 28 October 1975, p. 1, and 3 November 1975, p. 5; John Walsh, "Brigham Young University: Challenging the Federal Patron," *Science,* 16 January 1976, p. 160; "Mormon Colleges Say They'll Ignore Six Title IX Rules," *Higher Education and National Affairs,* 24 October 1975, p. 4; and Judith Cummings, "College in Michigan Takes Stand Against Rule It Views as 'Federal Take-Over' of Campus," New York *Times,* 12 November 1975.

67. John Walsh, "Higher Education and Regulation: Counting Costs of Compliance," *Science,* 31 October 1975, p. 447.

Welfare stating that where religious concepts of the LDS Church conflict with the provisions of Regulation 9, the religious concepts will prevail. Other interpretations were made which correspond with the views of BYU. Thus, for the present the controversy has ended to the satisfaction of BYU.

Title IX Regulation as It Applies to the Role of Women at BYU

Brigham Young, the founder of BYU, stated that if he had to choose between educating his girls and his boys he would educate the girls because they were the ones who would be the mothers of his grandchildren and would have the most influence on future generations. Accordingly, BYU has always been a coeducational institution. Indeed, in its first class of twenty-nine students there were twenty girls. And, Martha Jane Knowlton Coray was an active participant on the first Board of Trustees.

Over the years BYU has maintained the same admissions standards for women and for men. BYU generally has more single women on campus than single men. Scholarships are awarded to women and men on the same basis of judgment, except where the donors designate one sex, which BYU feels is their right. There have been many more men than women on the faculty, but that is because there are many more men who have higher academic credentials than women. Women have been appointed full professors and academic deans.

When Dallin Oaks became president of BYU, one of his first actions was an investigation of the status of women employees at the University. In 1973, two years in advance of the final Title IX regulation, President Oaks discussed this matter with the faculty in the following language:

> Many of our women employees have had the impression that they are paid less than men of comparable qualifications, experience, and performance. . . . Consequently, during the last few months, in close cooperation with the deans and directors and other appropriate officials of the University, we have conducted a thorough review of the compensation paid to women in all parts of the Univer-

sity, comparing them with the compensation paid to men of comparable experience, education, and performance. Where these reviews showed that adjustments needed to be made . . . they are being made, effective no later than the first of September.

Another concern voiced by our women employees was the general attitude of the University and the Church toward the employment of women, especially married women, and more especially married women with children in the home. What is our policy when the law requires that we not discriminate in the employment, promotion, and compensation of women, but our Church leaders have urged mothers with young children not to work?

That matter has now been clarified. In a letter dated May 14, 1973, the officers of our Board of Trustees, who are the First Presidency of the Church, have given this inspired direction, which not only defines our employment policy but also gives special direction to every teacher in this institution. I quote the middle two paragraphs from that letter:

> As you are aware, the leaders of the Church have consistently taught that mothers who have young children in the home should devote their primary energies to the companionship and training of their children and care of their families and should not seek employment outside the home unless there is no other way that the family's basic needs can be provided. As we view the distressing conditions in our society, many of which we attribute to the weakening of influences of the home, we earnestly desire that all members of The Church of Jesus Christ of Latter-day Saints — as well as all persons everywhere — would follow this counsel. We expect the teachers in the Church Educational System to continue to teach this principle, just as we expect them to uphold and teach all of the principles of the gospel taught by the leaders of the Church.
>
> Our counsel that mothers should not be employed outside the home except in extraordinary circumstances is not contrary to the laws mentioned above since these teachings concern matters of belief on

> which we are content to teach the membership correct principles and let them govern themselves. Since the law does concern the actions of employers, the administrators of our Church schools, colleges, and university in all actions on the hiring, promotion, and compensation of women should scrupulously observe the requirements of the law.

Two committees were named with instructions to make direct reports to the administration. One, an ad hoc committee designated as the "Task Force on Women's Studies," which was chaired by Dr. Margaret H. Hoopes, associate professor of Child Development and Family Relations, was organized in February 1974. Its main function was to investigate whether there was any discrimination against women of the faculty. The other, chaired by MacCene Grimmett, administrative officer in charge of payrolls, was appointed in March 1974 with authority to investigate the question of whether there was any discrimination against women in the administrative and nonacademic staff, as well as against women in general on the University campus. This committee sent a questionnaire to 762 representative men and women on the University payroll to obtain their attitudes. The reports revealed that there were a few disparities in remuneration between men and women. Corrective actions were immediately taken.

President Oaks also announced the appointment of Marilyn Arnold, a member of the English Department faculty, to serve as assistant to the president for special projects, with a special responsibility to assist the administration in working with groups throughout the University charged with implementation of initiatives designed to assist women students and employees.

Thus, by the time the school's formal opposition to the Title IX regulations was announced, substantial progress had already been made in improving attitudes and policies that otherwise might have been sources of complaints of sex discrimination at the University.

Leadership of BYU

If, as some have suggested,[68] the opposition of BYU and Hillsdale to the Title IX regulation causes HEW to reevaluate its overall stand regarding private education, their action may have lasting national significance.

Because it is by far the largest church-related and largest private university (on a single campus) in the country, because it is one of the few institutions which has struggled to hold to its original purpose of providing a Christian education and has resisted secularization, because its Trustees have insisted that it remain free and not beholden to government, because it has not succumbed to the temptation to accept federal aid, and because it is supported by the resources of the Mormon Church, BYU seems to have been thrust into the position of leader and champion of those institutions which believe in the continued existence of independent private higher education and in the maintenance of the highest quality our educational institutions are collectively capable of producing. The election of Dallin Oaks as the eighth president of the American Association of Presidents of Independent Colleges and Universities not long after BYU's Title IX announcement further suggests that BYU is continuing to be looked to for leadership at a critical juncture.[69] This leadership comes at a time when there is widespread dissatisfaction with the unprecedented regulations and controls emanating from Washington:

According to *U.S. News and World Report,*

> Nearly 400 federal programs now directly affect higher education. About 50 executive agencies and two dozen congressional committees crank out bills, regulations, program guidelines, criteria standards and audit re-

---

68. "There is some talk that HEW might beat a strategic withdrawal, now that there seems to be an awakening in the press and public over what is at stake" ("Private Colleges at Bay," *Wall Street Journal,* 4 December 1975).
69. BYU's president (either Wilkinson or Oaks) has been an officer or director of this organization for seven of its eight years of existence. Both have been president.

> quirements for colleges and universities....
>
> An affirmative-action plan drawn up by the University of California at Berkeley to guarantee equality of educational and employment opportunities alone required 70,000 statistical calculations. At the University of North Carolina, 10 reports required by HEW in one year swamped its computer facilities to the exclusion of all other work.... One report from Greensboro to the Office of Civil Rights was 1,187 pages in length and weighed more than 12 pounds....
>
> Compliance with five federal programs is costing Harvard up to 8.3 million dollars a year.[70]

In his 1975 annual report, President Derek C. Bok of Harvard expressed alarm at government actions that strike directly " 'at the central academic functions of colleges and universities.' After reciting a long list of examples he argues that government rules 'diminish initiative and experimentation,' 'threaten to impinge upon diversity of the system' and 'transfer authority from experienced educational leaders to inexperienced public officials, thus increasing the likelihood and magnifying the impact and cost of mistakes.' "[71]

In his annual report for 1974-75, the president of Yale stated:

> We have been insistent that criminal and administrative regulations should not go beyond what is rationally required by their stated purpose. We must be no less vigilant about the use of spending power as a lever to extend regulation beyond the accountability reasonably related to purposes for which the support is given. This is crucial if we seek to remain a society which respects localism, which respects volunteerism, which respects the diversity of private initiative.[72]

70. "Another Campus Revolt — This Time against Washington," *U.S. News and World Report,* 5 July 1976, p. 91.
71. Derek C. Bok, "The President's Report, 1974-75," Harvard University, 1975.
72. Kingman Brewster, Jr., "The Report of the President, Yale University: 1974-75," Yale University, 1975, pp. 19, 22.

The 19 April 1976 issue of *Chronicle of Higher Education* stated:

> A quartet of presidents of universities in the nation's capitol — American, Catholic, George Washington, and Georgetown — recently issued what they styled "A 1976 Declaration of Independence," protesting "recent government policies and behavior toward education," which, in their opinion, "have threatened [the] valued independence and . . . shaken the foundations of our system of higher education in this country." These presidents saw "an intensification of these interventionist trends." Referring particularly to what they called "the myriad, pedantic, and sometimes contradictory requirements imposed by government regulation," their statement reaffirmed their "intention to maintain institutional independence from any external intervention which threatens the integrity of [their] institutions."[73]

Despite these furious objections and despite staggering costs, practically all educational institutions can do little about putting an end to spiraling governmental regulations because they have been and still are the sponsors and recipients of a gigantic federal aid program: "Since 1960, more than 50 billion in Government dollars has flowed from Washington, D.C., to the campuses of the nation." In view of this enormous expenditure, Secretary Mathews has justified the government's regulatory action by stating: "Somebody has to monitor all this spending."[74]

Of all the large private institutions in the country, BYU is probably the best suited to fight federal encroachment. Brigham Young University presidents have responded to that responsibility. Even before the enactment of Title IX, President Wilkinson spoke frequently throughout the country against federal encroachment, and President Oaks has done the same. In one of his addresses, President Oaks pointed out

73. "A 1976 Declaration of Independence," *Chronicle of Higher Education*, 19 April 1976, p. 5.
74. Ibid.

that administrative agencies have been responsible for much of the government's flagrant interference: "The fourth branch branch derives its power not from the consent of the governed, but from their powerlessness. As a practical matter, even elected representatives rarely can reverse agency action."[75]

The University's influence has increased, and as its stature has become more evident, its leaders have received more and more invitations to speak to prestigious and influential groups in the nation against the encroachment of federal regulations.

By way of action, President Oaks has called a national meeting for the presidents of all independent colleges to discuss Title IX and other governmental controls. This meeting should prove productive.

In what was considered more than a mere accreditation review, the Accreditation Committee of 1976 highly complimented BYU for its leadership in opposition to governmental regulations:

> As one of the largest private institutions with a religious commitment, Brigham Young University has earned the gratitude of all such private as well as public institutions by drawing the line beyond which federal regulation and control must not be permitted to extend.
>
> The Committee urges the institution to continue its efforts to bring about a national consensus on the balance that must be obtained between the rights and responsibilities of the federal government and those of individual colleges and universities.[76]

If the shifting winds of political and social policy ultimately push BYU into a formal legal confrontation, the name of the University could become permanently associated with either

---

75. Dallin H. Oaks, "A Private University Looks at Government Regulation," an address by Dallin H. Oaks before the National Association of College and University Attorneys, Dallas, Texas, 18 June 1976.
76. "Report to the Commission on Colleges of the Northwest Association of Schools and Colleges," Evaluation Committee Report, Brigham Young University, Provo, Utah, 23-25 March 1976, Dallin H. Oaks Presidential Papers, BYU Archives.

the demise or the reestablishment of independent higher education in the United States. In the words of President Roche of Hillsdale, "The issue at stake is not equal treatment for minority groups or women. Academia is far ahead of HEW in that area. The issue is whether academic freedom and independent education are to endure in America."[77]

President John Howard of Rockford College in Illinois has expressed the same thought:

> Government has imposed a policy which says that academic competence shall no longer be the supreme determining factor in faculty appointments. Academic freedom is now a thing of the past, and federal subsidy has been the bludgeon employed to demolish it.

Whatever the ultimate outcome of this important controversy, it is obvious that in its centennial year Brigham Young University is providing the leadership for a continuance of free independent private higher education in this country. In its 100 years of existence, BYU has emerged from a struggling elementary school of twenty-nine elementary students, with only a limited chance of survival, and with only scrimpy, parsimonious, voluntary support from a church which was scorned throughout the country, to a university looked upon by independent universities as a leader in maintaining independence from government, and with a basis of solid financial support from the same church, now honored and respected, and which eighty years ago officially adopted BYU as its own. It is therefore fortunate that BYU has become as good and as strong as it is. It is even more important than ever that BYU become as good and as strong as it can be.

---

77. Ralph Kinney Bennett, "Colleges under the Federal Gun," *Reader's Digest,* May 1976, p. 130.

53

The Promise of the Oaks Years

The University's accomplishments during the period of the Oaks Administration, as in other administrations, represent the aggregate achievements and contributions of faculty, administrators, staff, and students — named and unnamed. But it is appropriate at this point to make some observations about the personal contribution of Dallin H. Oaks. It is also appropriate to begin this section with some reflections about where the University is after one hundred years and where it may yet go, particularly as thoughts about those larger questions may be influenced by more specific inquiries concerning the last five years of the first century.

The short-range and long-range elements in these two levels of analysis coincide more naturally than one might ordinarily expect. The coincidence arises from the conclusion that Oaks's greatest personal contribution may well be the effect of his example upon spiritual and intellectual attitudes, both at BYU and in the larger Mormon community. His example has meaning, not only because of his own peculiar combination of academic, administrative, and spiritual talents, but more significantly because he symbolizes a development in the intellectual history of Mormonism. Because his example is typical of the growing achievements and attitudes of other Mormon scholars and teachers, a concluding comment about him also serves as a take-off point for comment about the Mormon intellectual community in 1976.

In *The Mormons,*[1] a relatively objective description of twentieth-century Mormonism, Thomas O'Dea suggests that "perhaps Mormonism's greatest and most significant problem is its encounter with modern secular thought."[2] O'Dea accurately notes the Church's emphasis on education from its earliest beginning. However, he writes, "Little did they realize that in placing their hopes in education they were at the same time creating the 'transmission belt' that would bring into Zion all the doubts and uncertainties that, in another century, were to beset the gentile world."[3] Specifically, O'Dea is identifying the risk that "by encouraging education and giving it a central place in both its own activities and its world view, Mormonism exposed itself more vulnerably to the danger"[4] of an intellectual apostasy. He continues:

> This is especially the case, since the Mormon appreciation of education emphasized higher education and thereby encouraged contact between Mormon youth and those very elements in modern thought that are bound to act as a solvent on certain aspects of Mormon beliefs. The Mormon youth, who usually comes from a background of rural and quite literal Mormonism, finds that his entrance into the university is an introduction to the doubt

---

1. Thomas F. O'Dea, *The Mormons* (Chicago: University of Chicago Press, 1957). Thomas Francis O'Dea was born in Massachusetts in 1915 and was educated at Harvard University. Six years after receiving his Ph.D. in sociology from Harvard, O'Dea moved to Salt Lake City and was a professor of sociology from 1959 to 1964 at the University of Utah. It was while living in Salt Lake City that he was first exposed to Mormonism. Though he expressed an active interest in the Mormon Church, he never became a member. O'Dea died in 1974 after having written extensively on many diverse aspects of Mormonism.
2. Ibid., p. 222.
3. Ibid., p. 225.
4. Ibid., p. 226.

> and confusion that his first real encounter with secular culture entails. He has been taught by the Mormon faith to seek knowledge and to value it; yet it is precisely this course, so acceptable to and so honored by his religion, that is bound to bring religious crisis to him and profound danger to his religious belief. . . .
>
> Clearly, the dilemma of education versus apostasy is one to which Mormonism has as yet found no genuine solution. The church remains, however, committed to the encouragement of education, and it attempts in the ways we have indicated to meet the complications that such education brings in its wake. Mormonism as a way of life has to its credit that it has created a genuine intellectual group of considerable proportions in relation to the general size and rural composition of the community as a whole. But these intellectuals find themselves very often in a condition of inner conflict. Torn between a loyalty to the Mormon tradition and a commitment to modern thought, affected by both a genuine attachment to their own group and its way of life and the intellectual dispositions of the modern temper, these men find their own Mormonism a great problem to themselves.[5]

It seemed to O'Dea, writing in 1957, that the primary response of the Church to those risks was the seminary and institute system. The potential effect of BYU is mentioned only casually, as O'Dea considers at length the various sources of strain and conflict relating to the problem which he has given such a significant place in his analysis of modern-day Mormonism. He concludes his discussion of the issue as follows:

> We can only conclude that the encounter of Mormonism and modern secular learning is still taking place. It is a spectacle of the present, of which no history can as yet be written. Upon its outcome will depend in a deeper sense the future of Mormonism. A final loss of the intellectual would be a wound from which the Church could hardly recover. A liberalization of belief and an aban-

5. Ibid., pp. 226-27, 235-36.

> donment of traditional positions in faith would transform, if not destroy, Mormonism. These potentialities slumber fitfully and insecurely within the present state of prolonged but regularized crisis.[6]

What O'Dea might not have anticipated was that a goodly number of those Mormon youths of whom he spoke, who usually come from a background of "rural and quite literal Mormonism" into the college and graduate schools of the country, would emerge before too many years having dealt with and understood the intellectual world at its most demanding level, but finding that their literalistic religious commitments had been strengthened rather than weakened by the encounter. Were an intellectual history of Mormonism to be written, it would have to acknowledge that the young and energetic faculty at Brigham Young University in 1976 might, in its combination of faithfulness to the Church and competency of mind, answer O'Dea's concerns more thoroughly than he imagined.

Dallin Oaks is but one example of such a fruitful synthesis between mind and spirit, a symbol of the reconciliation that seemed unfathomable to O'Dea. Oaks has emerged loyal, orthodox, and competent from his encounters with some of the great minds and issues of modern times. He has returned to the land of his "rural and quite literal Mormonism" to give not only intellectual, but also moral and spiritual leadership to a community of believing scholars who have turned O'Dea's source of conflict into a source of great strength.

The suggestion of the foregoing paragraphs is a bold one, "subject to correction in fact, and to revision as perspective lengthens."[7] However, the suggestion is that the BYU of the early 1970s, represented by a widespread sense of intellectual and spiritual strength across the campus, may constitute a resolution of the "education versus apostasy" dilemma that O'Dea thought would have a profound impact upon "the future of Mormonism." If this is so, it is not because BYU

---

6. Ibid., p. 240.
7. *See* chapter 45.

scholars have found some subtle way to outwit or circumvent the authoritarianism, the literalism, or the lay leadership of the Church. Quite the contrary. Their honest acknowledgement of that authority, literalism, and prophetic leadership means, rather, that the scholars have put their own work in perspective. In 1976 there is a feeling that neither the solidarity of the University community behind the values of the Church nor the aggregate skill of the faculty and students has ever been so fine.

In addition to these observations about what Dallin Oaks may symbolize for the Latter-day Saint community, some attempt should be made to evaluate more specifically his performance as president of the University. In making that attempt, it has been instructive to look for some criteria beyond the BYU environment against which to measure his work.

As other universities in the United States have chosen new presidents in the aftermath of the campus unrest of the 1960s, one observer has written that higher education has sought open, candid "men of low profile," characterized by "an ability to mediate rather than to polarize."[8] The President's Commission on Campus Unrest, expressing a similar preference, was pointed in its recommendations to boards of trustees about "their most important decision — the university president":

> Above all, the administrator must keep open every possible channel of talk with students. He must have an open mind, for much that students say is valuable; he must have a cryptographer's mind, for much that they say comes in code words and postures; he must have an honest mind, for the worst crime in dealing with the young is to lie to them; he must have a tough mind, for he will frequently, for reasons either invisible or simply unintelligible to his hearers, have to say "No." Above all he must have a compassionate spirit — for youth is neither a disease nor a crime, though to its elders it may be one of

8. J. Kirk Sale, "Men of Low Profile," *Change* (July-August 1970), p. 36.

the world's major puzzles.[9]

Oaks's personal style seems to fit this model. He once identified his own philosophy of leadership by comparing it to other basic approaches. One approach he called "compliance," by which a leader persuades people to comply with his requests by adjusting rewards and punishments according to the level of compliance. A second method he labelled "identification," in which the leader attempts to influence followers to take his advice because of the personal regard they have for him. The third method is that of "internalization," by which a leader helps his followers to receive a personal conviction of the values and beliefs on which the program is based so the follower will be

> self-motivated and the structure and basis of leadership will not be upset by changes in leadership personnel. The essential difference between leadership by the process of identification and leadership by the process of internalization is suggested in the following anonymous saying: "A good leader inspires other men with confidence in him. A great leader inspires other men with confidence in themselves."[10]

Oaks's preference for the internalization philosophy has influenced his view of the faculty role, as well as his view of the role of other members of the University community.[11] Oaks has encouraged innovation from students, faculty, and staff whenever possible. He has seen his role as that of creating an atmosphere in which creative and workable suggestions can be made and then giving support to those suggestions that have merit.

His leadership style places a premium on efficiency, as

---

9. The President's Commission on Campus Unrest, *Campus Unrest* (Washington: U.S. Government Printing Office, 1970), p. 209.
10. Dallin H. Oaks, "Come Follow Me," a speech given at the Primary Annual Conference, 4 April 1974, Dallin H. Oaks personal files. The leadership styles mentioned here were first described by BYU professor William G. Dyer in his book *The Sensitive Manipulator* (Provo, Utah: Brigham Young University Press, 1972).
11. *See* chapter 46.

indicated by his "closure" philosophy in resolving problems as quickly as an analysis of the facts permits. Neal Maxwell has described Oaks's leadership style as anticipatory, identifying an ability to "look ahead and see those things that need to be dealt with while they are still manageable and before they come crowding in, in a hurly-burly way."[12]

In view of the demanding routine and tedious dispensing of "royal functions" that inevitably accompany a college president, Oaks has also displayed a remarkably constant mood of cheerfulness and control. Not threatened in frank and forceful dialogue over the merits of an idea, he treats others as equals rather than adversaries and therefore finds little difficulty in changing his own position when persuaded by clear reasoning.

It might be added that the president's optimism and sense of humor have generally made communication easier. This side of his personality has not been communicated as fully in large public gatherings as it has been in more intimate contexts, where he is able to put almost any person or group at ease; but even in his opening remarks to the BYU student body he managed these lines that show a light touch, as well as a sense of the subtle hint:

> All who know and admire President Wilkinson will be able to appreciate the sense of humility and challenge I feel at being selected to follow this great man. However, I am sure all will recognize that I will do some things quite differently from President Wilkinson. For example, my *financial* condition will not permit me to start out for a salary of one dollar per year. And my *physical* condition will not permit me to do 47 pushups at basketball games.[13]

His wit also found an opening during the general fall faculty meeting in 1974 when it was suggested that it would be

---

12. Neal A. Maxwell, "Building Bridges Outward," *Excellence in Learning* (Brigham Young University, 1973), p. 15.
13. Dallin H. Oaks, "A New President Speaks to BYU," *Speeches of the Year* (Provo, Utah: Brigham Young University Press, 1971), p. 4.

delightfully appropriate if the faculty were to grow beards during the BYU Centennial year, in honor of the occasion. Said the president to his faculty: "I think it is a splendid suggestion, and in keeping with the historical flavor of the idea, I'm sure we could arrange for the salaries of those who grow beards to be paid in kind, with corn, beets, and potatoes."

The biographical sketch of President Oaks in chapter 45 provides evidence of his background as both a scholar and a teacher.[14] Much of what is said in this evaluative section stresses his administrative skills. The mere presence of both scholarly and administrative talents makes him something of an exception:

> Universities and colleges are still attempting to find scholars to be their presidents — and good luck to them. It is unlikely that five percent of these searches will end with a choice who is both a productive scholar and a good administrator. The two vocations are nearly mutually exclusive and the few who qualify no longer find a president's salary or activity an improvement over the professorial way of life.[15]

Apparently, BYU had its share of good fortune in Oaks's selection. Indeed, his experience with and commitment to scholarship has strengthened his ability to give leadership to a university in which he had no prior teaching experience. The American Academy of Arts and Sciences, in its Assembly on University Goals and Governance, concluded that the ideal president would be "both a member of the faculty and its

14. In addition to what is outlined in that chapter about Oaks's pre-BYU work in teaching and research, he has continued to do both since coming to BYU. He has taught courses in Book of Mormon in Religious Instruction and in his legal specialty, trusts, in the J. Reuben Clark Law School. Ten years of collaborative research and writing with BYU history professor Marvin S. Hill culminated in the October 1975 publication by the University of Illinois Press of Oaks and Hill, *Carthage Conspiracy,* a 250-page account of the trial of the accused assassins of Joseph Smith.
15. Stanley Salmen, *Duties of Administrators in Higher Education* (New York: The Macmillan Company, 1971), p. 34.

Dallin H. Oaks addressing
the Orem, Utah, Chamber
of Commerce.

leader," which demands sufficient first-hand academic experience to "be sensitive to the educational and intellectual needs and missions of the academic community."[16] As president, Oaks has gradually assumed leadership of the University faculty, conveying an understanding of the needs, aspirations, and frustrations commonly felt among university teachers. This kind of leadership has had an effect on the roles of Oaks's two primary vice-presidents,[17] but it is generally a positive development in BYU's academic maturation.

The Oaks Administration has made some serious attempts to remove some of the ambiguity inherent in university organization by clarifying roles, duties, and expectations among faculty, administrators, and others. That process has also clarified the implications of the University's commitments to both the religious and the professional sectors. And while it is too early to evaluate it fully, there is evidence of an attitudinal shift among faculty and students in favor of greater academic productivity without any loss of religious perspective.

Oaks's conclusion to the 1974 Annual Faculty Report contained a statement illustrative of his perspective about the religious element at BYU:

> "The ideal professorial model . . . is someone introspective and disciplined enough to find great psychic satisfaction in the lonely pursuit of new knowledge, someone secure enough to work effectively with others in team research and academic committees, someone gregarious enough to love students, someone articulate enough to do inspired teaching, and someone concerned enough to indulge in a variety of public services." . . . To that last prescription for the ideal professorial model at BYU I would add: someone worthy enough and faithful enough to enjoy the continuous companionship of the Holy Ghost in all teaching and other activities.[18]

---

16. Carnegie Commission on Higher Education, *Governance of Higher Education,* p. 143.
17. *See* chapter 46.
18. Dallin H. Oaks, "Annual Report to the Faculty," *A Wise Steward* (Brigham Young University, 1974), p. 23.

Oaks's academic commitment, important as it is to him, is the servant rather than the master of his religious commitment. After the appearance in 1974 of a widely circulated article in the *Los Angeles Times* describing BYU's efforts to upgrade its academic standards, some Church members became concerned that the University might be abandoning its traditional spiritual values in its search for academic accomplishment. The president's comments to the faculty about that problem further reflected his priorities:

> We need to take care that we are not misunderstood as abandoning the spiritual values that make us unique. We risk this misunderstanding not only with our alumni and other friends who view us from afar, but even within the University family and among the ranks of our own faculty. Some who do not want to participate in the extraordinary effort necessary to be unarguably good in our various disciplines may accuse us of abandoning our unique values in order to reach for values recognizable by the world.
>
> We are all agreed that the price of achievement under standards recognizable by the world is too high if it uproots us from our own standards. Let us acknowledge candidly that this could happen, or could be thought to have happened, and use that knowledge as a means of guarding against the result or the misunderstanding. Far from abandoning our standards, I believe . . . that this is a time when we should reaffirm them and be more candid in expressing them. I believe, in short, that we can both hold to our traditional values and successfully attain accomplishments more understandable to people who do not share these values.[19]

Changes made at BYU since 1971 have frequently been consistent with the recommendations of recent studies of higher education, even though the administration does not appear to have followed consciously those recommendations. Oaks's leadership style, his scholarly background, his personal

19. Ibid., p. 21.

traits, and his effect on attitudes in the University community, by his example as well as his policies, suggest that by both national and local criteria the Oaks years have thus far been good ones for BYU.

In fairness, it must be asked whether the Oaks Administration has produced or will produce lasting, substantive changes. To date, his administration has necessarily concerned itself with matters of planting. The more difficult matters of cultivation and harvest are yet to come. Therefore, some questions should be raised about the Oaks presidency that might be pondered by some future historian. As an open man of energy and balance, was Oaks too balanced to carry on the momentum generated during the early 1970s? This caution has been raised about the approach of university presidential search committees in the seventies:

> In selecting men of low profile, universities are constantly turning away from men of vision, men of foresight, men of innovation and radical perspective — and it may be that these are the characteristics which are vital to fundamental change. It may just be that what is really needed now are not men of low profile, however tempting, but men of revolutionary vision, men who can turn the universities around rather than keep them functioning.[20]

Those questions could be asked about Dallin Oaks. Some have also thought he was at times too pedantic in the way he dealt with the enforcement of dress and grooming standards and perhaps too didactic in some of his hard-hitting talks on subjects such as honesty.[21] A few have wondered whether he has been colorful enough or imaginative enough to be more than smoothly efficient in his leadership. Still others have raised the question whether what has happened might not have been somewhat inevitable. Some long-time members of

---

20. J. Kirk Sale, "Men of Low Profile," *Change,* p. 39.
21. The sources for the personal impressions contained in this portion of the text were numerous formal interviews with deans, directors of administrative areas, faculty members, and others, conducted in the spring and summer of 1974 by Bruce T. Reese and Bruce C. Hafen.

the BYU community have at least wondered whether there were not enough good people already at BYU to do much of what has been done under *any* new president. Encouraging the active participation of others has been a high priority goal for Oaks, but how much personal responsibility is his for uniting and moving the faculty remains an open question.

Whatever questions are raised about the meaning and effectiveness of the Oaks Administration, in the minds of most members of the University community in 1975, Dallin Oaks is more than a nice man of low profile. The developments at BYU since he came should speak for themselves. The most serious question in evaluating his administration is how much the impression of an apparently solid beginning must be discounted because of the absence of historical perspective.

The larger and potentially more significant questions about the meaning of the '70s for BYU have to do, not with the administration, but with the faculty and students. As mentioned earlier, there is only so much power in rhetoric, reorganizations, policy proclamations, personal example, and moving descriptions of destiny. Even attitudinal changes are meaningful only if they are lasting enough to bear fruit. It is still true of universities that "the heart of the matter lies beyond all regulation." It can be argued that even the best of what has been accomplished since 1971 is still in the nature of mechanics, stage-setting, pump-priming, and multiple reaffirmations of what has always been obvious about BYU — it has great potential, potential for genuine independence, the potential for value-oriented education of high academic quality, the potential for wholeness, the potential to have a great impact on American society — and all this at a time when there is increasing doubt whether American higher education has sufficient positive potential to warrant realistic hopes for the future. It is good to have potential; and without question, BYU has enough of it to capture the imagination of both friends and strangers. The very idea of the place is exciting. It has been since it was first dreamed about:

> Can you imagine with me that perhaps on one of those nights as some of the pioneers came across the prairies,

Presidents Dallin H. Oaks
and Spencer W. Kimball
together at BYU.

> one or two of the older youngsters who liked books (or even Brigham himself, who liked books) might have sat beneath the stars and said . . . "Do you think that one day there might be a great university in Zion? A great school, with all the books, and laboratories, and teachers — where the Saints might come from all around the world to learn together? Just think — all those books and the Spirit too." An impossible dream? They might have thought so. But the dream has come true.[22]

In 1976 the fulfillment of that dream seems closer than ever before, especially when the astonishing progress of one hundred years is so vividly set before us, proving that dreams do come true.

A time comes, however, when so much is made of potential that potential itself can be mistaken for what it seems to promise. Articulate descriptions of excellence can be mistaken for excellence. But ultimately, excellence is action, not pronouncement. That is especially true at a university, where all that finally matters very much is what is *discovered,* by teacher or by student. In the words of Richard L. Evans, a former member of the BYU Board of Trustees, "Sooner or later in life there comes a time when it is performance that counts. Not promises, not possibilities, not potentialities — but performance." It is with that thought firmly in mind that Brigham Young University, after a century of life rich in history, rich in achievement, and rich in potential, must turn its face to the future, to a century hungry for the *performance* of true greatness.

---

22. Bruce C. Hafen, "Reflections on Being at BYU," *Best Lectures, 1973-1974* (Associated Students of Brigham Young University Academics Office, 22 January 1974), pp. 52-53.

54

A Fruitful Tree: A Century of Love, Truth, and Service

Centennial Emblem and Motto

Responding to a century of tradition, the BYU Centennial Committee adopted as its Centennial Emblem "The Fruitful Tree" and as its motto "Love of God, Pursuit of Truth, and Service to Mankind." These together, as shown in the accompanying illustration, represent both the traditions and the aspirations of Brigham Young University.

Love of God

One of the Pharisee lawyers, in an effort to embarrass or entrap the Savior, asked him, "Master, which is the great commandment in the law?"

> Jesus said unto him, Thou shalt love the Lord thy God with all thy heart, and with all thy soul, and with all thy mind.
>
> This is the first and great commandment.
>
> And the second is like unto it, Thou shalt love thy neighbour as thyself.
>
> On these two commandments hang all the law and the prophets.[1]

With this guidance, the founders of Brigham Young University recognized from the outset that a university dedicated to the Lord should be founded on the love of God. BYU was designed to be "a school of the prophets," a divinely led institution where students and faculty would meet on the common grounds of faithful, studious preparation, on the grounds of love and service — the divine pattern for happy living which God has revealed for all who will enter his Kingdom. The founders of BYU aspired to qualify for the benediction from heaven given to an earlier school of the prophets: "I, the Lord, will cause them to bring forth as a very fruitful tree which is planted in a goodly land, by a pure stream, that yieldeth much precious fruit" (D&C 97:9). This fruitful tree is described in the Book of Mormon as representing "the love of God which sheddeth itself abroad in the hearts of the children of men" (1 Nephi 11:21-22), and it is the core of Brigham Young University's success during its first century.

In clinging to the ideals which constitute this love of God, BYU has sought to avoid the tragic decline of spiritual training in American universities recently emphasized by Charles H. Malik, former president of the United Nations General Assembly, who, after referring to annual reports of presidents and administrators of institutions of higher education, commented:

---

1. Matthew 22:35-40.

> I search in vain in these reports for any reference to the fact that character, personal integrity, spiritual depth, the highest moral standards, the wonderful living values of the great tradition, have anything to do with the business of the university or with the world of learning. Now scholarship, freedom and creative research certainly befit a university. But the root of all evil is when these are absolute . . . and values and morals and spirit and integrity are only relative . . . .
>
> The soul of the learned these days is quite empty — empty to the bare bones. The students will rebel, not knowing why they are rebelling or what they are rebelling against, although they think they do. For they have come to the great banquet of being, seeking food and fullness, and are turned away empty.[2]

In the place of these lost spiritual values there has emerged a spiritual malaise which has engulfed our society. This has had its influence at BYU as elsewhere. But BYU has struggled for a century to forge into reality its audacious school-of-the-prophets dream — a dream which insists that its students, regardless of current trends and influences, shall never forget the primary aim of their education — love of God.

William James stated that the Alpha and Omega of a university is "the tone of it" and that this tone is "set by human personalities exclusively." A kindred thought was expressed by Robert Gordon Sproul, president of the University of California (1930-58):

> The truly great university is not a thing of books and papers, test tubes and reports, grades, and mechanisms. It is a creature of the spirit built out of the lives of men — faculty men, student men [and women]. It is founded on great loyalties as well as on great intellects.[3]

BYU's men and women, who have kept their feet on Utah

---

2. Charles H. Malik, "Education in Upheaval: The Christian's Responsibility," *Creative Help for Daily Living* 21 (September 1970): 18.
3. From a talk by Gordon B. Hinckley to BYU faculty and staff, 28 August 1975.

Valley sod while their aspirations topped Mount Timpanogos, would add to President Sproul's statement "The truly great University is founded on a testimony of the divinity of the Lord Jesus Christ." The Trustees, the administration and faculty, and the students on the whole have recognized that the right *idea* of education is an institution where all are in harmony with divine commandments.

Keeping the Commandments

At BYU this permeating love of God is not merely theoretical. "If ye love me," said the Savior, "keep my commandments" (John 14:15). That the love of God has influenced the lifestyle of BYU students is evidenced by their compliance with commandments which are ignored by many who profess to be Christians.

In general, all people who profess Christianity keep some of the Lord's commandments, yet there are certain commandments from which the world, even the Christian world, has generally departed, commandments which are nevertheless observed more fully by BYU students than by students at many other institutions of higher learning. Devoted adherence to the Savior's commandments demonstrates personal commitment to love of God. Let us cite several examples:

The first example is the First Commandment given to man — to "Be fruitful, and multiply, and replenish the earth, and subdue it."[4] This commandment "has never [been] changed, abrogated, or annulled; but it has continued in force throughout all the generations of mankind."[5] Bearing children and rearing them in righteousness has been a cardinal principle of the LDS Church and thus of BYU students throughout its history. Every President of the Church has spoken out in support of this commandment. Over a hundred years ago, in language even more applicable to the present situation, Brigham Young declared:

---

4. Genesis 1:28.
5. Joseph F. Smith, "The Righteousness of Marriage and Its Opposite," *The Juvenile Instructor*, 37:400.

> To check the increase of our race has its advocates among the influential and powerful circles of society in our nation and in other nations. The same practice existed forty-five years ago, and various devices were used by married persons to prevent the expenses and responsibilities of a family of children, which they must have incurred had they suffered nature's laws to rule preeminent. That which was practised then in fear and against a reproving conscience, is now boldly trumpeted abroad as one of the best means of ameliorating the miseries and sorrows of humanity. . . . The wife of the servant man is the mother of eight or ten healthy children, while the wife of his master is the mother of one or two poor, sickly children, devoid of vitality and constitution, and if daughters, unfit, in their turn, to be mothers, and the health and vitality which nature has denied them through the irregularities of their parents are not repaired in the least by their education.[6]

President David O. McKay gave expression to the same concept in the following language: "The principal reason for marriage is to rear a family. Failure to do so is one of the conditions that causes love to wilt and eventually to die."[7] For a number of years the Population Reference Bureau, Inc., of Washington, D.C., compiled an annual record of the number of children born to both men and women graduates of ap-

---

6. Brigham Young, in *Journal of Discourses*, 26 vols. (Liverpool, England: Albert Carrington, 1869; photo lithographic reprint, 1966), 12:120.
7. David O. McKay, "The Home Front," *The Improvement Era*, November 1943, p. 657. President Stephen L Richards has given this warning: "To warn of a greater danger I must speak of it more specifically. I do so most reverently. If it shall please the Lord to send to your home a goodly number of children, I hope, I pray, you will not deny them entrance. If you should, it would cause you infinite sorrow and remorse. One has said that he could wish his worst enemy no more hell than this, that in the life to come someone might approach him and say, 'I might have done good beyond computation, but if I came at all I had to come through your home and you were not man enough or woman enough to receive me. You broke down the frail footway on which I must cross and then you thought you had done a clever thing' " (The Church of Jesus Christ of Latter-day Saints, *Conference Reports*, October 1941, p. 108).

proximately 150 universities in the United States and found that, over the years, graduates of Brigham Young University had observed more fully the commandment to multiply and replenish the earth than graduates of any other institution of higher learning in the nation. This was illustrated by a news release of 6 June 1955, characteristic of other years, stating: "Brigham Young University . . . was announced as winner of the 'baby sweepstakes' competition among U.S. college graduates."[8]

Graduates of Utah State Agricultural College and the University of Utah, in which students are preponderantly Mormon, also had a high rating, but lower than that of BYU. The performance of the three Utah universities in general and BYU in particular led Robert C. Cook, director of the Population Reference Bureau, to write President Wilkinson on 31 May 1955:

> It is a remarkable record. When college graduates on the average are falling quite far short of replacing themselves, the graduates of these three Mormon universities have consistently shown a fertility well above replacement. Since in the kind of world we live in, there is an even greater need for people with a high level of competence and ability, the importance of this can hardly be overestimated. I sometimes tell my genetics classes at George Washington University that a college diploma comes high. Speaking statistically it amounts to almost semisterilization! That is not true in Utah. You should be very proud that this is so.[9]

This continuing record of BYU graduates stands in marked contrast to the attitude of those individuals who today consider themselves to be superior in knowledge to the Lord of

---

8. "BYU Graduates Win 'Baby Sweepstakes,' " Brigham Young University News Release, 6 June 1955, Wilkinson Presidential Papers, BYU Archives.
9. Ernest L. Wilkinson, "Charge to the Graduates," *Speeches of the Year* (Provo: Brigham Young University Press, 1955), BYU Archives, pp. 18-19. Unfortunately, the Population Reference Bureau no longer makes a study of the comparative size of families of college graduates.

our creation. Indeed, since the development of the "pill," the rate of reproduction in the United States, according to some reports, does not even amount to replacement.[10] It is not unusual at BYU for distinguished members of the faculty to have from seven to ten or more children. As this volume goes to press there are seventy-eight couples on the staff (faculty and other employees) who have from nine to fourteen children. Childless couples often adopt children (in one case as many as eight).

A second example of keeping God's commandments by BYU students is the high premium placed on chastity. Both its founding church and BYU have taught that "Sex immorality stands next to murder in the category of personal crimes"; it is "most abominable above all sins save it be the shedding of innocent blood or denying the Holy Ghost" (Alma 39:5). Strict adherence to chaste and virtuous living has applied to both sexes; a single standard of morality has been a basic principle of conduct for BYU students. This does not mean that there are no students who violate this principle, but the instances are relatively few; and when they do occur, the participants are subject to disfellowship or excommunication from the Church and dismissal from school.

The world, on the other hand, has long countenanced a double standard of morality. While believing, generally, that women should remain virtuous, the world has tolerated loose conduct on the part of men. The trend is toward increasing looseness by both sexes. Even though in America there are still Christian-oriented statutes on the books which forbid adultery, fornication, and other forms of sexual immorality, rarely

---

10. This trend, although not as pronounced then as now, led Theodore Roosevelt as early as 1916 to exclaim, "Voluntary sterility among married men and women of good life is, even more than military or physical cowardice in the ordinary man, the capital sin of civilization, whether in France or Scandinavia, New England or New Zealand. If the best classes do not reproduce themselves the nation of course will go down" (Ernest L. Wilkinson, "Charge to the Graduates," *Speeches of the Year* [Provo: Brigham Young University Press, 1955], BYU Archives, p. 30).

are people prosecuted for these offenses. Indeed, vigorous and widespread attempts are now being made throughout the country to eliminate these offenses from recognized categories of crime and to make these God-forbidden practices a legal and acceptable way of life.

On a related front, the LDS Church and students at BYU are profoundly opposed to the current agitation for and practice of abortion. The First Presidency of the Church has stated:

> The Church opposes abortion and counsels its members not to submit to or perform an abortion except in the rare cases where, in the opinion of competent medical counsel, the life or good health of the mother is seriously endangered, or where the pregnancy was caused by rape and produces serious emotional trauma in the mother. . . . Abortion must be considered one of the most revolting and sinful practices in this day.[11]

President Spencer W. Kimball has referred to this practice in the following words:

> We deplore the reported million unborn children who will lose their lives in this country this year. Certainly the women who yield to this ugly sin and the sin which often generated it, and those who assist them, should remember that retribution is *sure*. It is *sure*.
>
> We marry for eternity. We are serious about this. We become parents and bring wanted children into the world and rear and train them to righteousness.
>
> We are aghast at the reports of young people going to surgery to limit their families and the reputed number of parents who encourage . . . vasectomy. Remember that the coming of the Lord approaches, and some difficult-to-answer questions will be asked by a divine Judge who will be hard to satisfy with silly explanations and rationalizations. He will judge justly, you may be sure.[12]

---

11. *The Ensign*, March 1973, p. 64.
12. Spencer W. Kimball, "God Will Not Be Mocked," *The Ensign*, November 1974, p. 9.

As an indication that BYU students have heeded this advice, the director of the BYU Health Service and Medical Clinic has reported that during his twelve years in his present position not a single case of abortion among BYU students has come to his attention. In contrast, there were an estimated 800,000 reported abortions in the United States during 1973, and the number is growing.[13] Nor has there come to his attention a single case of sterilization for women or vasectomy for men.

A fourth illustration of the determination of BYU students to "keep the commandments" concerns the Sabbath. At BYU more than ninety percent of the students faithfully observe the Sabbath day by attending two or more meetings in the 130 branches of the LDS Church located on and off campus. Indeed, there are as many students attending church on Sunday on the BYU campus as there are students attending school on any of the other days of the week. The Sabbath is also honored by students' general refusal to attend movies, engage in athletic contests, or participate in other activities demeaning to the Lord's day. When, for instance, several years ago the BYU baseball team won a berth in a national baseball championship tournament, they withdrew from the tournament because they would have been required to play on Sunday. Consistent with the Lord's commandment, all athletic facilities at BYU are closed on the Sabbath. This contrasts with the general trend of our day where even those who profess to be Christians consider the Sabbath as a day for recreation and pleasure.

Still another indication of the love of God among BYU students is their abstinence from the use of alcohol and tobacco. This practice is in response to a revelation given to the Prophet Joseph Smith more than 140 years ago, in which the Lord, not by way of commandment, but by way of counsel, said that these substances were not good for man.[14] Although this was given by way of advice only, the Saints, in a subse-

---

13. "The Abortion Battle," *Newsweek*, 4 February 1974, p. 57.
14. This was interpreted to include tea and coffee. *See* D&C 89:7-8.

quent conference of the entire Church, accepted it as a commandment.[15] The BYU campus is therefore probably the only university campus in the country today where there is no smoking and no use of alcohol. No liquor of any kind is permitted or sold on campus. Indeed, none of the cafeterias or eating places on campus serves tea, coffee, or cola drinks, and the use of them by students in their homes is minimal.

In contrast to BYU students' observance of this God-given law of health, in 1968-69 there were 144,400 known deaths in the United States from the use of alcohol[16] and at least 81,000 reported deaths caused by tobacco or other irritants causing lung cancer.[17] In refraining from using alcohol and tobacco, BYU students demonstrate respect for their bodies as temples of God.

This respect for their bodies has also led BYU students to sustain the LDS standards of strict abstinence from drug abuse. Rarely does a BYU student abuse his body by the use of these addictive substances.

Another significant Christian virtue practiced by BYU students is the voluntary payment of tithing (one-tenth of their incomes) to their Church. This practice is older than Israel. Abraham, a patriarch, paid tithes to Melchizedek, the priest of the most high God (Genesis 14:18-20); Jacob (Israel) covenanted to "give the tenth" unto the Lord (Genesis 28:20-22). The same commandment was enjoined upon the children of Israel after they had been brought out of Egypt (Leviticus 27:30, 32), and it was continued as a commandment. Tithing was still practiced at the time of our Lord's personal ministry, approved and commended by Him, and continued as a church function during the Apostolic period and for a considerable time thereafter. Church officials at BYU report that between eighty-five and ninety percent of BYU students show their love for God by payment of tithing,

---

15. "Minutes of the General Conference," *Millennial Star* 14(1852):35.
16. Metropolitan Life Insurance Company, *Statistical Bulletin*, vol. 55, July 1974, p. 2.
17. American Cancer Society, *Cancer Facts and Figures '75* (American Cancer Society, Inc., 1974), p. 18.

thereby fulfilling an implicit covenant they make as members of the Church.

Another praiseworthy tenet observed by BYU students is that of honoring and upholding the law. The twelfth Article of Faith of the LDS Church proclaims, "We believe in being subject to kings, presidents, rulers and magistrates, in obeying, honoring, and sustaining the law."[18] During the divisive campus upheavals and disturbances of the 1960s and early 1970s, BYU remained productive and at peace — a tribute to students and faculty who fully supported the traditional "love of God" precepts of the school.

Still another cardinal virtue of students of the Mormon faith, taught and in general practiced at BYU, is that of the students being self-reliant, self-supporting, and not dependent on the government for their sustenance. The majority of the students, even though they may be in poor economic circumstances while attending college, still prefer not to accept government aid. If they need financial help, the Church has a welfare plan which will take care of them. The Church and school believe that while it is the duty of the people to support the government, it is not the duty of the government to support the people.

While the administrators, faculty, and students at BYU do not delude themselves into believing that all of its students — or staff — have yet arrived at the lofty goal of observing all the commandments, it is apparent that the vast majority of students and faculty have sought to demonstrate their love of God by following the commandments. The nine just enumerated are those which obviously are often ignored by others professing the Christian faith.

University Policy

This allegiance to the love of God through following His commandments is implicit in other matters that touch University vision and policy, including the University's sustained

18. James E. Talmage, *Articles of Faith* (The Church of Jesus Christ of Latter-day Saints, 1924), p. 413.

insistence on ever higher academic standards; on viewing students as individuals, not as numbers or ciphers; on leaving to the faculty the freedom to develop and implement their varied programs within the framework of Christian principles; and insistence on a workable honor code based on those principles. Such overt and subtle policies make for phenomena: for the phenomenon of 20,000 or more students unitedly cheering a basketball team on Saturday night and, twelve hours later, reverently, freely, and joyously worshipping together; the phenomenon of faculty, staff, students, and visitors joining in frequent spiritual devotionals; the phenomenon, seen at no other university, of a school which converts, each Sabbath, more than one hundred of its largest classrooms into chapels filled several times each Sunday with worshipping students; the phenomenon of professors shedding their academic titles in favor of "brother" or "sister"; the phenomenon of a school which accords status, promotion, and other accolades, not only because of the writing and research of its faculty, but because of its faculty's excellence in espousing and in living lives based on Christian principles; the phenomenon of a school which seeks to demonstrate, through its immaculate buildings and grounds, that there is a close relationship between spiritual sensitivity and the order and sanctity of one's surroundings.

In contemporary higher education there is often an implicit — and highly organized — objection to all this. Some seem to feel that love of God and love of man are not appropriate concerns in a mature university, that they are at best a private luxury and at worst an impediment to genuine personal and institutional growth. This objection can be refuted on its own ground. Whatever may be the outcome of present-day studies on the psychology of learning, the springs of student motivation, or the sources of creativity, one thing has been presumed, and in many cases demonstrated, at BYU: the student responds little to how much his teacher knows until he knows how much his teacher cares — cares about caring, cares for and with him, cares about manifesting such care in his teaching and research.

Outside Appraisals and Comments of Distinguished Visitors

Outside appraisals of the institution (sometimes disparaging) have said there is something intimate, even something familial, that characterizes BYU classrooms. Although BYU, as an enterprise, has stood for discipline, excellence, and technical mastery, it has stood for other relationships of love that open the mind. After a visit to campus the Swedish theologian Nels F. S. Ferre said that all over the world he had discovered committed individuals, but at BYU he had found (and this in spite of international and intercultural gulfs) a "committed community." A visitor from the Far East, walking across campus, reported "few neurotic faces." The humanist-philosopher Sydney Hook commented: "I would trust your young men more than any I have met in the world." An expert in comparative religion declared that he felt "more vitality per square inch" in his seminars with the faculty and students at BYU than elsewhere. A distinguished Briton saw something "wholehogmatic" about BYU students he met. David Reisman asserted that behind BYU's peaceful facade, and in contrast with the disorder and in some cases the chaos of universities elsewhere, there is obviously not just strong but also deeply humane leadership. After a study of private universities in this country, the Danforth Foundation team for Religion in Higher Education concluded that, comparatively, BYU was doing more than any other to make Christianity a permeating part of its program.[19]

Student Responses

For many BYU students the school displays subtle but important inward differences from other universities. At BYU, academic life is more than a career; it is a mission, and the student experiences crucial distinctions between intellectual stimulation and spiritual emulation, between twisting the

---

19. Manning M. Pattillo and Donald M. Mackenzie, *Church Sponsored Higher Education in the United States*, pp. 187-89.

University into a theater for political protest and building it into a community of cooperative creativity.

BYU's attempts at reunion, at pulling together diverse worlds, are difficult and, therefore, of all its aspirations, the easiest to abandon. In an attempt to avoid the vitiating effects of what they consider an untenable dualism of the sacred and secular, many educational reformers have recently attempted an "entente" of the two, placing them at least side-by-side, as is shown by newly created and large departments of religion in many state universities. But the axiom at BYU is that in the end there can be no distinction. The educational future does not belong to those who withdraw from or secularize the sacred, but to those who sacramentalize the secular. Every aspiration and activity must be an important effort to achieve harmony. How fruitful BYU has been in its first century may require keener perception and better instruments of judgment than are yet within reach. But BYU's second century begins with a vast and open assurance that the "living waters" that are essential to the living tree are there, that "until we have perfect love," we are, regardless of reputation, only shadows under the sun of truth. In the final analysis the entire University enterprise — its classrooms, its laboratories, and perhaps most of all the long hours spent in one-to-one counseling — is a sacramental act, a form of worship. Even the University's demanding drudgery is a manifestation of the love of God for man and the love of man for God.

The Pursuit of Truth

The second part of the motto for the BYU Centennial year is "The Pursuit of Truth." On this subject the BYU student has access to and is taught not only the secular knowledge available elsewhere, but also modern-day revelation from God — the source of all truth. Mormon philosophy harmonizes with those schools of thought which posit the existence of a wide margin between absolute truth (which is known to God as a fixed postulate of cosmic reality) and those fragments of truth as they appear to the human intellect with its limited comprehension, its finite capacity for analysis, and its restricted powers of observation. Mormon philosophy further presupposes that since absolute, perfect truth is attained only by a divine intelligence, it becomes the task of human scholarship to test any and all secular knowledge through the prism of divine revelation, when such is available.

It is, of course, axiomatic that truth never contradicts itself; therefore, when the BYU scholar finds an apparent contradiction between what science and human reason have pronounced to be true and what God has revealed, he treats this contradiction as a temporary aberration which he knows will be resolved eventually in favor of what God has revealed. This means that at BYU there is a strong priority granted to *revealed* knowledge over secular knowledge. The student accepts divine revelation as springing from the source of absolute truth; whereas, ever-changing secular knowledge must always remain entirely relative to the latest research.

The BYU concept of absolute truth is simply an extrapolation of a definition given by divine revelation: "Truth is *knowledge* of things as they are, as they were, and as they are to come" (D&C 93:24; italics added). It is spelled out with even greater clarity in the words of Jacob, a Book of Mormon prophet of the sixth century, B.C., who said: "For the Spirit speaketh the truth and lieth not. Wherefore, it speaketh of things as they *really are,* and of things as they *really will be*" (Jacob 4:13; italics added). In other words, truth in its totality, in its perfection, is equated with an intrinsic, all-encompassing knowledge of the universe. The scripture states that these realities are fixed both as to time and space; therefore, a perfect knowledge such as God possesses becomes an eternal, absolute truth that will never change in all the aeons of future infinity. "Truth abideth and hath no end," the Mormon scriptures read (D&C 88:66). Another scripture promises that by pursuing knowledge and practicing principles of God-like conduct, man will ultimately attain a knowledge of *all* truth, precisely as God has done (D&C 93:26-28).

Although many non-Mormon scholars will not concede that truth and knowledge can come from divine revelation, Mormon scholars and others insist that "truth" in its ultimate sense can be comprehended only by a divine, omniscient intelligence. It then becomes man's task to approximate as nearly as possible God's knowledge of truth. As Thomas Aquinas emphasized, "Natural things are said to be true insofar as they express the likeness of the ideas that are in the divine mind." To achieve this it is necessary to hone the sharp edge of research and scholarship to the finest point.

Mormon scholars give full credence to the scripture in which God says, "I am the Spirit of truth" (D&C 93:26). That is why He is called the "God of Truth" (Deuteronomy 32:4). He reveals himself to "bear witness unto the truth" (John 18:37). He is described as being "full of grace and truth" (John 1:14). His "law is the truth" (Psalm 119:142). His "commandments are truth" (Psalm 119:151). Once these premises are accepted as a fundamental postulate it becomes an inescapable necessity to attribute to each revelation from God the highest possible priority in the pursuit of truth. This makes BYU scholars responsible for a careful scrutiny of knowledge on two distinct but ultimately harmonious levels, the secular and the divine. This explains why Mormon philosophy considers it intellectually crippling to restrict research to either of these areas. Truth must be gleaned from both dimensions.

The Advantages of the Dual Approach

The advantages of this dual approach to the discovery of truth are readily demonstrable. More often than not, divine revelation precedes the secular discovery of truth by decades or even centuries. This history permits only a few illustrations of this truth.

Search for Truth in the Field of Health

As early as 27 February 1833, it was revealed to Joseph Smith that there is a syndrome of physiologically dangerous components in alcohol, tobacco, and certain hot drinks (D&C 89). It took science nearly a century to verify the soundness of this revelation, which is known in Mormon literature as the Word of Wisdom. Recent statistical studies of the health level of those who practice these standards, as compared with those who do not, dramatically demonstrate the literal significance of both the Lord's admonition and the favorable results He promised in this revelation.

Search for Truth in the Field of Political Science

Modern revelation also has disclosed a pattern for sound government which the American experiment with freedom has vindicated. While many historians insist that the United States Constitution merely represents a series of compromises, the Mormon belief is that in its drafting the Founding Fathers were endowed with wisdom from on high. Indeed, in a revelation given to the Prophet Joseph Smith in 1833 the Lord revealed that He had "established the Constitution of this land by the hands of *wise men* [he] had raised up for this very purpose." The Prophet Joseph Smith later reaffirmed this by declaring that "The Constitution of the United States is a glorious standard; it is founded in the wisdom of God. It is a heavenly banner."[20] At another time he declared that he was the greatest advocate of the Constitution on earth.[21] Succeeding prophets of the Church have all acknowledged the divine origin of the Constitution; this has become one of the most firmly established tenets of the Church, and it is one of the cardinal principles of political science taught to all students at BYU. The Church believes that "No government can exist in peace, except such laws are framed and held inviolate as will secure to each individual the free exercise of conscience, the right and control of property, and the protection of life,"[22] and that the Constitution is capable of securing "the rights and protection of all flesh, according to just and holy principles."[23]

The Mormon viewpoint further asserts that the present Constitution was designed to require a proper balance be-

---

20. Mark E. Petersen, *The Great Prologue*, p. 75; and *Teachings of the Prophet Joseph Smith*, p. 47.
21. *Teachings of the Prophet Joseph Smith*, p. 147.
22. D&C 134:2.
23. D&C 101:77.

tween the executive, legislative, and judicial branches of our government and that so far as possible each should be a check on the others from the use of excessive power. This squares with the revelation by the Lord to Joseph Smith in which He states, "We have learned by sad experience that it is the nature and disposition of almost all men, as soon as they get a little authority, as they suppose, they will immediately begin to exercise unrighteous dominion."[24] Indeed, the desire to curtail excessive governmental power was in the minds of our Constitutional Fathers. Thomas Jefferson, for instance, said, "In questions of power, then, let no more be heard of confidence in man, but bind him down from mischief by the chains of the Constitution."[25] James Madison wrote in the *Federalist Papers*,

> The interest of the man must be connected with the constitutional rights of the place. It may be a reflection on human nature that such devices should be necessary to control the abuses of government. But what is government itself but the greatest of all reflections on human nature? If men were angels, no government would be necessary. If angels were to govern men, neither external nor internal controls on government would be necessary.[26]

The Church's profound belief in the sacred nature of the Constitution (not in all of its interpretations) is fortified by the related distinctive belief of the Church that all of the signers of the Declaration of Independence (the forerunner of the Constitution) appeared to President Wilford Woodruff, the third President of the Church, in the St. George Temple *demanding* that he should attend to the ordinances of the Lord in their behalf to assure them of their salvation.[27]

---

24. D&C 121:39.
25. Andrew A. Lipscomb, ed., *The Writings of Thomas Jefferson*, 24 vols. (The Thomas Jefferson Memorial Association, 1904), 17:389.
26. James Madison, *The Federalist Papers*, Clinton Rossiter, ed. (New York: New American Library, 1961), p. 322.
27. President Woodruff's precise testimony to this appearance is as follows: I am going to bear my testimony to this assembly, if I never do it

The Search for Truth in the Social Sciences

Because human nature does not change, each generation must be disciplined in the same basic principles: self-control, personal responsibility, basic morality, and learning to live peaceably with one another. Social and cultural institutions continually change, but these fundamental requirements for a civilized society do not. No amount of human engineering or psychological experimentation has been able to improve upon the revelations of God concerning the principal requirements for human happiness and social well-being, as given in the Ten Commandments and the Sermon on the Mount. These are reinforced by modern revelation taught at BYU. Standards of self-reliance, honesty, sobriety, morality, compassion for those in need, the giving of honest labor, the payment of honest wages, the strengthening of the family, the requirement of reparation rather than imprisonment for the commission of lesser crimes, the governing of mankind through covenant societies, the principles required for the establishment of justice, the emphasis on conservation, cleanliness, and beauty — all these from the hand of God — provide the social scientist with the only reliable tools for structuring families, societies, and nations. While Mormon scholars pretend to no higher role than implementing what divine revelation and human experience have demonstrated to be sound, they insist on the opportunity to demonstrate the reliability of what God has revealed for human happiness in complex social relationships.

---

again in my life, that those men who laid the foundation of this American government and signed the Declaration of Independence were the best spirits the God of heaven could find on the face of the earth. . . . Every one of those men that signed the Declaration of Independence, with General Washington, called upon me, as an Apostle of the Lord Jesus Christ, in the Temple at St. George, two consecutive nights, and demanded at my hands that I should go forth and attend to the ordinances of the House of God for them. . . . Brother McAllister baptized me for all those men, and then I told those brethren that it was their duty to go into the Temple and labor until they had got endowments for all of them. They did it.

The Search for Truth in the Physical Sciences

Brigham Young, the founder of BYU, gave every encouragement to members of the Church to study not only the arts, but also the physical sciences. After stating that it is "the business of the Elders of this Church . . . to gather up all the truths in the world pertaining to . . . the sciences, and to philosophy,"[28] he stated: "We are only just approaching the shores of the vast ocean of information that pertains to this physical world, to say nothing of that which pertains to the heavens."[29] He also said: "In these respects we differ from the Christian world, for our religion will not clash with or contradict the facts of science in any particular. You may take geology, for instance, and it is a true science; not that I would say for a moment that all the conclusions and deductions of its professors are true, but its leading principles are."[30] Because this philosophy has been that of the Church from its beginning, Latter-day Saints have produced statistically large numbers of scientists as compared to the proportion of Mormons in the population of the United States.[31]

Here again students at BYU have the advantage of being taught both ancient and modern revelation. Twenty centuries before Christ a revelation to Abraham disclosed the whole intricate operation of what appears to have been our own galaxy. In the center he was shown Kolob, a great stellar giant which Abraham was told the Lord "set . . . to govern all those which belong to the same order as that upon which thou [Abraham] standest [the earth]" (Book of Abraham 3:3). Abraham was shown the wheels within wheels of the vast organization of stellar systems and the "set time" of the important ones. He saw one system rise above another until it

---

28. Brigham Young, "Intelligence, Etc.," *Journal of Discourses*, 7:283.
29. Brigham Young, "Necessity of Paying Due Attention to Temporal Duties, & c," *Journal of Discourses*, 9:167.
30. Brigham Young, "Attending Meetings — Religion & Science — Geology — The Creator," *Journal of Discourses*, 14:116.
31. Kenneth R. Hardy, "Social Origins of American Scientists and Scholars," *Science*, 9 August 1974, pp. 497-506.

reached the central power plant called Kolob that operates according to "the reckoning of the Lord's time; which Kolob is set nigh unto the throne of God, to govern all those planets which belong to the same order as that upon which thou standest" (Book of Abraham 3:9). The ancient patriarch then concludes, "Thus I, Abraham, talked with the Lord, face to face, as one man talketh with another; and he told me of the works which his hands had made" (verse 11). A few hundred years later a similar revelation was given to Moses, and he noted that among the vast creations of God there were many "lands," each of which was called an "earth," and "there were inhabitants on the face thereof" (Book of Moses 1:29). When Moses asked about these many creations and these numerous inhabited planets, God replied, "Only an account of this earth, and the inhabitants thereof, give I unto you. For behold, there are many worlds that have passed away by the word of my power. And there are many that now stand, and innumerable are they unto man; but all things are numbered unto me, for they are mine and I know them" (Book of Moses 1:35).

These revelations were early accepted by Mormon scholars, who were long ridiculed for their concept of "many inhabited planets." But not any more. Science is getting close enough to realize that the whole idea is not only plausible but highly probable. Harlow Shapely, well-known astronomer from the Harvard University observatory, was one of the first to postulate the idea that there may be hundreds of thousands of planets similar to the earth and capable of supporting life. When he visited Brigham Young University to speak at a forum assembly in 1965 he was astonished to learn that his "revolutionary concept of other inhabited planets" had been taught in Mormon schools for over a century.[32]

Divine revelation given to the Prophet Joseph Smith also disclosed many fascinating insights into the nature of light, particularly as a communicating medium.[33] Dean Armin J.

32. Armin J. Hill to Ernest L. Wilkinson, 10 July 1975, Wilkinson Presidential Papers.
33. *See*, for example, D&C 88:11-13.

Hill of the College of Engineering Science and Technology at BYU points out that no one would have guessed in Joseph Smith's day that men would eventually discover that "light is our most powerful communicating medium. A single beam of light in the visible wave-length can convey all the information which can be received by the two eyes of 200 million people."[34]

The Task of Establishing Credibility

Mormon scholars have learned that while science is in the process of catching up with revealed truth, anyone who relies upon revelation as a source of knowledge and action runs the risk of being considered by his academic peers in secular-oriented institutions of higher learning as both unscientific and unscholarly. Nevertheless, Mormon academicians have observed such an undeviating pattern of fulfilled expectations in relying on advance knowledge from a divine source that they press forward with the complete assurance that time is on the side of truth and that eventually all that God has revealed will be vindicated. Rather than rule out divine revelation as a source of truth to accommodate their critics, they prefer to take advantage of this superior source of truth while winning the confidence of their peers in the secular field through demonstration of scholarly excellence. Brigham Young expressed this aspiration as follows:

> If, on the Sabbath day, when we are assembled here to worship the Lord, one of the Elders should be prompted to give us a lecture on any branch of education with which he is acquainted, is it outside the pale of our religion? I think not. If any of the Elders are disposed to give a lecture to parents and children on letters, on the rudiments of the English language, it is in my religion, it is a part of my faith. Or if an Elder shall give us a lecture upon astronomy, chemistry, or geology, our religion embraces it all. It matters not what the subject be, if it tends to improve the mind, exalt the feelings, and enlarge the

34. Armin J. Hill to Ernest L. Wilkinson, 10 July 1975, Wilkinson Presidential Papers.

> capacity. The truth that is in all the arts and sciences forms a part of our religion.[35]

Service to Mankind

The third part of BYU's Centennial slogan is "Service to Mankind." This instinct for service has led BYU to sponsor many programs or projects beyond the confines of the campus, as the University offers its service to nations on every continent, to local communities, and to the LDS Church.

BYU Participation in the Point Four Program in Iran

During the first year of President Wilkinson's administration at BYU, the University was invited to participate in the Point Four Program in Iran which was under the direction of Franklin S. Harris, who had served as president of Brigham Young University for twenty-four years and president of Utah State Agricultural College for five years.[36] The United States government also sought the aid of the University of Utah and Utah State Agricultural College in planning, staffing, and operating the program. The objective of assisting Iran to remain among the free nations of the world, oriented to the West, and helping the people of Iran to help themselves to a better standard of living was achieved. Despite political crises, incited opposition, and many tense days, the vast majority of Iran's eighteen million people and her officials welcomed the Point Four Program and helped make it a success.

William E. Warne, who followed Franklin S. Harris as U.S. Country Director in Iran, was asked by Empress Soroya, "Why Point Four?" This was his reply:

> The United States of America feels that it has been blessed by God and that its people have inherited their

35. Brigham Young, "Comprehensiveness of True Religion — The Saints But Stewards," *Journal of Discourses*, 1:334-35.
36. The Point Four Program was first begun under the name of the Iranian-United States Joint Commission for Rural Improvement. Its name was later changed to the Technical Cooperation Administration for Iran, and finally to the United States Operation Mission to Iran, under the International Cooperation Administration.

> culture, energy, ingenuity and their ability to live peacefully side by side from those who emigrated to America from all parts of the earth. America, therefore, in token of her gratitude, is giving some of herself to help others to help themselves, believing that when other people can witness that they, too, are going ahead to a better future, greater hopes will come to the common man, and peace will be buttressed within every village throughout the world. America is striving, therefore, to help the people of Iran to help themselves through improved agriculture, more education, and better health. These objectives are in line with the aspirations of men everywhere that their children may live, grow up in health to labor usefully and have a chance better than that of their fathers to find happiness.[37]

The Iranian school system was plagued with a multitude of weaknesses, the most serious of which dealt with administration, school organization, curriculum, teacher training, and the prevailing educational philosophy. BYU sent four groups of educators to assist in correcting those weaknesses. The initial group of six educators from Brigham Young University, sent in 1951, assisted in upgrading elementary education, establishing tribal schools, and getting the Point Four Program in operation.[38]

In 1953, a second contingent of twelve educators arrived in Tehran to work primarily in the field of secondary education in the various regions of Iran.[39]

In the fall of 1957 a third group of BYU personnel landed

---

37. William E. Warne, *Mission for Peace* (Indianapolis: The Bobbs-Merrill Company, Inc., 1956), p. 306.
38. Those in the first group were Max J. Berryessa, Reed H. Bradford, Douglas C. Brown, Glen S. Gagon, Dean A. Peterson, and Troy A. Walker.
39. This group consisted of John E. Bean, J. Richard Brown, A. John Clarke, Rissa Clarke, Vern Kupfer, Boyd H. McAfee, A. Reed Morrill, Damaris Morrill, James A. Nuttall, John W. Payne, Robert Van Drimmelen, and Kenneth H. Young.

Max Berryessa, Reed
Bradford, and Dean Peterson
discussing their work with the
Point Four Program in Iran.

in Tehran.[40] This group was successful in establishing and upgrading educational programs at the National Teachers College, known as Daneshsaraye Ali. This college was given a special charter by the Iranian Parliament to develop good teachers, supervisors, administrators, and researchers to meet the mounting needs of the nation.

The educators in the third BYU group had effected an excellent beginning for the National Teachers College by the time they left in 1959 and the final BYU group arrived to carry on the program.[41]

Following the return of the fourth group of educators in 1961, Dr. A. John Clarke was the last from BYU to go to Iran. He served (on his second tour of duty) from August 1962 to August 1964 as a secondary school curriculum and higher education adviser.

Assistance to Arab Development Society

Another area in which BYU has played a helpful role in assisting worthy activities off campus was in providing cattle for the Arab Development Society under the direction of Musa Bey Alami.

The Arab Development Society is a small group of publicly minded private Jordanians, under the inspired leadership of Musa Bey Alami, who have operated an experimental farm and vocational training school at Jericho since 1951 to train

40. The group included Edith B. Bauer, adviser in secondary teacher education; Caseel Burke, adviser in elementary education; Malno A. Reichert, adviser in homemaking and family living; Morris A. Shirts, adviser in instructional media; and Golden L. Woolf, director of the program.

41. In this final group from BYU were Dean B. Farnsworth, adviser in library development and related teacher education; Royce P. Flandro, adviser in curriculum materials development; David B. Geddes, adviser in teacher education in physical education, recreation, and health; Reed A. Morrill, adviser in teacher education on the secondary school level (returning for a second tour of duty); John E. Ord, adviser in teacher education on the elementary school level; Malno A. Reichert, adviser in homemaking and family living (returning for a second tour of duty); and Golden L. Woolf, general training adviser (returning for a second tour of duty).

future farmers for work under the unique climatic conditions of the Jordan Valley, which is over 1,000 feet below sea level and has a rainfall of less than four inches per year. The students of this school are Arab refugee orphans. The school has trained several hundred of these boys to become good farmers. On the occasion of his visit to the Middle East in the summer of 1959, President Wilkinson invited Mr. Alami to come to BYU, which he did in 1960. While in Provo, Musa Alami appealed to President Wilkinson for help in getting some dairy cattle to start a producing herd. The BYU Board of Trustees approved the plan to sponsor the entire project without outside financial aid.

Deciding that it was too expensive to ship the cows all the way from Utah, Professor Seymour Mikkelsen of the BYU faculty, accompanied by his wife, Orel, left BYU in January 1961, purchased twenty-seven head of top Friesian cattle in Holland, and shipped them to Jordan. A crowd of Arab Development Society leaders, government officials, and representatives of the U.S. Operations Mission were on hand to welcome the herd, which was trucked in good condition from the seaport of Aqaba to the refugee school at Jordan.[42] The dairy herd prospered and was one of the important innovations in Jericho. Up to that time the students at the school had never tasted milk. The farm and school, despite the political upheavals, is still operating, and Mr. Alami, as recently as 3 September 1975, again expressed his gratitude for the dairy herd.

Student Service to Local Communities

As was previously mentioned in chapter 48, BYU students have rendered service to local communities since 1875. Volunteer service by Brigham Young University students during the 1975-76 school year amounted to 25,167 hours, which led the nation's colleges and universities in volunteer work. In

42. Norman Burns, "First Pioneer Modern Dairy in Jordan," 3 March 1961, Wilkinson Presidential Papers. *See also* "Onetime Desert Land Becomes Dairy Farm," BYU *Daily Universe*, 30 June 1961.

BYU Professor Seymour Mikklesen, who assisted in the establishment of a dairy herd in Jordan.

recognition of this effort, BYU's Student Community Service program was awarded a silver bowl by the Community Service Agency of Utah County and the Volunteer Action Council.[43]

Ambassadors of Good Will

BYU has served the continental United States, South America, Europe, and Asia in the performing arts by producing and sending high-class dramatic art and musical troupes to these areas.[44]

The Program Bureau

A prime example of services being rendered by students as ambassadors of goodwill to the world, the Program Bureau is an outgrowth of the old Public Service Bureau established in part in 1919-20 by Ernest L. Wilkinson while he was a student at BYU. It was designed to provide an outlet for students interested in variety talent and to develop and provide wholesome entertainment for positive purposes. Originally, the Program Bureau was run by students alone with an appointed student head and student directors, but as the school grew the administration found need for professional direction. Accordingly, in 1952, Janie Thompson, a former BYU graduate in music, was chosen to organize the Bureau on its present basis. Her name has become synonymous with Program Bureau and the enthusiasm, color, dash, youthful exuberance, and talent for which it has become famous. Janie is a born entertainer. While a student at BYU during World War II, she helped produce assemblies, floor shows, and musicals. After graduation she was one of one hundred girls selected by the Army from throughout the United States to tour Europe and entertain the GI's overseas. She taught music professionally in Utah, California, and New York.[45] A talented pianist, singer, talent coach, song leader, and choreographer posses-

---

43. "BYU Students Donate More Service Time Than Any Other School in U.S.," *California Intermountain News,* 29 July 1976.
44. *See* Volume 3, chapters 38 and 43.
45. Janie Thompson biographical file, BYU Archives.

Janie Thompson, director of
BYU's Program Bureau.

sing an outgoing personality, Janie Thompson has been the spark plug, the inspiration, and the initiator of the Program Bureau's amazing performances, which have enlivened audiences around the world in recent years.

From 1952 until 1956 the Program Bureau was used largely as an aid in recruiting efforts aimed at increasing BYU enrollment and improving the positive image of the school. This effort was translated into roughly six hundred variety shows sponsored annually by the Program Bureau under Janie Thompson's direction. In the 1953-54 school year, for example, the Bureau put on 252 Church shows, 217 civic shows, 68 performances at high schools, and 16 appearances at hospitals, making a total of 553 performances before a combined audience of 186,000. Most of the performances were in the Intermountain West.[46]

By 1956 the pace was almost too much for Janie to bear physically and emotionally; she needed a rest. Furthermore, there had developed friction between the Music Department and the Program Bureau. Program Bureau shows were not designed for classical musicians but were of a popular nature. Discouraged by the ensuing criticism of sophisticated musicians, Janie Thompson, after four years and 2,463 shows, resigned on 1 January 1957.[47] In her own words, she went to New York "to get some peace and quiet after Provo."[48]

For three years in New York, Janie Thompson coached talent shows, taught music, and trained many leading performers, especially male and female choral groups. However, she missed BYU and BYU missed her. Three years in New York also convinced Janie of the influence for good that clean, wholesome entertainment can have in the lives of impressionable young people. Responding favorably to an invitation to return to BYU, she wrote:

---

46. "Annual Report of the Student Program Bureau, 1953-54," BYU Program Bureau files.
47. BYU Presidency Meeting Minutes, 15 November 1956, BYU Archives.
48. BYU *Daily Universe*, 18 November 1968.

> Personally, I have come to regard the medium of entertainment as one of the most powerful and influential mediums that exists. . . .
>
> With the Program Bureau, you have provided us with a very fine "chance" to try and combat some of this . . . [unwholesome] influence. This is primarily why I am so dedicated to what we are trying to do. I feel we have a real . . . responsibility to sell "our products" . . . and by that I mean everything that the BYU and the Church stand for. When we put a show up there on the stage, to me it is like the gospel in action where everyone can see it.[49]

Because of the scope of her activity, Janie was ably assisted by, among others, James ("Jimmy") Lawrence, formerly sportscaster and program director of KOVO radio. Lawrence contributed much to the success of the Program Bureau with his excellent behind-the-scenes scheduling and business management.

For the Program Bureau, the years before 1960 were characterized by comparatively small local spheres of performance promoting public relations for the University and recruiting. Between 1960 and the end of 1974 the Bureau broadened its scope of activity, becoming more diversified, professional, and international in tone. Variety groups of the Bureau visited Europe seventeen times, the Orient eleven times, Greenland twice, the Caribbean twice, and the Middle East, South Africa, and South America once each, for a total of thirty-five foreign tours.[50]

The first international tour invitation was by the Department of Defense (at its expense) in 1960 to make a fifteen-thousand-mile tour of the Orient to entertain American military personnel. The Program Bureau responded by producing "Curtain Time," a ninety-minute variety show. This tour

49. Janie Thompson to Ernest L. Wilkinson, 11 January 1963, Wilkinson Presidential Papers.
50. Richard E. Bennett, transcribed interview with John Kinnear, 31 January 1975, Centennial History files, BYU Archives.

was so successful that the invitation was again extended in 1962 to return to the Orient. In 1963 the show (which became known as "Curtain Time USA") had become so popular that it toured the American military bases in Europe.

Typical of the compliments extended to the Program Bureau over the years is the following from a government official after the whirlwind tour of "Curtain Time USA" through Ceylon:

> Here in Ceylon our image of American youth is what we get only from Elvis Presley records, rock and roll, and second rate Hollywood films. We see American youth with a cigarette in one hand, a glass of alcohol in the other and highly spoiled by wealth as they race around in their flashy cars.
>
> But this group from BYU represents the larger, finer element of American youth . . . who will prevail. For they do not smoke or drink and their customs and manners . . . are of modesty and bearing.[51]

Adlai Stevenson, upon seeing the 1965 performance of "Curtain Time USA," said that "I am completely captured: These glorious young people have represented superbly the ideals of my country. . . . They should be sent on a nationwide tour to show Americans what Americans can do and produce."[52]

Theodore Burton, then President of the European Mission, referring to a 1963 "Curtain Time USA" production in Mannheim, West Germany, wrote:

> The talent was so good and the whole presentation on such a high level that everyone [more than 700 in attendance] was enthusiastic about it. In the past our Church has been regarded as a "back-alley sect." . . . Now this wonderful program from such a large LDS University has opened up everyone's eyes. From a public rela-

---

51. "Program Bureau's 'Curtain Time' Receives Rave Reviews in Ceylon," BYU *Daily Universe*, 18 March 1965.
52. "Song and Dance Goes a Long Way," *Monday Magazine*, 13 January 1975, p. 15.

Members of BYU's Curtain
Time USA troupe that toured
the Orient in 1962.

BYU Folk Dancers performing
in Belgium.

> tions viewpoint this tour has been a tremendous help to us.[53]

From a mission president in Korea came this appraisal: "I can honestly say that this group from the Program Bureau did more in two hours to advance the cause of MIA in Korea, than we have been able to do in two years."[54]

International Folk Dancers

As ambassadors of goodwill the International Folk Dancers, under the skilled leadership of Mary B. Jensen, have made equally favorable impressions abroad. W. Tapley Bennett, Jr., former U.S. Ambassador to Portugal, after seeing the International Folk Dancers appear in the Portugal National Agricultural Fair at the International Folk Festival, wrote Senator Wallace F. Bennett:

> Several Portuguese groups took part in some or all of these affairs and there were groups from several European countries including Belgium, Bulgaria, France, Ireland, Italy and Spain. True to communist practice, the Bulgarians sent a highly skilled, professional group; other national groups were well coordinated and of long experience. But our young people from Brigham Young University were unquestionably the big hit. . . . I don't think we need to worry about the broad appeal of our country for people abroad when we have outstanding representatives like the Brigham Young University group traveling and making friends.[55]

On another occasion, while touring the Orient in 1964, the combined Program Bureau-Folk Dance troupe was invited to perform on board the large American aircraft carrier *Kitty Hawk*. Following the performance "the Captain jumped to the

---

53. Theodore M. Burton to Ernest L. Wilkinson, 8 August 1963, Wilkinson Presidential Papers.
54. Gail E. Carr to the MIA General Board, 5 July 1964, Wilkinson Presidential Papers.
55. W. Tapley Bennett to Wallace F. Bennett, 28 June 1967, Wilkinson Presidential Papers.

stage and was very lavish in his praise and thanks . . . expressing how much good he thought productions like these did, and exclaiming his own gratitude for the cleanness of the show and the fine example of American youth that was exhibited."[56]

After the folk dancers had toured Austria, the information coordinator of the Austrian Mission wrote:

> This fine group was one of the biggest helps we've received in the missionary work in Vienna in a long time. They presented not only a great showing of dancing ability but also, and equally as important, a type of clean cut, real, down-to-earth freshness that really spotlighted the "fruits" of Mormonism. The members of the Church in Austria, as well as our investigators and friends, need to be shown the Church as it is on a world-wide basis. The Folk Dancers did just that — and in a superb manner![57]

Wherever these touring performers appeared they were ambassadors of goodwill for America. From Tokyo to Israel, from England to South Africa, from Labrador to Hawaii, they were held in high regard. A more extended discussion of the International Folk Dancers is given in Volume 3, chapter 38.

The A Cappella Choir

The BYU A Cappella Choir was the first non-Catholic choir to sing in the Notre Dame Cathedral in Paris (1970), and they did so well under the direction of Dr. Ralph Woodward that they were invited to return in 1972. In fact, the choir has performed in major cathedrals throughout Europe with great success. Some of the honors gained by the choir include being named "Best International Choir" at the Linz Centennial Festival in Linz, Austria, in 1972.

---

56. Janie Thompson, "BYU Orient Tour — 1964," unpublished report, Wilkinson Presidential Papers.
57. "American Folk Dancers," report of the 1966 Folk Dancers Tour, Program Bureau records, p. 117.

International Sports Activity

BYU has acquired an international reputation by sending its basketball and golf teams to sports-loving audiences of South America and Europe. Indeed, some South American countries have adopted the BYU basketball team as their own (*see* Volume 3, chapter 39). In 1974 the BYU baseball team participated in an international tour to Italy.

Impact of All BYU Groups

As a representative of the United States to servicemen abroad, and to foreign lands, BYU student-performers have left a lasting impression. On every tour, special performances were sandwiched in for LDS Church congregations, MIA's, and other Church gatherings. Messages of gratitude praising the efforts of BYU groups assisting the Church have been prolific. In recent years there has developed a demand to have shows broadcast over national and overseas television networks. The 1973 tour of the Young Ambassadors, a Program Bureau group, to South America was frequently televised by Brazilian and Argentine television stations; it was estimated that eighty-eight million viewers watched these young people perform.[58]

All of the Program Bureau overseas tours until 1970 were sponsored either by the Department of Defense and/or the Department of State. Drama Department tours were sponsored by the Department of Defense, in conjunction with the National Music Council. The American Folk Dancers and A Cappella Choir tours were funded primarily by the students involved in those tours, but with support from folk and music festivals located in the countries visited and, on occasion, by missions of The Church of Jesus Christ of Latter-day Saints. Later, in some cases Program Bureau tours were funded almost entirely out of income earned by the performing groups themselves. The Young Ambassadors conducted the

---

58. Richard E. Bennett, transcribed interview with John Kinnear, 31 January 1975.

first self-funded tour to Central and South America in 1973. The Sounds of Freedom and the Folk Dancers experienced their first self-funded tours in 1974, and the Lamanite Generation toured Central and South America in 1975. The Lamanite Generation tour, featuring performances of American Indians studying at BYU, was described by Janie Thompson as "the most significant tour in my entire career" due to its great impact on Indian peoples south of the United States border.

Church Activity of Students and Alumni

The training students have received while at BYU has motivated them when they left to serve their Church wherever they reside. A survey of the 1974-75 *Church Directory* conducted by the Alumni Association indicated that although less than five percent of the Church membership has attended BYU, BYU alumni comprise almost twenty-five percent of the General Authorities, more than forty percent of the regional representatives of the Twelve, almost twenty-three percent of stake presidents, and almost twenty-four percent of all bishops.[59]

Auxiliary organizations of the Church are receiving the same support. Illustrative is a letter from Mrs. Belle S. Spafford, long-time president of the Relief Society, who wrote to President-Emeritus Wilkinson on the occasion of Alice Wilkinson's release from the Relief Society General Board after serving fourteen years:

> Looking back over the more than 29 years I served as President of the Relief Society of the Church, there stand out in bold relief a few events that have proved highly significant in advancing the work of the Society. . . .
>
> Holding a position of distinction among these events was the establishment of a stake with wards and branches on the Brigham Young University campus and the or-

59. "Report on BYU Alumni in Positions of Church Leadership," 25 September 1975, Centennial History papers, BYU Archives.

ganization of campus Relief Societies. . . . Campus Relief Societies are proving to be a reservoir of intelligent, trained leadership for the Society in many parts of the world.

As the young women leave the colleges they take with them leadership experience, a depth of understanding of the purpose of the organization, a knowledge of its fundamental procedures, and an abiding testimony of its divine origin. . . .

I have met them and seen them in action in many parts of the world, and I marveled at all they have to offer. For example, I met one young woman on the BYU campus a few years ago who had just been called to be a Relief Society President. She was unfamiliar with the organization and dubious about her qualifications to serve as President; however, she responded to the call. The next time I met her she was competently presiding over Relief Society in a branch on a military base in Japan. Later I met her once again, a member of a Relief Society stake board in San Antonio, Texas. Now I am told she is a Stake Relief Society president in one of the large centers in the United States. Humble, competent, completely dedicated, she is offering the women with whom she works the rich fruits of her experience at BYU in a campus Relief Society.[60]

Faculty Contributions to the Church

The BYU faculty is not only characterized by its improving academic excellence, but also by its recurring ecclesiastical participation within the Mormon Church. Many faculty members have been "called" to serve in leadership positions, both locally and afar. Others have been commissioned to fulfill specific Church needs such as writing manuals, composing and directing pageants, and translating materials. Concurrently, in a different vein, an ever-growing cadre has voluntarily yet energetically embarked upon individualized

60. Belle S. Spafford, "An Evaluation of BYU Campus Relief Societies," April 1975, Centennial History papers, BYU Archives.

studies within their own areas of specialization to comment upon or critically interpret some phase of the broad magnetic field of Mormonism.

The creation of the first BYU student stake in 1956, and eventually its twelve successors, provided sudden new Church positions for faculty to fill. Specifically, it was urged that generally "The Stake President should be appointed from the faculty," which would insure "complete unity between the School Administration and the Stake President."[61] The selection of a faculty member (Antoine K. Romney) as the first Stake President was a strong impetus to the selection of faculty bishops and high councilors. Two of the three members of the first stake presidency were from the University. Of the University. Of the original twelve bishops, all but three were BYU faculty or staff. Seven of the twelve high councilors were also BYU personnel. It was common for a student to have as his bishop one of his regular coursework instructors.

A computer report based on personnel data sheets of faculty and administrative staff summarized the number of faculty and administrative staff who have fulfilled Church assignments during the period from 1950 to 1975:[62]

General Authorities	3
Regional Representatives	24
Members of General Church Boards	112
Members of General Church Committees	125
Mission Presidents	34
Counselors to Mission Presidents	98
Stake Presidents	45
Counselors to Stake Presidents	108
Bishops	398
Counselors to Bishops	668

61. Ernest L. Wilkinson to Henry D. Moyle and Adam S. Bennion, 9 November 1954, Wilkinson Presidential Papers.

62. These data are approximated and not meant to be exact. Some previous faculty who passed away were not included in this computer tabulation. Furthermore, some of the data represents a faculty member's participation before coming to BYU. If anything, these figures are conservative (David H. Yarn, Jr., to Robert K. Thomas, 19 March 1975, BYU Archives).

Stake Mission Presidents	102
Stake Missionaries	355
Temple Workers	78
Branch Presidents	275

Preparation of Priesthood and Auxiliary Manuals

Many faculty members have been commissioned to fulfill special assignments, such as writing manuals. In 1968, for example, at least twenty-eight faculty were writing priesthood or auxiliary manuals for the Church.[63] The assistance rendered is suggested by a letter from the Relief Society General Presidency to President Wilkinson in 1958:

> Two of our courses of study . . . are written by your faculty members. . . . Both courses are exceptionally good and enthusiastically received by Relief Society members. . . .
>
> We have also had excellent help in our homemaking courses from your faculty members. . . .
>
> It is a wonderful thing, Dr. Wilkinson, for an auxiliary of the Church to have access to the professional services which are made available to us by the Brigham Young University. . . . Those who work with us give us not only high quality work, but they evidence a spirit of genuine interest in our organization and a desire to serve us to the best of their abilities.[64]

Special Projects

Faculty members have exercised their talents and skills in many other ways. Dr. Harold Hansen of the Speech Department has directed the very successful "Hill Cumorah Pageant" staged yearly in upstate New York. Crawford Gates, a former member of the BYU faculty, has written musical

---

63. BYU Board of Trustees Minutes, 5 May 1968; BYU Archives.
64. Belle S. Spafford, Marianne C. Sharp, and Louise W. Madsen to Ernest L. Wilkinson, 15 October 1958, Wilkinson Presidential Papers, BYU Archives.

scores for the Hill Cumorah Pageant and other productions, such as "Promised Valley" and "Sand in Their Shoes." BYU has also been of great assistance in language translation, especially as the Church becomes increasingly international.

Computer-assisted Language Processing Program

Recently, as indicated in chapter 47, a very important Computer-assisted Language Processing Program has been instituted at BYU, with Dr. Eldon Lydle as director. By 1975, with the Church translating annually into 15 languages more than 17,000 pages of material, the need for faster translation processes was immediate. The three essentials of the BYU language computer program are:

1. Devising a special code for expressing the meaning of sentences unambiguously.
2. Programming the computer to interact with a human in converting sentences to this special code.
3. Programming the computer to convert this special code back into natural language sentences.[65]

The aim of the system is to develop computer-assisted simultaneous translation into many languages.

The BYU Asian Studies faculty, under the direction of Dr. Spencer J. Palmer, produced a significant document entitled *The Educational Needs of The Church of Jesus Christ of Latter-day Saints in Asia*, designed to assist the Church in meeting the future educational needs of an increasing percentage of its worldwide membership.

Consultants, Advisers, and Researchers

In addition to answering Church calls for service and participating in Church-commissioned projects, faculty members have also served as consultants, advisers, and researchers upon official request. One good example of this form of

65. Melvin Smith and D.K. Jarvis, "The Brigham Young University Project in Computer-assisted Language Processing," slide presentation, printed copy in BYU Archives.

assistance was the establishment in 1957 by the Board of Trustees of a Bureau or Institute of Church Studies "for the purpose, in part, of assisting the General Authorities in research and other problems."[66] The Bureau primarily emphasized statistical studies, delving into such multifaceted fields as Church membership (including estimated growth patterns, areas of greatest growth, and concentration), Church school system and BYU enrollments, and many more. Dr. Howard C. Nielson of the Statistics Department was in charge of the program. Always an informal and lightly budgeted affair, the Bureau of Church Studies eventually evolved into the Institute of Mormon Studies and the Institute of Church Studies. The former, under the direction of Dr. Truman G. Madsen, was concerned primarily with Mormon doctrinal studies. The latter, under Dr. Daniel Ludlow, emphasized research in Church history. Institutional Research, under Leland H. Campbell, has made many statistical studies for the school and the Church.

Independent Research and Writing

In addition to all of the above, the faculty has made significant contributions to the Church by means of its own independent research and writing. *BYU Studies*, started in 1959 as a professional quarterly underwritten by the school, has published scholarly articles from many fields of learning. Dr. Clinton Larson served as managing editor from 1959 to 1963; Dean B. Farnsworth, 1964 to 1966; Charles Tate, 1967 to present. *BYU Studies* has featured many articles about the Church, including Vasco M. Tanner's "Charles Darwin After One Hundred Years" (Autumn 1959), Clinton Larson's poetic drama entitled "The Mantle of the Prophet" (Spring-Summer 1960), Karl Young's "Early Mormon Troubles in Mexico" (Spring-Summer 1964), Robert J. Matthews's "A Study of the Text of Joseph Smith's Inspired Version of the Bible" (Autumn 1968), Marvin S. Hill's "Joseph Smith and the

66. BYU Board of Trustees Minutes, 27 September 1957, BYU Archives.

1826 Trial" (Winter 1972), and many more. Now in its eighteenth year, *BYU Studies* has become a highly respected voice of LDS scholars, professional in content and design. More recently, the Charles Redd Monograph Series for Western U.S. History has afforded an opportunity for the publication of many additional articles and papers on the Mormon heritage in the West.

Contributions to Church Journals

Faculty members have also contributed articles on phases of Mormon doctrine, history, and life to other journals as well, including *Ensign, New Era, Dialogue, Sunstone,* and *Exponent II*. From 1951 to 1975 inclusive, faculty members authored 831 books. Of these, 419 were textbooks in various disciplines.

The formation on 1 November 1972 of the Richard L. Evans Chair of Christian Understanding, with Dr. Truman G. Madsen as director, heralded a step toward increased communication and understanding between the LDS academic community and religious scholars and institutions throughout the nation and around the world. The ever-growing manuscript collection in the Harold B. Lee Library possesses an impressive variety of primary sources in Church history. The papers of Reed Smoot, J. Reuben Clark, Jr., Wallace F. Bennett, and the diaries of James E. Talmage, to name but a few, form the core of a beckoning, unplumbed manuscript collection.

Mormon Festival of Arts and Related Activities

Besides these kinds of offerings, BYU has used the exciting medium of the fine arts to give, through art, music, literature, dance, and drama, a new expression of and perspective on Mormonism. Although the message of the gospel has found articulation over the years in poetry, music, and art, not until the last decade has a group within the College of Fine Arts attempted to produce festivals of Mormon art which included all of the artistic media.

The impetus behind this Festival began in 1967 among an

informal group of faculty and students who met on Sunday evenings to discuss art and Mormon belief. Dale Fletcher, leader of the movement, articulated clearly the idea that "Mormon arts should be dedicated to the upbuilding of the kingdom of God on earth."[67]

An address by Elder Spencer W. Kimball at a preschool conference of BYU faculty and staff in September 1967 added encouragement. Said the future president of the Church:

> If we strive for perfection, the best and greatest, and are never satisfied with mediocrity, we can excel. In the field of both composition and performance, why cannot the students from here write a greater oratorio than Handel's *Messiah*? The best has not yet been composed nor produced. They can use the coming of Christ to the Nephites as the material for a greater masterpiece. Our BYU artists tomorrow may write and sing of Christ's spectacular return to the American continent in power and great glory, and his establishment of the kingdom of God on the earth in our own dispensation. No Handel (1685-1759) nor other composer of the past or present or future could ever do justice to this great event. How could one ever portray in words and music the glories of the coming of the Father and the Son and the restoration of the doctrines and the priesthood and the keys unless he were an inspired Latter-day Saint, schooled in the history and doctrines and revelations and with rich musical ability and background and training? Why cannot the BYU bring forth this producer?[68]

Thus encouraged, Dean Lorin F. Wheelwright and his successor, Lael J. Woodbury, put into motion the plans and preparations that eventually culminated in the first Festival of Mormon Arts in 1969. This Festival set the stage for future productions with its art exhibits, choral and orchestra concerts, writing and publishing symposia, drama productions,

---

67. Lorin F. Wheelwright, Preface to *Mormon Arts*, vol. 1, BYU Archives.
68. Spencer W. Kimball, "Education for Eternity," *Fall Faculty Workshop* (Brigham Young University, 12 September 1967), pp. 14-15.

operas and recitals, and a Mormon Arts Ball. Every year since 1969 the College of Fine Arts has staged the Festival with greater participation and excellence.

Music Department faculty have contributed toward upgrading the Church hymnal. The Church Music Committee, under the direction of Dr. Harold Goodman, will shortly be producing a new hymn book for the Church.

BYU thus seeks to develop a Mormon historical awareness, social conscience, cultural heritage, and doctrinal expertise. In an academic sense, BYU is becoming a microscope on the Church, while continuing to be a telescope on the universe, ever seeking to explain the religious phenomenon of Mormonism.

Motion Pictures

The Department of Motion Picture Production has also rendered special services to the Church. The department originated in 1953 when President Wilkinson was able to persuade Wetzel "Judge" Whitaker to leave his work at Walt Disney Studios and organize a motion picture department on campus.[69] The impetus behind the program was also provided by the requests of General Authorities for motion pictures on various aspects of the gospel to teach doctrines, introduce new programs, and, in the words of President Wilkinson, "do justice to the great faith-promoting stories that exist in our Church history."[70]

Members of the Church continue to be witnesses to the many excellent films produced by the Department of Motion Picture Production. The Presiding Bishop's Office, Deseret Sunday School Union, Church Education offices, Relief Society, Primary, Historical Department, Genealogical Society, and almost every major administrative unit of the Church has sponsored the production of special movies and filmstrips.

---

69. "Y Film Producer Discusses Past, Future," BYU *Daily Universe*, 20 July 1976.
70. Ernest L. Wilkinson to the First Presidency, 1 June 1960, Wilkinson Presidential Papers.

How Near to the Angels, a 1956 movie on preparing for eternal marriage, was "one of the first large films of the department."[71] *Feed My Sheep* (1957) emphasized improved Sunday School teaching, and *Unto the Least of These* featured the Relief Society Visiting Teaching Program. In 1963 the studios produced another milestone in *The Windows of Heaven*, a historical presentation on the principle of tithing. These and other movies represented new marks of professionalism, more expert screen writing, acting, and photography. Each was "a step up."[72] 1964 saw the release of the Church's well-known missionary film *Man's Search For Happiness*, made popular by its showing at the 1965 New York World's Fair. *Johnny Lingo* (1968), *Are You Listening?* (1972), and *Cipher in the Snow* (1974) represent some of the most recent and most widely acclaimed movies. From the time of its establishment until mid-1976, the BYU Department of Motion Picture Production produced for the Church more than 125 movies and 90 filmstrips.

Family Movie of the Year

From 1966 until 1968, on the initial suggestion of Jay Todd, formerly of the Program Bureau, BYU organized a Family Movie of the Year Award in conjunction with the *Improvement Era*, KSL radio and television, and the *Deseret News*, all Church-controlled operations.[73] The purpose was to make an award to the movie of the year that best epitomized qualities of family unity, love, and inspiring personal relationships. The 1966 award went to *The Sound of Music*; in 1967 it went to *Follow Me, Boys*; and in 1968 it went to *To Sir With Love*. The festivities usually included a student assembly and award banquet. In 1969 no movie seemed worthy; no award was given, and the program was not thereafter revived.

---

71. Richard E. Bennett transcribed interview with Wetzel ("Judge") Whitaker and Scott Whitaker, 31 January 1975, Centennial History Papers, BYU Archives.
72. Ibid.
73. Jay M. Todd to Ernest L. Wilkinson, 29 December 1965, Wilkinson Presidential Papers.

Church Building Projects

BYU and its staff have also lent a helpful hand to Church building projects. The training and expertise of Sam Brewster, Ben Lewis, and Fred A. Schwendiman (to name but three of many) have been drawn upon to assist in such diverse programs as planning the LDS housing units at Utah State University, developing the cafeteria plans in the new Church Office Building, drawing up blueprints and other work for the new Language Training Mission complex, and advising on scores of other projects.

Assisting the Church Missionary Program

One of the ways BYU assists the Church Missionary Program is in the voluntary conversion of students to the gospel of Jesus Christ. While no precise figure has been kept, faculty members and administrators estimate that approximately one-half of non-Mormon students attending BYU either join the Church while they are on campus or after they return to their homes. This they have done despite admonitions to students at the beginning of each school year that while Mormon students should be as friendly with non-Mormons as possible, no pressure should be applied to non-Mormons to join the LDS Church, for they have the same rights as Mormons to their religious beliefs.

Religion Classes and Social Encouragement

From its beginning, Brigham Young University has also made a major contribution to the effectiveness and vitality of the worldwide proselyting emphasis of the Mormon Church. Over the years, Religious Instruction has sponsored classes designed specifically for prospective missionaries in order to provide them a knowledge of the scriptures and understanding of their own faith.

The existence of BYU stakes and branches with around nine thousand returned missionaries has accentuated the atmosphere of youthful devotion and dedication of young men and women of missionary age (nineteen for men and twenty-one for women) to the Church. Not to be forgotten is the constructive influence of many women students who encourage their boy friends or fiances to go on missions before proceeding with marriage. Thus, BYU is a training ground for thousands of future missionaries.

Genealogical Research and Activity

Besides the large missionary and Indian programs by which BYU has assisted the Church, there are many other important areas where BYU makes an important contribution. One is genealogical research.

One of the cardinal religious beliefs of Latter-day Saints is that in the hereafter, those who in this life have not had an opportunity to accept the restored gospel of Jesus Christ will have an opportunity to become converted and accept it in the "spirit world." But since the saving ordinances of baptism, confirmation, ordination, and eternal marriage are earthly ceremonies, they must be done here by proxy for those who have passed away. This is commonly called "temple work" and cannot be done until adequate genealogical data have been compiled so as to properly identify the individual. The result is that the LDS Church has the largest genealogical library in the world. In some cases, such as that of Denmark, it has a genealogical record of natives of that country comparable to the genealogical records of Denmark itself.

BYU has long had course offerings in genealogy to assist members of the Church in searching out the records of their ancestors, but in recent years BYU has inherited a more distinct role to play in genealogical education. For a few years a bachelor's degree was offered by the College of Industrial Technology. However, lack of a sizeable professional market for those holding the degree caused the program to be cut back to a two-year certificate.

Outside the classroom, other genealogical aids have been instituted both for students and local residents. The largest branch library of the Genealogical Society Library in Salt Lake City has been in operation in the Harold B. Lee Library since

May 1965. Its budget equals the combined budgets of twenty-five average branch libraries.[74] This branch library, although housed in the BYU Library, is independent of the University. But rental space is made available free by the school and, as is the case of the Language Training Mission, BYU cooperates in its administration. The library is funded and directed by a regional board.

By 1973, total genealogical offerings at BYU (not including those at the branch library) constituted what is now called the Institute for Genealogical Studies (formerly the Genealogical Research Center). The Institute is divided into three areas: academic teaching (fundamentals, advanced research), demography (training in population origins), and professional research assistance. The BYU-budgeted Family History Services is a professional research office that accepts patron accounts for reasonable fees.[75]

Besides these services, BYU hosts various family and genealogical research seminars throughout the year. In 1975, for example, the Office of Continuing Education sponsored a week-long annual Genealogical Seminar on campus that treated almost every phase of genealogical work. Approximately 3,000 patrons participated. The establishment by the Church of a temple in Provo in 1972 has greatly increased the interest and activity of the BYU faculty and students in genealogical work. Although in existence only five years, the Provo Temple has the greatest activity of any of the temples of the Church. The facility has around one thousand temple workers, and nearly one and one-half million temple ordinances are performed there each year. While students are not recruited as temple workers because it would conflict with their studies, thousands of them actively participate in temple sessions. BYU hopes in the future to greatly increase its genealogical service to the Church and its members.

---

74. Transcribed interview of Roger Flick by Richard E. Bennett, 2 June 1975, Centennial History Papers, BYU Archives, p. 1.
75. Ibid.

Educational Guidance Center

Another service administered primarily through BYU for the benefit of the youth of the Church is the Educational Admissions Guidance Center, established in 1965 to assist college-age LDS students in exercising appropriate educational options. Depending on their individual needs, some were counselled to go to BYU, Ricks, BYU — Hawaii, state schools where strong LDS institutes existed, or to technical colleges.[76]

In time the program was amplified to include an Educational Information and Guidance Center under the direction of Dr. Lynn Eric Johnson; it became a veritable beehive, dispensing career information to all who sought it. Special conferences, telelectures, addresses, and radio broadcasts were held in many areas of Canada and the United States, advising LDS students not only on school selection, but on career opportunities. It has been of particular assistance to high school students, missionaries in the field, and servicemen.[77]

Language Training Mission

Looking to the future, the greatest service BYU will contribute to the Church may very well be its administration of the Language Training Mission, the history, present status, and immediate future of which are discussed in chapter 50. Summarily stated, within the immediate future (five to ten years) it is expected that the LTM will train 24,000 missionaries a year who will serve in all the foreign missions of the Church (sixty-four at present and increasing every year). Already the LTM teaches twenty-three foreign languages, and the number will undoubtedly increase from year to year. In the words of President Harold B. Lee, "The approval of this new project

76. First Presidency to all presidents of missions and stakes, 5 May 1965, Wilkinson Presidential Papers.
77. Lynn Johnson, "Educational Information and Guidance Center Annual Report, September 1969 to August 1970," in the possession of Lynn Eric Johnson.

will have the effect of making Provo the language capital of the world, with Brigham Young University the focal point." He also said, "The approval of this project is not the end, it is just the beginning."[78]

Centennial Motto and Emblem

The Centennial emblem and motto of the first one hundred years, "Dedicated to Love of God, Pursuit of Truth, and Service to Mankind" are more than symbols. Rooted in the soils of Mormon religion and theology, the Church University is bearing rich dividends for the Church, for the community, for the students, and for many nations. In its love of God the school has not forgotten to observe the commandments. In its pursuit of truth the University has observed the prophetic advice to seek wisdom. In its service to mankind BYU has followed the admonition of the Master: "Inasmuch as ye have done it unto one of the least of these my brethren, ye have done it unto me."[79]

---

78. Ben E. Lewis to Ernest L. Wilkinson, 18 March 1975, Wilkinson Presidential Papers.
79. Matthew 25:40.

55

A University of Destiny

The Mission of BYU

Since the founding of Brigham Young Academy in 1875 there never has been any doubt about the purpose and mission of LDS Church schools, especially Brigham Young University. That mission and purpose is to teach the gospel of Jesus Christ — Christianity in its fullness — to every student as an essential and motivating part of his education. Four days after signing the Deed of Trust which conveyed land for the establishment of the Academy, Brigham Young wrote his son Alfales, who was studying at the University of Michigan,

> I have deeded my property on that place on which the University building stands to a Board of Trustees, composed of Smoot, Harrington and others for the purpose of endowing a college, to be called Brigham Young's Academy of Provo. . . . I hope to see an Academy established there . . . at which the children of the Latter-day Saints can receive a good education unmixed with the pernicious, atheistic influences that are found in so many of the higher schools of the country.[1]

1. Brigham Young to Alfales Young, 20 October 1875, Brigham Young Papers, Church Historical Department.

In 1888, President Wilford Woodruff reiterated the same purpose:

> The time has arrived when the proper education of our children should be taken in hand by us as a people. Religious training is practically excluded from the District Schools. The perusal of books that we value as divine records is forbidden. Our children, if left to the training they receive in these schools, will grow up entirely ignorant of those principles of salvation for which the Latter-day Saints have made so many sacrifices. To permit this condition of things to exist among us would be criminal.[2]

In 1945, almost three-quarters of a century later, President Heber J. Grant reemphasized what Brigham Young had in mind: "In this school we are seeking to implant in the hearts of the young men and the young women an absolute testimony of the divinity of Jesus Christ and of the restitution again to the earth of the plan of salvation."[3] President J. Reuben Clark, Jr., counselor to presidents Heber J. Grant, George Albert Smith, and David O. McKay, stated at the inauguration of Howard S. McDonald as president of BYU in 1945 that Brigham Young University "has a . . . dual aim and purpose — secular learning, the lesser value, and spiritual development, the greater. These two values must be always together, neither would be perfect without the other, but the spiritual values, being basic and eternal, must always prevail, for the spiritual values are built upon absolute truth."[4]

Similar expressions have been made by each of the presidents of the Church, including Spencer W. Kimball, the present President of the LDS Church:

> This institution has no justification for its existence unless it builds character, creates and develops faith, and makes

2. James R. Clark, ed., *Messages of the First Presidency of The Church of Jesus Christ of Latter-day Saints*, 5 vols. (Salt Lake City: Bookcraft, 1965-71), 3:168.
3. "President Grant Promoted Wide Education," *The Y News*, 21 May 1945.
4. J. Reuben Clark, Jr., "The Mission of Brigham Young University," *Brigham Young University Quarterly*, 1 August 1949, p. 10.

> men and women of strength and courage, fortitude and service — men and women who will become stalwarts in the Kingdom and bear witness of the Restoration and the divinity of the Gospel."[5]

On another occasion, President Kimball stated:

> The uniqueness of Brigham Young University lies in its special role — education for eternity — which it must carry in addition to the usual tasks of a university. This means concern — curricular and behavioral — for not only the "whole man" but for the "eternal man." Where all universities seek to preserve the heritage of knowledge that history has washed to their feet, this faculty has a double heritage — the preserving of knowledge of men and the revealed truths sent from heaven.[6]

Members of the Council of the Twelve have expressed similar convictions. Elder John A. Widtsoe, who once served on the faculty of BYU and was later president of both Utah State Agricultural College and the University of Utah, wrote in 1949, "There are many institutions of learning, which foster splendidly the learning gains of the centuries. But, there is only one offering full collegiate training, Brigham Young University, in which the wisdom of men is saturated and made alive with the wisdom of the gospel of Jesus Christ — the gospel restored through Joseph Smith."[7] Elder George Q. Morris, also a member of the Council of the Twelve, told the BYU student body on 11 January 1955, "You are attending a university that is absolutely unique in all the world. As I have said before, it is called the Brigham Young University, but it is the University of the Kingdom of God, and that is its uniqueness."[8]

---

5. Spencer W. Kimball, "A Style of Our Own!" *Church News,* 28 February 1951, p. 4.
6. Spencer W. Kimball, *Education for Eternity* (Provo, Utah: Brigham Young University Press, 1967), pp. 1-2.
7. John A. Widtsoe, "Commencement Day at Brigham Young University," *The Improvement Era,* July 1949, p. 449.
8. George Q. Morris, "Church Doctrine," *Speeches of the Year* (Brigham Young University, 1955), p. 1.

Perhaps the most forthright statement about the mission of BYU was made by Elder Boyd K. Packer, an assistant to the Quorum of the Twelve who later became a member of that body. On the occasion of the dedication of the Daniel H. Wells Building on 29 April 1969, he said, "Brigham Young University is unique among all universities. It is a private school and it is established for a special spiritual purpose." Then, after quoting the president of another university, ironically also established by a religious group, who stated, "We can best serve as a neutral territory — a kind of arbiter where people can come to reason," Elder Packer commented:

> This could not be said of Brigham Young University. For this University is not neutral; it is committed; it is one-sided; it is prejudiced, if you will, in favor of the gospel of Jesus Christ.
>
> This is not a playing field where good and evil can come and joust with one another until one may win. Evil will find no invitation to contest here. This is a training ground for one team. Here you are coached and given signals preparatory for the great game, and we might say the great battle, of life. The scouts and the coaches of the opposing team are not welcome here.[9]

Visions of the Fulfillment of BYU's Mission

The ultimate fulfillment of the purpose and mission of the Church and its University also seems never to have been doubted by Mormon leaders. President John Taylor, who succeeded Brigham Young as President of the Church, had no hesitancy in proclaiming the destiny of LDS schools. As early as 13 April 1879, he prophesied, "You will see the day that Zion will be as far ahead of the outside world in everything pertaining to learning of every kind as we are today in regard to religious matters.[10]

---

9. Boyd K. Packer, "A Dedication — To Faith," *Speeches of the Year* (Provo, Utah: Brigham Young University Press, 1969), pp. 3-4.
10. John Taylor in *Journal of Discourses,* 26 vols. (London: Latter-day Saints' Book Depot, 1855-86), 21:100.

During the presidency of David O. McKay, the First Presidency, in a letter to all stake presidents and bishops, recorded their deep convictions about BYU's future;

> Because of its combination of revealed and secular learning, Brigham Young University is destined to become, if not the largest, at least the most proficient institution of learning in the world, producing scholars with testimonies of the truth who will become leaders in science, industry, art, education, letters, and government.[11]

Elder Spencer W. Kimball (now President of the LDS Church) told the BYU student body in 1951:

> It is a glorious privilege, my young brothers and sisters, to be attending this, the greatest university in all the world. There is no other one that can compare with it. There are many universities with greater enrollment, larger faculty and more elaborate facilities, institutions which develop the mind — but this one is designed to teach the mind, the heart and the spirit. Here you have the privilege not only of following the regular academic subjects, but to learn how eventually to exalt yourselves and to help yourselves to become Gods.[12]

Presidents Heber J. Grant,[13] Joseph Fielding Smith,[14] and Harold B. Lee,[15] and Elder Matthew Cowley[16] all bore similar testimony that BYU would become the greatest institution of higher learning in the world. George H. Brimhall reported that Francis M. Lyman of the Quorum of the Twelve Apostles,

---

11. The First Presidency to all stake presidents, 4 November 1957, Wilkinson Presidential Papers.
12. Spencer W. Kimball, "A Style of Our Own!" *Church News,* 28 February 1951, p. 4.
13. BYU Board of Trustees to Franklin S. Harris, 7 February 1945, Harris Presidential Papers, BYU Archives.
14. Joseph Fielding Smith, "Alumni Meeting Address," 8 April 1950, BYU Archives, p. 1.
15. Harold B. Lee, "$425,000 Student Building Displayed," *Church News,* 28 March 1953, p. 4.
16. Matthew Cowley, "Elder Cowley at BYU," *Church News,* 4 June 1952, p. 4.

in addressing BYU students, said: "This school will be needed in the millennium."[17]

The presidents of BYU have had the same prophetic beliefs. During his seventeen years as principal of Brigham Young Academy, Karl G. Maeser, among other statements, declared: "I should be ungrateful if I did not place myself on record as being conscious that the Brigham Young Academy has been a chosen instrument in the hands of the Lord God of Israel, to plant the seed for an educational system that will spread its ramifications throughout all the borders of Zion, penetrating with its benign influence every fireside of the Saints, and opening to our youth the avenues to all intelligence, knowledge, and power."[18]

Making Dreams Come True

During the earlier years of the University the seemingly extravagant superlatives employed by the builders of BYU to describe its prophetic destiny must have aroused great outbursts of humorous disdain among the school's detractors. During the first three-quarters of a century of the history of BYU few could have foreseen what has been accomplished in the last quarter-century of the school's existence. Great strides have been made toward fulfilling the prophetic utterances in their entirety. All the various administrations, despite what seemed insurmountable barriers on many occasions, have contributed to that end.

---

17. George H. Brimhall, "The Founding and Growth of a Great School," *The Utah Genealogical and Historical Magazine,* January 1926, p. 10.
18. Reinhard Maeser, *Karl G. Maeser* (Provo, Utah: Brigham Young University, 1928), pp. 125-26. Seven years later, George H. Brimhall wrote, "The school depends not on man, or any set of man. God planted it and we are but gardeners to take care of it" (George H. Brimhall to Benjamin Cluff, Jr., 13 December 1902, Cluff Presidential Papers, BYU Archives). In his first speech to the BYU student body, President Franklin S. Harris proclaimed: "This institution will become the greatest on earth, as it now is in many respects. This is the Temple of Learning and it is to be pre-eminent in scholarship and leadership" (Franklin S. Harris, Maiden Speech to the BYU Student Body, 28 April 1921, Franklin S. Harris biographical file, BYU Ar-

The Dusenberry Administration

The founding of Brigham Young Academy by Brigham Young in Provo rather than Salt Lake City was undoubtedly due to the educational endeavors of Warren and Wilson Dusenberry. They had founded two schools, both of which were eminently successful, even though they were unable to survive financially. Warren was principal of the Timpanogos Branch of the University of Deseret, which also had to close because of lack of financial support by the parent institution (*see* chapter 3). Because of his successful educational experience it was only natural that Dusenberry should have been chosen as the first principal of BYA, although it was under-

---

chives). When he was criticized for purchasing additional land for the school, President Harris told his secretary, Dean A. Peterson, "I can never purchase enough land to provide for the future growth and development of this campus" (Ernest L. Wilkinson conference with Dean A. Peterson, 26 September 1974). Presidents McDonald, Wilkinson, and Oaks have all expressed similar beliefs as to the future of BYU. Howard S. McDonald said Brigham Young University "has been organized not only to teach the academic learning of the world, but also to teach the Gospel of Jesus Christ. If faculty and students grasp the significance of these great aims and strive to accomplish them this University will grow into a mighty institution of learning" (Howard S. McDonald, "The Future of Brigham Young University," speech given about 1947, Howard S. McDonald Presidential Papers, BYU Archives). On 5 February 1971 President Wilkinson devoted an entire address to sustaining the prophetic utterance of the First Presidency that BYU "*will* become the most proficient institution of higher learning in the world" (Ernest L. Wilkinson, "The Unique Role of BYU among Universities of America," *Speeches of the Year* [Provo, Utah: Brigham Young University Press, 1970], p. 3). President Oaks later joined in expressing similar faith, but added, "It will not be gained without unity and love and personal effort toward perfection" (Dallin H. Oaks, "The University Community," *Intercom* 1 [September 1973]:2). Even the accreditation committee of 1966, which made certain criticisms of BYU, concluded, "The University will undoubtedly earn its rightful place as one of the great universities in the United States of America" ("Report of the Visitation Committee to the Commissioner on Higher Education of the Northwest Association of Secondary and Higher Schools at Brigham Young University, 26 to 29 April 1966," Wilkinson Presidential Papers, BYU Archives, pp. 71-72).

Warren N. Dusenberry,
first principal of Brigham
Young Academy.

stood that he would serve only until a permanent principal was appointed. To him, three financial educational failures were probably enough. He preferred to go into the practice of law where he would not have to push wheelbarrows around to collect produce for tuition but could obtain adequate fees on which to live.

The Maeser Administration

Maeser's administration was plagued from the beginning with insufficient funds on which to operate the school. Its only property consisted of the Lewis Building and the land deeded by President Brigham Young. He intended to provide other financial support for the school, and at the time of his death on 29 August 1877 he had another deed of property to BYA on his desk which he never got around to signing. After President Young's death the school was dependent on tuition and gifts it might receive. With only twenty-nine beginning students who paid only four dollars per term in a community with many financial problems, the outlook was bleak. Even with an average of seventy students through four successive terms the first year, the tuition did not even pay Maeser's salary ($1,200), let alone provide salaries for other faculty members or for operating the school. Thus, in the very first year of Maeser's administration it became painfully apparent that the Academy would go the way of the Timpanogos Branch if it could not recruit more students and attract the general support of Utah Stake residents. With almost superhuman effort and the leadership of Abraham O. Smoot, president of the Board of Trustees, in recruiting students and obtaining contributions from Utah County residents and the Church, the school managed for the next eight years to survive.

As if this burden were not enough to bear, on the night of 27 January 1884 a fire of undetermined origin destroyed the entire Lewis Building. Since Brigham Young, founder and benefactor, was no longer alive to aid the school, many

Karl G. Maeser with his
family in 1898.

thought that the fire meant the end of the Academy.[19] Accosting Professor Maeser on the street, Reed Smoot said, "Oh, Brother Maeser, the Academy has burned." Maeser answered, "No such thing, it's only the building."[20]

From then until 1896 the school almost went under on at least six occasions. One year the teachers taught without pay, and during other years they waited long periods for their meager salaries.[21]

On 14 April 1886, Brother Maeser wrote President John Taylor:

> As all the teachers have been forced to incur debts, and the financial condition of the Academy gives them no hope of meeting their obligations, nor to support their families until the commencement of the new academic year in August, and there being even then no prospect of better times, they all will be under the necessity of seeking positions elsewhere immediately after the close of the present term.[22]

But they survived that year, although conditions became even worse.

On 4 May 1887, clearly evidencing his discouragement and exasperation, Karl G. Maeser penned the following pathetic lines to L. John Nuttall:

> The affairs of this institution are in such an unsettled condition financially and executively, that I cannot see my way clear at any point. . . . This one point is certain that it cannot go on much longer in the way in which it has vegetated during the last two years, in as much as the teachers have no security that the institution may not have to stop in the middle of the school year for lack of funds. . . . I am *worn out* and *sick in spirit,* dear Brother, about this dragging and planless condition of things, and

---

19. *See* Volume 1, p. 125.
20. Ibid.
21. *See* Volume 1, pp. 137-40.
22. Karl G. Maeser to John Taylor, 14 April 1886, Maeser Presidential Papers, BYU Archives.

> with all my love for this Academy, I feel that I owe it to my very life, which is needlessly wearing out here in an apparently hopeless task, to accept any change that will promise to me opportunities for permanent usefulness.[23]

At one time during these financial crises, Karl G. Maeser informed his wife and daughter that because of lack of sufficient money on which to live, he was going to accept a position at the University of Deseret. Accordingly, his wife and daughter got things packed and sat on their trunks. When the daughter finally mustered enough courage to ask her father when they were moving, his response was, "I have changed my mind. I have had a dream — I have seen Temple Hill filled with buildings — great temples of learning, and I have decided to remain and do my part in contributing to the fulfillment of that dream." Maeser repeated this story to his daughter on many occasions.[24]

During Maeser's entire administration he and his colleagues struggled from day to day to keep the institution afloat so that his dream could eventually come true (*see* chapters 4 to 8).

The Cluff Administration

The financial problems that had plagued Maeser deepened when Cluff became principal in 1892. Even President Smoot, who had financially saved the Academy on many instances, either by his own funds or by appealing to the Brethren in Salt Lake, with whom he had great influence, felt that if Utah Stake could not pay the school's outstanding debts the Academy would probably be removed from Provo. It appeared that nothing could save the school.[25] Indeed, plans were already being made for the establishment of a Church

23. Karl G. Maeser to L. John Nuttall, 4 May 1887, box 1, folder 3, Maeser Presidential Papers, BYU Archives.
24. Ernest L. Wilkinson, conference with Eva Maeser Crandall, May 1960.
25. Utah Stake High Council Minutes, 2 September 1892, LDS Church Historical Department.

University in Salt Lake City which would become the center of LDS Church education and relegate BYA to a position of decreasing importance. *Circular Eight,* released by the Church Board of Education, announced that Brigham Young Academy would be authorized to carry on normal (teacher training) work only. With a $100,000 building erected but not paid for, the BYA Board of Trustees faced bankruptcy. As the school faced financial collapse, a rumor spread that the Catholic Church was going to buy the Academy's property and take over the school's operation. Except for the national financial panic of 1893, which made both the Church University in Salt Lake City and the purchase of BYA by the Catholic Church impossible, it is likely that the Church University in Salt Lake City would have become a reality, and it is possible that a Catholic university would have been established in Provo. In either event Brigham Young University might never have come into existence.

Even though neither of these things happened the Academy was still living on borrowed money, and when the notes began to fall due, its survival was once again in question. A. O. Smoot was now in ill health, and the financial panic had so depleted his resources that he was unable to come to the rescue. Smoot urged that the Church incorporate Brigham Young Academy and assume its financial obligations, but the idea was not approved. By 23 June 1892 the school had a net indebtedness of $61,107, and Cluff was told that the Church could in no way help assume the debts. In addition to these debts, in September 1892 the Board of Trustees learned that the Church General Board of Education had allocated only $3,600 to Brigham Young Academy for the 1892-93 school year. A separate appropriation of $5,000 was made to the Normal School, but these combined funds of $8,600 were scarcely adequate to operate the Normal Department alone, and this money could not be used to pay the school's debts. It appeared that nothing could save the school. Appropriately, the closing song at the Founders Day Celebration of 1892 was "The Sinking Ship."

The next two years brought similar critical financial prob-

Benjamin Cluff, Jr., third president of Brigham Young University. This photograph was taken on President Cluff's eighty-eighth birthday in 1946.

lems. As the school faced financial collapse in 1895, Smoot arose from his death bed and made a special trip to Salt Lake City for help. He partially succeeded but died two weeks later. With the death of President Smoot, on whom both Maeser and Cluff relied for community and Church succor for the school's continuance, most supporters had given up hope of the Academy's survival.[26]

Up to that time the school had been threatened with termination on six different occasions. It was at this critical juncture that President Cluff recorded, "One evening while returning from a walk down town and while studying deeply over the future of the Academy, the thought came to me like an inspiration: 'give the school to the Church.' Immediately my mind was at rest. I knew that it was the right thing to do."[27] Although this same suggestion had been made and rejected a number of times in the past, the Board of Trustees succeeded in obtaining permission to incorporate the school on 18 July 1896.

However, incorporation of Brigham Young Academy by the Church only temporarily quieted fears that BYA would be closed. By the fall of 1900 there were a number of serious obstacles still threatening the progress of Brigham Young Academy. The Board of Trustees, which had always been firmly united behind Maeser and influential with the authorities in Salt Lake City, had begun to weaken in effectiveness. BYA facilities were in serious need of repair. Salaries were so low that many of the leading teachers and professors were considering leaving BYA for better pay elsewhere. At one time the First Presidency actually decided to curtail certain programs at BYA and make it a "feeder" to the University of Utah. This aroused the ire of President Cluff, who did not hesitate to express himself. Because of the advent of another serious depression which also seriously impaired the financial

---

26. *See* Volume 1, pp. 239-43.
27. Eugene L. Roberts and Mrs. Eldon Reed Cluff, "Benjamin Cluff, Jr.," typescript history in BYU Archives, pp. 84-85.

capacity of the University of Utah, this decision was never really put into effect.[28]

Brimhall Administration

Financial crises continued throughout the Brimhall Administration. There were, however, those who maintained a positive attitude and had an optimistic vision of the future. Thus, President Edwin S. Hinckley, shortly after the turn of the century, predicted that the campus of Brigham Young University would one day extend to Rock Canyon.[29] Counting the Language Training Mission, which is served by BYU teachers as a part of their University work, the campus now extends nearly that distance. But Hinckley's optimism did not alter the bleak economic outlook. By 1911 the school administration had continued to spend money that it did not have until its debts became a threat to Brigham Young University's existence. But the faculty took inspiration from the fact that in 1912 the University graduated its first four-year graduating class, with eighteen members. The president of the class was B. F. Larsen, who later chaired the BYU Art Department for thirty years. The students chose Alfred Kelly, a young teacher critic in the Training School, to give the graduation speech.

In a speech given on 25 May 1962, entitled "Fifty Years Ago," B. F. Larsen related that when Kelly was introduced, he rose and stood in silence for a moment. Some thought he had lost his power of speech. When he gained his composure, he explained that he had been much concerned over his speech, that he had written and discarded it several times:

> Finally one morning with a feeling of desperation he walked toward Temple Hill. He stopped to rest and think when he reached the hill top.
>
> He looked at the incomplete Maeser Building in front

---

28. *See* Volume 1, pp. 348-49.
29. J. Edward Johnson, "Edwin S. Hinckley as an Administrator," *Edwin Smith Hinckley Centennial Tributes* (Provo, Utah: Brigham Young University Press, 1968), p. 19.

David Starr Jordan with
President George H.
Brimhall during one of
Jordan's visits to Provo.

of him, hoping that inspiration would come from this intimate view, but he felt only grim disappointment. The sky was radiant with the morning light but the silhouetted building seemed dark and a symbol of gloom.

Kelly turned to view the valley which was still in shadow. He gazed at the building with the hope that this intimate view would give direction to the solution of his problem. But no inspiration came. Then he turned toward the valley which was in shadow.

Suddenly the light from the rising sun illuminated the western hills with an unusual golden glow. The light gradually descended from the hill tops and slowly advanced to the spot where Kelly stood.

He partially closed his eyes and was startled. He stood as if transformed. The advancing sunlight suddenly assumed the appearance of people. The trees, the bushes, the ripples on the surface of Utah lake, everything in the valley disappeared. Only people were there, young people moving toward Temple Hill. Hundreds of people, thousands of young people came into view advancing with the warm sunlight to the place where this campus is now built.

Finally when this apparition reached Kelly, Temple Hill was bathed in sunlight. The whole of the present campus was illumined beyond the power of description and Kelly saw buildings here, not homes but temples of learning, large buildings, beautiful buildings, buildings which covered the top of this hill.

The people who came with the sunlight from the valley below and from the far places beyond were students. They carried books in their arms.

They entered these many temples of learning and when they came out again they raised their eyes heavenward; their faces were toward the east. Their countenances bore a smile of hope, of faith. They were cheerful and confident. Their walk was light but firm as they again became a part of the sunlight as it moved to the top of Y mountain and disappeared from view.[30]

---

30. B. F. Larsen, "Fifty Years Ago," speech given at a BYU Alumni meeting, 25 May 1962, B. F. Larsen biographical file, BYU Archives, p. 4.

At the time of Kelly's address it was contemplated that the east end of Temple Hill, where the University now stands, would be divided into building lots and sold. A new subdivision of Provo City, to be named "Manavu," had already been planned, and President Brimhall had expected Kelly to sponsor the sale of these lots. Brimhall was indignant that no such effort had been made, and he tried to save the day by giving a fiery speech of his own. Nevertheless, after Kelly's speech this plan was abandoned, and Temple Hill was preserved for BYU.

This did not end the financial worries. By 1914 the situation became so acute that there were unofficial reports that the school was to be closed and moved to Salt Lake City to be consolidated with Latter-day Saints University.[31] By April 1915, Reed Smoot recorded in his diary that BYU owed $104,000 in overdue debts.[32] Furthermore, the accounting officer of the Church Board of Education notified the school that it had grossly overestimated the value of its few assets. The only salvation from this financial crisis was a low-interest loan from the Church-owned Utah-Idaho Sugar Company in the amount of $127,000. This was arranged through the personal solicitation of President Joseph F. Smith. Coupled with the personal financial assistance of Jesse Knight, this permitted the school to continue. Subsequent conditions in Provo forced the University to apply for extensions of time on the loan from Utah-Idaho Sugar Company. BYU also asked the Church to pay the interest on the loan. By July 1918,

---

31. " 'Uncle Jesse' Knight's Gift," Provo *Daily Herald,* 24 September 1914: "There has been talk of consolidating this school with the LDSU and concentrating both in Salt Lake City. . . . The theory is advanced that if both schools were operated under one head there would be a greater saving of money to the Church." The editorial noted that Jesse Knight's generosity to the school would probably enable it to remain in Provo. *See also* "A Great University," Provo *Daily Herald,* 15 October 1914. There was no mention of the rumored move in Church Board of Education minutes, BYU Board minutes, or in Brimhall's papers.

32. Diary of Reed Smoot, 14 April 1915, BYU Library Special Collections.

indebtedness had grown to $113,500. Having little confidence that BYU would ever be able to pay its debts, the First Presidency of the Church chose to liquidate the debts of the school in exchange for BYU's limited assets. This saved BYU from financial collapse (*see* Volume 1, chapters 12 through 14).

The Harris Administration

Despite the brilliant beginning of the Harris Administration, during which time the new president organized several colleges and it looked like the school would come into its own, a new series of financial crises asserted themselves. On 18 March 1926, Superintendent Adam S. Bennion recommended that Brigham Young University be organized on the basis of a senior college and a junior college and that the junior college be taken over by Provo City or Utah County. While he was willing that a small but eminently superior Church University should continue, he proposed that "the enthusiasm to build a great Church University" should be discouraged.[33] In a subsequent meeting of the General Church Board of Education on 23 March 1926, President Heber J. Grant stated that "I doubt if we will be able to maintain the higher institutions at all." He reported that the cost of maintaining Church schools had vastly increased, but the tithing of the Church had not. Between 1921 and 1926, President Franklin S. Harris was never quite sure of the role of BYU. While he publicly proclaimed that BYU would never close, he had internal fears. In obvious frustration he wrote to John T. Wahlquist that he wished "the Brethren would tell me what they want done to the BYU — am I to starve it, am I to phase it out, or am I supposed to make it a reputable institution?"[34]

Pessimism increased in 1928 when the General Church Board of Education decided "that the policy of the Church

33. General Church Board of Education Minutes, 18 March 1926.
34. John T. Wahlquist to Ernest L. Wilkinson, 6 April 1971, Wilkinson Presidential Papers.

A. W. Ivins, Franklin S. Harris, and Heber J. Grant together in 1923.

was to eliminate Church schools as fast as circumstances would permit."[35] Between 1931 and 1934 the LDS Church turned Weber College at Ogden, Snow College at Ephraim, and Dixie College at St. George over to the State of Utah, and the Gila Academy at Thatcher, Arizona, over to the county (the county later turned it over to the state). Although enrollment at BYU rose from 1,009 in 1924 to 2,459 in 1934, appropriations from the General Church Board of Education remained around $200,000 each year. Faculty members were required to take salary cuts of ten percent and thirteen percent (*see* Volume 2, chapters 15 through 22).

Profoundly disturbed over rumors that BYU would close, Sidney B. Sperry, a member of the religion faculty, said he once awakened in the middle of the night and saw a vision of Brigham Young University in the future. He saw beautiful modern buildings extending along the entire East Bench and great crowds of people going to and from the University. He also saw a temple, seemingly indicating that BYU was going to remain a Church institution. The following morning Sperry advised a number of his colleagues of his vision and insisted that the Church was not going to give up BYU. In relating his experience Dr. Sperry said, "I know that BYU is destined to be one of the great universities in the world, and that some day we will have a Temple here."[36]

The McDonald Administration

Notwithstanding the vision of Maeser, the prophetic prediction of Hinckley, and the visions of Kelly and Sperry, further considerations were given to the discontinuance of BYU. As late as 1945, when Howard S. McDonald was appointed president of BYU, he was asked by President J.

35. General Church Board of Education Minutes, 22 March 1928 and 20 February 1929.
36. Memorandum of conference between W. Cleon Skousen and Sidney B. Sperry, 1951; and memorandum of conference between Ernest L. Wilkinson and Sidney B. Sperry, 26 September 1975, Wilkinson Presidential Papers.

President Howard S. McDonald (at top of stairs) with other BYU administrators on an inspection tour of Wymount Village student housing units around 1947.

Ernest L. Wilkinson greeting
Joseph Fielding Smith, Jr.,
and his wife, Jessie Evans
Smith, after an assembly
at BYU.

Reuben Clark, Jr., to make a study to determine whether BYU should continue. McDonald reported orally, urging that the University be perpetuated with much greater financial support than in the past.[37] His report that it should be continued resolved that threat.

The Wilkinson Administration

Even during the Wilkinson Administration the suggestion was made from time to time by outsiders that by turning BYU over to the state the Church could be spared its large cost of operation. The Church leaders' firm rejection of this idea is reflected in the multimillion-dollar appropriations which have made possible the remarkable growth of BYU in buildings and educational services.

The Oaks Administration

No suggestion of any kind has been made concerning BYU's discontinuance during the Oaks Administration. The only real threat to the University has been a growing challenge to its independence resulting from broad regulations issued by the federal government involving all schools which have accepted any vestige of federal aid. While BYU does not itself accept federal aid except for research where it gives an honest *quid pro quo,* some of its students have availed themselves of federal loans, and the bold federal contention is that this constitutes an acceptance of federal aid by BYU. President Oaks has responded that the school will resist this federal intrusion into the affairs of the school which violates its status as a private institution (*see* chapter 52).

Contributions of Various Presidents

The visions of Maeser, Kelly, and Sperry and the prophetic utterances of President Edwin H. Hinckley did not magically produce the beautiful campus now existing on Temple Hill.

---

37. Howard S. McDonald to Ernest L. Wilkinson, 6 July 1975, Wilkinson Presidential Papers.

Dallin H. Oaks listening to
President Harold B. Lee.

That was accomplished only by the privation, perseverance, and loyal sacrifice of the administration, faculty, and staff for one hundred years, in addition to the leadership of the school's principals and presidents and the support of the Board of Trustees.

The founder of Brigham Young University, along with its eight presidents, have all made unique contributions to the success of the institution. President Brigham Young founded the school, gave it its first home, and charted its course with his simple instructions to Maeser that he should not teach anything except under the inspiration of the Spirit of God. Dusenberry's contribution consisted of providing the climate in Provo for the establishment of an educational institution which eventually became BYA.

Karl G. Maeser was the master teacher and spiritual architect of BYU. Following faithfully the instructions of President Brigham Young, he gave the school a religious foundation which has guided the institution over its entire one-hundred-year history. His administration, however, would never have endured without the guidance and financial statesmanship of Abraham O. Smoot.[38]

Although often at odds with Karl G. Maeser, Benjamin Cluff, Jr., was an educational innovator who brought progressive ideas to the campus and successfully fused them with the spiritual motivation of Karl G. Maeser. Where others had failed, he persuaded Church leaders to incorporate BYU as an official subsidiary of the LDS Church. Without this important change the future growth of BYU, and possibly its existence, would have been impossible.[39]

George H. Brimhall, who was in the good graces of both Maeser and Cluff, began building what he and others considered to be a great educational faculty. This thrust was temporarily stalled by the modernism controversy of 1911. Many thought this meant the end of BYU, but it did not, and although the school was not yet organized in the pattern of a

38. *See* Volume 1, chapters 4 through 7.
39. *See* Volume 1, chapters 8 through 11.

modern university (some still thought of BYU as a glorified high school), it produced many outstanding graduates who distinguished themselves in various professions. Brimhall was an eloquent speaker and, like Maeser, moved his students and others to great accomplishments. In addition to these contributions, Brimhall was a great stabilizer of the University.[40] Like Abraham O. Smoot during the Maeser Administration, Jesse Knight came to the financial rescue of the Brimhall Administration on many occasions.

Franklin S. Harris, who served longer than any other president, was responsible for molding BYU into the beginning of a great modern university. He organized the first colleges on campus and was successful in recruiting a faculty with superior training and advanced degrees. With his educational background (he was the first president of BYU to hold a doctor's degree), perseverance, and magnetic personality, he was able to have BYU approved by important national accrediting associations so that the school was recognized as a university. He contributed greatly to the overall advancement of higher education throughout Utah and was an international personality, having traveled more abroad and rendered more international service than any other president of the school.[41]

The four years of Howard S. McDonald's administration were times of turbulence due to the return of the veterans from World War II. In three years they increased the size of the student body four-fold. With great energy, McDonald was able to provide temporary housing for the new students. He completely reorganized student services, making them more professional and functional. His greatest accomplishment probably consisted in creating an awareness among the Trustees of the need for an extensive building program. This was manifested during his own short administration by the construction of the Carl F. Eyring Science Center and the George Albert Smith Fieldhouse. In many ways this laid the

40. *See* Volume 1, chapters 12 through 14.
41. *See* Volume 2, chapters 15 through 22.

groundwork for the progress to be made later, during the administration of Ernest L. Wilkinson.[42]

With this foundation laid by his six predecessors, coupled with the growth of the Church, improved economic conditions, and the unusual support of President David O. McKay and the Board of Trustees, Ernest L. Wilkinson made his contribution by building, in terms of full-time students, the nation's largest private university. Under his administration the dreams of Maeser, Hinckley, Kelly, Sperry, and others concerning the building of great tabernacles of learning on Temple Hill became a reality; some seventy-seven permanent and eighty-two temporary buildings were constructed during his presidency. Of more importance, the growth in size and quality of the student body paralleled the physical growth of the campus. The size and professional stature of the faculty and the intellectual standards of the University also increased. Also under his administration and on his recommendation, ten stakes and 104 branches of the LDS Church were established on campus. This he considered his greatest contribution. Since then the number of student units has increased to twelve stakes and 130 branches.[43]

President Dallin H. Oaks, who has been in office only five years, has already left his imprint on the University. He has continued the building program of his predecessor with the enlargement of the bookstore, construction of the Law School (authorized during the Wilkinson Administration), and erection of a new library addition equal in size to the original structure. He has also witnessed the construction by the Church of the Language Training Mission near the University and has announced a drive for funds to construct a large graduate school of management. Of more importance, he has accelerated the intellectual renaissance of the faculty and is striving for perfection of performance in all areas of the University.[44]

---

42. *See* Volume 2, chapters 23 and 24.
43. *See* Volume 2, chapters 25 through 30 and Volume 3, chapters 31 through 44.
44. *See* chapters 45 through 53.

Thus, each president of Brigham Young University has employed his talents in solving problems and meeting challenges peculiar to his own administration. During the combined administrations of Maeser, Cluff, Brimhall, Harris, and McDonald (seventy-four years) there were more than twenty recorded occasions when Brigham Young Academy or Brigham Young University was threatened with termination. Only by the heroic and unselfish efforts of its early teachers and Trustees and by the ultimate inspiration and judgment of the leaders of the Church did it survive.

Having survived that many crises, the school seems within the past twenty-six years to have reached a seasoned maturity, with 284 permanent and 85 temporary buildings on one of the most beautiful campuses in the world; with a combined student body on and off campus, including those in Continuing Education, of over 300,000 registrants; with the student body of 25,000 at Provo alone including more than 9,000 returned missionaries; with an active Alumni Association of over 150,000 members; and with more than 1,200 members of the regular faculty.

During the last quarter of a century the school has founded the first College of Family Living in the country; established a College of Industrial and Technical Education, the first of its kind to be officially accredited by the National Engineers' Council for Professional Development; become a recognized national leader in the education of American Indians; founded a law school which soon asserted its quality; and is now planning a graduate school of management. In addition, twelve stakes and 130 branches of the LDS Church have been established at BYU, giving the school the reputation for leading all colleges in America in the religious training of its students. Along with this, the University has now become a champion of private colleges in opposing the federal government's attempt to curtail their freedom of operation (*see* chapter 52).

If one had stood on Center Street in the days of Karl G. Maeser gazing at the old Lewis Building, if one had walked along what is now University Avenue peering at the proud

Academy Building on lower campus in the days of Cluff, or if one had climbed Temple Hill when Wilkinson first came to BYU, the most fanciful imagination scarcely would have guessed what BYU would become by its centennial year. The development of a tiny pioneer academy into America's largest private university in terms of full-time students fulfills to a great extent the prophetic vision of its prophet-founder and his self-sacrificing successors.

Prospects for the Future

Despite the struggles and near death of BYU on many occasions during the first century of its existence, as related above, the University is on its way to fulfilling the prophetic destiny envisioned by presidents of the Church, various General Authorities, its eight presidents, and the faithful members of the University community. The many advances which remain to be made may not require the same kind of privation as in the past, but strenuous effort, personal sacrifice, and professional dedication will continue to be required as the University moves closer to its prophetic goal.

The writers of this history make no pretense of knowing or adequately perceiving all that this University can become by the end of its second century, but there are certain trends which already point toward dimensions of future achievement. The following are a few examples.

Intensifying the Teaching of the Gospel of Jesus Christ

The University must intensify its efforts to teach the gospel of Jesus Christ, which embraces all truth. In the words of William E. Berrett,

> There is a noticeable hunger in the land for a vital, living religion. In this awakening religious fervor, Brigham Young University holds a unique position. . . . It is especially . . . in this area of learning that honest men will beat a path to the doors of a University that is not ashamed of the Gospel of Jesus Christ.[45]

---

45. William E. Berrett to Ernest L. Wilkinson, March 1975, Wilkinson Presidential Papers.

The University must continue to teach that man is a child of God and has the potential to become like God. The emphasis on free agency, excellence in personal performance, service to others, the worth of hard work, and the avoidance of the dole and personal reliance on government must all find expression in the programs of the University.[46] The University should always have as its objective the statement of Karl G. Maeser to President John Taylor: "There is one thing, Pres. Taylor, I will guarantee, that is, that no infidels will go from my school."[47]

A World Center for Religion Teacher Training

Achievement of the basic goals of the institution will require a great enlargement of its programs for the preparation of institute and seminary teachers. The tremendous growth of the institutes and seminaries of the Church will give BYU a much greater role in teacher training. During the 1974-75 year there were 498 institutes serving 73,643 students and more than a thousand seminaries serving 174,018 students. The training of teachers for this system must have top priority. Dr. Joseph F. Merrill, former Church commissioner of education and a member of the Council of the Twelve, stated in an address to the BYU student body shortly after the seminary system was instituted:

> The Church has established a great seminary system — the greatest one in America. A seminary system without a university to head it would be like a U.S. navy without Annapolis, without the naval academy. A navy must have officers and officers must be trained. The Naval Academy is therefore an indispensable unit in the Navy. And just so is a university an essential unit in our seminary system. For our seminary teachers must be specifically trained for their work. The Brigham Young University is our training school.[48]

46. Ben E. Lewis to Ernest L. Wilkinson, 18 March 1975, Wilkinson Presidential Papers.
47. *Journal of Discourses,* 20:48.
48. Joseph F. Merrill, "Brigham Young University, Past, Present and Future," *Deseret News,* 20 December 1928.

Pioneering New Programs

BYU will undoubtedly be an innovator of many bold new programs. As Franklin S. Harris expressed it, the school must constantly find new ways to train leaders:

> What this particular university must aim to do is to train for leadership in its highest forms: leadership in the Church itself, leadership in social affairs, leadership in business, leadership in art, leadership in citizenship, in fact leadership in all that will contribute to the betterment of the world and the happiness of its people.[49]

Dallin H. Oaks has said:

> Brigham Young University is more than a university in the conventional sense. Its domain spans the limits of human experience, spiritual as well as physical, practice as well as precept. . . . It is concerned with teaching . . . the fundamentals of spiritual and secular knowledge.
>
> That is the nature of the challenge to this University.[50]

Writing New Textbooks

In the past the work load of members of the faculty, and in some cases their lack of adequate professional training, has required the use of textbooks which were not fully suited to BYU. However, the improved salary schedule and economic conditions during the Wilkinson Administration gave faculty members sufficient time to begin writing texts and other books related to their fields of learning. Thus, from 1951 to 1975, faculty members authored 831 books. Of these, 419 were textbooks in various disciplines. While this is a good start, it is only a beginning. The accomplishment of the mission of BYU will require the authorship of many textbooks designed especially for BYU, Church institutes, and high school seminaries. In the words of William E. Berrett, "In the future BYU professors must . . . launch out as leaders in their

---

49. "Pres.-Elect Harris Writes on Future of School," *White and Blue,* 25 May 1921.
50. Dallin H. Oaks, "Naming of a New President," *Speeches of the Year* (Provo, Utah: Brigham Young University Press, 1971), p. 6.

respective fields. The union of faith and science has its greatest chance at this University. Textbooks in Sociology, Archaeology, Geology, Psychology, etc., must be written with a bold new view."[51]

President Oaks gave further emphasis to this in an address which he delivered at the preschool faculty workshop on 27 August 1975:

> I must not leave this review of creative activities without reemphasizing my conviction that our most important creative activity is one that strengthens our effectiveness as a teaching institution. Indeed, this is the principal justification for all our research and our other creative activities. The writing of more effective textbooks is, in my view, a creative activity of vital importance, and one that has been neglected in some of our departments. I echo here and underline my total agreement with President Ezra Taft Benson's remarks last December that "on this campus, in due time, there will be an increasing number of textbooks written by inspired men of the Church. There will be less and less a tendency to subscribe to the false teachings of men."[52] Where the textbooks available for teaching in a particular area do not measure up to the standards we desire, whether because of inadequate professional content, values inferior to our own, or because of failure to treat matters of value that we believe to be relevant for that subject matter, I urge the colleges and departments to manage their resources so that this significant omission can be repaired as soon as possible by our own scholars. Until I am formally advised to the contrary, I will assume that every academic department at BYU has both the resources and the professional qualifications to prepare its own texts where necessary.[53]

---

51. William E. Berrett to Ernest L. Wilkinson, March 1975, Wilkinson Presidential Papers.
52. Ezra Taft Benson, "Jesus Christ — Gifts and Expectations," *Speeches of the Year* (Provo, Utah: Brigham Young University Press, 1975), p. 305.
53. Dallin H. Oaks, "Accomplishments, Prospects, and Problems in the Centennial Year," 1975 Fall Faculty Conference, BYU Archives.

Oaks told deans and department chairmen, "If you do not have faculty capable of writing texts in your field, it is your duty to help us identify the poorest performers in the department, get rid of them, and hire faculty who can. We are a *University,* not a high school or a junior college."[54]

Setting a New Level of Quality in the Arts

In the field of fine arts, Mormon teachers should be able to produce dramatic, musical, and artistic productions that would inspire students and patrons of the arts to achieve higher and more noble goals. On 27 September 1967, Elder Spencer W. Kimball told the faculty:

> For years I have been waiting for someone to do justice in recording in song and story and painting and sculpture the story of the restoration, the reestablishment of the kingdom of God on earth, the struggles and frustrations; the apostasies and inner revolutions and counter revolutions of those first decades; of the exodus; of the counter reactions; of the transitions; of the persecution days; of the plural marriage and the underground; of the miracle man, Joseph Smith, of whom we sing "Oh, what rapture filled his bosom, for he saw the living God!"; and of the giant colonizer and builder, Brigham Young, by whom this University was organized and for whom it was named.
>
> The story of Mormonism has never yet been written nor painted nor sculptured nor spoken. It remains for inspired hearts and talented fingers *yet* to reveal themselves. They must be faithful, inspired, active Church members to give life and feeling and true perspective to a subject so worthy. Such masterpieces should run for months in every movie center, cover every part of the globe in the tongue of the people, written by great artists, purified by the best critics.
>
> Our writers, our moving picture specialists, with the inspiration of heaven, should tomorrow be able to produce a masterpiece which would live forever. Our own

---

54. BYU *Daily Universe,* 13 December 1974.

talent, obsessed with dynamism from a CAUSE, could put into such a story life and heartbeats and emotions and love and pathos, drama, suffering, love, fear, courage, and the great leader, the mighty modern Moses who led a people farther than from Egypt to Jericho, who knew miracles as great as the stream from the rock at Horeb, manna in the desert, giant grapes, rain when needed, battles won against great odds. And the great miracle prophet, the founder of this University, would never die.

Take a Nicodemus and put Joseph Smith's spirit in him and what do you have? Take a daVinci or a Michelangelo or a Shakespeare and give him a total knowledge of the plan of salvation of God and personal revelation and cleanse him, and then take a look at the statues he will carve, and the murals he will paint, and the masterpieces he will produce. Take a Handel with his purposeful effort, his superb talent, his earnest desire to properly depict the story, and give him inward vision of the whole true story and revelation and what a master you have![55]

Providing Leadership in Political and Social Sciences

In the field of humanities, BYU textbooks should have the same ennobling objectives President Kimball yearned for in the fine arts. This is also true of the social sciences. Certainly, in the field of sociology, BYU teachers should be able to give powerful insight into the consequences that flow from righteous as well as iniquitous practices that have existed in the civilizations of the past. In the field of political science, President John Taylor has advised that "the elders of Israel [should] . . . understand that they have something to do with the world politically as well as religiously, that it is as much their duty to study correct political principles as well as religious."[56] He also said, "Besides the preaching of the Gospel, we have another mission, namely, the perpetuation of the

---

55. Spencer W. Kimball, *Education for Eternity* (Provo, Utah: Brigham Young University Press, 1967), pp. 18-19.
56. *Journal of Discourses,* 9:340.

free agency of man and the maintenance of liberty, freedom, and the rights of man."[57]

Improving Teaching Methods

Just as the school will need to write its own textbooks, it will need to discover and institute new and more effective methods of teaching. As William E. Berrett expressed it, "With the type of students drawn to BYU, experimentation with many new methods of learning, away from the traditional lockstep methods, is not only possible but will become a must."[58] Hollis Scott, University archivist, has noted that "The advent of video disc, new improvements in computer science, the laser beam, automation, and new energy sources will open up new vistas of learning and dissemination of knowledge."[59]

Continuing Education

During its second century of operation, BYU must fulfill to an even greater extent its slogan that "The World Is Our Campus." There are unlimited possibilities for its expansion. The program must utilize more and more local LDS leadership in all parts of the world, supplementing leadership from the Provo campus. According to William E. Berrett, this means organization of courses by BYU professors to be taught by local talent for college credit in many areas of the world. It may become quite different from personal correspondence courses (which should be continued) and quite different from the semester abroad programs which involve only BYU students. The program should probably involve an expansion of services similar to those carried on in BYU off-campus centers.[60]

---

57. Ibid., 23:63.
58. William E. Berrett to Ernest L. Wilkinson, March 1975, Wilkinson Presidential Papers.
59. Hollis Scott to Ernest L. Wilkinson, 25 March 1975, Wilkinson Presidential Papers.
60. William E. Berrett to Ernest L. Wilkinson, March 1975, Wilkinson Presidential Papers.

Expansion of the role of Continuing Education will accommodate national trends: "Recent government statistics show that between 1969 and 1972, the rate of increase in numbers of collegiate part-time students was three and one-half times as great as for full-time students. In 1972, 57.5 percent of all postsecondary students were attending school on a part-time basis."[61]

In the opinion of Dr. Dean A. Peterson, administrative assistant to President Dallin H. Oaks, "Many additional overseas BYU Centers should be established to help fill worldwide educational needs. BYU will be a world center of excellence."[62] Ben E. Lewis, executive vice-president of BYU, is enthusiastic about the prospects for BYU's Continuing Education program:

> The work of our University professors through the organization of Continuing Education in developing programs and taking them to the people where the end product is to teach them to read and write is having remarkable results. The teaching of English as a second language will provide means for communication which should help people to have greater understanding and to live at peace with each other.[63]

Ezra Taft Benson Agriculture and Food Institute

With the establishment of the Ezra Taft Benson Agriculture and Food Institute, the University is now ready to render greater service than its past facilities permitted. As Vice-President Ben Lewis suggests: "The University has great opportunity through research activities to provide information and instruction as related to making the soil productive and promoting the adoption of sound health practices. In close cooperation with the Church missionary and welfare services

61. Stanley A. Peterson to Ernest L. Wilkinson, 20 March 1975, Wilkinson Presidential Papers.
62. Dean A. Peterson to Ernest L. Wilkinson, 1 April 1975, Wilkinson Presidential Papers.
63. Ben E. Lewis to Ernest L. Wilkinson, 18 March 1975, Wilkinson Presidential Papers.

Ezra Taft Benson, President of the Quorum of the Twelve Apostles of the LDS Church. The recently established Ezra Taft Benson Agriculture and Food Institute was named in his honor.

there are unlimited opportunities to better the lives of people to the point of making them far more meaningful."[64]

Based on the inspired programs of the Church which founded and maintain BYU, the Agriculture and Food Institute will assist the countries of the world in making better use of their agricultural resources to feed a growing population without restricting the size of individual families. The Institute will support the words of the Lord as reflected by President Benson in a speech given on 23 September 1975 when his name was given to the Institute:

> Throughout the world — and I have seen most of it — there are vast resources waiting to be used for the betterment of mankind. *The objective of this institute is to use the human, physical, and spiritual resources of BYU to help the people of the world help themselves improve their quality of life. . . .*
>
> The institute will be an agency of experimentation whereby the agricultural resources of the various lands can be evaluated, new technology applied, nutritional needs studied. Then, the beneficial results of this research can be implemented at the proper time through the worldwide priesthood channels of the Church, correlated through existing developing welfare services programs.
>
> In this manner, the delivery system for these programs will enjoy the effectiveness of the priesthood leadership throughout the world. The people will be taught to help themselves. And that is a vital part of God's plan.[65]

The philosophy of President Benson finds support in the words of the Lord:

> For, behold, the beasts of the field and the fowls of the air, and that which cometh of the earth, is ordained for the use of man for food and for raiment, and that he might have in abundance. (D & C 49:19.)

---

64. Ibid.
65. *See* "Y Food Institute Created to Fill Wide Church Needs," BYU *Daily Universe,* 24 September 1975.

> And I have made the earth rich, and behold it is my footstool. (D & C 38:17.)

His views also receive corroboration and support from a book entitled *Population, Resources, and the Future,* edited by three professors at BYU (Howard M. Bahr, Bruce A. Chadwick, and Darwin L. Thomas).[66] One of the chapters of the book, entitled "Prospects for Abundance: The Food-Supply Question," is written by Dr. Philip F. Low, professor of agronomy at Purdue University. Dr. Low says, "A common statement is that the world is or will soon be overpopulated. In considering this statement, it is legitimate to ask the questions: overpopulated with reference to what, and according to whose values or ethics?"[67] According to Dr. Low,

> There are about 7.8 billion acres of potentially arable (cultivatable) land in the world, of which more than half, about 4.4 billion acres, are not yet cultivated (President's Science Advisory Committee, 1967:405-469; Kellogg and Orvedal, 1968:14-17). These figures are conservative and do not include land that could be brought under cultivation if desalinized sea water or soil-warming systems were available.[68]

In Dr. Low's view, "The technology exists or can be developed to produce enough food for the world's people both now and in the foreseeable future. The real question is whether or not we will take advantage of this technology. In other words, providing food for all mankind is more a matter of will than of ability."[69]

The interest of the Institute extends beyond the better production of food. It has already sent a task force of nine volunteers under the leadership of Lon J. Wallace to

---

66. This is the type of book which it is contemplated will be continually written by members of the BYU faculty over the next one hundred years.
67. Howard M. Bahr, Bruce A. Chadwick, and Darwin L. Thomas, *Population, Resources, and the Future* (Provo, Utah: Brigham Young University Press, 1972), p. 75.
68. Ibid., p. 65.
69. Ibid., p. 78.

Guatemala to assist in reconstructing buildings devastated by the recent earthquake in which more than 2,000 persons were killed, of which 15 were LDS Church members, and in which more than 3,000 persons were injured and left homeless. This small contingent plans to build between twenty-five and forty one-room homes for the survivors. This is only a small indication of what the Church, with its devoted concept of voluntary service, could do in the future.[70]

Better Opportunities for Women

Brigham Young University has always been a leader in providing educational opportunities for women. Anticipating modern educational thought, the school provided coeducational training from its beginning. Brigham Young declared that if he had to choose between the education of his daughters and his sons, he would choose to educate his daughters for they would have the most influence in training the rising generations.[71]

Over the years, women have been admitted to all the academic programs on the BYU campus. Women have graduated in agriculture, animal husbandry, and preveterinary programs.[72] Except where donors have placed certain restrictions on their gifts, scholarships and grants are open to women as well as to men. Surprisingly enough, women were participants in intercollegiate athletic teams at BYU before men. At the present time there are more single women on the BYU campus than men. Women are also employed along with men on the building and grounds crews.

While women students at BYU are taught that their most important mission in life is to be mothers and to raise a Christian family, they are also given vocational and professional training to enrich their family activities and provide them with marketable skills. As President Oaks has observed,

---

70. "Guatemala Volunteers Doing Well, Reports Say," BYU *Daily Universe,* 25 May 1976.
71. *See* Volume 1, p. 191.
72. BYU does not have a veterinary school.

> One of the most important purposes of a university education is to prepare men and women to be responsible and intelligent leaders and participants in the life of their families, in their Church and in their communities. That kind of education is needed by young men and women alike. . . . We make no distinction between young men and young women in our conviction about the importance of an education and in our commitment to providing that education.[73]

With the added attention now being given to women, BYU will undoubtedly originate many programs of special interest to them.

Scientific Goals

In earlier years the University did not have the funds for proper scientific research, and until the advent of the Carl F. Eyring Center in 1950 there were very few facilities. At its dedication on 17 October 1950, Dean Eyring commented that within that very building some student might discover the cure for leukemia, from which Eyring was slowly dying at the time (he passed away on 3 January 1951). Now, practically all areas of science and engineering have good laboratory facilities at BYU.

School of Social Work

While the matter was never resolved by formal action, the Board of Trustees at one time during the Wilkinson Administration favored the establishment of a College of Social Work — one whose graduates would exemplify the standards and ideals of the Church in this area to rely more on self, the family, and Church rather than on government. Because of other commitments and a lack of trained persons in the Church available at that time to be on the faculty, no action was taken on the establishment of this school. But with the

---

73. Dallin H. Oaks, "Statement on the Education of Women at Brigham Young University," 9 September 1975, BYU Archives.

increased reliance by other schools of social service on the government, it is possible that consideration may be given to this proposal in the future unless it is felt that an Institute of Behavorial Sciences or some other educational program would better serve the purposes of the Church. The proposed school would be in partnership with the home and help to establish the sanctity and responsibility of family life.

Improved Moral and Intellectual Standards

The editors of this Centennial History think it is safe to say that the moral and intellectual climate of the University has continually improved during the school's first one hundred years and that during the University's next one hundred years it will undoubtedly improve and continue to refine itself. William E. Berrett wrote in 1975:

> BYU in the future will become more and more distinctive as to its student body. The contrast with other universities as to moral standards will become more marked. With the screening of admissions made possible by the curtailment of numbers, the intellectual level of BYU students should gain national and international recognition.[74]

In 1952, shortly before his death, Dr. John A. Widtsoe wrote in his book *In a Sunlit Land:* "If the BYU fulfills its destiny it will more and more draw students from the whole world to seek revealed truth and worthwhile practical knowledge. Its message must be given to all people. The BYU must look up to the skies; it must have the courage to challenge, if needs be, the whole world."[75] During the Wilkinson Administration alone, students from 106 foreign countries and all states of the Union registered at the Y. They will come from more countries in the future. Those who are members of the Church will, on their return to their homes, provide leadership for the Church; others will be ambassadors of good will

---

74. William E. Berrett to Ernest L. Wilkinson, March 1975, Wilkinson Presidential Papers.
75. John A. Widtsoe, *In a Sunlit Land* (Salt Lake City: Deseret News Press, 1952), p. 96.

who will make it easier to establish the Church in their countries.

Views of President Oaks As to the Future

In a recent memorandum requested by the editors, President Oaks gave his views about the future of BYU:

> As I look ahead to the Second Century of BYU, and feel the momentum and direction of present growth, I see the University holding to its present spiritual and educational ideals, and increasing its effectiveness in the education of our young people. But the most important growth in the stature and performance of the University in the Second Century will be in the area of research and creative work — pushing back the frontiers of knowledge, especially in areas of preeminent importance for the Church and Kingdom of God. The Wilkinson administration took the first steps toward that goal in building the physical plant, strengthening the faculty, and beginning the creation of several special research entities to encourage faculty creative work and to provide an administrative organization to manage that work apart from the formal academic departments and colleges, though the relations with those departments and colleges must remain close. Thus, the formation of the Research Division was an extremely important step. We took a further step in that direction by naming Leo Vernon as an Assistant Academic Vice-President for Research, and by establishing a pattern in which our various research entities — especially those whose operations affect more than one college — report to Vernon on their research activities. Your [Wilkinson's] establishment of the Center for Business and Economic Research, the Charles Redd Center for Western Studies (just being established as I became president), and the Language Research Center were examples of the early development of research entities. . . .
>
> The establishment of the Law School, which bridged our administrations, is another event of immense importance in terms of the research and creative role of Brigham Young University in the Second Century. I have always believed that the role of the Law School in assem-

> bling a faculty and stimulating top legal scholarship by persons spiritually committed to our form of government and to the interests of the Kingdom of God would turn out to be just as important as a contribution to our government and the Kingdom as its role in training the graduates of the Law School. I see the Law School as a giant research institute in law.

President Oaks then outlined in a modest way some of the research activities initiated in his short administration:

> The Institute of Ancient Studies was organized to provide a focus for scholarship on ancient documents of great religious significance.
>
> The Center for Religious Studies has just been formed to give better coordination and focus to the activities previously carried on by the Institute of Mormon Studies and the Book of Mormon Institute, which were established during the Wilkinson administration, and to the Richard L. Evans Chair of Christian Understanding, established during my administration.
>
> A Family Research Center was established about two years ago in connection with the College of Social Sciences and the College of Family Living in order to provide research in the institution and structure of the family and other family-related topics.
>
> The Graduate School of Management will provide a special research focus that will provide in the field of management (of obvious importance to the increasingly complex and worldwide Church) the same kind of research impetus that the Law School will provide in its sphere. . . .
>
> During the past year we approved and announced a Center for Communications Research, which will sponsor basic research into the theory and practice of communication of ideas, not just across cultures (as some aspects of the Language Research Center do) but within a common culture.
>
> We have just obtained Trustee approval of . . . an Institute of Education, to be established in connection with the College of Education . . . to serve as an organizational

vehicle and stimulus for research into the theory of learning and the practice of teaching with special emphasis on the teaching of moral values, and also to serve as an organizational home for certain activities . . . dealing with instructional research, evaluation, and testing.

We are currently giving some serious administrative consideration to . . . some type of Institute for Research in the Behavioral Sciences. This would serve as a focus for the kind of basic behavioral research that we need in order to provide the scientific basis and experience necessary to construct and use a unique Mormon approach to human behavior, which would have immense ramifications in the teaching and practice of many disciplines.[76]

President Spencer W. Kimball's Second Century Address

On 10 October 1975 the principal address commemorating the founding of Brigham Young University was given by President Spencer W. Kimball, President of the LDS Church, at the Centennial Founders Day Convocation. This was a comprehensive statement of the purposes and destiny of BYU. President Kimball reiterated the Latter-day Saint belief

---

76. It is obvious that the editor of this history is pleased with the views of President Oaks, for as a young student editor in 1921 the editor wrote in *White and Blue,* which was then the student newspaper, "Brigham Young University should be the great Church laboratory for social . . . work. The scope of social service work should be enlarged and the entire population of the Church should be influenced directly by what the school is doing. The best teachers in the Church — experts in different lines of work — should be brought here to reinforce the now loyal faculty. If the Church wants scientific and authoritative treatises of its social and other problems, it should then submit them to the heads of the various departments for investigation. In this way the Church, as a whole, as well as Y students, would reap direct benefits (*White and Blue,* 5 January 1921). Whether these institutes will fulfill the objectives suggested by the young editor of *White and Blue* fifty-five years ago, or the more sophisticated and meaningful proposals of President Oaks today, only time will tell. There may be other programs which will be originated by the First Presidency and General Authorities which will be much more productive in achieving the ultimate destiny of BYU.

in education by quoting from the founder of this institution:

> Learn everything that the children of men know, and be prepared for the most refined society upon the face of the earth, then improve on this until we are prepared and permitted to enter the society of the blessed — the holy angels, that dwell in the presence of God.[77]

Making it plain that this education must be well-rounded education, he quoted from President David O. McKay:

> The university is not a dictionary, a dispensary, nor is it a department store. It is more than a storehouse of knowledge and more than a community of scholars. The University life is essentially an exercise in thinking, preparing, and living.

Adding to this educational concept, President Kimball said:

> We do not want BYU ever to become an educational factory. It must concern itself with not only the dispensing of facts, but with the preparation of its students to take their place in society as thinking, thoughtful, and sensitive individuals who, in paraphrasing the motto of your Centennial, come here dedicated to love of God, pursuit of truth, and service to mankind.[78]

Stressing the divine responsibility of the faculty at BYU, he stated:

> The faculty has a double heritage which they must pass along: the secular knowledge that history has washed to the feet of mankind with the new knowledge brought by scholarly research — but also the vital and revealed truths that have been sent to us from heaven. . . .
>
> Your double heritage and dual concerns with the secular and the spiritual require you to be "bi-lingual." As LDS scholars you must speak with authority and excellence to your professional colleagues in the language of

---

77. Spencer W. Kimball, *Second Century Address* (Provo, Utah: Brigham Young University Press, 1975), p. 5.
78. Ibid., p. 6.

Spencer W. Kimball,
President of the LDS
Church and the BYU Board
of Trustees since 1973.

> scholarship, and you must also be literate in the language of spiritual things.[79]

Placing great emphasis on the Christian uniqueness of the University, he declared:

> We expect . . . that Brigham Young University will "become a leader among the great universities of the world." To that expectation I would add — Become a unique university in all the world![80]
>
> BYU is being made even more unique, not because what we are doing is changing, but because of the general abandonment by other universities of their efforts to lift the daily behavior and morality of their students. . . .
>
> This University is not of the world any more than the Church is of the world, and it must not be made over in the image of the world.[81]

Making it plain that the faculty must be men of faith, he quoted from President John Taylor:

> Whatever you do, be careful in your selection of teachers. We do not want infidels to mold the minds of our children. They are a precious charge bestowed upon us by the Lord, and we cannot be too careful in rearing and training them. I would rather have my children taught the simple rudiments of a common education by men of God, and have them under their influence, than have them taught in the most abtruse sciences by men who have not the fear of God in their hearts.[82]

Referring directly to the educational objective which BYU must envision for the future, he urged that it strive to become "an educational Everest":

> There are many ways in which BYU can tower above other universities — not simply because of the size of its student body or its beautiful campus — but because of the

---

79. Ibid., pp. 1-2.
80. Ibid., p. 11.
81. Ibid., p. 3.
82. Ibid., p. 5.

> unique light BYU can send forth into the educational world. Your light must have a special glow, for while you will do many things in the programs of this University that are done elsewhere, these same things can and must be done better here than others do them. You will also do some special things here that are left undone by other institutions.[83]

Applying this to the curriculum of the University, he urged that BYU

> become the last remaining bastion of resistance to the invading ideologies that seek control of curriculum as well as classroom. We do not resist such ideas because we fear them, but because they are false.[84]

As the need for industry and patience in the pursuit of excellence continues on the BYU campus, and elsewhere in the educational system, President Kimball commented that

> We must remember the great lesson taught to Oliver Cowdery who desired a special outcome — just as we desire a remarkable blessing and outcome for BYU in the Second Century. Oliver Cowdery wished to be able to translate with ease and without real effort. He was reminded that he erred, in that he 'took no thought save it was to ask' (D&C 9:7). We must do more than ask the Lord for excellence. Perspiration must precede inspiration; there must be effort before there is excellence. We must do more than pray for these outcomes at BYU, though we must surely pray. We must take thought. We must make effort. We must be patient. We must be professional. We must be spiritual. Then, in the process of time, this will become the fully anointed University of the Lord about which so much has been spoken in the past.[85]

He also emphasized the need for linguists:

> One peak of educational excellence that is highly relevant to the needs of the Church is the realm of language. BYU

83. Ibid., p. 1.
84. Ibid., p. 2.
85. Ibid., p. 8.

> should become the acknowledged language capital of the world in terms of our academic competency and through the marvelous "laboratory" that sends young men and women forth to service in the mission field. I refer, of course, to the Language Training Mission. There is no reason why this University could not become the place where, perhaps more than anywhere else, the concern for literacy and the teaching of English as a second language is firmly headquartered in terms of unarguable competency as well as deep concern.[86]

Referring to the present loss of freedom by many universities because of their reliance on the government for monetary support and guidance rather than reliance on the Lord for spiritual direction, President Kimball stated:

> Too many universities have given themselves over to such massive federal funding that they should not wonder why they have submitted to an authority they can no longer control. Far too many no longer assume that nations are responsible to heaven for the acts of the state. Far too many now see the Rights of Man as merely access rights to the property and money of others, and not as the rights traditionally thought of as being crucial to our freedom.
>
> He noted that the labors of the past are not sufficient:
>
> It will take just as much sacrifice and dedication to preserve these principles in the second century of BYU, and even more than were required to begin this institution in the first place — when it was once but a grade school, and then an academy supported by a stake of the Church. If we were to abandon our ideals, would there be any left to take up the torch of some of the principles I have attempted to describe?[87]

He warned that it "would require more sacrifice and dedication to preserve" the objectives and standards of BYU in the second century than "required to begin the institution." He suggested that this "can sometimes be done by sharing our

---

86. Ibid., p. 9.
87. Ibid., pp. 7-8.

concerns with thoughtful scholars who share our concerns" and thus "multiply our influence and give hope to others who may assume they are alone." But he warned that in other situations "in order to be unique in the years that lie ahead" we may have to break with certain patterns of the educational establishment." "Our scholars, therefore, must be sentries as well as teachers." Characteristic of other addresses he has made, he therefore urged the administration, faculty, and students to lengthen their stride, quicken their pace, and continue their journey, for "dreams are never self-executing."

He urged that those associated with this University must keep themselves seaworthy and sailing, especially with reference to the centers of research that have been established on this campus, ranging from family and language research, on through to research on food, agriculture, and ancient studies, as well as translation projects. He said that "Much more needs to be done," but that the school "must 'not run faster or labor more than you have strength and means provided' (D&C 10:4)":[88]

> I see even more than was the case nearly a decade ago [when he then spoke to the faculty] a widening gap between this University and other universities both in terms of purposes and in terms of directions. Much has happened in the intervening eight years to make that statement justifiable. More and more is being done, as I hoped it would, to have here "the greatest collection of artifacts, records, writings . . . in the world."[89]

President Kimball predicted that "There will rise brilliant stars in drama, literature, music, sculpture, painting, science, and in all the scholarly graces. This University can be the refining host for many such individuals who will touch men and women the world over long after they have left this campus."[90] He quoted Brigham Young as stating that there is "no music in hell," from which he insisted that our art must be

88. Ibid., p. 5.
89. Ibid., p. 4.
90. Ibid.

the kind which edifies man, which takes into account his immortal nature, and which prepares him for heaven, not hell.[91]

To achieve the University's purposes in the second century he warned that BYU must be patient. Just as the City of Enoch took decades to reach its pinnacle of performance in what the Lord described as occurring "in the process of time (Moses 7:21)," so he said the quest for excellence at BYU must also occur "in the process of time."[92]

He also urged that to accomplish its objectives the Y must be kept free as a university; that state and federal governments and people are better served by free colleges and universities than by institutions that are compliant out of fears over funding. Quoting President Wilkinson that "attendance at BYU is a privilege and not a right, and . . . students who attend must expect to live its standards or forfeit the privilege,"[93] President Kimball noted that "because fewer [in percentage of total Church membership] will attend BYU [in the future], its obligation will be greater"; that many of its objectives are now "hidden from our immediate view" and will be until "we have climbed the hill just ahead of us."[94]

He assured his audience that the Church will continue to make greater use of BYU. Finally, he asserted that the institution cannot escape its rendezvous with history, as stated by President John Taylor:

> You will see the day that Zion will be as far ahead of the outside world in everything pertaining to learning of every kind as we are today in regard to religious matters.[95]

Cognizant that suggestions are often made to the President of the Church which do not seem compatible with the prophet's own inspiration, President Kimball made it plain that suggestions given in the right spirit are always

---

91. Ibid., p. 9.
92. Ibid., p. 4.
93. Ibid., p. 7.
94. Ibid., p. 9.
95. Ibid., p. 6.

welcome, but that only the prophet may set "the basic direction for this University":

> We want, through your administration, to receive all your suggestions for making BYU even better. I hope none will presume on the prerogatives of the prophets of God to set the basic direction for this University. No man comes to the demanding position of the Presidency of the Church except his heart and mind are constantly open to the impressions, insights, and revelations of God. No one is more anxious than the Brethren who stand at the head of this Church to receive such guidance as the Lord would give them for the benefit of mankind and for the people of the Church. Thus, it is important to remember what we have in the revelations of the Lord: "And thou shalt not command him who is at thy head, and at the head of the Church" (D&C 28:6)."[96]

The Road Ahead

As many at BYU have recognized, building a "unique" institution of higher learning is a prolonged and sometimes painful process. There is still a great difference between the destiny which the leaders of BYU have predicted and the present status of the school. BYU economics professor Clayne Pope has written:

> It is fine for us to remind ourselves of the destiny of the University, but we must understand the need for patient progress. We should soberly ask ourselves if we at BYU are committed to the trek or simply enthralled with the idea of a destiny.[97]

The editors of this history agree with this analysis and anticipate that there will be other Mount Everests to climb. The problems of the future may be different than those of the past, and, as President Kimball has said, their solution will

96. Ibid., p. 3. President Kimball's entire address and his dedication of the carillon tower, which occurred the same day, are found in the appendices to this volume.
97. Clayne Pope, "No Shortcuts to Greatness," *Monday Magazine*, 27 January 1975, p. 2.

The Carillon Bell Tower,
constructed as a part of
BYU's centennial
celebration. The tower is
symbolic of the University's
accomplishments during its
first one hundred years,
as well as its expectations
for the future.

require more "sacrifice and dedication" than those of the past. Nevertheless, in view of the past history of the institution the editors are of the conviction that under the leadership of the living prophets of the Church, Brigham Young University, as it enters its second century, has every expectation of demonstrating, through continuous effort, that it will measure up to the prophetic utterances made in its behalf — that it will continue to provide for its students "education for eternity."

Errata

1. The dust jacket, foreword, preface, and page 746 of the one-volume history stated that Brigham Young University is the largest private university in the country. This is repeated in the foreword and preface of Volume 1 of the four-volume history. It would have been more accurate to state that in terms of full-time students Brigham Young University is the largest private university in the country and that the Provo campus, in terms of full-time students, is the largest private campus in the country. Northeastern University in Massachusetts has more students, but a large percentage of them are part-time students, and they are scattered over three campuses.

2. The editors' attention has been called to the omission of the name of Dr. William J. Snow, distinguished professor of history, who served from 1904 to 1941, from the list of teachers on the faculty of BYU from 1876 to 1921 included in Volume 1 of the four-volume history. The editors regret this omission, for Dr. Snow was one of the stalwarts on the faculty.

3. The editors also discovered that Volume 1 of the four-volume history omits discussion of the second marriage of President George H. Brimhall. In 1885 he married, as his

second wife, Flora Robinson. Eight children resulted from this union: Dean R., Fay R., Fawn R., Ruth Afton, Paul R., Alta R., Golden H., and Arco R. When combined with the six children from George's first marriage, this made a total of fourteen Brimhall children.

4. During the time the history of BYU under President Howard S. McDonald was being written, the editor was never able to find a letter in which President McDonald summarized the accomplishments of his administration. The letter was thought to have been written in 1949, the year of his resignation. It now turns out that the letter, which was dated 22 April 1953, was addressed to Mrs. LaVieve H. Earl, who was an officer of the Alumni Association. This communication is included in Volume 4 as Appendix 45.

Appendices

Appendix 29
Biographical Sketches of Certain Important Figures in Recent BYU History

Recent Presidents of the BYU Board of Trustees

Heber Jeddy Grant was born in Salt Lake City on 22 November 1856, the son of Jedediah Morgan Grant and Rachel Ridgeway Ivins. His father, at the time mayor of Salt Lake City and second counselor in the First Presidency to President Brigham Young, lay dying of typhoid fever and what physicians then called "lung fever" (probably pneumonia). When Heber, his last child, was nine days old, "Jeddy" Grant succumbed at the age of forty. His death came at the beginning of a campaign he seemed to spearhead aimed at the "Reformation" and rededication of the Latter-day Saints.

Rachel Grant supported herself and her young son by sewing and taking in boarders. Though a frail youngster and economically handicapped, Heber determined early to accomplish whatever goals he might set for himself, as if he sensed in his paternal heritage the necessity to succeed. Whatever he undertook, whether it was baseball, singing, penmanship, or bookkeeping, the tall, thin boy was determined to master it. Indeed, his perseverance took on a legendary quality. By the age of nineteen he had obtained his first employment as bookkeeper and policy clerk for a Wells Fargo agent. A year later he purchased the "good will" of the agent's insurance agency in Salt Lake City and also became assistant cashier of Zion's Savings Bank and Trust Company in Salt Lake City.

In the meantime he had attended the Thirteenth Ward school in Salt Lake City and studied under Dr. John R. Park at the University of Deseret. A year following his marriage to Lucy Stringham in 1877, Heber J. Grant joined the faculty of the University of Deseret to teach penmanship and bookkeeping and to assist Dr. Park in the school's administration. His brief experience at the university profoundly influenced his outlook and future regard for education.

In the fall of 1880, at the early age of twenty-four, Heber Grant was sustained as President of the Tooele Stake of the LDS Church, a calling which took him from his business and teaching in Salt Lake City and one which recharted the course of his life. After two years in Tooele, Elder Grant was called in October 1882 as an apostle by President John Taylor.

In 1884 he married Augusta Winters (May 6) and Emily Wells (May 7). In 1897 he suffered acute appendicitis but survived the illness after a year's struggle. In the course of three years he buried two young sons and his first wife (Lucy). His third wife (Emily) died in 1908, leaving Heber and Augusta with ten daughters from the three families.

During the two decades following his appointment as an apostle, Elder Grant's assignments with the Quorum of the Twelve were enriched by extensive business involvements. During the depression of the early 1890s, he used his reputation and skill as a businessman to obtain loans for the Church and its related business activities at a time when banks were failing and credit was nearly impossible. He also encouraged the development of home industries and preached continually the ideals of hard work and sound personal management, both in temporal and spiritual affairs.

The First Presidency assigned Heber J. Grant in 1901 to open the Japanese Mission. After two years there, he was reassigned to the presidency of the European Mission, with headquarters in England, where he stayed an additional three years. Returning to Salt Lake City early in 1907, he again assumed his active role in business which had by then extended through virtually every facet of Utah finance and industry, including directorships and executive positions in such businesses as Zion's Cooperative Mercantile Institution, the insurance firm of Heber J. Grant & Company, the Salt Lake Herald Company, Provo Woolen Mills Company, the Deseret National Bank, the Salt Lake Theater Company, the Consolidated Wagon and Machine Company, and the Home Fire Insurance Company of Utah.

For ten years Elder Grant established a heavy routine of work divided between his ecclesiastical and business responsibilities. When, on 23 November 1916, he succeeded Francis M. Lyman as president of the Quorum of the Twelve, his Church leadership role became more pronounced; on 23 November 1918 he assumed the mantle of the prophet as successor to President Joseph F. Smith.

The administration of Heber J. Grant as president of the LDS Church spanned nearly twenty-seven years, longer than any President. It was a period of continual change and development as the Latter-day Saints moved more fully into the mainstream of American life and expanded internationally. President Grant gave particular emphasis to the Word of Wisdom and individual financial responsibility. President Grant, with his two counselors, David O. McKay and J. Reuben Clark, Jr., instituted the far-reaching Church Welfare System, which, perhaps more than anything else, contributed to a change of attitude in the United States toward the previously denigrated Latter-day Saints. But the President himself was another important element in this process of change as he traveled widely, lending his prestige and charm to the cause of the Church and its members.

Another important legacy of the Heber J. Grant era (which ended with his death on 14 May 1945) was involved in the growth and evolution of the Church Educational System. President Grant believed that Church schools had a mission of "making Latter-day Saints." Immediately after assuming the Church presidency, he instituted a series of changes in the Church school system, including the appointment of David O. McKay as Church commissioner of education, with Stephen L Richards and Richard R. Lyman as his counselors and Adam S. Bennion as superintendent, all of whom had had extensive educational experience. This professionalization of the system's management led to many improvements in the operation of the schools. He often expressed regret that he had little education himself.

After becoming president of the Board of Trustees of BYU, President Grant, on the recommendation of Elder Stephen L Richards and his assistants (President McKay was on a trip around the world), called Franklin S. Harris in April 1921 to head BYU, informing him of his wish that "this school . . . be all that it is possible to be, to be worthy of its founder, and to be worthy of the Church." The Grant era in Church history corresponded graphically with that of President Harris at BYU (1921-45), a period rich in growth and development because of the efforts and vision of both men.

Unfortunately, during President Grant's administration the Church experienced two serious depressions, the first in the early 1920s and the second the Great Depression which began in the late 1920s and continued during most of the 1930s. So serious was the financial impact of these crises on the Church that during the first one the Church closed most of its academies and during the second transferred all its junior colleges, excepting Ricks College in Idaho, to the states of Utah and Arizona.

But at BYU, President Grant supported the construction of a new library, which was subsequently named for him at its dedication in October 1926 during BYU's semicentennial celebration. The Heber J. Grant Library was a fitting monument to both the president's support of the institution and his love for books, thousands of which he gave to friends for their edification and pleasure. His generosity also caused him to make a number of donations to BYU. On the occasion of one such gift in 1938, he wrote: "I wish I could find a gold mine so that I could endow the Brigham Young University and it could double its capacity." BYU had few friends as firm and as dedicated as Heber Jeddy Grant.

George Albert Smith was the second son of Sarah Farr and John Henry Smith. Born 4 April 1870, the boy grew up in Salt Lake City. His grandfather, who lived nearby until his death in 1875, was Elder George A. Smith, cousin of the Prophet Joseph Smith, apostle, and first counselor to President Brigham Young. His father, John Henry Smith, followed his father into the Quorum of the Twelve in 1880 when George Albert was ten.

After attending ward schools in Salt Lake City, George Albert, at the age of twelve, went to board in Provo so he could study at Brigham Young Academy under Professor Karl G. Maeser. Though the economic burden of his father's mission call to England a year later cut short his experience at BYA, George Albert never forgot the winter he spent listening to the wisdom of the pioneer educator. "I love the memory of Brother Maeser," he wrote in 1928. "I think I have spoken of him more than any other man, perhaps, among those who have contributed to my education." After working at ZCMI and its clothing factory during his father's mission (1883-85), the fifteen-year-old returned to school, this time as a student of Dr. John R. Park at Deseret University. Despite his desire for learning and his love for books, George Albert's eye injury, suffered while he was traveling for ZCMI, forced him to forego a higher education beyond taking some law courses by correspondence.

George Albert Smith returned to ZCMI as a salesman after leaving school for good at the age of nineteen. His work took him through much of the West. In 1891, when he was twenty-one, he was called to be a missionary to the youth of Southern Utah in behalf of the Mutual Improvement Association.

Following his marriage to Lucy Emily Woodruff in the Manti Temple in May 1892, George Albert left on a mission to the Southern States, where he labored mostly in Tennessee under President J. Golden Kimball. Upon his return after two years in the mission field, he again found employment with ZCMI that lasted until January 1898 when he was appointed receiver of the

United States Land Office for Utah. He remained in that position until 8 October 1903, when President Joseph F. Smith called him to take a seat with his father on the Council of the Twelve Apostles.

His initial assignments as a member of the Twelve related to programs for the youth of the Church. Early in 1904 he was named to the general board of the YMMIA, a work which eventually brought him to the position of general superintendent of the organization in 1921. Elder Smith was excited about the development of the worldwide scouting movement and the founding in 1910 of the Boy Scouts of America. He worked closely with the National Council of the Boy Scouts of America, and scouting became an integral part of the Church program for boys. In 1931, Elder Smith was elected a member of the national executive board of the BSA; he was awarded the Silver Beaver award by the Salt Lake Council of the BSA in 1932 and the Silver Buffalo award of the National Council in 1934.

The young apostle was also active in the Sons of the American Revolution and the management and acquisition of Church historic sites. In February 1909 a severe illness struck that incapacitated him for two years and weakened him for the remainder of his life. His father, John Henry Smith, then serving as president of the Quorum of the Twelve, died on 13 October 1911.

Upon his recovery from illness, George Albert became an influential member of the international farmers movement, serving as president of the International Irrigation Congress (1916), of the International Dry Farm Congress (1917), and of the International Farm Congress (1918). In January 1919 he received a call from President Heber J. Grant to preside over the European Mission. After two years in Liverpool, he returned home to become general superintendent of the YMMIA. The next two decades were full of more travels and more honors for the now seasoned Church leader. In addition to his scouting awards, he was elected (1922) vice-president of the National Society of the Sons of the American Revolution and (1930) president of the Utah Pioneer Trails and Landmarks Association.

After the death of his wife in the fall of 1937, Elder Smith left on an extended tour of the missions in the South Pacific, returning the next summer to renew his activities but now without a companion. For five years he immersed himself in his duties, and in July 1943 he succeeded Elder Rudger Clawson as president of the Quorum of the Twelve. Two years later, on 14 May 1945, President Heber J. Grant died at his home in Salt Lake City, and George Albert Smith assumed the reins of leadership as eighth President of the Church, being sustained by the Twelve on May 21.

As President of the Church, George Albert Smith continued his wide travel. His administration was known for its extroverted flavor as President Smith extended his hand to a wealth of new friends during his term, including national political leaders. During the Church's pioneer centennial in 1947, he presided over a celebration that brought wide attention to the Church and its history. He also spent considerable time and effort seeing to the welfare of Church members scattered across areas of the globe that had been ravaged in World War II. Appealing for peace and brotherhood in a world increasingly plagued with distrust and fear, President Smith guided

Mormonism through a period of frightening world change. He died on 4 April 1951, his eighty-first birthday.

A few months after the death of President Smith, officials of the Church and Brigham Young University dedicated a new athletic facility in Provo, naming it the George Albert Smith Fieldhouse, after the late prophet. It was a fitting memorial to a man who loved young people. He was particularly anxious for the success and effectiveness of BYU. "I feel that the BYU is one of the greatest institutions in the Church," he said in 1949. Perhaps the most important event in his administration with regard to the Church Educational System was the appointment in 1950 of Dr. Ernest L. Wilkinson as president of Brigham Young University. Dr. Wilkinson accepted the challenging position because President Smith persuaded him that the First Presidency wanted the school "to become the greatest educational institution in the world."

David Oman McKay was born in Huntsville, Utah, on 8 September 1873, the son of David and Jennette Evelyn Evans McKay. Young David grew up in a religious atmosphere, as his father, though living in Huntsville, was bishop of Eden Ward for many years and was then bishop of Huntsville Ward. David O. McKay received his early education at the public school in his native Huntsville and at Weber Stake Academy in Ogden. Before entering the University of Utah, he taught at the Huntsville Elementary School for one year. The summer before entering the University he earned money by carrying the daily newspaper and mail by horseback sixteen miles to the mining town of La Plata, Utah. It was on these long rides that he memorized choice bits of literature which he used to such good effect in later life in his sermons.

In 1897 he was graduated from the University of Utah with a teaching certificate as president of his class and valedictorian. After his graduation he was called on a mission to Great Britain, where he served in the Scottish District. In 1898 he was selected president of that district.

On his release in 1900 he was appointed assistant superintendent of the Sunday School board of Weber Stake. While he held this office the stake initiated uniform preparation of lessons by preparation meetings, stake board visiting, and learning the fundamentals of outlining lessons. That same year he was appointed registrar and instructor in literature and pedagogy at Weber Stake Academy. He was made principal in 1902, which position he held until 1908.

In 1906, at the young age of thirty-three, he was called to be a member of the Council of the Twelve Apostles. During the same year he was called to be second assistant to President Joseph F. Smith as superintendent of the General Sunday School Board. He was named first counselor in 1909 and general superintendent from 1918 until 1934. Under his direction the gospel teaching features initiated in Weber Stake became general practice throughout the Sunday Schools of the Church.

In 1920 he began a year-long worldwide tour of the missions of the Church with President Hugh J. Cannon of Liberty Stake.

From 3 November 1922 to December 1924 he was president of the European Mission. At the same time he acted as president of the British

Mission. During this time the wave of antagonism toward the Church, which had been particularly noticeable in the newspapers, became modified, and the Church began taking roots in England and Europe. His concept of the Church as a worldwide institution, with Zion meaning the "pure in heart," began to take hold.

On 11 October 1934 he was sustained as second counselor to President Heber J. Grant in the First Presidency of the Church. On 21 May 1945 he was named second counselor to President George Albert Smith. On 30 September 1950 he was sustained as President of the Council of the Twelve Apostles, and on 9 April 1951 he was sustained as President of the Church.

Having been called to the Council of the Twelve when he was principal of a Church academy, David O. McKay was looked to in the councils of the Church for educational leadership. He was immediately appointed to the General Church Board of Education (1906). From 1908 to 1923 he was president of the board of trustees of Weber Academy, which became Weber Normal College, Weber College, and later, after having been transferred from the Church to the state, Weber State College. In 1919 he was named Church commissioner of education. A mosaic at the Church College of Hawaii (now BYU — Hawaii) shows him and President Hugh J. Cannon of Liberty Stake foretelling in 1920 the establishment of the Church College of Hawaii. He had the pleasure of dedicating it thirty-eight years later in Laie, Oahu, Hawaii.

President McKay was a regent of the University of Utah in 1921 and 1922 and a trustee of Utah State Agricultural College (Utah State University) in 1941. He received the Silver Buffalo award of the Boy Scouts of America in 1953, along with several honorary degrees — among them an M.A. degree from BYU in 1922, an LLD from Utah State Agricultural College in 1950, and a doctor of letters degree from both the University of Utah and Temple University in 1951. He was an honorary member of the International College of Surgeons.

He became President of the Board of Trustees of Brigham Young University in 1951, serving until the time of his death in 1970. It was during this time, and under his leadership, that Brigham Young University witnessed its most remarkable growth and achieved national and international recognition.

In 1951, Brigham Young University had 5,957 full-time students. In 1969 it had 27,220 full-time students, and the school had erected almost one hundred major buildings in that time span. On one occasion President Wilkinson wrote him that, except for his leadership and support, the school would never have made the remarkable progress which it did. During his administration the campus of Ricks College was greatly enlarged, and also the Church colleges of Hawaii and New Zealand were opened. Five schools were opened in Santiago, Chile; thirty-six elementary and two high schools were started in Mexico; and others were completed at Pago Pago and Tahiti. A Language Training Mission was established at BYU, Ricks, and the Church College of Hawaii during his administration.

While he was President he presided over the construction of more than 3,750 church building projects throughout the world, a number far greater than the total built by the Church during all the years of its existence prior to

1951. By the time of his death, an additional 650 buildings were under construction or in the planning stages. The buildings completed during his administration included five temples: Switzerland, Los Angeles, London, New Zealand, and Oakland. Three more were in the planning stages. Of the buildings constructed as of January 1970, more than 2,000 of them were ward and branch chapels. On the average, 204 were built per year. More than 90 were seminary and institute buildings. On the Brigham Young University campus in Provo more than 80 academic buildings and over 200 housing units were constructed.

President McKay died on 18 January 1970 at the age of ninety-six.

Joseph Fielding Smith, tenth President of The Church of Jesus Christ of Latter-day Saints, an apostle from 1910 until his death in 1972, served as a member of the Board of Trustees of Brigham Young University longer than any other member. His life spanned the time from the covered wagon days to the jet plane era. He found delight in flying and sometimes in taking over the controls of a military jet as honorary colonel and later as honorary brigadier general in the Utah Air National Guard, all this while he was in his eighties.

He was born in the lineage of prophets, his grandfather having been Hyrum Smith, brother of Joseph Smith. His father, Joseph F. Smith, was the sixth President of the LDS Church.

President Smith was an enthusiastic sponsor of the acquisition of the vast genealogical collection of vital data of the present Genealogical Society of the Church. From 1934 until 1964, he was the president of this society and its predecessor, the Genealogical Society of Utah. During those years the foundation was laid for the gathering of information in the United States and in foreign countries. The Society has become the largest depository of genealogical information in the world. Joseph Fielding Smith was the originator of the *Utah Genealogical and Historical Magazine,* published by the Society.

His zest for education began early in life and never abated. He was interested in many areas of education but particularly in religion. His associates asserted that he was the best doctrinarian and historian of the Church during his lifetime. On his eightieth birthday the Quorum of the Twelve referred to "his profound gospel writings," stating that "in his theological dissertations, he has given to his associates and to the Church a rich legacy which will immortalize his name among the faithful" *(Improvement Era)* 59, [July 1956]: 495). Twenty-five books came from his pen, including *The Way to Perfection; The Progress of Man; Essentials of Church History; Man, His Origin and Destiny;* three volumes of *Doctrines of Salvation* compiled by Bruce R. McConkie; and the five volumes of *Answers to Gospel Questions,* a compilation of articles appearing for many years in the *Improvement Era.*

His forthrightness, courage, and ability were well expressed in the following tribute from his Quorum associates in 1956:

> President Joseph Fielding Smith has inherited in rich measure the dauntless courage and the unswerving devotion to duty which have characterized the lives of his noble ancestors. For more than forty-six

> years as a member of the Council of the Twelve he has been a fearless defender of the faith and an untiring preacher of the gospel of repentance. In his vigorous denunciation of the theories of men which would negate the truths of the restored gospel, he has often drawn the criticism of some of the exponents of the theories he has assailed, but seldom has he failed to win the admiration and respect of his severest critics because of his scholarship and the consistency of his course, which is as undeviating as the stars of heaven. No one has ever had occasion to question where he stood on any controversial issue. (*Improvement Era,* 59 [July 1956]: 495.)

President Smith measured man's discovered knowledge by the yardstick of the scriptures. Although he did not always agree with the theories pronounced by educators, his desire was to see the youth of the Church receive an opportunity to become educated under optimum conditions. He believed that a balance should be struck between secular knowledge and spiritual insight obtained from an understanding of the scriptures.

In 1912 he became a member of the BYU Board of Trustees and in 1939 a member of the Executive Committee, continuing in that position until he became President of the Church in 1972. While he was chairman of the Executive Committee, President Smith met with President Wilkinson and his committee often to chart the way for BYU's phenomenal growth.

President Smith's interest in history began early in life and increased over the years. He rose from his position as an employee in the Church Historian's Office to become assistant Church historian and then Church Historian and Recorder, serving in the latter office for a period of almost fifty years. In 1966, BYU established an American church history collection in his honor.

Among the other awards received from BYU, he was given an honorary Doctor of Letters degree in 1951 and a Special Service Award in June 1960.

For many years he was in the presidency of the Salt Lake Temple, serving for a time as president. While President of the Church he laid the cornerstone for the Provo Temple and later gave the dedicatory prayer. The Ogden Temple was also dedicated during his presidency.

His fifty-three months as President brought many changes to the Church. Among the programs developed were meetinghouse libraries, teacher development, and the prospective elder program. Other developments included a restructured Social Services Department and a Department of Internal Communications to correlate programs and produce and distribute all manuals, handbooks, and Church magazines. The first area conference ever held by the Church was presided over by President Smith in London, England.

During his presidency the J. Reuben Clark Law School was announced for Brigham Young University.

President Joseph Fielding Smith's death on 2 July 1972 closed a life of dedication characterized by the love of the Lord, signified by keeping his commandments; by loyalty to the Prophet Joseph Smith and the gospel truths restored through him; and by his own gospel scholarship and spiritual insight, manifesting pure religion by example as well as by precept.

Harold Bingham Lee was born on 28 March 1899 in Clifton, Oneida County, Idaho, a son of Samuel Marion and Louise Emeline Bingham Lee. One of six children, he grew up on the family farm. He married Fern Lucinda Tanner on 14 November 1923 in the Salt Lake Temple. She died on 24 September 1962. He later married Freda Joan Jensen on 17 June 1963. President Lee had two daughters, Mrs. L. Brent (Helen) Goates, Salt Lake City, and Mrs. Ernest J. (Maurine) Wilkins, who died in 1966. The Lees had ten grandchildren.

President Lee attended the Oneida Stake Academy from 1912 to 1916 and Albion State Normal College, which later was merged with Idaho State University, receiving a teacher's certificate in 1917. He became principal of an Idaho school at the age of seventeen, and after further study at the University of Utah from 1922 to 1923, he became a principal in the Granite School District in Salt Lake City from 1923 to 1928.

He began his prominent Church career as a missionary in the Western States Mission from 1920 to 1922, serving most of the time as a conference (district) president. He later taught a youth group in Poplar Grove Ward, Pioneer Stake, was both ward and stake Sunday School superintendent, was Pioneer Stake superintendent of religion classes (now the Church seminary program), and served as a member of the Pioneer Stake high council, as a counselor in the stake presidency and as Pioneer Stake President.

President Lee resigned his school position in 1928 to become Intermountain manager for Foundation Press. He was appointed to the Salt Lake City Commission on 1 December 1932 and won reelection on 7 November 1933. Meanwhile, as stake president he had organized Pioneer Stake Bishop's Storehouse early in 1932 to care for the needy and unemployed of the Church within the stake. At the request of the Church's First Presidency and in recognition of his great welfare activities as president of the Pioneer Stake, he resigned from the city commission on 1 January 1937 to become managing director of the newly organized Church Welfare Program, a position he held for twenty-two years.

After his ordination as an apostle in April 1941, President Lee served the Church as chairman of the Military Relations Committee, as an adviser to the Primary and the Relief Society general boards, as chairman of the General Melchizedek Priesthood Committee, as adviser to the General Music Committee, as a member of the Executive Committee of the Brigham Young University Board of Trustees, and as chairman of the Correlation Executive Committee.

This prominent Church official was recognized with honorary degrees from all three major universities in Utah; he received an honorary Doctor of Humanities in 1953 from Utah State Agricultural College (now Utah State University), an honorary Doctor of Christian Service from Brigham Young University in 1955, and an honorary Doctor of Humanities degree from the University of Utah in 1965.

President Lee was an officer and director of several national and Utah business corporations. He was chairman of the board of Zion's First National Bank, first vice-chairman of the board of Beneficial Life Insurance Company, vice-chairman of the board of directors of Utah-Idaho Sugar Company, vice-chairman and director of ZCMI, vice-chairman and director of Zion's Securities Corporation, first vice-president and director of Deseret Management Corporation, director of Union Pacific Railroad, and director of the Equitable Life Assurance Society of the United States. He also served on the board of governors of the American Red Cross. In 1972, President Lee was elected chairman of the board of ZCMI, Beneficial Life Insurance Company, and Hotel Utah Company and was named director of Zion's Utah Bancorporation.

He was the author of a book, *Youth and the Church* (now called *Decisions for Successful Living)* which reprinted a series of radio talks over station KSL in Salt Lake City. He also wrote the books *Stand Ye in Holy Places* and *Ye Are the Light of the World.*

On 23 January 1970 he was called as first counselor to President Joseph Fielding Smith and was appointed President of the Council of the Twleve.

On Wednesday, 26 December 1973, shortly before 9:00 p.m., President Harold B. Lee died in the LDS Hospital in Salt Lake City of lung and heart arrest.

After the death of President Joseph Fielding Smith on 2 July 1972, President Harold B. Lee was ordained and set apart as the eleventh President of The Church of Jesus Christ of Latter-day Saints in the Salt Lake Temple, with President N. Eldon Tanner as first counselor and President Marion G. Romney as second counselor. President Spencer W. Kimball, who was called as President of the Council of the Twelve, was voice in ordaining and setting apart President Lee.

Although Harold B. Lee was President of the Church for less than eighteen months, the shortest administration in this dispensation, they were eighteen months of strong, vigorous activity. Many of the programs initiated during his administration will leave their mark on the Church and its members for years to come.

Spencer W. Kimball, born in Salt Lake City in 1895, was taken with his family to the Gila Valley in Arizona when he was three years old. His father, Andrew Kimball, had been called to preside over the St. Joseph Stake, which covered Southeastern Arizona and an adjacent area in New Mexico.

Andrew Kimball, by virtue of his position as stake president, also bore primary responsibility for the Church-operated academy, known as Gila Stake Academy, which provided high school training for the area. When Spencer grew older he attended this Academy. Each year he was class president and outstanding student. Despite his size he led the basketball team with his quickness and shooting ability. Upon graduation he served as a missionary in the Central States Mission, carved out of the old Indian Territory Mission. His father had for ten years been president of the Indian Territory Mission in Oklahoma and Missouri, visiting it periodically and then returning home to support his family. After his mission, Spencer returned to school, starting college at the University of Arizona. In the fall of 1917 he decided to transfer to BYU.

As he stepped off the train at Provo he hoped to save a little money by lugging his baggage to the University. When he finally neared the building, exhausted, he was startled to see strange-looking men, dressed in drab clothes, tending the grounds. Two or three seemed to peer at him from behind the bushes. He then remembered that the state mental hospital was also in Provo. He had been about to register at the wrong institution.

His attendance at BYU lasted only a few weeks; he received a physical examination and notice to report back to Arizona for induction into the army. While he waited for his contingent to be activated, Spencer courted and married Camilla Eyring. Her family had moved to Arizona after being driven from the Mormon colonies in Mexico by the revolution of 1912. She later went to BYU to finish high school and to qualify as a home economics teacher. In the fall of 1917 she had returned to Arizona to teach at Gila Stake Academy.

After their marriage, Spencer obtained a job working as a bank teller while he waited for his contingent to be called up, but the war ended without his being called to serve. He worked for a number of years in banks as teller, branch manager, and assistant cashier. In 1927 he left to establish an insurance and realty firm.

Immediately after his marriage, Spencer was called to serve as his father's stake clerk. He also served on the board of education of Gila Junior College. When his father died in 1924, Spencer was made a counselor to the new stake president. He continued to be deeply involved in the affairs of the college until the Church turned it over to the State of Arizona during the Great Depression. In 1936, Melvin J. Ballard came to divide the St. Joseph Stake, and he called Spencer to be the first president of the new Mt. Graham Stake, which extended from Safford, Arizona, to El Paso, Texas, 250 miles away.

In 1943, Spencer received a telephone call from J. Reuben Clark, Jr., counselor in the First Presidency, informing him that he had been called as a member of the Quorum of the Twelve Apostles. The news left him shaken, wondering about his competence to fill so important a role. Yet he was willing to respond with his full energies to any call from President Heber J. Grant. At age forty-eight he uprooted his family and moved to Salt Lake City from Arizona, becoming the first General Authority to be called from so far away.

From the beginning of his service as a General Authority he renewed contact with BYU and was appointed a member of the Board of Trustees in 1950, just before the beginning of the administration of Ernest L. Wilkinson. He has given both presidents Wilkinson and Oaks his inspirational support.

From the beginning of his tenure as an apostle he filled assignments to speak to the faculty and student body. Probably no speaking assignments caused him more anxiety since he felt a need to bring a message of substance suitable for his audience. The fact that he had not himself been able to finish college left him feeling somewhat self-conscious and concerned that some critical people might discount his message for this irrelevant reason, despite the fact that his extensive self-education represented a much greater accomplishment than a few years of formal training. Despite his fears, his addresses were among the most influential given during his tenure as an apostle. "A Style of Our Own" called for modesty and resulted in a rush to "Kimballize" bare-shouldered or low-cut evening gowns. "Tragedy or Destiny" explored the puzzle of what seems to mortals to be untimely death.

"John and Mary" posed for young people the challenge of keeping themselves chaste for marriage and preparing for family life. "Education for Eternity" spelled out the great role and prophetic future of BYU. It gave the school a new compass by which to measure its future.

In 1969, Spencer received an honorary doctorate from BYU. This recognition gave him great pleasure, representing to him acceptance by the educational community, despite his jeremiads. Honorary degrees from other institutions followed.

When he had the time, he loved to read and study. During his recuperation from a major heart attack in 1949 he created a scroll which extended across the room on which he correlated for his own better understanding the lines of secular and religious history from the beginning. He encouraged his wife to continue taking college and institute classes through the years, despite other claims on her time. He valued education for his family. His daughter and three sons have ten college degrees among them. Three of the four are teachers, one in primary education and two as law professors (one at BYU). Their parents simply expected them to excel and gave every support to their academic pursuits. Even so, Spencer always felt concern that their intellectual life should not become an intellectualism which had no place for faith. He felt that academic learning and faith in God could enhance one another, but he had no doubt about which was the more important.

His efforts at writing turned primarily toward preparation of sermons, but he did devote his spare time for years to preparation of *The Miracle of Forgiveness,* which is a profound dissertation on the process of repentance.

In December 1973, upon the death of Harold B. Lee, Spencer W. Kimball became the twelfth President of the LDS Church. No man has had such an inpact on the Church in such a short time. Because of air transportation he has been able to travel much more than a million miles in his calling. His time as President of the Church has seen a burgeoning of area conferences, with meetings in South America, the Far East, the South Pacific, Europe, and Australia. New temples have been announced for South America, Asia, and the American Northwest. Under his leadership the First Quorum of Seventy has been reactivated. Oriental, European, and American Indian General Authorities have been named. A new vision of international missionary work was opened up, with a sudden major increase in the number of missionaries serving full-time missions (there are now approximately 23,000 of them) and an emphasis on making it possible for saints to serve missions in their own countries, where they already know the language and the culture. A series of solemn assemblies have been held to call upon priesthood leaders for renewed dedication to living and teaching the gospel.

Few men have dealt so well with the adversity of ill health, including, among other illnesses, a major heart attack, cancer of the throat requiring removal of one and part of the other vocal cord, leaving him with a tenuous voice; and open heart surgery. His uncomplaining attitude leaves most people unaware of his condition, even when he can barely stand the pain. Indeed, the most striking characteristic of President Kimball is his seemingly inexhaustible reservoirs of strength. Few if any Church leaders ever worked as tirelessly in formal Church work and in individual counseling.

Throughout his life his stamina has been legendary. Even at the age of eighty he continues to set a fast tempo for his brethren, urging them to lengthen their stride and quicken their pace.

Wives of Recent Presidents of BYU

F. Estella Spilsbury Harris, wife of President Franklin S. Harris, served as first lady of Brigham Young University for twenty-four years. She fully supported her husband in his responsibilities and always managed her household affairs so that she could attend campus functions. She was likewise dedicated to the Utah State Agricultural College at Logan, Utah, for the five years her husband served as president there. The care which she gave her children, while at the same time carrying on her duties outside the home, is attested by the rectitude of their lives.

Sister Harris was born in Toquerville, Utah, on 17 February 1884, to George Moroni and Roselia Haight Spilsbury. There were twelve children in the family. She enjoyed the labors and joys of living in a small community in a closely knit family group. All members shared in pioneer tasks of living — drying fruit, carrying water from the ditch, washing, ironing, and cleaning — as they also shared enjoyment in picnics, horseback riding, candy pulls, and barn dances. The everyday life was appreciated, but Estella had fixed her mind on achieving a goal in education that she continued to pursue throughout her life. She rejoiced when she was able to attend a graded school in Sandy, Utah. She also attended the Branch Normal School in Cedar City. She enlarged her abilities by studying dressmaking and music in Salt Lake City until she became ill with typhoid fever. Estella recovered, but a brother and sister died from typhoid. Only six of the twelve children lived to adulthood.

In 1905, Estella entered Brigham Young University. She was a good student and also was active in social and cultural groups. In 1907 she graduated with a Kindergarten Normal Diploma and taught school for one year in Price, Utah.

The next year she married Franklin Harris; their romance had begun at BYU. They had a family of two sons and four daughters. Their oldest son, Franklin Stewart Harris, Jr., is presently doing upper air research for NASA in Hampton, Virginia. He married Maurine Steed after his first wife, Mabel Bost Harris, died. Franklin, Jr., has distinguished himself by writing numerous articles and publications. The other son, Chauncey Dennison Harris, was a Rhodes Scholar and is now vice-president for academic resources at the University of Chicago. Married to Edith Young, he also has published several scientific articles and written books.

The four daughters are Arlene (Mrs. Roscoe A. Grover) of Salt Lake City, who has a master's degree in English and a library certificate; Helen (Mrs. Ralph W. Jenson) of Lafayette, California; Leah (Mrs. Vernon D. Jenson) of Pocatello, Idaho; and Mildred (Mrs. Ralph O. Bradley) of Salt Lake City.

Much credit for her children's success must go to the teachings and training of Sister Harris. She held up the goal of a college education to them and set them a proper example by graduating from Brigham Young University with a bachelor of science degree in 1941 along with her youngest daughter.

She was widely traveled, sacrificing her own ease to accompany her husband on his studies and travels for some years as adviser to the government of Iran and as director of the American program in that country.

Sister Harris was a devoted Latter-day Saint. She served faithfully in Church positions; she supported cultural activities, sharing her knowledge through book reviews and travel lectures; and she was a fine example to young women.

She died in 1973 at the age of eighty-nine.

Ella Gibbs McDonald was a woman who looked "well to the ways of her household," and President McDonald could echo the words of Proverbs: "The heart of her husband doth safely trust in her" (Proverbs 31:11).

She was born on 5 July 1894 on a farm just north of Brigham City in Box Elder County, Utah, the oldest in a family of six daughters and three sons born to Joseph Smith and Hulda Korth Gibbs. She had instilled into her the beauty of honest and earnest toil. She helped with the farm and household chores while she learned and followed the principles of the gospel. In her youth she served as secretary in the Primary, the Sunday School, and YWMIA. This indicated a recognition of her careful observation and the exactitude of her recording.

During her senior year in high school she was called by President Joseph F. Smith to go on a mission to the Eastern States. Her first assignment in 1915 was to the West Pennsylvania Conference, whose president was Howard S. McDonald. She was president of the first Relief Society organization in Pittsburgh, Pennsylvania, and she completed her mission in Baltimore, Maryland. Throughout her life she remained devoted to Relief Society and filled her many important callings faithfully and well.

After her return home in 1917, Howard S. McDonald sought her out, and their marriage was solemnized in the Salt Lake Temple on 26 September 1917.

They were living in Logan, Utah, while President McDonald studied engineering at Utah State Agricultural College, when World War I called him to France. Sister McDonald returned home to her mother, where her first daughter, Ruth, was born. Ruth was some months old before her father returned and saw her. In 1923 a second daughter, Melva, was born in Logan while President McDonald was teaching mathematics at Utah State Agricultural College.

While Howard was working for his doctorate degree at the University of California at Berkeley, Sister McDonald, who was a meticulous homemaker, enjoyed the arts of embroidery and crocheting and taught these skills to her daughters. Although she was away from her beloved mother, they kept in close touch through letters.

Following this period in California, President McDonald returned to Utah as superintendent of schools in Salt Lake City. Upon being named president of Brigham Young University, he and his family moved to Provo. The four years she spent at the University were very enjoyable to Sister McDonald.

A second return to California was welcomed as it brought her close again to her married daughters and their treasured children. Her daughters had won scholastic honors. Ruth, married to L. Bryce Boyer, M.D., has a doctorate in anthropology and is now teaching at the College of Arts and Crafts in Oakland, California. Melva, who married Douglas H. Orgill, Ph.D., has a master's degree and is now teaching home economics at City College in Long Beach, California. Sister McDonald's grandchildren treasure her memory because of her gentleness and tender care for them.

The crowning delight of Sister McDonald's life came in 1963 when her husband was called to be president of the Salt Lake Temple and she became the matron. She felt that her entire life had been in preparation for this call. She was beloved in her calling, and her labors were attended by the Spirit of the Lord.

She always respected the priesthood, and throughout her married life her husband sought her counsel and respected her perception of people. She was a humble and devoted Latter-day Saint wife and mother: "Her children arise up, and call her blessed; her husband also, and he praiseth her" (Proverbs 31:28). Sister McDonald founded her life on eternal truth and had joy therein. She died on 18 December 1966 in Salt Lake City and was buried in the family plot at Forest Lawn Memorial Park, Cypress, California.

Alice Ludlow Wilkinson, wife of President Ernest L. Wilkinson, was first lady at Brigham Young University for twenty years (1951-71). During that time she endeared herself to the students, supported the school in its activities, and inaugurated Sunday evening socials at the President's Home, where students with like interests could become acquainted with each other. One year she was chosen "Woman of the Year" by the women students.

Sister Wilkinson has been loyal and supportive to her husband all through their married life. She has been an exemplary wife. With her marked talent in literature and speech, she held teaching positions, along with her responsibilities of motherhood, just as long as her husband needed that kind of support. When his schooling was over she welcomed the opportunity to remain home with the children. The oldest was born while President Wilkinson was still attending law school in Washington, D.C. Sister Wilkinson bore the financial hardships of their early married life uncomplainingly, and she continued her same modest demeanor and manner when affluence came to them in later years. President Wilkinson has sought her good judgment and counsel in the problems that have arisen throughout their lives together.

Alice lived during her youth and girlhood in Spanish Fork, Utah. She is the daughter of Nathaniel and Margaret Jones Ludlow, who had four girls and four boys. Sister Wilkinson remembers her father driving out to his acres of hay, grain, beans, and sugar beets, first in a horsedrawn wagon and later in an old Ford. An English grandfather celebrated Christmas with so many of his descendants that there would have to be three and four sittings at the tables. It was a closeknit family.

As Alice grew up she learned to play the piano, was active in dramatics, and engaged in sports. Her major and minor in college were English and speech, but she married before she graduated. She met her future husband when he became her campaign manager when she ran for student body vice-president. She paraphrases his words as follows: "In trying to convince others of my qualifications he said he convinced himself." After serving as vice-president, she taught the next year in both the Provo junior high and high schools instead of graduating. At the conclusion of that year they were married.

The Wilkinsons moved to Washington, D.C., where Ernest obtained a law degree from George Washington University. They both taught school in order for him to be able to complete his schooling. Sister Wilkinson continued to teach in Washington while he studied at Harvard to obtain an advanced doctorate degree. The family then moved to New Jersey and soon to New York for a number of years before settling back in Washington, D.C.

Through all her years in the East, Sister Wilkinson was a devoted Church member, holding numerous important Church positions, especially in the Relief Society in Washington, D.C., and New York. When the family moved to Provo she became the first Relief Society president of the original campus stake. She was called to the General Board of the Relief Society in 1960, where she served admirably until 1974. She was chairman of a number of important committees.

There are five Wilkinson children: Ernest Ludlow, M.D., is a specialist in vascular heart diseases married to Marjorie Nielson. Marian, wife of Gordon F. Jensen, has a master's degree. Alice, wife of Floyd Anderson, majored in English for three years at Brigham Young University. Her first husband, John K. Mangum, was killed in an airplane accident. Another son, David L., was a Rhodes Scholar who obtained his law degree from the University of California and is now assistant attorney general for the State of Utah. Douglas D. is married to Rosalie Gilbert. He graduated from the University of Utah Law School and is now practicing law in Salt Lake City.

Sister Wilkinson can look back with satisfaction and joy on the accomplishments of her life. She has lived unselfishly for the good of her family and in service to her fellow men.

June Dixon Oaks, wife of President Dallin H. Oaks, is relatively young in years and probably will ever be young in spirit. She has accepted the responsibility of being the first lady at the Brigham Young University with becoming modesty and yet with enthusiasm. She has a motherly concern toward all the young women on campus. She has a lively interest in them and their accomplishments, accepting invitations to speak to groups on campus as her time permits. Young women look to her for advice on how a wife can best support her husband, how to be a student wife and mother, and how to strive for one's full potential. Her life experiences qualify her to speak authoritatively on these subjects. She has dedicated her efforts to the success of her husband. Even with children in the home, once the financial condition of the family permitted, June again began work toward a college degree. In 1965, fourteen years and five children after she first enrolled at BYU, she received her bachelor's degree. It had been a family effort. The greatest joy the family has received, however, since they returned to BYU has been the birth of their sixth child, Jenny June, the first child to be born in the President's Home on campus. All six Oaks children have been born by Caesarian section.

Sister Oaks was only nineteen when she married, but she and her husband at once undertook the rearing of a family. Throughout her eventful life she has prayerfully weighed choices and devoted herself at a particular time to those matters of most concern in an eternal perspective.

She was born in Spanish Fork, one of six children of Charles H. and True Call Dixon. As a young girl she and her twin sister Jean traveled over Utah County doing routines of tap and creative dance. They played two-piano duets and were very active in women's sports. Since June returned to BYU she has become a devotee of tennis, which she thoroughly enjoys. Her family life is one of togetherness, and the Oakses have camped overnight in twenty-five of the forty-seven United States in which they have traveled. In addition to her activity in sports, June is a homemaker, a collector of antiques, and she enjoys homemaking skills such as quilting. She also reupholsters and refinishes furniture.

Her full life includes study and teaching in the educational and cultural fields. Her interests were varied during the sixteen years the Oakses resided in Chicago. Just prior to returning to BYU she did some substitute teaching in the inner-city schools of Chicago that she thoroughly enjoyed. Often the family accompanied her on culture appreciation visits to the art museum, Field Museum of Natural History, and the Museum of Science and Industry as well as to the Brookfield Zoo. They also enjoyed Washington, D.C., when they resided there for a year.

The warp and woof of the Oaks family's life has been the gospel of Jesus Christ. The influence and power of a Latter-day Saint mother reflects the devotion June has always given to fulfilling calls to serve in the Mutual Improvement Association, the Primary, and the Relief Society in both ward and stake positions. She has been a Relief Society visiting teacher for eighteen years and now is serving as a social relations teacher in her ward Relief Society.

The interests and teachings of June and Dallin are revealed in the interests of the children, four girls and two boys. Sharmon (Mrs. Jack D. Ward) is a graduate honor student and a registered nurse. Her husband is a student in the J. Reuben Clark Law School. Cheri (Mrs. Louis E. Ringger) graduated in recreational therapy and is a talented singer. Her husband is a graduate in engineering, Lloyd D. is a freshman at BYU and plans to serve a mission. He is an Eagle Scout and earned his Duty to God Award. Dallin D., who attends high school, plays the French horn and is an Eagle Scout. TruAnn attends junior high, plays the piano and violin, and loves sports. Jenny June, the baby, is the pride and joy of her family.

Sister Oaks is approachable and has a warm personality. She carries her great responsibilities with dignity and honor and endears herself to those with whom she associates. She is a true helpmeet to President Oaks.

Acting Presidents of BYU

Leonard John Nuttall, Jr., was born 6 July 1887 in Salt Lake City, Utah, the first son and third child born to L. John and Christina Little Nuttall, who had a total of thirteen children. L. John was named after his famous grandfather, who was the private secretary to President John Taylor and President Wilford Woodruff. He attended elementary and secondary schools in Pleasant Grove.

He began his career as an educator in 1906 as principal at Pleasant Grove, where he served until 1908. He was a critic teacher from 1908 to 1910 at the Brigham Young Training School.

L. John married Fannie Burns of Puma, Arizona, in 1911. They became the parents of eleven children, all of whom received college degrees. He graduated from Columbia University with his bachelor's and master's degrees in 1911 and 1912. In 1912 he became a high school teacher in Payson, where he taught until 1915. After serving as principal in Spanish Fork for a year, he began two years of service as superintendent of the Iron County School District. In 1919 he was appointed superintendent of the Nebo School District, where he worked for the next three years.

In 1922 he was appointed dean of the College of Education at BYU, where he served until 1930. In 1926-27 he served as acting president of the University in the absence of President Franklin S. Harris, who was on a world tour.

Nuttall received his Ph.D. from Columbia University in 1929. He then accepted the position of director of the Stewart Training School, associated with the University of Utah, where he worked for two years until 1932. In 1932 he was appointed superintendent of the Salt Lake City Schools, which position he held until his death on 18 April 1944. After his death Howard S. McDonald was appointed to succeed him.

Brother Nuttall's life was tremendously motivated by education. He was president of the Utah Education Association (1922-23) and served as chairman of the Appraisal Committee of the American Association of School Administration and vice-chairman of the Salt Lake Youth Council. He undoubtedly was one of the most outstanding and dedicated educators ever to be affiliated with BYU.

Edward Henry Holt was born in South Jordan, Utah, in 1872. From an early age he had interests in clerical work as he served as secretary in the Primary, Aaronic Priesthood, Sunday School, MIA, and later as ward and stake clerk. From the time he was fifteen to the time of his death at age sixty-six, no two years went by that he did not hold some clerical position. He graduated from Brigham Young Academy in 1893 and became an instructor in phonography and typewriting. He married Edith Holdaway in 1895.

From 1894 to 1938 he was secretary to the faculty, serving under three University presidents: Benjamin Cluff, George H. Brimhall, and Franklin S. Harris. In 1895 he was appointed assistant professor of business education. In 1902 he became a professor of business education. In 1906 he became treasurer to the Board of Trustees. In 1907 he was appointed secretary of the University Council, and in 1915 he was named department head of business education and secretary-treasurer of the Board of Trustees.

During World War I when times were exceedingly hard and BYU struggled for its very existence, Brother Holt, as treasurer, struggled to pay the faculty their salaries or find scrip to substitute for cash. As treasurer he knew the financial condition of all faculty families. Many times he sought help from those who had a little more to tide over those with less.

In 1929 he was appointed acting president of the University while President Franklin S. Harris was on his trip to Russia.

Brother Holt also held positions as president, vice-president, and secretary of the Alumni Association at various times between 1905 and 1923.

Even with so much time dedicated to service to the University, Brother Holt received three mission calls. He was released from all three callings because of his obligations to the University during times of stress. He died at the age of sixty-six, leaving behind a wonderful record of service to Brigham Young University.

Christen Jensen was born on 4 February 1881 in Salt Lake City, Utah. His parents, Christen Jensen, Sr., and Nel Sina Johnsen, were immigrants from Denmark. Brother Jensen received his elementary and secondary schooling in Salt Lake City and was a leading student at Salt Lake High School. He took the normal course at the University of Utah and then taught school in Riverton, Midvale, and Pleasant Green for four years. While he was teaching in Midvale he met another teacher, Juliaette Bateman, who shared with him a common interest in music. They were married on 17 August 1904.

He received his B.A. degree from the University of Utah, graduating in 1907. During the following year he attained the rather unique distinction of being the first graduate from a Utah college to receive a Master of Arts degree from Harvard in a single year of work. From 1914 to 1921, Brother Jensen continued his education by attending summer school, and he graduated magna cum laude with his Ph.D. from the University of Chicago in 1921.

In 1908, Brother Jensen began fifty-three years of service as a faculty member at Brigham Young University by accepting the position of assistant professor of history and political science. During this long period of service Brother Jensen distinguished himself not only as a teacher but also as an administrator, serving twice as acting president of the University. In 1911 he became professor and head of the History and Political Science Department, a position he held for thirty-eight years. He was appointed dean of the Graduate School in 1929 and held this position for twenty years. He also served as the acting dean for three colleges on campus: the College of Applied Sciences, the College of Arts and Sciences, and the Graduate School.

From 1939 to 1940, President Franklin S. Harris was in Iran, and Brother Jensen was selected as acting president of the University in his absence. In 1949 he became dean-emeritus of the Graduate School, and after retiring and moving to Salt Lake City, he was called back to become acting president of the University in the interim period between the administrations of Howard S. McDonald and Ernest L. Wilkinson (1949-51). Under his direction the Eyring Science Center was completed and dedicated, and plans for the George Albert Smith Fieldhouse were approved. Emphasis on scholarship and the meticulous observance of University standards characterized his administration, as did stability and sound judgment.

In paying tribute to Christen Jensen, President Ernest L. Wilkinson has written, "During the interval existing between the time I was appointed in July of 1950 and September of the same year, when the announcement was made, I corresponded continuously with him. . . . When I came to the campus he opened up his desk and had two massive drawers of letters and correspondence, all requiring decisions which he had felt that it was improper for him as acting president to make. In his modesty, he never wanted to trespass upon the prerogative of another even though he had much more wisdom to make these decisions than I. . . . May I finally add that when, without experience, I took over my present office, I found no one more helpful or loyal to me in the administration of my office."

In describing Brother Jensen's earlier administration during the absence of President Harris, President Wilkinson wrote: "Certain pressures were exercised in an effort to curtail the program of Brigham Young University and in particular the functions of the president. A weak acting president easily could have succumbed, but President Jensen stood like a rock of Gibraltar and when President Harris returned, handed over to him the authorities and power of his office fully intact. I have heard President J. Reuben Clark, Jr., many times congratulate President Jensen on his loyalty to his chief, President Harris, while he was out of the country."

Brother Jensen was as devoted to his Church as he was to his profession, and he rendered service in countless capacities. He was president and teacher in the several priesthood quorums, as well as the Sunday School and YMMIA. He served on three different high councils and was first counselor in the Utah Stake Presidency for five and one-half years. Under the appointment of the First Presidency he also served as chairman of the Church Reading Committee for three years. At the time of his death on 17 August 1961 he was serving as patriarch to the East Provo Stake.

Earl Clarkson Crockett was born in Preston, Idaho, in 1903. After receiving his B.S. degree in economics with honors from the University of Utah in 1927, he taught in the Idaho schools for two years. He then attended the University of California at Berkeley and received his Ph.D. in economics in 1931. While at the University of California he served as a teaching fellow. He then spent three years as assistant professor of finance at the University of North Dakota. He served as assistant, associate, and full professor of economics at the University of Colorado, where he was made acting dean of the graduate school, chairman of the Department of Social Sciences, and assistant to the vice-president. The university bestowed upon him the Robert Stern Award for outstanding teaching and the University Research Lectureship, which is the highest honor the faculty gives. He was also awarded the Alumni Medal for extraordinary service outside of his university positions. During World War II he was a principal economist on the War Production Planning Board in Washington, D.C. He also served as a consultant for the Colorado General Assembly, the Governor's Commission on the Aged, the Civil Service Commission, the Colorado State Tax Commission, and the Public Welfare Department under three governors. He wrote a text for the high schools entitled *Problems of American Democracy.*

In 1957 he was appointed academic vice-president of Brigham Young

University. During his eleven years in the administration from 1957 to 1968, Vice-President Crockett was instrumental in a great expansion of University staff and faculty programs. Under his direction the BYU Honors Program, faculty research fellowships, new master's degree programs, and numerous doctoral degree programs were established. He was largely responsible for the adoption of the semester system. He also pursued research on problems of motivation, recruitment, and morale of faculty, along with studies of teaching loads, faculty evaluation, and faculty participation in University administration.

From January to December 1964 he served as acting president of the University, during which time President Wilkinson had resigned to run for the Senate. In 1968, Dr. Crockett resigned from his administrative responsibilities to go abroad to teach for the University of Maryland for a year and then resume the role of a full-time teacher. He believed that "the best job in the University was that of a full-time professor."

In 1966 he was made chairman of the Higher Commission of the Northwest Association of Secondary and Higher Schools.

Dr. Crockett dearly loved his years at Brigham Young University. In an assembly address to the student body in 1964 he defined the letters BYU, saying,

> B stands for an important bridge students may cross which leads from a condition of lesser knowledge to that of greater knowledge, wisdom, and a strong spiritual faith in God. B also stands for balanced educational programs, banners for courageous living, and beauty of campus buildings and beauty of mind, body, soul. Y stands for the young who possess youthful enthusiasm, high ideals and a thirst for knowledge. It also stands for a yield harvest of earning credits and knowledge, wisdom and ideals acquired and carried away. U stands for the uniqueness of the university that has fine purpose and objectives, that is church-related and guided, that has an outstanding faculty and outstanding student body. U also stands for the unconquerable spirit, unbounded determination, undying loyalty, unsurpassed scholarship, and unceasing faith which thrives at Brigham Young University.

President Crockett died unexpectedly in his sleep on 2 December 1975.

Vice-Presidents of BYU

William E. Berrett, lawyer, educator, and author, served Brigham Young University over a twenty-five year period, from 1948 to 1973, culminating a career of forty-eight years of service to Church, state, and nation in various capacities. Born in the old pioneer village of Union, formerly Fort Union, in Salt Lake Valley, Utah, on 2 June 1902, his early education was in the schools of the Jordan School District.

Attending the University of Utah, he graduated with honors in 1924. He was a member of Tau Kappa Alpha national debating fraternity, Delta Theta Phi law fraternity, and Phi Kappa Phi scholastic fraternity. He continued graduate work in the University of Utah Law School but found it advisable, because of financial difficulties, to accept a teaching position as principal of the LDS Church seminary at Roosevelt, Utah, in 1925. In 1932 he returned to the University of Utah, receiving an LLB degree in 1933 (later changed to an LLD). During the interval between 1927 and 1933, in addition to his teaching, he did graduate work at Brigham Young University during six summer sessions, providing his first connection with that school.

Admitted to the Utah State Bar in 1937, he remained an active member, but the Church Educational System drew him repeatedly into educational assignments, where he served as administrator of various seminaries and as institute teacher and director at LDS Business College.

Elder Berrett's writing career began in 1936 with the publication of text books for the Church schools and as editor in the Church Department of Education. The early texts produced included *The Restored Church,* now (1975) in its sixteenth edition and translated into seventeen languages; *Doctrines of the Restored Church; Teachings of the Book of Mormon; Teachings of the Doctrine and Covenants;* and *The Gospel Message,* all of which have been translated into numerous languages. He later was coauthor with Alma Burton of three volumes of *Readings in LDS Church History.*

For nine years he taught outgoing missionaries in the Mission Home in Salt Lake City. During this period he also gave two series of radio talks for the Church.

In 1943 he was appointed special prosecuting attorney for the Office of Price Administration, Utah Division, where he served until 1946, when he was appointed assistant United States attorney, serving the Fourth Judicial District, Territory of Alaska. Late in 1947 he resigned that position and returned to Salt Lake City to begin a private law practice. For the next three years he also wrote a daily editorial for the *Deseret News.*

Berrett served the Church as a Sunday School superintendent, a member of various stake auxiliary boards, a member of the Deseret Sunday School General Board (1935-46 and 1947-53), first councilor in the East Millcreek Stake Presidency (1945-46), and a member of the Fairbanks Branch Presidency in Alaska (1946-47).

In the fall of 1947, Howard S. McDonald, president of Brigham Young University, persuaded him to accept a position as associate professor of Church history. In 1951 he became full professor. In that same year Ernest L. Wilkinson came to BYU and the activities of William E. Berrett became involved with that administration. His first administrative assignment was to obtain an ROTC unit for the University, which culminated in establishing the AFROTC. For the next fifteen years Berrett served as liaison officer for the University, representing the president in most affairs pertaining to the AFROTC and the Selective Service. From 1951 to 1953 he also served the president in recruiting new faculty members for the rapidly growing school.

In the summer of 1953 he was appointed vice-president of the University, in charge of religious education, and as vice-administrator of all Church seminaries and institutes of religion, which were then brought into the Unified Church School System. With the full support and urging of the administrator there began a rapid expansion of seminaries and institutes of religion which, over the next two decades, was to cover the Church throughout the world.

In 1960, Governor Clyde appointed Berrett as a member of the Utah

Committee on Children and Youth, and in that year he was a delegate to the White House Conference on Children and Youth. He continued as a member of the Utah Committee, serving as its chairman in 1962-65. During these years he also served as a member of the National Committee on Children and Youth.

In 1965, with the separation of the BYU administration from the Church Educational System, Berrett became administrator of seminaries and institutes of religion. In that year Brigham Young University honored him with an honorary Doctor of Laws degree.

In October 1970 he was retired from the administrative field, but he returned to teaching as professor of religion at BYU. In 1972 he was appointed by the Church Board of Education to write a comprehensive history of seminaries and institutes of religion. This task, ending in the summer of 1973, resulted in the production of six volumes, all of which still remain in manuscript form (1975).

For his work with the AFROTC, he was awarded a plaque for distinguished services by the United States Air Force. He also received a citation by Tau Kappa Alpha national debating fraternity for services to humanity. He now serves as a patriarch of the Church.

He is married to the former Eleanor Callister, and they have four children, seventeen grandchildren, and one great-grandson.

William F. Edwards was born in Emery, Utah, on 26 April 1906, a son of William Foster Edwards and Ann Rhodelin Williams. His father died before William F. was born, leaving Mrs. Edwards to support her baby and his two older brothers. He attended Brigham Young University from 1924 to 1928, working his way through school and at the same time serving as president of his junior and senior classes. The vice-president of his senior class was Catherine Eyring of Colonia Juarez, Mexico. They were married in the Salt Lake Temple in September 1929. They are parents of six married children and have thirty-six grandchildren.

Continuing his education at Columbia and New York universities, Edwards graduated in 1930 with a master of science degree and in 1937 with a doctor of commercial science degree from New York University Graduate School of Business. Concurrent with his graduate studies, he worked full time in the New York financial district.

Dr. Edwards was an organizer and research partner of a large investment counseling firm in New York City from 1939 to 1946. In 1946 he became director of research and senior investment officer of a group of large mutual funds. During these years he gained recognition in the New York financial field, where he was a frequent speaker, as well as contributor to financial magazines. In 1948 he was awarded the prestigious New York University Alumni Meritorious Service Award.

In November 1950, President-elect Wilkinson announced the appointment of Dr. Edwards as Dean of the College of Commerce at BYU, effective January 1951. Edwards accepted this position at a little more than a tithe of what he was making in the Wall Street commercial district. This was the beginning of a new career at forty-four. In addition to being a dean and a teacher, he soon found himself assisting the new president in areas such as student housing, salary problems, and retirement programs. In mid-1953, in addition to continuing as dean, he was appointed vice-president of finance and business administration of BYU and the Unified Church School System.

In January 1955, Dr. Edwards was called by President David O. McKay to do a series of studies and to counsel the Brethren in the temporal and business affairs of the Church. During the next two years he divided his time between his three appointments at BYU and the Church. In January 1957 he was released from the educational assignments and appointed secretary of finance to the First Presidency. *Business Week* commented on this assignment: "[President] McKay created the office of Financial Secretary to the First Presidency. To fill the job, he named Dr. William F. Edwards, a Mormon with a brilliant career not only in the Church but also in the New York financial community."

Dr. Edwards was elected a trustee of the College Retirement Equities Fund in 1959 for a four-year term. In 1961 he was appointed a board member of the Utah Public Employees Retirement Programs and was helpful in establishing an investment program for these important funds.

Another challenging assignment in the area of education — in addition to his regular work — came in 1957-59 when he was appointed codirector of a study directed toward solving the problems of higher education in Utah. Beginning as early as 1895, many studies had been made, and the State Legislature gave frequent consideration to the unification or coordination of the state institutions of higher learning. The problem kept growing, but the solution was not forthcoming. The ongoing assignment culminated in establishing the Coordinating Council of Higher Education in 1959, with Dr. Edwards as its first chairman. It was necessary for him to resign from the Council in 1960 when he was appointed professor of finance (part-time) at the University of Utah. At the same time, after ten years of full-time service with BYU and the Church, Dr. Edwards reentered business. He became executive vice-president of First Security Investment Company and vice-president of First Security Bank, Salt Lake City, while continuing his part-time teaching assignment. In June 1971, Dr. Edwards retired from the investment-banking business and was appointed distinguished professor in the Driggs Chair of Finance of BYU. Dr. Edwards received from BYU the Distinguished Service Award of the Alumni Association in 1957 and the Jesse Knight Industrial Citizenship Award in 1968 for his many years of exceptional services in the fields of banking, finance, and education, as well as for his devotion to BYU and the Church. In 1976, he and his wife, Catherine Eyring Edwards, were awarded the Joseph F. Smith Family Living Award. They have six children and thirty-six grandchildren.

Dr. Edwards was president of the New York Stake when appointed to his position at BYU. At the time of this writing, he is a sealer-supervisor in the Provo Temple, a Sunday School teacher, a member of the board of directors of Bonneville International Corporation, and chairman of the Finance Committee and a director of Eyring Research Institute.

Ben E. Lewis was born on 6 November 1913. From the time of his birth he developed a love for work, a good sense of humor, and an enthusiasm for completing each task he undertakes. He graduated from high school at the age of fifteen, worked for five years, filled an LDS mission, and then entered BYU. He was junior class president and then president of the BYU student body during his senior year. He graduated in 1940 with high honors in banking and finance. In 1942 he received his master's degree from the University of Denver, where he had been awarded a fellowship from the Alfred P. Sloan Foundation. He has worked in the banking firms of Utah Savings and Trust Company in Salt Lake City and the Farmers and Merchants Bank in Provo. He assisted in the development of a centralized accounting system for the State of Illinois. He has worked for the Bureau of Labor Statistics and as budget and procedures officer in the Office of the Administrator of the National Housing Agency. From 1945 to 1952 he was budget director in charge of sales and promotion for the Hot Shoppes Restaurants, Inc., later known as the Marriott Corporation.

In 1952, Ben Lewis came to BYU, where his duties included the direction of BYU food services, housing, press, dairy, farms, motion picture and photo studios, and the acquisition and management of properties of the University and those acquired for the Church as possible junior college sites. The dollar gross income of these and other auxiliary operations later placed under the supervision of Lewis increased nearly fifty times from 1952 to the present. He served as chairman of the Campus Planning Committee, which had major responsibility in the planning and construction of buildings and facilities for the burgeoning University. In 1961 he was appointed vice-president in charge of all Auxiliary Services, and in 1969 he became executive vice-president. He also served as acting president when University President Ernest L. Wilkinson was away, as well as taking on some administrational duties to allow the president more time on policy matters. Under President Dallin H. Oaks his responsibilities as executive vice-president include the areas of finance, personnel services, physical plant, athletics, housing, food services, bookstore, special events, laundries, farm operations, campus planning and development, University press, warehousing, receiving, laundries, property acquisition and management, and Language Training Mission facilities. From this recital it is evident that Ben Lewis has been an important administrator of the University during its period of most extensive expansion. In recognition of his services he was, in 1970, awarded an honorary Doctor of Laws degree by the University.

In addition to his responsibilities at the University, he is currently serving as chairman of the Development Committee of the Development Office of the Church. He is a member of numerous boards, including the Hotel Utah, Deseret Book Company, State Savings and Loan Association, Utah Valley Hospital, the Provo Advisory Board for Walker Bank and Trust Company, and Taylors, Inc., in Provo. He served for several years on the Provo City Planning Commission and is a member of the Provo Kiwanis Club.

Over the years he has been active in the Boy Scout organization, having served as a scoutmaster, district chairman, and chairman of the Provo area. He is a recipient of the Silver Beaver Award.

Ben Lewis has been a president of a seventies quorum, a member of two bishoprics, and a member of the high council in the Washington, Sharon, and Sharon East Stakes. He served for sixteen years as president of the

Sharon East Stake. At the time of his appointment as stake president in 1955 the stake (then known as the East Sharon Stake) had a membership of less than 3,000 individuals, residing in five different wards. When he was released in 1971 it had a membership of over 8,500, residing in eighteen wards, making it one of the largest stakes in the Church. He also filled a regular full-time mission and two stake missions. He has served on the Executive Committee of the General Sunday School Board and is currently serving as a Regional Representative of the Quorum of the Twelve Apostles, where his present assignment is to the San Fernando and Ventura Regions.

He is married to Barbara Wootton; they are the parents of five children and three foster children.

Harvey L. Taylor was born on 28 August 1894 in Harrisville, Utah, the only son of Harvey Daniel Taylor and Letty May Saunders. His father died when Harvey was ten months old, leaving his mother without money or property. Through her strong will, determination, hard work, and unwavering faith, she not only provided life's necessities but instilled in her young son ideals of decent living and service to his fellow men.

Harvey received his education in the schools of Weber County; Weber Academy; the University of Utah, where he received his B.S. degree; and Columbia University, where he earned his M.A. degree. He also did graduate study at Stanford and at State Teachers College in Greeley, Colorado. He received an honorary LLD degree from Arizona State University. He was principal and teacher in the public schools of Weber and Summit counties. He taught in both Weber Academy and Weber College, and he taught the first LDS seminary classes in the Ogden area.

While at Weber, Adam S. Bennion, commissioner of Church schools, asked him to serve as president of Gila Junior College in Thatcher, Arizona, a position he held for six years. After Gila College was closed by the Church, Harvey accepted a position as superintendent of Mesa Union High School. Later, upon consolidation of several school districts, Harvey was appointed superintendent of Mesa Public Schools. He held these two positions for twenty years.

While in Mesa, he served as vice-president of the Arizona Education Association, president of the Arizona School Administration Association, president of Arizona School Superintendents Association, an eight-year member of the Arizona North Central Accrediting Commission, organizer of the Arizona Association of Student Councils, and vice-president of the National Association of Student Councils.

Not only did he serve Mesa's educational system but also her community system. For sixteen years he was chairman of Mesa Parks and Playgrounds Board and chairman of Arizona Colony Board for Mentally Handicapped Children. He served on the Arizona Youth Council, Governor's Safety Council for both Arizona and Utah, Mesa Planning Board, Mesa's Little Theatre Board, and as president of the Stafford, Arizona, Rotary club.

In January 1953, President Ernest L. Wilkinson chose him as his executive assistant. He later was appointed vice-president of Brigham Young University and vice-chancellor of the LDS Unified Church School System under President Wilkinson.

When Wilkinson resigned as president of BYU and chancellor of the Church School System in 1964, Taylor was made acting chancellor of the entire Church school system. When Wilkinson returned to his post as president of BYU, Taylor became administrator of all seminaries and institutes and all Church schools (except BYU), which included Ricks College, LDS Business College, Church College of Hawaii, and schools in Mexico, South America, and the South Pacific. The system at that time had a total enrollment of over 250,000 students.

Harvey Taylor received many honors, such as the Silver Beaver Award and a fifty-year Service Award for his active participation in the Boy Scouts of America. He received Mesa's first Most Valuable Citizen Award. The Mesa City recreational field was named Taylor Field after him. He won the Arizona State Farmer Award and the Phoenix, Arizona, Rotary Club Orchid Award for service to youth. He was an honorary member of Alpha Phi Omega (national scouting fraternity), Blue Key (national honor fraternity), BYU Circle K Club (student service organization), and Archon (national honor fraternity). He received the BYU Distinguished Alumni Award in 1965 and the Ricks College Distinguished Service Award in 1967. He received the Arizona Governor's Award of Honor to a Distinguished Citizen for Meritorious Service, the Weber State College Alumni Meritorious Service Award, the State of Utah Third Juvenile District Court Distinguished Service to Youth Award, and an Honorary Master M-Men Award for distinguished service to youth.

Harvey has been listed in *Who's Who in America* since 1965, along with *Who's Who in Western Education*, *Who's Who in American Education*, and Sloan's *History of Arizona*.

His long life of Church service includes thirty years as Sunday School teacher and many other leadership positions, including membership on two high councils and time as ward and stake superintendent of Sunday Schools and YMMIA organizations. He has served as teacher trainer and priesthood leader in many quorums.

He married Lucelle Rhees in the Salt Lake Temple in 1916. They are the parents of four children, all with collegiate degrees. They have twelve grandchildren and twelve great-grandchildren.

When he retired in 1971 after fifty years of service in education, Harvey Taylor was assigned by the new commissioner of Church schools to write the story of LDS Church schools. This assignment he completed in two volumes in 1972.

Robert K. Thomas was born in Sunnyside, Utah, in July 1918 and is, as he says, "the first generation out of the coal mines." In 1927 his family moved to Oregon, and he grew up in the little seacoast town of Coos Bay. As an undergraduate he attended the University of Oregon and then transferred to Reed College in Portland, where he was graduated with a B.A. in humanities and elected to Phi Beta Kappa. Moving to Eugene, Oregon, to pursue graduate work at the University of Oregon, he met and married Shirley Ann Wilkes and received his M.A. in English. He taught briefly at the University of Oregon before leaving for further graduate work at Columbia University in New York City. In 1951 he took a teaching position at Brigham Young University in the English Department. Thomas won a Danforth Teacher Grant in 1957-58 — the first given to a member of the Church — which he used to continue his doctoral program at Columbia. He completed his Ph.D. in American literature in 1967.

An authority on literature and religion, Thomas completed an undergraduate thesis at Reed on the literature of the Book of Mormon and a master's thesis on Thoreau and Christianity. His dissertation at Columbia was an examination of the effect of space and time on the writings of Henry David Thoreau.

At BYU, Thomas developed courses in general semantics and the Bible as literature. In 1959 he was named director of the Honors Program and was the "founding father" of this program for gifted students at BYU. In 1961 he was recognized by the students as the outstanding teacher for that year. In 1962 he coached the BYU General Electric College Bowl team which won four of its five matches.

He was appointed by President Ernest L. Wilkinson to be assistant vice-president at Brigham Young University in 1966, and during that year he received the Maeser Award for Distinguished Teaching. He became academic vice-president in 1967, replacing Earl Crockett, who was retiring. In off-campus positions Thomas has been particularly active in the general accreditation of senior colleges and universities, having served on the Higher Commission of the Northwest Association of Secondary and Higher Schools for ten years and on the board of trustees of that same organization for six years. With Bruce Clark he was the author of the popular five-volume work *Out of the Best Books*. In addition to membership in Phi Beta Kappa, he has also been elected to Phi Kappa Phi, Blue Key, and Phi Eta Sigma. He has written extensively for the Church and has served throughout the West as consultant on higher education administration. He is now president of the BYU Fourth Stake of the LDS Church.

Appendix 30

BYU Alumni Who Have Become Presidents or Chancellors of Colleges and Universities

Bakersfield College
  Burns L. Finlinson
Brigham Young University
  Benjamin H. Cluff, Jr.
  George H. Brimhall
  Franklin S. Harris (also Utah State Agricultural College)
  Christen Jensen (acting)
  L. John Nuttall, Jr. (acting)
  Edward H. Holt (acting)
  Ernest L. Wilkinson
  Dallin H. Oaks
University of California at Los Angeles
  Vern O. Knudsen (chancellor)
Chico State College/California State University at Chico
  Stanford Cazier
Church College of Hawaii
  Reuben D. Law
Church College of New Zealand
  Clifton Boyack
Dixie College
  Hugh M. Woodward
  Edgar M. Jenson
  Erastus S. Romney
  Joseph K. Nichols (twice)
  B. Glen Smith
  Matthew M. Bentley
  Arthur F. Bruhn
  Ferron C. Losee
College of Eastern Utah
  John W. Tucker
  Aaron E. Jones
  Dean M. McDonald
College of Ganado (Navajo Indian Reservation)
  George Lee
Eastern Arizona College (formerly Gila College)
  Eugene Hilton
  Edgar Fuller
  Monroe Clark
  Harvey L. Taylor
  Dean A. Curtis
LDS Business College (formerly LDS College and LDS University)
  Willard Done

Guy C. Wilson
Bryant S. Hinckley
University of Minnesota
O. Meredith Wilson
Montclair College
E. DeAlton Partridge
University of Oklahoma
Royden Dangerfield (acting)
University of Oregon
O. Meredith Wilson
Oregon College of Education
Leonard Rice
Ricks College
Andrew B. Christensen
George S. Romney
Hyrum Manwaring
John L. Clarke
San Jose State College
John T. Wahlquist
Snow College
Alma Greenwood
Newton Noyes
Wayne B. Hales
Milton H. Knudsen
James A. Nuttall
Lester B. Whetten
J. Elliot Cameron
Floyd S. Holm
J. Marvin Higbee
College of Southern Utah (Southern Utah State College)
Henry Oberhansley
Royden Braithwaite
University of Utah
James E. Talmage
A. Ray Olpin
James C. Fletcher
David P. Gardner
Utah State University
Joseph M. Tanner
Franklin S. Harris (also BYU)
H. Aldous Dixon (also Weber State College)
Utah Technical College, Salt Lake City
Jay L. Nelson
Central Utah Trade Technical College
Wilson Sorensen
Weber State College
Aaron W. Tracy
H. Aldous Dixon (also Utah State University)
Joseph J. Bishop

Appendix 31
BYU Stake Presidents, 1956-1975

President	Dates of Service
BYU Stake	
Antone K. Romney	1956-1960
BYU First Stake	
Wayne B. Hales	1960-1964
Raymond E. Beckham	1964-1969
Joseph T. Bentley	1969-1972
J. Duane Dudley	1972-
BYU Second Stake	
Bryan West Belnap	1960-1964
Clyde D. Sandgren	1964-1972
Lael J. Woodbury	1972-
BYU Third Stake	
William Noble Waite	1960-1964
Fred A. Schwendiman	1964-1972
R. Dermont Bell	1972-
BYU Fourth Stake	
William R. Siddoway	1964-1972
Ronald G. Hyde	1972-
BYU Fifth Stake	
A. Harold Goodman	1964-1971
Gordon M. Low	1971-
BYU Sixth Stake	
Wayne B. Hales	1964-1972
Jesse E. Stay	1972-
BYU Seventh Stake	
Dean A. Peterson	1967-1972
Paul Cheesman	1972-
BYU Eighth Stake	
David H. Yarn	1967-1973
Robert J. Smith	1973-
BYU Ninth Stake	
Carl D. Jones	1969-1973
Jae R. Ballif	1973-
BYU Tenth Stake	
Ivan J. Barrett	1969-1973
Donald N. Wright	1973-
BYU Eleventh Stake	
Gregory E. Austin	1975-
BYU Twelfth Stake	
C. Verl Clark	1975-

Appendix 32
BYU Alumni Association Presidents, 1893-1975

Name	Dates of Service
George H. Brimhall	26 May 1893-1894
Milton H. Hardy	24 May 1894-1895
Reed Smoot	23 May 1895-1896
May Bell Davis Thurman	21 May 1896-1897
Edwin S. Hinckley	28 May 1897-1898
Alfred L. Booth	27 May 1898-1899
Lars E. Eggertsen	26 May 1899-1900
J. Will Knight	31 May 1900-1901
John E. Booth	31 May 1901-1902
John C. Swenson	30 May 1902-1903
Joseph R. Murdock	27 May 1903-1904
Anthony C. Lund	25 May 1904-1905
Stephen L. Chipman	2 Jun 1905-1906
J. Will Knight	31 May 1906-1907
William E. Rydalch	31 May 1907-1908
Heber C. Jex	1908-1909
W. Lester Mangum	1909-1910
William E. Ryalen	1910-1911
Joseph B. Keller	1911-1912
Thomas N. Taylor	1912-1913
Edward H. Holt	1913-1915
Arthur Candland	1915-1916
R. Eugene Allen	1916-1919
Eugene L. Roberts	1919-1920
Henry Aldous Dixon	1920-1921
Herald R. Clark	25 May 1921-1922
Horace G. Merrill	2 Jun 1922-1923
Hugh M. Woodward	8 Jun 1923-1924
Edwin S. Hinckley	6 Jun 1924-1925
Oscar A. Kirkham	16 Oct 1925-1927
Richard R. Lyman	1927-1930
R. Leo Bird	1930-1933
Isaac E. Brockbank	1933-1935
Fred R. Hinckley	30 Jan 1935-1936
Earl J. Glade	15 Jun 1936-1938
Lynn S. Richards	19 Jan 1938-1938
J. Clifton Moffitt	28 Jun 1938-1939
Junius M. Jackson	14 Sep 1939-1940
Bryant S. Hinckley	18 Sep 1940-1941
George Albert Smith	30 Oct 1941-1942
Marion J. Greenwood	15 Oct 1942-1944
Don B. Colton	8 Apr 1944-1945
L. Weston Oaks	14 Jun 1945-1946
Harold R. Clark	14 Jun 1946-1947
Clyde D. Sandgren	3 Jun 1947-1951

Roy Broadbent	2 Jun 1951-1952
Wallace W. Brockbank	31 May 1952-1953
Raymond B. Holbrook	14 Jun 1953-1955
S. Lynn Richards	3 Jun 1955-1956
Grant Thorn	1 Jun 1956-1957
G. Robert Ruff	31 May 1957-1959
Clyde J. Summerhays	5 Jun 1959-1960
DaCosta Clark	3 Jun 1960-1961
E. Lamar Buckner	3 Jun 1961-1962
Sanford M. Bingham	25 May 1962-1963
Arch L. Madsen	31 May 1963-1964
Phillip V. Christensen	29 May 1964-1965
Harold H. Smith	28 May 1965-1967
William Sorensen	26 May 1967-1968
Howard C. Maycock	11 May 1968-1969
Ernest Ludlow Wilkinson	7 Apr 1969-1971
Don Alder	5 Apr 1971-1972
Fred L. Markham	7 Apr 1972-1973
Albert Choules, Jr.	1973-1974
Roy E. Christensen	1974-1975
Harold P. Christensen	1975-

Appendix 33
BYU Alumni Distinguished Service Award Recipients

1937
*Arthur L. Beeley
*Amy Brown Lyman
*Vern O. Knudsen
Harvey Fletcher
*Philo T. Farnsworth
*Alice Louise Reynolds
*Reed Smoot

1938-45
No awards given

1946
*Benjamin Cluff, Jr.
*N. L. Nelson
*Elsie C. Carroll
*George Albert Smith
*Bryant S. Hinckley
*J. Will Knight

1947
*A. L. Booth
*William H. King
*William J. Snow
*Annie Pike Greenwood

1948
*John C. Owensen
*T. N. Taylor
*Emma Lucy Gates Bowen
*Hermese Peterson
*Don B. Colton

1949
*George R. Hill
*Thomas L. Martin
*Eugene L. Roberts
*Ida Smoot Dusenberry
*Mima Murdock Broadbent

1950
*Rose B. Hayes
Howard S. McDonald
*Earl J. Glade
Ezra Taft Benson
*Eva M. Crandall

1951
*Arthur V. Watkins
*Amos N. Merrill
*Christen Jensen
*Jennie Brimhall Knight
Belle Smith Spafford
*Margaret Davis Swensen

1952
Colleen Kay Hutchings
*Issac A. Smoot
*Brent L. Larsen
Florence Jepperson Madsen

1953
*Herald R. Clark
*Leah Dunford Widtsoe
*Andrew T. Rasmussen
*LeRoy J. Robertson
*Alsina Brimhall Holbrook

1954
*Alex Hedquist
*Hyrum W. Manwaring
Vesta Pierce Crawford
David J. Wilson
*William H. Boyle

1955
*Henry Aldous Dixon
A. Ray Olpin
A. Sherman Christensen
Kathryn B. Pardoe
*Howard R. Driggs

**Deceased*

1956
O. Meredith Wilson
*Aetmesia Redd Romney
*Joseph K. Nicholes
*John E. Hayes
*Fred G. Warnick

1957
Clawson Y. Cannon, Sr.
*Maybell Thurman Davis
*L. Weston Oaks
William F. Edwards
*Oscar A. Kirkham

1958
*T. Earl Pardoe
*Estella Spilsbury Harris
*George Q. Morris
*Wayne Mayhew
*Stella Pugmire Rich
*Lucy A. Phillips

1959
Wayne B. Hales
Lynn S. Richards
*Angelyn M. W. Wadley
Robert H. Hinckley
Kiefer B. Sauls
Myrtle Austin

1960
G. Roy Fugal
Rhea Alberta H. Christensen
*Ray E. Dillman
Richard P. Condie
Alice Ludlow Wilkinson
Henry D. Taylor

1961
*Jennie Knight Mangum
*Milton Reed Hunter
O. Preston Robison
O. Leslie Stone
Grant Thorn
A. Theodore Tuttle

1962
Marion G. Romney
*H. Franklin Madsen
*Wilma Boyle Bunker
*Dilworth Walker
Arch L. Madsen

1963
LeRoy R. Hafen
*Ann Woodbury Hafen
*DeAlton Partridge
*James R. Price
Ernest L. Wilkinson

1964
*Clarence Cottam
Carolin Eyring Miner
Wesley P. Lloyd
J. Earl Garrett
J. Clifton Moffitt

1965
*Lorena C. Fletcher
Stella Harris Oaks
Boyd K. Packer
*Amasa Lyman Clark
Fred L. Markham
Harvey L. Taylor

1966
Hannah Cropper Ashby
*Edith Young Booth
DaCosta Clark
James A. Cullimore
Kenneth A. Randall
Rudger H. Walker

1967
Raymond E. Beckham
Carl Christensen
Chesley G. Peterson
Leona Holbrook
Ora Pate Stewart

1968
Robert M. Ashby
Redd Braithwaite
J. Edward Johnson

*Charles Redd
Algie E. Ballif

1969
T. Ray Broadbent
*Bertha Kleinman
George H. Mortimer
H. Roland Tietjen
Stanley H. Watts

1970
Oakley S. Evans
*H. Grant Vest
Samuel P. Smoot
Vasco M. Tanner
Roy E. Christensen

1971
John Boyde Page
S. Eugene Dalton
Clyde D. Sandgren
Antone K. Romney
Helen Hinckley Jones

1972
Nyle C. Brady
Verda Mae Fuller Christensen
Loren Charles Dunn
Wallace H. Gardner
Harold H. Smith

1973
Arta Romney Ballif
Rafael E. Castillo
Don M. Alder
Owen Raynal Long

1974
Fern Chipman Eyring Fletcher
Crawford Marion Gates
Frank William Gay
Saing Silalahi
Mark B. Weed

Appendix 34

BYU Emeritus Club Presidents, 1941-1975

President	Years of Service
Richard R. Lyman	1941-1944
Bryant S. Hinckley	1944-1947
Frank Evans	1947-1948
I.A. Smoot	1948-1949
John C. Swensen	1949-1950
Joseph Nelson	1950-1951
Fred C. Graham	1951-1952
Eugene L. Roberts	1952-1953
Francis W. Kirkham	1953-1954
Leah D. Widstoe	1954-1955
Genevieve Day Larsen	1955-1956
Alonza N. Leonard	1956-1957
Oscar A. Kirkham	1957-1958
Harvey Fletcher	1958-1959
Wells T. Brockbank	1959-1960
Nellie Oliver Parker	1959-1960
Ray Dillman	1960-1961
George H. Higgs	1961-1964
Elvon C. Jackson	1964-1965
C. Melvin Paulson	1965-1966
H. Roland Tietjen	1966-1967
T. Earl Pardoe	1967-1968
David J. Wilson	1968-1971
Stanley S. Cheever	1971-1973
Wayne B. Hales	1973-1975
Vasco M. Tanner	1975-

Appendix 35
Deans of BYU Colleges during the Wilkinson and Oaks Administrations

College of Biological and Agricultural Sciences	
A. Lester Allen	1971-
Rudger H. Walker	1961-70
Merrill J. Hallam	1960
Raymond B. Farnsworth	1956-59
Clarence Cottam	1954-55
College of Applied Science	
Thomas L. Martin	1951-54
College of Business	
Merrill J. Bateman	1975-
Bryce B. Orton	1974-75
Weldon J. Taylor	1959-74
College of Commerce	
Weldon J. Taylor	1958-59
William F. Edwards	1951-57
Continuing Education	
Stanley A. Peterson	1972-
Harold Glen Clark	1966-71
Adult Education and Extension Services	
Harold Glen Clark	1957-66
College of Education	
Curtis Van Alfen	1974-
Stephen L. Alley	1971-73
Antone K. Romney	1963-70
A. John Clarke	1961-62
Asahel D. Woodruff	1956-60
Reuben D. Law	1951-55
Engineering Sciences and Technology	
Armin J. Hill	1973-
Industrial and Technical Education	
Ernest C. Jeppsen	1966-72
College of Family Living	
Blaine R. Porter	1969-
Virginia Cutler	1963-68
Jack B. Trunnell	1959-62
Marion C. Pfund	1956-59
Royden C. Braithwaite	1954-55
College of Fine Arts and Communications	
Lael J. Woodbury	1974-
Lorin F. Wheelwright	1969-74
Conan E. Mathews	1964-68
College of Fine Arts	
Conan E. Mathews	1961-64
Gerrit de Jong, Jr.	1951-60

General Studies	
C. Terry Warner	1974-
General College	
Lester B. Whetten	1967-73
Ernest C. Jeppsen	1965-66
Wayne B. Hales	1959-64
Graduate School	
Chauncey C. Riddle	1970-
Wesley P. Lloyd	1960-69
A. Smith Pond	1957-59
George Hansen	1954-56
Christen Jensen	1953
Asahel D. Woodruff	1951-52
Humanities	
Bruce B. Clark	1966-
College of Humanities and Social Sciences	
John T. Bernhard	1964-66
Reed H. Bradford	1961-63
Leonard W. Rice	1957-60
A. Smith Pond	1956
Antone K. Romney	1955
Asahel D. Woodruff	1954
Law	
Rex E. Lee	1972-
Nursing	
Maxine J. Cope	1972-
Elaine Murphy	1968-71
Lennia Morrison	1966-67
Beulah Ream Allen	1961-65
L. Bernice Chapman	1959-60
Physical and Mathematical Sciences	
Jae R. Ballif	1973-
College of Physical and Engineering Sciences	
Armin J. Hill	1958-73
Harvey Fletcher	1954-57
Physical Education	
Clayne K. Jensen	1974-
Milton F. Hartvigsen	1960-74
College of Recreation, Health, Physical Education, and Athletics	
Milton F. Hartvigsen	1956-60
Jay B. Nash	1955
Religious Instruction	
Ellis T. Rasmussen	1976-
Jeffrey R. Holland	1974-76
Roy W. Doxey	1972-73
Daniel H. Ludlow	1968-71
B. West Belnap	1964-67
David H. Yarn, Jr.	1959-63

Social Sciences	
Martin B. Hickman	1970-
John T. Bernhard	1966-68

Appendix 36

Deans and Directors of Important Nonacademic Areas at BYU

Admissions and Records (Dean)
- Robert Spencer (Asst. Dean, 1969-70; Dean, Aug. 1971-present)
- Frank McKean (Oct. 1970-May 1971)
- William R. Siddoway (1965-70; title changed to Dean in 1965)
- Lynn Eric Johnson (Acting Director, 1964-65)
- William R. Siddoway (Director, 1962-64)
- Alma P. Burton (1959-62)
- Bliss Crandall (1955-57)

Alumni Relations (Director)
- Ronald G. Hyde (1966-present)
- Raymond E. Beckham (1954-65)
- Cleon Skousen (1951-53)

Assistant Vice-President — Physical Plant
- Fred Schwendiman (1974-present; various other roles, 1953-74)
- Sam F. Brewster (Director of Physical Plant, 1957-74)
- Leland Perry (1946-47 and 1952-57)

Security (Chief)
- Robert Kelshaw (1974-present)
- Swen Nielsen (1961-73)
- Leonard Christensen (1952-60)

Development (Director)
- Donald T. Nelson (Acting Director, 1971; Director, 1973-present)
- Richard C. Stratford (1970-71)
- David B. Haight (1970; previously was Assistant to President)
- Raymond E. Beckham (1965-70)
- Noble Waite (1958-61)

Computer Services (Director)
- Gary Carlson (1963-present; Academic and Administrative combined)
- Ed Dean (Academic, 1958-63)
- Dave Bachelor (Administrative, 1958-63)
- Bliss Crandall (Administrative, 1955-58)
- Rulon Brough (1953-55)

Continuing Education (Dean)
- Stanley Peterson (1971-present)
- Harold Glen Clark (1946-72)

Dean of Student Life
- J. Elliot Cameron (1962-present)
- Wesley Lloyd (1938-62; title changed to Dean of Student Life, 1945)
- Wesley Lloyd (Acting Dean of Men, 1937-38)
- A. Rex Johnson (Apr. -Aug. 1937)

Dean of Women
- Lucile O. Petty (1971-72)
- Klea Worsley (Counselor for Women, 1960-70)
- Lillian C. Booth (Counselor for Women, 1951-59)

Health Center (Director)
Cloyd Hofheins (1964-present)
Jack Trunnell (1962-63)
Richard Nimer (1958-62)
Allan Barker (1956-58)
Ariel Williams (1952-56)
Financial Services (Director)
Lyman Durfee (1967-present)
Joseph T. Bentley (1958-67; on faculty, 1967-71)
Broadcast Services
Bruce L. Christensen (1970-present)
Earl J. Glade, Jr. (1966-70)
Personnel Services (Director)
B. Keith Duffin (1952-present)
University Relations
Bruce L. Olson (1973-present; in position in Admissions and Records, 1966-73)
Heber G. Wolsey (1969-73)
Stephen R. Covey (1965-69)
Lester B. Whetten (1956-65; changed to Univ. Relations, 1956)
Dean A. Peterson (Director of Public Relations and Publications, Jan.-Dec. 1955)
University Press (Director)
Ernest L. Olson (1957-present)
Ernest L. Wilkinson Center
Lyle Curtis (1964-present)

Appendix 37
BYU Department Chairmen, 1906-1975

Accounting Department	
Leon W. Woodfield	1970-
Karl M. Skousen	1968-69
Bryce E. Orton	1962-67
Robert J. Smith	1959-61
H. Verlan Andersen	1957-58
Joseph F. Bentley	1955-56
Robert J. Smith	1952-54
Accounting and Business Administration	
Harrison Val Hoyt	1936-51
Herald R. Clark	1931-35
Harrison Val Hoyt	1930
Aerospace Studies Department	
Colonel Richard B. Jensen	1974-
Colonel Richard A. Baldwin	1973
Colonel L.H. Johnson	1970-72
Lt. Colonel Jesse E. Lloyd	1968-69
Lt. Colonel Paul H. Sharp	1966-67
Air Science	
Lt. Colonel Donald E. McDulloch	1964-65
Lt. Colonel William J. Gibson	1959-63
Colonel Barnett S. Allen	1956-58
Lt. Colonel Jesse E. Stay	1952-55
Agricultural Economics Department	
Lowell Wood	1970-
Carlton Infanger	1968-69
Ivan Corbridge	1959-67
Glen L. Nelson	1958
Ivan Corbridge	1956-57
A. Smith Pond	1947-55
Harrison Val Hoyt	1942-46
A. Smith Pond	1941
Agricultural Engineering	
Ernest D. Partridge	1921-23
Agriculture	
Thomas L. Martin	1921-23
Amos N. Merrill	1911-20
William H. Homer, Jr.	1907-10
John A. Widtsoe	1906
Agriculture Education Department	
Rudger H. Walker	1966-70
Agronomy and Horticulture	
Laren R. Robison	1972-
Rudger H. Walker	1966-71
Agronomy	
Raymond B. Farnsworth	1961-68

R. Chase Allred	1958-60
Merrill J. Hallam	1955-57
Raymond B. Farnsworth	1952-54
Thomas L. Martin	1922-51
American Indian Studies	
Royce P. Flandro	1972-74
Animal Science	
Leon Orme	1974-
R. Phil Shumway	1964-73
Animal Husbandry	
Lawrence Morris	1955-63
Grant S. Richards	1947-54
H. Grant Ivins	1929-46
Clawson Y. Cannon	1922-28
Anthropology and Archaeology	
Merlin G. Myers	1968-
Ross T. Christensen	1966-67
Archaeology	
Ross T. Christensen	1960-66
M. Wells Jakeman	1947-59
Art and Design	
W. Douglas Stout	1972-
Art	
Floyd E. Breinholt	1970-71
Glen A. Turner	1966-69
Richard L. Gunn	1962-65
J. Roman Andrus	1960-61
Bent F. Larsen	1937-54
Elbert H. Eastmond	1906-36
Asian Studies	
Spencer Palmer	1970-
Lanier Britsch	1968-69
Paul Hyer	1966-67
Athletics. See Intercollegiate Athletics.	
Bacteriology. See Microbiology.	
Banking. See Finances and Banking.	
Bible and Modern Scriptures	
Howard H. Barron	1961-66
Daniel H. Ludlow	1959-60
Eldin Ricks	1958
Roy W. Doxey	1954-57
Sidney B. Sperry	1941-53
Biblical Languages	
Andrew Christensen	1912-19
Biblical Literature	
Andrew Christensen	1912-19
Biology	
Charles H. Carroll	1924-25
Martin P. Henderson	1915-23

Charles H. Carroll	1913-14
Andrew Rasmussen	1911-12
Ralph V. Chamberlin	1908-10
Botany and Range Sciences	
Kimball T. Harper	1974-
Benjamin W. Wood	1973
Dayna L. Stocks	1970-72
Botany	
Earl M. Christensen	1966-69
Bertrand F. Harrison	1961-65
Kent H. McKnight	1958-60
Bertrand F. Harrison	1937-57
Edna Snow	1936
Bertrand F. Harrison	1934-35
Thomas L. Martin	1931-33
Walter P. Cottam	1930
A.O. Garrett	1929
Walter P. Cottam	-29
Business Administration.	
See Accounting and Business Administration.	
Business Education	
George E. Nelson	1970-
Max D. Waters	1966-69
Lars G. Crandall	1964-65
Business Education and Office Management	
Richard D. Bell	1961-63
Edward Christensen	1960
Lars G. Crandall	1959
Edward L. Christensen	1957-58
Lars G. Crandall	1956
Business Education	
Thatcher Jones	1920-21
Edward H. Holt	1919
Business Management	
Eran A. Call	1970-
L. Brent Eagar	1966-69
Sterling D. Sessions	1964-65
Parley M. Pratt	1961-63
Clinton L. Oaks	1958-60
Richard L. Smith	1952-57
Career Education	
Richard A. Heaps	1974-
Career Orientation	
William D. Goodson	1972-73
Chemical Engineering Sciences	
L. Douglas Smoot	1972-
Bill J. Pope	1966-71
Dee H. Barker	1961-65
James J. Christensen	1960

Billings Brown	1958-59
H. Smith Broadbent	1957
Chemistry	
Richard T. Hawkins	1972-
LeRoi K. Nelson	1968-71
J. Rex Goates	1966-67
Loren C. Bryner	1964-65
Albert Swensen	1960-63
Keith P. Anderson	1958-59
H. Smith Broadbent	1955-57
Joseph K. Nicholes	1946-56
Charles E. Maw	1907-45
Child Development and Family Relations	
J. Joel Moss	1970-
Duane M. Laws	1966-69
Family Life Education	
Blaine R. Porter	1964-66
Human Development and Family Relations	
Blaine R. Porter	1956-60
Marion C. Pfund	1955
Civil Engineering Sciences	
James Barton	1972-
D. Allan Firmage	1970-72
Cliff S. Barton	1962-69
Ralph L. Rollins	1960-61
Dean K. Fuhriman	1959
Harry Hodson	1957-58
Church History and Doctrine	
Lamar Berrett	1970-75
Church History	
Russell R. Rich	1953-59
Hugh Nibley	1951-52
Russel B. Swensen	1921-46
Clothing and Textiles	
Charlene Lind	1974-
Eleanor Jorgensen	1966-73
Margaret Childs	1961-65
Eleanor Jorgensen	1959-60
Margaret S. Potter	1956-58
Eleanor Jorgensen	1955
Maud Tuckfield	1927-29
Vilate Elliott	1922-25
Communications	
M. Dallas Burnett	1975-
Edwin O. Haroldsen	1972-74
J. Morris Richards	1966-71
Oliver R. Smith	1964-65
Journalism	
Jean R. Paulson	1961-64

Oliver R. Smith	1950-60
T. Earl Pardoe	1945-46
Carlton Culmsee	1939-44
Harrison R. Merrill	1936-38
Computer Science	
C. Edwin Dean	1970-
Gary Carlson	1966-69
Devotional Assemblies	
Dean A. Peterson	1970-73
Stephen R. Covey	1966-69
Drafting	
William H. Snell	1924-31
Dramatic Arts. See Speech and Dramatic Arts.	
Economics. See also History and Economics.	
Wayne W. Clark	1973-
Larry Wimmer	1970-72
Wayne W. Clark	1966-69
Richard Wirthlin	1964-65
Willard Doxey	1961-63
Glen L. Nelson	1959-60
Elmer Miller	1956-57
A. Smith Pond	1952-55
Elmer Miller	1935-51
Russell Swenson	1930-33
Clarence S. Boyle	1929
Harrison Val Hoyt	1927-28
Russell Swenson	1921-25
Economics and Sociology	
Russell Swenson	1919-20
Economics, Sociology, and Commerce	
John C. Swensen	1912-18
Economics and Home Management	
Vesta W. Barnett	1957-60
Beth S. Henman	1956
Economics and Management of the Home	
Marion C. Pfund	1955-56
Education, Graduate. See Graduate Department of Education and Teacher Education.	
Educational Administration	
Ralph B. Smith	1972-
Keith R. Oakes	1958-72
Percy E. Burrup	1956-57
Owen L. Barnett	1955
Reuben D. Law	1948-54
Asael C. Lambert	1931-47
Joseph Sudweeks	1929-30
L. John Nuttall	1924-28
Hugh M. Woodward	1922-23

Elementary Education	
Floyd Sucher	1974-
Max J. Berryessa	1972-73
Hazel B. Bowen	1954-55
Reed Morrill	1951-53
LeRoy Bishop	1947-50
Reuben D. Law	1937-46
William H. Boyle	1929-36
L. John Nuttall	1922-28
Pedagogy	
James L. Brown	
Secondary Education	
Wally Allred	1972-
Golden L. Woolfe	1953-54
A. John Clarke	1950-52
Golden L. Woolfe	1945-49
Amos N. Merrill	1929-44
L. John Nuttall	1927-28
Amos N. Merrill	1922-25
Education Personnel and Guidance	
Wesley P. Lloyd	1953-54
Educational Philosophy and Programs	
Stephen L. Alley	1958-62
Educational Philosophy and History	
Wesley P. Lloyd	1953-54
Philosophy of Education and Guidance	
Wesley P. Lloyd	1946-53
Philosophy of Education	
Wesley P. Lloyd	1937-46
Hugh M. Woodward	1929-36
Guy C. Wilson	1927-28
Hugh M. Woodward	1922-25
Educational Research and Service	
Lester N. Downing	1961-62
Robert L. Egbert	1955-60
Educational Sociology	
John C. Swensen	1922-23
Educational Values and Programs	
Keith R. Oakes	1957-58
Electrical Engineering Sciences	
Ferril A. Losee	1966-
Darrell J. Monson	1960-65
Jens J. Jonsson	1957-59
Engineering Sciences	
Jens J. Jonsson	1955-57
Harvey Fletcher	1953-54
Engineering	
William F. Ward	1906

English	
Richard H. Cracroft	1975-
Marshall R. Craig	1973-75
Dale H. West	1966-72
Bruce B. Clark	1960-65
Ralph A. Britsch	1958-59
Leonard W. Rice	1955-57
Parley A. Christensen	1933-54
Alfred Osmond	1929-32
Parley A. Christensen	1924-28
Alfred Osmond	1906-23
Environmental Design	
Milo Ray Baughman	1970-73
European Studies	
Edwin B. Morrell	1970-
Family Economics. See Home Management.	
Family Life Education. See Child Development and Family Relations.	
Family Living, General, In-charge	
Virginia Poulson	1958-59
Finance and Banking	
Howard D. Lowe	1956-58
Herald R. Clark	1931-55
John C. Swensen	1921-25
Food Science and Nutrition	
John M. Hill	1974-
John H. Johnson	1970-73
Food and Nutrition	
Marion Bennion	1962-69
Sadie D. Morris	1961
Marion Bennion	1955-60
Foods and Nutrition	
Effie Warnick	1927-29
Elizabeth Cannon	1924-25
Ethel Cutler	1922-23
Forum Assemblies	
J. LaVar Bateman	1968-73
Herald R. Clark	1966-67
Genealogy	
Norman E. Wright	1968-75
General Studies	
William D. Goodson	1974-75
General Curriculum	
Willis M. Banks	1968-73
Geography	
Robert L. Layton	1968-75
Floyd Millet	1966-67
Robert L. Layton	1961-65

Albert L. Fisher	1959-60
Elliot Tuttle	1955-58
Geology	
W. Revell Phillips	1973-75
J. Keith Rigby	1970-72
Lehi F. Hintze	1960-69
Harold J. Bissell	1955-57
Geology and Geography	
George H. Hansen	1929-54
Murray O. Hayes	1927-28
Fred Buss	1915-25
Geological Science	
Edwin S. Hinckley	1908-14
Geology and Geological Engineering Science	
Lehi F. Hintze	1962-68
Kenneth C. Bullock	1957-61
Graduate Department of Education	
Curtis Van Alfen	1968-70
Robert L. Egbert	1964-67
Keith R. Oakes	1962-63
Health Sciences	
Ray Watters	1970-
Health and Safety Education	
Ray Watters	1960-69
Health Education	
David D. Geddes	1958-59
Health Education and Safety	
David D. Geddes	1956-57
Clarence Robison	1955
Health, Physical Education, and Recreation	
Charles J. Hart	1948-55
History. See also Political Science.	
Ted J. Warner	1973-
DeLamar Jensen	1968-72
Eugene Campbell	1960-67
Richard C. Poll	1959
Eugene Campbell	1958
Richard D. Poll	1955-57
Russel B. Swensen	1949-54
Christen Jensen	1929-48
William Snow	1924-28
Christen Jensen	1921-23
History and Economics	
John C. Swensen	1906-20
History and Philosophy of Religion	
Truman G. Madsen	1959-64
Theology and Philosophy	
Truman G. Madsen	1957-59

David H. Yarn	1956
Theology and Religious Philosophy	
David H. Yarn	1951-56
Sidney B. Sperry	1948-50
J. Wyley Sessions	1941-47
Theology	
George H. Brimhall	1924-25
Theology and Religion	
George H. Brimhall	1920-21
Joseph B. Keeler	1914-19
George H. Brimhall	1913
Joseph B. Keeler	1911-12
Theology	
George H. Brimhall	1906
Home Economics	
Irene S. Barlow	1949-55
Christen Jensen	1948
Effie Warnick	1937-47
Margaret Swenson	1936
Effie Warnick	1930-35
Vilate Elliott	1929
Ethel Cutler	1920-23
Home Economics Education	
Ruth Brasher	1970-
Virginia Poulson	1968-69
Homemaking Education	
Virginia Poulson	1959-68
Ethel Lee Jewell	1958
Virginia Poulson	1956-57
Marion C. Pfund	1955
Family Economics and Home Management. See also Economics and Home Management.	
Gary D. Hansen	1973-
Virginia Cutler	1970-72
Housing and Home Management	
Jennieve Poulson	1964-70
Stephen Stanford	1960-63
Housing and Design	
Elizabeth L. Gardner	1957-60
Beth S. Hinman	1956
Marion C. Pfund	1955
Household Administration	
Effie Warnick	1924-29
Ethel Cutler	1922-23
Household Arts	
Margaret H. Eastmond	1914-21
Household Economics	
May Ward	1907-13
Christina D. Young	1906

Ladies Work Department	
Laura Foote	1888
Jennie Tanner	1885-87
Zina Y. Williams	1879-84
Honors	
C. Terry Warner	1973-
Horticulture	
Ernest F. Reimschussel	1964-68
Horticulture and Horticulture Specialities	
Ernest F. Reimschussel	1958-64
Clarence D. Ashton	1955-57
Horticulture and Landscape Architecture	
Clarence D. Ashton	1951-57
Robert H. Daines	1948-50
Melbourne D. Wallace	1945-47
George H. Smeath	1944
Charles Harris	1943
George H. Smeath	1942
Seth L. Shaw	1940-41
Horticulture	
Seth L. Shaw	1937-39
Laval S. Morris	1936
Seth L. Shaw	1933-35
Landscape Architecture	
Laval S. Morris	1933-39
Horticulture	
Laval S. Morris	1930-32
Melvin C. Merrill	1924-25
Human Development. See Child Development and Family Relations.	
Humanities and Comparative Literature	
Todd Britsch	1970-
Indian Studies. See American Indian Studies.	
Industrial Education. See also Technical Institute and Technology.	
William E. McKell	1972-
Edwin C. Hinckley	1966-71
Ross J. McArthur	1961-65
Guy Pierce	1960
Industrial Arts and Drawing	
Guy Pierce	1958-60
Lavell Gamett	1955-57
William H. Snell	1954
Industrial Arts and Graphics	
William H. Snell	1953-54
Industrial Arts	
William H. Snell	1952-53
Institute of Government Service	
Stewart L. Grow	1961-68

Intercollegiate Athletics	
Floyd Millet	1964-68
Edwin R. Kimball	1957-63
Interior Design	
Phyllis Allen	1973-75
International Relations	
Stanley A. Taylor	1970-
Ray C. Hillam	1966-69
Journalism. See Communications.	
Landscape Architecture. See Horticulture and Landscape Architecture.	
Asian and Slavic Languages	
Donworth V. Gubler	1972-
Classical, Biblical, and Middle Eastern Languages	
J. Reuben Clark, III	1968-
Languages	
R. Max Rogers	1964-68
H. Darrell Taylor	1960-63
Harold W. Lee	1958-59
Arthur R. Watkins	1957
Modern and Classical Languages	
Arthur R. Watkins	1954-57
Harold W. Lee	1952-53
Benjamin F. Cummings	1930-51
Gerrit de Jong	1927-29
Benjamin F. Cummings	1920-25
Modern Languages	
Dean R. Brimhall	1915-19
C. Elmer Barrett	1914
James L. Barker	1913
Andrew B. Christensen	1911-12
James L. Barker	1910
Ancient Languages	
W.H. Chamberlin	1911-19
Foreign Languages	
James L. Barker	1907
French and Italian	
Norman C. Turner	1972-
John A. Green	1970-71
Thomas H. Brown	1968-69
Germanic Languages	
Arthur R. Watkins	1970-72
Thomas Rogers	1968-69
Spanish and Portuguese	
M. Carl Gibson	1968-
Latin American Studies	
Lyman S. Shreeve	1972-
Wesley W. Craig	1968-71
Lyman S. Shreeve	1966-67

Law Enforcement Education	
Charles Fletcher	1968-73
Library and Information Sciences	
H. Thayne Johnson	1968
Library Science	
Hattie M. Knight	1956-68
Naoma Rich	1953-55
Library	
Anna Ollorton	1920-21
Linguistics	
Soren F. Cox	1973-
Robert W. Blair	1968-72
Marketing	
Weldon J. Taylor	1947-58
Harrison Val Hoyt	1939-46
Elmer Miller	1938
A. Rex Johnson	1933-37
Mathematics	
Kenneth L. Hillam	1964-
Harvey J. Fletcher	1958-63
Milton Marshall	1953-57
Carl F. Eyring	1939-51
Milton Marshall	1938
Carl F. Eyring	1931-37
Milton Marshall	1929-31
Carl F. Eyring	1916-29
Harvey Fletcher	1914-15
Andrew S. Gibbons	1913
William F. Ward	1912
Chester Snow	1911
William F. Ward	1907-10
Ernest D. Partridge	1906
Mechanical Engineering Sciences	
John M. Simonsen	1968-
Milton G. Wille	1966-67
John N. Cannon	1962-65
John M. Simonsen	1958-61
Leland K. Baxter	1957
Mechanic Arts	
William H. Snell	1937-52
George H. Havsen	1936
William H. Snell	1923-35
Mechanics	
Carl F. Eyring	1919-23
Microbiology	
David M. Donaldson	1972-
Don H. Larsen	1968-71
Bacteriology	
Don H. Larsen	1966-68

Richard D. Sagers	1961-65
David M. Donaldson	1959-60
Don H. Larsen	1955-58
Jay V. Beck	1951-54
Dean A. Anderson	1950
Thomas L. Martin	1935-49
Military Science	
Colonel Bartley E. Day	1968-
Music	
A. Harold Goodman	1966-
Crawford Gates	1961-65
John R. Halliday	1948-60
LeRoy J. Robertson	1946-47
Florence Jepperson-Madsen	1936-45
LeRoy J. Robertson	1935
Florence Jepperson-Madsen	1930-34
Robert Sauer	1927-29
Florence Jepperson-Madsen	1924-25
Florence Jepperson	1921-23
Clair W. Reid	1917-20
Anthony C. Lund	1908-16
Anthon C. Lund	1899
John J. McClellan	1898
Ottilie Maeser	1886-97
Nettie Southworth	1883-85
Office Management. See Business Education and Office Management.	
Organizational Behavior	
William G. Dyer	1970-
Personal Development Program	
David M. Sorenson	1973-
Vern H. Jensen	1972
Philosophy. See also History and Philosophy of Religion. See also Psychology.	
Noel B. Reynolds	1972-
C. Terry Warner	1970-71
Chauncey Riddle	1966-69
Nels L. Nelson	1906-09
Physical Education (Men)	
Elmo S. Roundy	1970-
David D. Geddes	1962-69
Charles J. Hart	1960-61
Blauer L. Bangerter	1959
Charles J. Hart	1937-48; 1955-58
G. Ott Romney	1930-36
Charles J. Hart	1929
Eugene L. Roberts	1911-28
Physical Culture	
Fred Bennion	1908

Clayton T. Teetzel	1906-07
Physical Education (Women)	
Phyllis C. Jacobson	1972-
Leona Holbrook	1955-71
Physical Science	
Lane Compton	1966-
Chester Snow	1907-20
Charles E. Maw	1906
Physics and Astronomy	
B. Kent Harrison	1973-
Physics	
John H. Gardner	1966-73
Dwight R. Dixon	1964-65
John H. Gardner	1961-63
E. John Eastmond	1959-60
Wayne B. Hales	1955-58
Milton Marshall	1953-54
Physics and Mathematics	
Milton Marshall	1951-53
Physics	
Carl F. Eyring	1939-51
Milton Marshall	1938
Carl F. Eyring	1930-37
Milton Marshall	1929
Carl F. Eyring	1916-28
Harvey Fletcher	1911-15
Chester Snow	1907-10
Astronomy	
Fred Buss	1916-20
Harvey Fletcher	1914-15
Political Science	
Ray C. Hillam	1970-
Edwin B. Morrell	1968-69
John T. Bernhard	1966-67
Jesse W. Reeder	1964-65
Mark W. Cannon	1961-63
Stewart L. Grow	1957-60
Richard D. Poll	1955-56
Russel B. Swensen	1953-54
History and Political Science	
Russel B. Swensen	1950-53
Political Science	
Christen Jensen	1936-48
Thomas C. Romney	1924-28
Christen Jensen	1921-23
History and Political Science	
Christen Jensen	1920-21
History and Government	
W.E. Morgan	1916-19

Christen Jensen	1912-15
Provisional Registration	
William D. Goodson	1966-72
Psychology	
Darhl M. Pedersen	1968-
Kenneth R. Hardy	1966-67
Robert J. Howell	1961-65
Mark K. Allen	1953-60
Asahel D. Woodruff	1952
M. Wilford Poulson	1940-51; 1924-29
Hugh M. Woodward	1921-23
Dean R. Brimhall	1918-20
Psychology and Philosophy	
W.H. Chamberlin	1911-18
Joseph Peterson	1909-10
Range Sciences. See Botany and Range Sciences.	
Recreation Education	
William J. Hafen	1970-
Israel Heaton	1956-59
Social and Recreational Leadership	
Eugene L. Roberts	1921-23
Religion. See History and Philosophy of Religion.	
Religious Instruction — Ancient Scripture	
Robert C. Patch	1972-
Ellis T. Rasmussen	1970-71
Religious Instruction — Graduate Studies	
Chauncey Riddle	1964-70
Religious Instruction — Undergraduate Studies	
Roy W. Doxey	1964-70
Religious Education	
Chauncey Riddle	1962-64
B. West Belnap	1959-61
Guy C. Wilson	1933-39
George H. Brimhall	1929-32
William H. Snell	1927-28
Rural School Economics	
Lowry Nelson	1929-31
Russian Studies	
Melvin P. Mabey	1966-70
Secretarial Training	
Lars G. Crandall	1955-56
Evan M. Croft	1949-54
Secretarial Practice	
Evan M. Croft	1947-49
Clarence S. Boyle	1942-46
Office Practice	
Evan M. Croft	1939-42
Edward H. Holt	1930-38
G. Lynn Lloyd	1929

Bertha Roberts	1927-28
Edward H. Holt	1921-25
Sociology. See also Economics and Sociology.	
Evan T. Peterson	1970-
John R. Christiansen	1968-69
Joseph N. Symons	1966-67
Sociology and Anthropology	
Joseph N. Symons	1961-65
Reed Bradford	1960
Sociology	
Reed Bradford	1955-60
Ariel S. Balliff	1948-54
Harold T. Christensen	1943-47
Clarence S. Boyle	1941-42
Russel Swensen	1930-40; 1921-25
Speech and Dramatic Arts	
Parley W. Newman	1972-
Lael J. Woodbury	1968-71
Speech	
Morris M. Clinger	1961-68
Dramatic Arts	
Lael J. Woodbury	1966-68
Harold I. Hansen	1961-65
Speech and Dramatic Arts	
Harold I. Hansen	1953-61
Speech	
Harold I. Hansen	1952-53
T. Earl Pardoe	1931-51
Alonzo J. Morley	1930
Public Speaking and Dramatic Arts	
Grace Stewart	1927-29
Kathryn Pardoe	1922-25
Public Speaking	
T. Earl Pardoe	1920-22
Special Elocution	
Laura Pearl Adams	1908-20
Miriam Nelke	1906-07
Statistics	
H. Gill Hilton	1970-
Dale O. Richards	1966-69
Melvin W. Carter	1964-65
Howard C. Nielson	1960-63
Teacher Education	
Stephen L. Alley	1964-70
Dean C. Christensen	1962-63
Instruction	
Dean C. Christensen	1959-62
Educational Instruction	
Dean C. Christensen	1959

Sterling G. Callahan	1956-58
Arthur Browne	1955
Education	
Reuben D. Law	1953-55
James L. Brown	1911-23
Henry Peterson	1909-10
George H. Brimhall	1906-08
Technical Institute	
Ernest C. Jeppsen	1964-73
Technical and Semiprofessional Institute	
Ernest C. Jeppsen	1961-64
Wayne B. Hales	1960
Technology. See also Industrial Education.	
Ross McArthur	1972-
Industrial Technology	
Ross McArthur	1966-72
Industrial Management	
Richard L. Smith	1957-58
Theology and Church Administration	
Rodney Turner	1962-64
LDS Theology, Church Organization, and Administration	
Rodney Turner	1960-61
G. Byron Done	1959
LDS Church Organization and Administration	
G. Byron Done	1957-59
Chauncey C. Riddle	1954-56
B. West Belnap	1952-53
Church Organization and Administration	
Wesley P. Lloyd	1941-50
University Studies	
David M. Sorenson	1974-
Spencer J. Condie	1973
Guided Studies	
Wayne R. Herlin	1968-73
Howard Reid	1966-67
Skills Improvement Services	
Howard Reid	1962-66
Vocational Education	
Amos N. Merrill	1922-23
Trades	
George C. Laney	1908
Orson D. Campbell	1906-07
Youth Leadership	
Thane J. Packer	1961-
Royal B. Stone	1958-60
Scouting Education	
Royal B. Stone	1956-58

Zoology	
Joseph R. Murphy	1970-
Zoology and Entomology	
A. Lester Allen	1966-70
D. Elden Beck	1962-65
C. Lynn Hayward	1958-61
Vasco M. Tanner	1927-57
Natural Science	
Edwin S. Hinckley	1906-20

Appendix 38
Honorary Degrees Awarded by BYU, 1875-1975

Name	Commencement	Honorary Degree Awarded
Karl G. Maeser	May 1889	Doctor of Letters and Didactics
Emmaline B. Wells	February 1912	Doctor of Literature
George H. Brimhall	June 1921	Doctor of Laws
Charles Penrose	June 1921	Doctor of Laws
David Oman McKay	June 1922	Master of Arts
James E. Talmage	June 1922	Doctor of Laws
George Sutherland	June 1941	Doctor of Laws
Franklin S. Harris	June 1945	Doctor of Laws
David Oman McKay	June 1951	Doctor of Humanities
Walther Mathesius	June 1951	Doctor of Science
Joseph Fielding Smith	June 1951	Doctor of Literature
Joshua Reuben Clark	June 1952	Doctor of Laws
Merlo John Pusey	June 1952	Doctor of Literature
Adam S. Bennion	June 1953	Doctor of Literature
Stephen L Richards	June 1953	Doctor of Laws
Harvey Fletcher	June 1954	Doctor of Science
Ezra Taft Benson	June 1955	Doctor of Public Service
Harold B. Lee	June 1955	Doctor of Christian Service
Irving S. Olds	June 1955	Doctor of Laws
John Francis Fitzpatrick	June 1956	Doctor of Public Service
Igor Gorin	June 1956	Doctor of Public Service
Belle Smith Spafford	June 1956	Doctor of Humanities
Nathan Eldon Tanner	June 1956	Doctor of Laws
Cecil B. DeMille	May 1957	Doctor of Laws
Glen E. Nelson	May 1957	Doctor of Science
Merrill N. Warnick	May 1957	Doctor of Public Service
Ernest L. Wilkinson	May 1957	Doctor of Laws
J. Willard Marriott	June 1958	Doctor of Laws
Dean Dinwoody	June 1959	Doctor of Laws
Nicholas G. Morgan	June 1959	Doctor of Humanities
George W. Romney	June 1959	Doctor of Laws
Carl Sandburg	June 1959	Doctor of Literature
David M. Kennedy	June 1960	Doctor of Laws
Robert Gordon Sproul	June 1960	Doctor of Laws
Leah Dunford Widtsoe	June 1960	Doctor of Humanities
Henry Dinwoody Moyle	June 1961	Doctor of Humanities
Barry Morris Goldwater	June 1961	Doctor of Laws
William Edward Alton Ochsner	June 1961	Doctor of Science
Christen Jensen	August 1961	Doctor of Laws
Joseph Kelly Nicholes	August 1961	Doctor of Science
Hugh B. Brown	May 1962	Doctor of Humanities
Erwin Dain Canham	May 1962	Doctor of Literature
Robert B. McClure	May 1962	Doctor of Laws

William Foxwell Albright	August 1962	Doctor of Humanities
George D. Marler	August 1962	Doctor of Science
Richard P. Condie	May 1963	Doctor of Music
John McChrystal Wallace	May 1963	Doctor of Laws
David J. Wilson	May 1963	Doctor of Laws
Lowell Thomas	May 1964	Doctor of Laws
Robert H. Hinckley	May 1964	Doctor of Laws
Henry Eyring	May 1965	Doctor of Science
William Edwin Berrett	May 1965	Doctor of Laws
Emerson Foote	May 1965	Doctor of Public Service
Herald R. Clark	May 1966	Doctor of Arts
Roger A. Freeman	May 1966	Doctor of Laws
Max Rafferty	May 1966	Doctor of Public Service
Frank Stanton	May 1966	Doctor of Laws
George M. Mardikian	May 1967	Doctor of Humanities
Norman Vincent Peale	May 1967	Doctor of Laws
Joseph H. Tippets	May 1967	Doctor of Public Service
Aziz Suryal Atiya	May 1968	Doctor of Laws
Howard Sharp Bennion	May 1968	Doctor of Engineering Science
Earl Clarkson Crockett	May 1968	Doctor of Laws
Philo Taylor Farnsworth	May 1968	Doctor of Science
James Cash Penney	May 1968	Doctor of Public Service
Alger B. Chapman	October 1968	Doctor of Public Service
Lee S. Bickmore	May 1969	Doctor of Public Service
Ernest Eberhard, Jr.	May 1969	Doctor of Humanities
Spencer W. Kimball	May 1969	Doctor of Laws
Wesley Parkinson Lloyd	May 1969	Doctor of Laws
Kenneth D. Wells	May 1969	Doctor of Public Service
John L. Clarke	August 1969	Doctor of Public Service
Charles Stewart Mott	January 1970	Doctor of Education
Sam F. Brewster	May 1970	Doctor of Public Service
Mark E. Petersen	May 1970	Doctor of Christian Service
Russell M. Nelson	May 1970	Doctor of Science
Ben E. Lewis	August 1970	Doctor of Business
Arthur V. Watkins	August 1970	Doctor of Laws
Robert Yeager	August 1970	Doctor of Business
G. LeRoy Fugal	August 1970	Doctor of Science
Lord Thompson of Fleet	August 1970	Doctor of Humanities
H. Tracy Hall	May 1971	Doctor of Science
Fred A. Rosenstock	May 1971	Doctor of Humanities
Wetzel O. Whitaker	May 1971	Doctor of Fine Arts
James A. Jensen	August 1971	Doctor of Science
Homer R. Warner	August 1971	Doctor of Science
Gareth William Lowe	May 1972	Doctor of Science
Delbert L. Stapley	May 1972	Doctor of Christian Service
William Wayne Keeler	April 1973	Doctor of Business
Wallace Foster Bennett	August 1973	Doctor of Public Service
LeGrand Richards	April 1974	Doctor of Christian Service

Rosel H. Hyde	April 1974	Doctor of Public Service
Marianne Clark Sharp	August 1974	Doctor of Humanities
G. Homer Durham	April 1975	Doctor of Public Service
Warren E. Burger	September 1975	Doctor of Laws
Lewis F. Powell	September 1975	Doctor of Laws
Marion G. Romney	September 1975	Doctor of Laws

Appendix 39
Chronology of Important Events in BYU History, 1875-1975

1875

October 16: Brigham Young executed a Deed of Trust for the founding of Brigham Young Academy.

November 22: The Board of Trustees was named and organized. The seven members appointed by Brigham Young were Abraham O. Smoot, Myron Tanner, Leonard Harrington, Harvey H. Cluff, Wilson Dusenberry, William Bringhurst, and Martha Jane Knowlton Coray. A.O. Smoot was elected president of the Board, with W.H. Dusenberry as secretary and Harvey H. Cluff as treasurer.

December 4: Warren N. Dusenberry was elected first principal of Brigham Young Academy by the Board.

1876

January 3: The first "experimental term" at BYA commenced.

April 21: Karl G. Maeser arrived in Provo and became the new principal of Brigham Young Academy. Warren Dusenberry resigned as principal of BYA, his administration having lasted a little over three months. At that time there were ninety-seven students and three teachers.

August 21: The first full year began with the dedication of the institution by Daniel H. Wells. There were 273 students enrolled.

1877

June 1: An additional endowment of property was made by Brigham Young to BYA. It amounted to 3.1 acres of land adjoining the land conveyed on 16 October 1875. By this action, Brigham Young Academy more than doubled its net worth.

August 29: Brigham Young died.

1878

February 1: The Domestic Department was organized to provide housing for non-Provo students.

1879

1880

1881

1882

May 9: Benjamin Cluff, Jr., returned to Utah after a three-and-one-half-year mission to Hawaii.

August 28: The LDS Church officially began assisting in financing the operation of Brigham Young Academy.

September 25: Benjamin Cluff, Jr., was hired as an instructor at Brigham Young Academy.

1883

July 7: Milton H. Hardy resigned as head of the Intermediate Department.

August 16: Benjamin Cluff, Jr., married Mary John.

1884

January 27: The Lewis Building was destroyed by fire.

March 2: John Taylor and other General Authorities visited Provo and selected a new site for BYA.

May 23: The property and grounds for the soon-to-be-constructed Education Building were dedicated.

August 29: Franklin S. Harris was born at Benjamin, Utah.

1885

October 24: A mathematical club was organized by Benjamin Cluff, Jr.

1886

November 21: A group of Provo businessmen organized a Beneficiary Fund to keep Brigham Young Academy financially solvent.

December 19 Benjamin Cluff, Jr., was set apart by John Taylor to continue his education at the University of Michigan.

1887

March 24: Karl G. Maeser pleaded guilty to the charge of unlawful cohabitation and was fined $300.

May 4: Karl G. Maeser contemplated abandoning the Academy, as did a number of the faculty, all of whom had worked without pay for some time.

1888

June 8: The Church Board of Education was organized.

July 27: Karl G. Maeser was appointed the first superintendent of the LDS Church school system.

1889

February 9: The Methodist Church disclosed plans to build a Methodist University in Provo at a cost of from $300,000 to $1,000,000.

December 21: The General Board of Education recognized Brigham Young Academy as the Latter-day Saints Normal College.

1890

1891

March 16: Wilford Woodruff wrote Benjamin Cluff, Jr., requesting that he join the faculty of the new LDS College in Salt Lake City. This infuriated the BYA Board of Trustees, resulting in President Woodruff's withdrawal of the invitation.

October 16: Founders Day was instituted at the suggestion of Benjamin Cluff, Jr.

1892

January 4: Karl G. Maeser delivered his farewell address, and the Education Building was dedicated. Benjamin Cluff, Jr., was appointed principal.

April 4: Karl G. Maeser and Benjamin Cluff, Jr., were appointed by the First Presidency to be members of a committee to help establish the Church University in Salt Lake City.

June 23:	Brigham Young Academy was $61,107 in debt.
1893	
May 26:	The Alumni Association was organized, with George H. Brimhall appointed its first president.
1894	
January 29:	President Wilford Woodruff officially abandoned the idea of founding a Church university.
July 18:	Howard S. McDonald was born in Salt Lake City.
1895	
March 6:	Abraham O. Smoot died.
May 22:	Brigham Young, Jr., replaced Abraham O. Smoot as president of the Board of Trustees.
July 20:	The title of principal was changed to president.
1896	
July 18:	New Articles of Incorporation were adopted with the Church as the sponsor for Brigham Young Academy.
October 16:	The College of Arts and Sciences was established.
1897	
August 2:	President Cluff suggested branches of the Academy be established in stakes that desired them.
1898	
September 26:	Facilities for the Beaver Branch of BYA were dedicated.
November 18:	George H. Brimhall became a member of the Board of Trustees.
December 28:	Benjamin Cluff, Jr., suggested the organization of the Academy Fund.
1899	
February 17:	Fund Day was inaugurated.
May 4:	Ernest L. Wilkinson was born in Ogden, Utah.
1900	
april 17:	The Cluff expedition to Mexico and South America began.
May 5:	The Cluff expedition entered Arizona.
September 19:	Athletic directors were appointed in basketball, baseball, and track.
October 12:	Football was banned from all Church academies.
1901	
February 15:	Karl G. Maeser died.
April 1:	Joseph F. Smith was appointed president of the Board of Trustees.
May 14:	Acting President George H. Brimhall submitted a plan for a training school and gymnasium.
October 16:	Doctors and lawyers of Provo offered to help establish medical and law schools at Brigham Young Academy.
1902	
January 11:	The Cluff expedition was asked by the First Presidency to return to Utah.
February 17:	The $35,000 Training School and gymnasium building was dedicated.

1903

May 9:	Brigham Young Academy won the first state intercollegiate athletic meet.
August 19:	Benjamin Cluff, Jr., failed to have Brigham Young Academy's name changed to Joseph Smith College.
September 22:	Benjamin Cluff, Jr., suggested that the name Brigham Young Academy be changed to Brigham Young University.
October 23:	Brigham Young Academy became Brigham Young University by decision of the First Presidency.
November 17:	Benjamin Cluff, Jr., resigned as president of Brigham Young University.

1904

April 16:	George H. Brimhall was appointed president of BYU.
October 26:	Joseph F. Smith offered the dedicatory prayer at the ceremony opening the $13,000 Missionary and Preparatory (Arts) Building.

1905

1906

October 16:	Jesse Knight donated 500 acres of land to BYU.

1907

October 12:	Jesse Knight secured water rights for BYU land.
November 1:	BYU made application to the Church to become the official Church university.

1908

January 16:	Temple Hill (upper campus) was dedicated.
May 3:	BYU was recognized as the official Church university.
June 3:	Officials broke ground for the construction of the Maeser Memorial Building.
October 6:	Students and faculty assembled at the grave of Karl G. Maeser to unveil a monument in his honor.

1909

February 11:	BYU was recognized as the Church Teachers College.
March 26:	The University was organized into departments.
May 17:	Students adopted a revised version of a proposed student body constitution, and the White and Blue political parties were originated.
August 31:	The BYU Alumni Association was incorporated.
October 16:	Joseph F. Smith laid the cornerstone of the $115,000 Maeser Memorial Building.

1910

October 25:	William Chamberlain spoke in a sacrament meeting on superstitions in the Bible.

1911

January 21:	Horace H. Cummings submitted a report to the Church Board of Education on "subversive teachings" at BYU.

1912

February 12:	The practice of conferring honorary degrees was inaugurated, and Emmeline B. Wells received the Doctor of

Literature degree.

August 29: George H. Brimhall recommended erection of an amusement hall — women's gymnasium to cost $29,212.

December 11: The Alumni Association purchased forty-two acres of land on Temple Hill from William H. Brereton.

1913

1914

June 15: The BYU administration was ordered by the Board of Trustees to liquidate the school's assets.

December 21: Jesse Knight endowed BYU with $100,000.

1915

1916

May 21: The Board of Trustees authorized conferring of master's degrees.

1917

May 2: Having been signed by a majority of college and high school students, a petition requesting that school be let out early so the male students could join the army was submitted to the administration.

December 18: A permanent BYU women's organization was initiated, with Mrs. Christen Jensen as president.

1918

August 1: Three BYU professors and forty students entered the Presidio of San Francisco for military training.

October 1: The Student Army Training Corps program commenced at BYU.

November 19: Heber J. Grant became the new President of the LDS Church.

December 23: The BYU Student Army Training Corps was disbanded.

1919

April 3: David O. McKay became the new commissioner of Church education, with Stephen L Richards and Richard R. Lyman as counselors.

July 16: Adam S. Bennion was appointed the new superintendent of Church schools.

1920

July 20: George H. Brimhall was requested to devote a portion of his time to the supervision of seminary work in the Church school system.

1921

March 14: Jesse Knight died.

April 28: A Research Division was established.

May 25: A new College of Commerce and Business Administration was approved by the Board of Trustees.

June 20: George H. Brimhall became professor emeritus of theology and was granted an honorary LLB degree.

July 1: Franklin S. Harris became the new president of BYU.

September 21: The *Y News* replaced the *White and Blue* as the official BYU student newspaper.

October 17:	The inauguration of Franklin S. Harris was held.
1922	
January 23:	The first BYU Leadership Week commenced.
April 4:	The high school building was officially named the Education Building.
July 14:	The first BYU Alpine Summer School commenced.
1923	
April 7:	BYU was accredited by the Northwest Association of Secondary and Higher Schools.
June 6:	The remaining Manavu property was transferred to BYU by the Alumni Association for $1 plus the incurred debt of almost $8,000 remaining on the property.
August 15:	Ernest L. Wilkinson and Alice Valera Ludlow were married in the Salt Lake Temple.
September 22:	BYU was admitted to membership in the American Council of Education.
October 1:	The name *Cougars* was adopted as a nickname for BYU athletes.
November 26:	The Carnegie retirement plan began for BYU staff members.
1924	
March 12:	The Executive Committee of the Board of Trustees decided that there would be no fraternities or sororities at BYU.
May 3:	BYU was admitted as a member of the National Association of Colleges and Universities.
August 18:	$125,000 was appropriated for construction of a new library.
October 16:	Groundbreaking ceremonies were held for the Heber J. Grant Library.
1925	
March 14:	The College of Fine Arts was established, with Gerrit de Jong as dean.
October 16:	The Heber J. Grant Library was dedicated.
1926	
January 27:	Publication of the monthly alumni magazine, *Y Alumnus,* began.
March 3:	John A. Widtsoe announced in a Church Board of Education meeting that a Church school system duplicating the public schools was ideal if the Church had the money.
April 7:	Adam S. Bennion, superintendent of Church schools, announced that the First Presidency had decided the Church would withdraw from the academic field and that all Church schools would soon be closed.
July 6:	Neal A. Maxwell was born in Salt Lake City.
October 27:	Franklin S. Harris arrived in Tokyo to attend the third Pan-Pacific Science Congress. L. John Nuttall, Jr., was named acting president of BYU.

1927

January 13: BYU was admitted to membership in the Association of American Colleges.

August 19: Franklin S. Harris and his wife Estella arrived in Provo after their year-long trip around the world.

November 5: A plan for organizing social units was adopted.

December 27: Joseph F. Merrill replaced Adam S. Bennion as superintendent of Church schools.

1928

January 14: The Beta Delta chapter of Alpha Kappa Psi, professional commerce fraternity, was organized at BYU.

March 22: Joseph F. Merrill was instructed by his superiors that the policy of the Church was to eliminate Church schools.

October 26: The $25,000 stadium was completed and dedicated.

November 20: BYU was accredited by the Association of American Universities.

1929

January 24: Benjamin Brown asked Franklin S. Harris to serve as chairman of the ICOR expedition to Russia.

February 20: The General Church Board of Education publicly announced its intention to close all Church schools.

May 2: It was announced by Church education officials that the continued employment of faculty members in violation of either the Word of Wisdom or the law of tithing would cease.

June 12: Franklin S. Harris and his secretary, Kiefer B. Sauls, left Salt Lake City on their way to Russia. Edward H. Holt was appointed acting president of BYU.

July 4: The ICOR expedition arrived in Moscow.

October 22: Franklin S. Harris and Kiefer Sauls arrived in London on their way home from Russia.

November 14: The Alumni Association was commissioned by Heber J. Grant to poll alumni to ascertain whether BYU should be closed.

1930

November 15: Franklin S. Harris visited several branches of the Church in Mexico, instructing them on agricultural techniques.

1931

January 31: The Phi chapter at BYU became the twentieth member of Beta Beta Beta, honorary international biology fraternity.

April 23: BYU administrative offices were transferred from the Education Building to the Maeser Memorial Building.

December 3: BYU and the Bureau of Research of the U.S. Forest Service made an agreement permitting Forest Service personnel to use University laboratories.

1932

April 15: The grandstand on Temple Hill was demolished by fire.

July 29:	George H. Brimhall died at age seventy-nine.
August 12:	Dallin H. Oaks was born in Provo, Utah.
1933	
May 11:	Faculty salaries were reduced by another twelve and one-half percent, making a total reduction for the Depression years of twenty-two and one-half percent.
July 1:	Weber College was transferred to the state.
1934	
1935	
October 16:	The George H. Brimhall building was dedicated by Heber J. Grant.
1936	
May 2:	Sigma Pi Sigma, national physics fraternity, installed a chapter at BYU.
1937	
June 9:	The Stadium House was paid for.
1938	
March 21:	Allen Hall was completed.
April 30:	Cornelius R. Peterson replaced H. Rex Johnson as Alumni Association general secretary.
August 8:	J. Reuben Clark, Jr., delivered an address on LDS educational philosophy.
1939	
February 2:	The BYU Board of Trustees was changed to be composed of General Authorities.
July 15:	Franklin S. Harris left for a government assignment in Iran.
September 12:	Franklin S. Harris met with the Shah of Iran.
November 8:	The Dame's Club was organized.
1940	
April 27:	Alice Wilkinson was the featured speaker at the annual Alumni Association banquet.
May 9:	Church leaders informed Franklin S. Harris that faculty members who had not paid a full tithe the prior year would not receive an increase in salary for the next school year.
July 2:	Franklin S. and Estella Harris left Iran.
1941	
January 1:	A faculty retirement plan was adopted by the Executive Committee of the Board of Trustees.
February 9:	Reed Smoot died at age seventy-nine.
June 3:	The Emeritus Club was organized.
August 31:	Franklin S. and Estella Harris arrived in Provo from their assignment in Iran.
October 16:	The Joseph Smith Memorial Building was dedicated.
December 17:	Franklin S. Harris urged students to avoid the hysteria of the war and stay in school.
1942	
March 13:	BYU began a Civilian Pilot Training Program with

twenty-eight students.

July 1: 300 army privates arrived at BYU to undertake the Army Specialized Training Program.

1943

1944

April 8: The Alumni Association began plans for a student union building.

October 28: The Board of Trustees of Utah State Agricultural College offered Franklin S. Harris the job of president of the college.

November 27: Franklin S. Harris informed the faculty that he had accepted the position of president of Utah State Agricultural College.

1945

February 21: The First Presidency decided it would no longer be wise to place the entire Church Educational System under the direction of one man; therefore, individual units of the Church system were granted autonomy.

March 29: Franklin R. Haymore replaced Ralph Britsch as general secretary of the Alumni Association.

June 30: Franklin S. Harris left BYU for his new job in Logan.

July 1: Howard S. McDonald became president of BYU.

1946

November 7: Harold Glen Clark replaced Franklin R. Haymore as general secretary of the Alumni Association.

1947

May 11: Groundbreaking took place for the Carl F. Eyring Science Center.

1948

March 11: Radio station KBYU began broadcasting.

September 30: The *Universe* replaced the *Y News* as the student newspaper.

1949

April 29: The Board of Trustees met in Salt Lake City to reincorporate Brigham Young University.

September 28: The Board of Trustees agreed to allow Howard S. McDonald to take the position of president of the Los Angeles State College of Applied Arts and Sciences if he so desired.

November 1: Dean Christen Jensen was called to be acting president of BYU.

1950

January 20: The Board of Trustees established that a course in American History and Government would be a requirement for graduation.

April 24: Christen Jensen was instructed by Church leaders to reduce BYU's budget by twenty percent for the coming year.

May 24: Joseph Fielding Smith officiated at groundbreaking

	ceremonies for the George Albert Smith Fieldhouse.
July 7:	The Executive Committee of the Board of Trustees recommended that Ernest L. Wilkinson be offered the position as president of BYU.
September 18:	George Albert Smith announced that Ernest L. Wilkinson would be the new president of BYU.
October 17:	The Eyring Science Center was dedicated by George Albert Smith.
1951	
February 15:	Governor J. Bracken Lee caused a bill to be introduced into the Utah State Senate that would turn state-owned colleges back to the Church.
March 15:	At a meeting of the Mountain States Athletic Conference, Ernest L. Wilkinson introduced an unsuccessful motion to abandon all subsidies for athletes.
May 28:	The Air Force ROTC program was activated at BYU.
June 1:	The total investment in physical plant facilities at BYU was estimated to be $6,150,440.
October 8:	Ernest L. Wilkinson was inaugurated as president of BYU.
December 1:	The $1 million George Albert Smith Fieldhouse opened.
1952	
May 9:	The BYU Board of Trustees announced the union of LDS Business College by BYU.
June 20:	The Board of Trustees approved the motion to make the McCune School of Music a branch of BYU.
1953	
April 16:	The Executive Committee of the Board of Trustees approved a motion to develop a campus master plan.
June 26:	Ernest L. Wilkinson's appointment as administrator of Church schools was officially confirmed by the Board of Trustees.
September 12:	A committee was appointed to reopen the bid for a student union building.
October 3:	Sixteen Heritage Halls units were completed at a cost of $3,032,000.
December 21:	The state legislature passed J. Bracken Lee's bill to turn state-owned colleges back to the Church.
1954	
May 26:	Sixteen Heritage Halls women's housing units were dedicated.
July 14:	The First Presidency announced the construction of a Church college in Hawaii.
October 1:	2,615 female students applied for 1,445 available on-campus living spaces.
December 14:	The David O. McKay Building was dedicated.
1955	
March 3:	Ernest L. Wilkinson recommended to the Executive

Committee of the Board of Trustees the formation of a stake on campus.

November 9: Approval was given to form a stake at BYU.

1956

January 8: The first BYU stake was organized.

July 4: Ernest L. Wilkinson met with Keys D. Metcalf, librarian emeritus of Harvard University, to consult on plans for a new library at BYU.

August 19: The *Universe* became a daily newspaper.

November 30: LDS Business College and the McCune School of Music and Art were eliminated as branches of BYU.

1957

January 1: Janie Thompson resigned from the Program Bureau.

April 19: The $2,200,000 Joseph F. Smith Family Living Center was completed.

May 7: The Benjamin Cluff, Jr., Plant Science Laboratory, the Harvey Fletcher Engineering Building, the Howard S. McDonald Student Health Center, eight Heritage Halls, and the Joseph F. Smith Family Living Center were dedicated.

July 11: David O. McKay decided not to move Ricks College to Idaho Falls.

August 15: A revised campus plan was presented to Ernest L. Wilkinson by a special planning committee.

November 22: Doctoral degrees were authorized.

1958

June 19: The LDS Church purchased 169 acres of land in Salt Lake City as the site for a junior college.

November 7: Helaman Halls men's dormitories were dedicated.

1959

1960

April 13: The William Snell Industrial Education Building was dedicated.

October 16: The Jesse Knight Building and two residence halls in the Helaman Halls group were dedicated.

1961

March 8: Groundbreaking ceremonies were held for the $220,000 Alumni House.

May 1: Ernest L. Wilkinson addressed the U.S. Chamber of Commerce in Washington, D.C., and was awarded the George Washington Medal by the Freedom Foundation of Valley Forge for his remarks.

June 2: The first doctoral degrees were awarded.

July 16: The Abraham O. Smoot Administration Building was completed.

August 22: Groundbreaking ceremonies for the $6,765,000 Ernest L. Wilkinson Center and Wymount Terrace were held.

September 6: The Board of Trustees announced that three stakes and

	twenty-eight wards would be adequate for BYU.
November 7:	The Chemical Engineering Department was fully accredited.
December 15:	Construction began on the $975,000 Physical Plant Building.
1962	
May 25:	The Alumni House was dedicated.
June 28:	Groundbreaking ceremonies for the Franklin S. Harris Fine Arts Center were held.
September 21:	The Physical Plant Building was completed.
October 10:	The Physical Plant Building, the Harold B. Lee Library, and the Abraham O. Smoot Administration Building were dedicated.
1963	
July 3:	Ernest L. Wilkinson presented a modified proposal for junior colleges to the Board of Trustees.
November 20:	Ernest L. Wilkinson announced to the Executive Committee of the Board of Trustees his intention to seek the 1964 Republican senatorial nomination.
1964	
January 9:	Ernest L. Wilkinson resigned as president of BYU. Earl C. Crockett became acting president.
May 3:	The number of BYU stakes was increased from three to six.
December 2:	Ernest L. Wilkinson was reappointed as president of BYU and chancellor of the Unified Church School System.
1965	
January 4:	Ernest L. Wilkinson was reappointed president of BYU.
February 8:	The positions of chancellor of the Church school system and president of BYU were separated. Ernest L. Wilkinson remained president of BYU, and Harvey L. Taylor was appointed acting administrator of The Church of Jesus Christ of Latter-day Saints Church Schools (the term "Unified" was dropped from the title).
April 3:	The Franklin S. Harris Fine Arts Center and the Ernest L. Wilkinson Center were dedicated by Joseph Fielding Smith.
May 28:	Associate degrees with the accompanying designation "technician" were granted by the General College.
November 8:	KBYU-TV went on the air.
1966	
April 26:	An accreditation team from the Northwest Association of Secondary and Higher Schools visited Brigham Young University.
1967	
September 1:	The University Press was organized.
November 1:	The Board of Trustees authorized the construction of the Marriott Center.

1968

October 2: The Indoor Tennis Court Building was completed.

1969

March 27: The civil rights director of the Department of Health, Education, and Welfare called BYU "one of the very finest schools we have visited."

November 12: President Kenneth Pitzer of Stanford University suspended all future relations with BYU because of BYU's policy on Blacks.

1970

January 18: David O. McKay died.

June 25: Kenneth Pitzer resigned as president of Stanford University.

August 1: Neal A. Maxwell became commissioner of Church schools.

1971

March 9: Harold B. Lee announced to the BYU student body the resignation of Ernest L. Wilkinson and the decision to establish a law school at BYU.

May 4: Dallin Oaks's name was presented to the Board of Trustees as the successor to Ernest L. Wilkinson.

July 24: Wyview Park was completed.

August 1: Dallin H. Oaks became president of BYU.

September 1: The Marriott Center was substantially completed.

November 9: Dallin Oaks announced that Rex E. Lee would be the founding dean of the J. Reuben Clark Law School.

1972

February 9: The Provo Temple was dedicated.

1973

February 4: The Marriott Activities Center was dedicated.

August 27: Opening ceremonies were held for the J. Reuben Clark Law School.

1974

February 19: The Engineering Building, James E. Talmage Math-Computer Building, and the Nicholes Chemistry Storage Building were dedicated by Delbert L. Stapley.

April 6: Neal A. Maxwell was sustained as an Assistant to the Twelve.

September 17: Spencer W. Kimball spoke to an audience of 24,265 at the Marriott Center.

1975

July 21: The Title IX regulation took effect.

September 5: The J. Reuben Clark Law School was dedicated.

October 10: Spencer W. Kimball delivered his Second Century Address at the special Centennial Convocation.

October 16: Dallin Oaks announced BYU's formal opposition to certain parts of the Title IX regulation.

Appendix 40
Principals of Brigham Young High School

Name	Dates of Service
George H. Brimhall	1895-1900
N.L. Nelson	1900-1904
Edwin S. Hinckley	1904-1909
William H. Boyle	1909-1926
A.C. Lambert	1926-1928
Edgar M. Jenson	1928-1935
Golden Woolf	1935-1946
A. John Clarke	1946-1948
Herbert Christensen	1948-1950
Wayne Sorensen	1950-1952
Rowan C. Stutz	1952-1954
Morris A. Shirts	1954-1957
Avard A. Rigby	1957-1959
Edwin A. Read	1959-1964
Lowell D. Thomson	1964-1968

Note: Prior to 1895 there was no separately designated principal of Brigham Young High School. The facility ceased operation after the 1967-68 school year.

Appendix 41

Brigham Young University Alumni Killed in Action in Viet Nam

Name	Home Town	Death Date
Bitton, Gary W.	Blackfoot, Idaho	10 January 1964
Bragg, Fred Garland, Jr.	Newark, Ohio	12 July 1967
Bretches, Raymond Dean	Santa Barbara, California	January 1968
Brown, Michael George	Parker, Idaho	19 September 1968
Chipman, Ralph Jim	American Fork, Utah	27 December 1972
De Celle, Robert E. II	Alameda, California	21 February 1971
Dewall, Howard Jacob	Salt Lake City, Utah	11 December 1967
Duce, Roger L.	Lancaster, California	10 May 1968
Duffin, Rey Lamar	Tooele, Utah	17 November 1967
Enos, Leonard Arvin	Scottsdale, Arizona	25 May 1967
Falconer, Paul B. III	Garden Grove, California	9 July 1968
Golden, Mervin Dennis	Boise, Idaho	9 June 1969
Hales, Raymon Draper	Mapleton, Utah	9 July 1969
Hansen, Craig H.	Soda Springs, Idaho	20 June 1969
Johnson, Kim William	Fresno, California	23 February 1968
Keown, Blair Logan	Murray, Utah	28 June 1968
King, Dennis Duane	Green River, Wyoming	20 February 1968
Littler, James Leslie III	Bartlesville, Oklahoma	3 July 1968
Meiners, Paul Albert	Burley, Idaho	2 March 1966
Moulton, Lester Neal	Victor, Idaho	25 May 1970
Mower, Gary Ruel	Fairview, Utah	21 May 1970
Newell, Gregg A.	Richfield, Utah	14 December 1969
Percival, Alton Dee	Roosevelt, Utah	28 January 1969
Powel, Lynn Kesler	Provo, Utah	21 August 1967
Rex, Robert Alan	Randolph, Utah	8 December 1968
Richins, Kim Jesse	Carmichael, California	before 4 March 1969
Robbins, Larry Oliver	Santaquin, Utah	13 May 1969
Romano, Jon August	New Providence, New Jersey	26 June 1969
Standring, Lauren W.	Reseda, California	August 1970
Stevenson, Jess Brent	Layton, Utah	9 March 1969
Wadsworth, John Lanier	Raleigh, North Carolina	8 July 1970
Walker, Henson Frank	Pleasant Grove, Utah	13 June 1969
Whiting, Ronald N.	Blackfoot, Idaho	16 January 1968
Yardley, Rodney B.	Clearfield, Utah	27 November 1968

Missing in Action

Evert, Lawrence G.	Chandler, Arizona	8 November 1967
Stephensen, Mark Lane	Riverton, Utah	1968
Strange, Floyd Wayne	Chico, California	2 December 1967
Wood, Don Charles	Provo, Utah	16 January 1966

Appendix 42

Cumulative Daytime Enrollment at BYU, 1876-77 to 1974-75

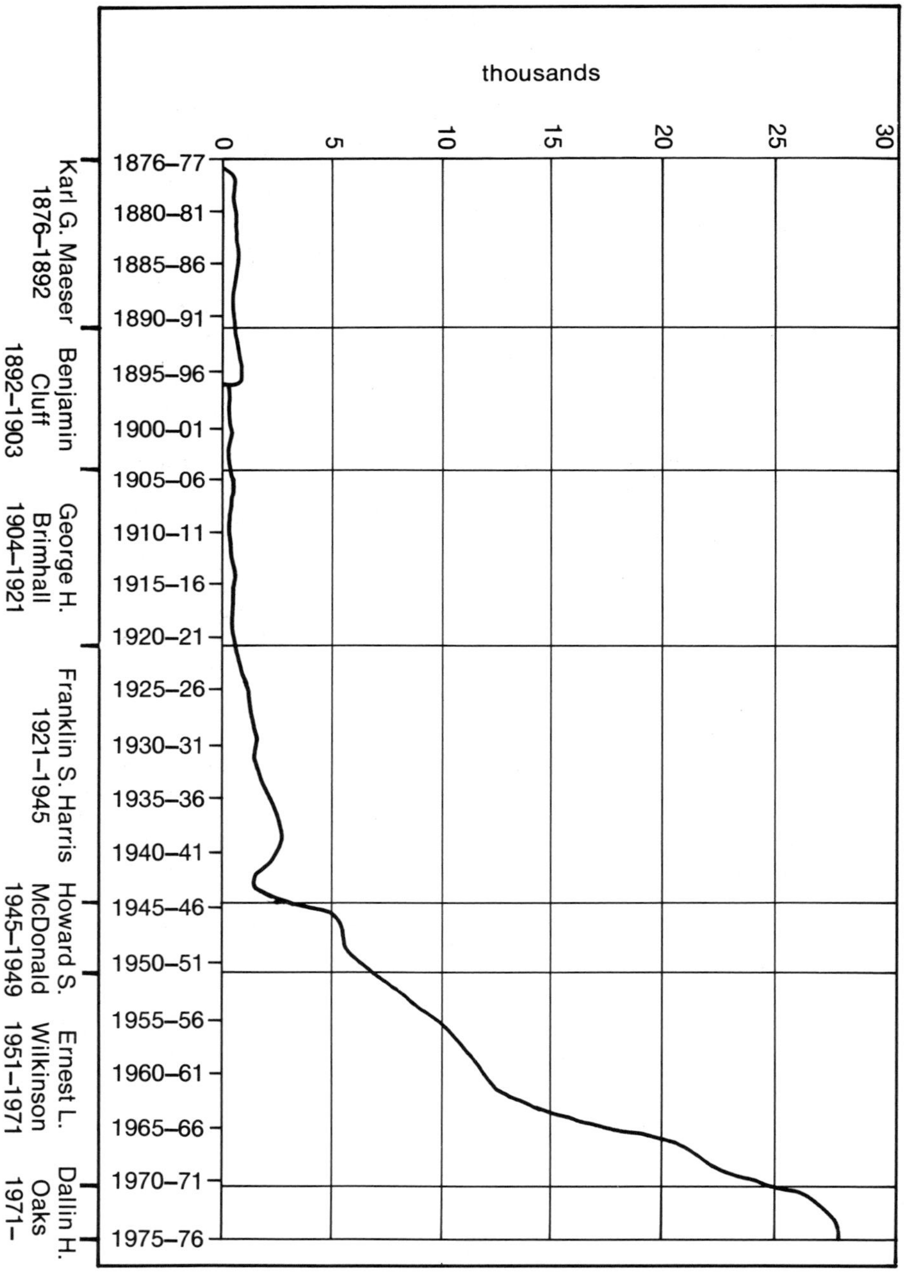

Appendix 43

Summary of Certificates and Degrees Awarded at BYU, 1876 to 31 August 1975

	Normal Cert.	Cert.	Assoc. Degree	Bach. Degree	Master's Degree	Special Graduate Cert.	Doctor's Degree	Juris Doctor	Honorary Degree	Total
Karl G. Maeser (1876–92)	—	243	—	—	—	—	—	—	1	244
Benjamin Cluff (1892–1903)	18	107	—	86	—	—	—	—	—	211
George H. Brimhall (1904–21)	442	421	—	301	2	—	—	—	3	1,169
Franklin S. Harris (1921–39)	1,207	4	—	3,151	251	—	—	—	2	4,615
Christen Jensen (1939–40)	64	—	—	362	28	—	—	—	—	454
Franklin S. Harris (1940–45)	95	—	—	1,056	50	—	—	—	2	1,203
Howard S. McDonald (1945–49)	—	—	—	1,979	135	—	—	—	—	2,114
Christen Jensen (1949–51)	—	—	—	840	74	—	—	—	—	914
Ernest L. Wilkinson (1951–64)	—	—	106*	15,986	1,633	2	24	—	40	17,791
Earl C. Crockett (1964)	—	—	66*	1,899	265	—	13	—	2	2,245
Ernest L. Wilkinson (1965–71)	—	—	1,100	21,517	3,480	2	310	—	34	26,443
Dallin H. Oaks (1971–75)	—	—	2,080	21,131	3,792	12	555	4	13	27,585
Grand Total	1,826	775	3,352	68,308	9,710	16	902	4	97	84,988

*Two-year certificates were replaced by the granting of associate degrees beginning in 1964–65.

Appendix 44

Buildings Dedicated at BYU, 1875-1975

Name of Building	Completion Date	Dedication Date	Dedicated By
Allen Hall	1938	26 May 1954	David O. McKay (with 22 other buildings)
Alumni House (Groundbreaking, 9 Mar. 1961)	1961	25 May 1962	Marion G. Romney
Amanda Knight Hall	Spring 1939	26 May 1954	David O. McKay (with 22 other buildings)
Arts Building	1904	26 Oct. 1904	Joseph F. Smith
(Originally named the Missionary and Preparatory Building; renamed the Arts Building and rededicated)		16 Jan. 1908	John Henry Smith
Auxiliary Maintenance Building (Contract date: Nov. 1967)	10 Oct. 1968	29 Apr. 1969	Boyd K. Packer
Brimhall (George H.) Building (Original structure was the Mechanic Arts Building. Groundbreaking: 8 Oct. 1918.	Summer 1919		
Complete renovation took place and two floors were added in 1935; named and dedicated the George H. Brimhall Building)	5 Jun. 1935	16 Oct. 1935	Heber J. Grant
Carillon Tower and Bells Spencer W. Kimball	1975	10 Oct. 1975	Spencer W. Kimball
Clark (J. Reuben) Law School	1975	5 Sept. 1975	Marion G. Romney
Clark (Herald R.) Building (Formal opening: 19 Mar. 1953)	1952	26 May 1954	David O. McKay
Cluff (Benjamin, Jr.) Plant Science Lab. (Construction began 1954)	Summer 1955	7 May 1957	Joseph Fielding Smith
College Hall	1898	26 May 1898	Joseph F. Smith
Deseret Towers			
Melvin J. Ballard Hall	1964	6 Oct. 1970	Ezra Taft Benson

Name of Building	Completion Date	Dedication Date	Dedicated By
Adam S. Bennion Hall	1964	6 Oct. 1970	Ezra Taft Benson
Charles A. Callis Hall	1964	6 Oct. 1970	Ezra Taft Benson
Charles W. Penrose Hall	1964	6 Oct. 1970	Ezra Taft Benson
George F. Richards Hall	1964	6 Oct. 1970	Ezra Taft Benson
Orson F. Whitney Hall	1964	6 Oct. 1970	Ezra Taft Benson
George Q. Morris Center	1964	6 Oct. 1970	Ezra Taft Benson
Education Building (Groundbreaking 21 May 1884. Originally known as the Academy Building, 1891; name changed to High School Building, 1898; name again changed to Education Building, 1922)	1891	4 Jan. 1892	George Q. Cannon
Engineering Sciences and Technology Building	1973	19 Feb. 1974	Delbert L. Stapley
Eyring (Carl F.) Science Center (Groundbreaking 11 May 1948. The building was originally named the Physical Science Center. It was renamed the Carl F. Eyring Physical Science Center on 16 May 1954 by David O. McKay.)	1950	17 Oct. 1950	George Albert Smith
Faculty Office Building	1968	6 Oct. 1970	Ezra Taft Benson
Fletcher (Harvey) Engineering Lab. (Additions made in 1954, 1955, and 1964)	1953	7 May 1957	Joseph Fielding Smith
Food Service and Receiving Building (Construction began 1 Nov. 1967)	10 Oct. 1968	29 Apr. 1969	Boyd K. Packer
Grant (Heber J.) Building (Originally the Heber J. Grant Library. Groundbreaking: 16 Oct. 1924)	1925	16 Oct. 1925	Heber J. Grant

Name of Building	Completion Date	Dedication Date	Dedicated By
Harris (Franklin S.) Fine Arts Center	Fall 1964	3 Apr. 1965	Joseph Fielding Smith
(Construction began 18 Jun. 1962)			
Helaman Halls			
(Construction began 22 Mar. 1957)			
Steven L. Chipman Hall	1958	7 Nov. 1958	Stephen L Richards
David John Hall	1958	7 Nov. 1958	Stephen L Richards
Thomas N. Taylor Hall	1958	7 Nov. 1958	Stephen L Richards
Ira N. Hinckley Family Hall	1958	7 Nov. 1958	Stephen L Richards
George Q. Cannon Center	1958	7 Nov. 1958	Stephen L Richards
William Budge Hall	1959	21 Oct. 1959	Henry D. Moyle
Marriner Wood Merrill Hall	1959	21 Oct. 1959	Henry D. Moyle
Jean Fossum May Hall	1970	6 Oct. 1970	Ezra Taft Benson
Heritage Halls			
Emma Lucy Gates Bowen Hall	1953	26 May 1954	David O. McKay
Mima Murdock Broadbent Hall	1953	26 May 1954	David O. McKay
Louie B. Felt Hall	1953	26 May 1954	David O. McKay
Ruth May Fox Hall	1953	26 May 1954	David O. McKay
Alice Merrill Horne Hall	1953	26 May 1954	David O. McKay
Estella Spilsbury Harris Hall	1953	26 May 1954	David O. McKay
Ann Mieth Maeser Hall	1953	26 May 1954	David O. McKay
Romania Pratt Penrose Hall	1953	26 May 1954	David O. McKay
Aurelia S. Rogers Hall	1953	26 May 1954	David O. McKay
Alice Robinson Richards Hall	1953	26 May 1954	David O. McKay
Ellis Reynolds Shipp Hall	1953	26 May 1954	David O. McKay
Louise Yates Robison Hall	1953	26 May 1954	David O. McKay
Emmeline B. Wells Hall	1953	26 May 1954	David O. McKay
Eliza R. Snow Hall	1953	26 May 1954	David O. McKay
Mary Fielding Smith Hall	1953	26 May 1954	David O. McKay
Lucy Mack Smith Hall	1953	26 May 1954	David O. McKay

Name of Building	Completion Date	Dedication Date	Dedicated By
Elsie C. Carroll Hall	1956	7 May 1957	Joseph Fielding Smith
Lavina C. Fugal Hall	1956	7 May 1957	Joseph Fielding Smith
Susa Young Gates Hall	1956	7 May 1957	Joseph Fielding Smith
Vilate M. Kimball Hall	1956	7 May 1957	Joseph Fielding Smith
Emily S. Richards Hall	1956	7 May 1957	Joseph Fielding Smith
Martha H. Tingey Hall	1956	7 May 1957	Joseph Fielding Smith
Elizabeth Ann Whitney Hall	1956	7 May 1957	Joseph Fielding Smith
Zina D. H. Young Hall	1956	7 May 1957	Joseph Fielding Smith
Indoor Tennis Courts	1968	6 Oct. 1970	Ezra Taft Benson
Knight (Jesse) Building (Groundbreaking 29 May 1959)	Fall 1960	10 Oct. 1960	Henry D. Moyle
Knight-Mangum Hall (Construction began 1946)	1947	26 May 1954	David O. McKay
Laundry (Auxiliary Services, Construction began 1 Nov. 1967)	10 Oct. 1968	29 Apr. 1969	Boyd K. Packer
Lee (Harold B.) Library (Library was originally named after J. Reuben Clark; named changed in 1974)	Sep. 1961	10 Oct. 1962	Hugh B. Brown
Lewis Building	(Building existed before BY Academy was established in 1875)		
Maeser (Karl G.) Memorial Building (Groundbreaking 16 Jan. 1908)	1911	30 May 1912	Joseph F. Smith
Maeser (Karl G.) Statue		7 Nov. 1958	Stephen L Richards
Marriott Center (Construction began 1968)	1971	4 Feb. 1973	Marion G. Romney
Martin (Thomas L.) Classroom Building (Construction began 10 Jul. 1968)	Summer 1969	6 Oct. 1970	Ezra Taft Benson
McDonald (Howard S.) Health Center (Construction began 1955)	1955	7 May 1957	Joseph Fielding Smith

Name of Building	Completion Date	Dedication Date	Dedicated By
McKay (David O.) Building (Construction began 8 Mar. 1954)	30 Nov. 1954	14 Dec. 1954	Stephen L Richards
Motion Picture Studio (Groundbreaking Apr. 1958)	1958	18 Feb. 1959	Carl W. Buehner
Nicholes Chemistry Stores Building	Jan. 1971	19 Feb. 1974	Delbert L. Stapley
Physical Plant Building (Construction began 15 Dec. 1961)	21 Sep. 1962	10 Oct. 1962	Hugh B. Brown
Richards (Stephen L) P.E. Building (Construction began 11 Dec. 1963)	Fall 1965	5 Nov. 1965	N. Eldon Tanner
Smith (George Albert) Fieldhouse (Groundbreaking 24 May 1950.	1951	26 May 1954	David O. McKay
The Smith Fieldhouse east addition was dedicated with the Richards P.E. Building;	1965	5 Nov. 1965	N. Eldon Tanner
west addition construction began 14 May 1959	24 Dec. 1959		
Joseph Smith Memorial Building (Construction began Jul. 1939. and renovations: 1964, 1965, 1966, and 1967)	1941	16 Oct. 1941	David O. McKay
Smith (Joseph F.) Family Living Center	1956	7 May 1957	Joseph Fielding Smith
Smoot (Abraham O.) Administration Bldg. (Construction began Oct. 1959)	16 Jul. 1961	10 Oct. 1962	Hugh B. Brown
Snell (William H.) Building (Groundbreaking 20 May 1959)	21 Dec. 1959	13 Apr. 1960	Thorpe B. Isaacson
Stadium	Fall 1964	6 Oct. 1970	Ezra Taft Benson
Talmage (James E.) Mathematical Sciences — Computer Building	28 Jan. 1971	19 Feb. 1974	Delbert L. Stapley
Training Building (Groundbreaking 28 Jun 1901)	1902	17 Feb. 1902	Joseph F. Smith

Name of Building	Completion Date	Dedication Date	Dedicated By
University Press Building (Construction began 1 Nov. 1967)	10 Oct. 1968	29 Apr. 1969	Boyd K. Packer
Wells (Daniel H.) ROTC Building	1968	29 Apr. 1969	Boyd K. Packer
Widtsoe (John A.) Building (Construction began 10 Jul. 1968)	Summer 1970	6 Oct. 1970	Ezra Taft Benson
Wilkinson (Ernest L.) Center (Construction began 16 Jun. 1961)	7 Apr. 1964	3 Apr. 1965	Joseph Fielding Smith
Wymount Terrace (married student housing)	1962-63		
Complex I	1962		
Sarah M. Kimball Hall		6 Oct. 1970	Ezra Taft Benson
Alice Louise Reynolds Hall		6 Oct. 1970	Ezra Taft Benson
Julina Lambson Smith Hall		6 Oct. 1970	Ezra Taft Benson
Complex II	1962		
Samuel O. Bennion Hall		6 Oct. 1970	Ezra Taft Benson
Antoine R. Ivins Hall		6 Oct. 1970	Ezra Taft Benson
J. Golden Kimball Hall		6 Oct. 1970	Ezra Taft Benson
Brigham H. Roberts Hall		6 Oct. 1970	Ezra Taft Benson
Complex III	1963		
Helen Spencer Williams Hall		6 Oct. 1970	Ezra Taft Benson
Complex IV	1963		
Charles W. Nibley Hall		6 Oct. 1970	Ezra Taft Benson
George Reynolds Hall		6 Oct. 1970	Ezra Taft Benson
Joseph L. Wirthlin Hall		6 Oct. 1970	Ezra Taft Benson
Levi Edgar Young Hall		6 Oct. 1970	Ezra Taft Benson
Complex V	1963		
William Clayton Hall		6 Oct. 1970	Ezra Taft Benson
John O. McClellan Hall		6 Oct. 1970	Ezra Taft Benson

Name of Building	Completion Date	Dedication Date	Dedicated By
Orson Pratt Hall		6 Oct. 1970	Ezra Taft Benson
Evan Stephens Hall		6 Oct. 1970	Ezra Taft Benson
Complex VI	1963		
Henry Aldous Dixon Hall		6 Oct. 1970	Ezra Taft Benson
Jacob Hamblin Hall		6 Oct. 1970	Ezra Taft Benson
George F. Sutherland Hall		6 Oct. 1970	Ezra Taft Benson
John C. Swensen Hall		6 Oct. 1970	Ezra Taft Benson
Complex VII	1962		
William J. Critchlow, Jr., Hall		6 Oct. 1970	Ezra Taft Benson
John Longden Hall		6 Oct. 1970	Ezra Taft Benson
Thomas E. McKay Hall		6 Oct. 1970	Ezra Taft Benson
Nicholas G. Smith Hall		6 Oct. 1970	Ezra Taft Benson
ZCMI Warehouse	(Building existed before BY Academy occupied it in 1884)		

Appendix 45

Howard S. McDonald's Assessment of the Accomplishments of His Own Administration

April 22, 1953

Mrs. LaVieve H. Earl
855 North University Avenue
Provo, Utah

Dear Sister Earl:

This is in answer to your letter of April 14, 1953, regarding the accomplishments during my administration of the Brigham Young University from 1945 to 1949. They are as follows:

Land Purchases

1) Twenty acres on Canyon Road for the Animal Husbandry Department.

2) About 15-20* acres where the North Building and Shops are located, just north of the Grove and south of the pear orchard.

3) About 5 or 10* acres just north of Wymount Village. Two houses are located on this property. They were converted to student housing. I think it was known as Neilson property.

   *Note: I do not remember the exact acreage. Kiefer Sauls could give it to you.

I wanted to buy other parcels of land but the Board of Trustees did not see fit to do so at that time.

Buildings Erected

1) Wymount Village, which housed 200 families and 200 single men students.

2) The North Building, transferred from the Small Arms Plant in Salt Lake City.

3) Printing Press Building, transferred from the Ogden Arsenal, and remodeled for school purposes.

4) Book Store Building, transferred from Ogden Arsenal, and remodeled for school purposes.

5) The Grove Cafeteria, transferred from Ogden Arsenal.

6) The Shop Building, transferred from the Small Arms Plant in Salt Lake City.

7) The Health Center Building, transferred from Ogden Arsenal, and remodeled for school purposes.

8) The transfer of Butler Huts from Stockton, California, remodeled to make up the Speech Building on the upper campus, a Science Building for B.Y.U. High School on lower campus, and a music building for the high school on the lower campus.

9) The new Upper Campus Dormitory, to house about 400 girl students.

10) The Social Hall on the Upper Campus to provide dancing space for 400 couples; also space for the B.Y.U. Music Department.

11) Installation of the Salt Lake Tabernacle Austin Organ in the Joseph Smith Auditorium.

12) The purchase of practice organs:
    1. Hammond Electric Organ.
    2. Moehler Pipe Organ.
    3. Schoenstein Pipe Organ.

13) The purchase of pianos:
    1. Steinway & Son (for President's home).
    2. Eight Baldwin grand pianos.
    3. About 12 new upright pianos for practice.

14) The erection of a Music Practice Building with 16 practice rooms, on the upper campus.

15) The erection of the Upper Campus Heating Plant with underground conduits to all parts of the upper campus.

16) The erection of a large quonset building for receiving, storage, and disbursing of equipment and supplies for the University.

17) The erection of a large quonset building for the processing of milk products — butter, bottled milk, cream and ice cream, etc.

18) The erection of a Laundry Plant for the campus.

19) The expansion of the stadium to twice the seating capacity.

20) The building of 8 modern tennis courts.

21) The erection of the new Physical Science Building — one of the best west of the Mississippi River.

22) The plans for the erection of the new Fieldhouse to seat 8,000 spectators.

Educational Program

1) The establishment of an efficient division of Student Personnel Service, one which has received recognition throughout the United States.

Under the Student Personnel Services, the following were reorganized:

1. Counseling and Guidance
2. Athletics
3. Attendance and Scholarship
4. Health Service
5. Scholarships and Awards
6. Student Employment
7. Student Housing
8. Student Loans
9. Student Publications

2) Study was in the process of curriculum revision for the University which also included a study of General Education for the University. This study was being made by a Committee of Administrators and Faculty Members.

3) The University was accredited by the National Society for the Study of Science.*

4) One of the finest herds of purebred Holstein cows was added to the program for educational purposes.

Musical Achievements

1) The Minneapolis Symphony Orchestra, under the direction of Dmitri Mitropolous, appeared two times, rendering two concerts each time.

2) The Philadelphia Symphony, under the direction of Eugene Ormandy, appeared once, giving two concerts.

3) The Los Angeles Symphony Orchestra, under the direction of Alfred Wallenstein, appeared for one week, rendering eight concerts.

4) The French Orchestra, under the direction of Charles Munch, appeared once, and rendered two concerts.

---

*Note: For the correct title of accrediting organization, consult Professor Joseph Nichols of the Chemistry Department.

5) Soloists such as Pinza, Traubel, Heifetz and Marion Anderson appeared on the stage.

6) The B.Y.U. Chorus, under the direction of Dr. and Mrs. Franklin Madsen, thrilled the General Conference audiences in 1947, 1948 and 1949.

7) We must not forget the many appearances of the Utah Symphony Orchestra, under the direction of Maurice Abravanel.

Faculty

The enrollment of the Brigham Young University grew from about 1600 students in the fall of 1945 to over 5500 students in the fall of 1949; therefore, many new faculty members were required.

1) I was proud of the scholastic background of the new members of the faculty. The University was strengthened academically in the additions.

2) LeRoy Robertson won the $25,000 Reickhold award for music composition.

Spirituality

In 1945, a small Sunday School was conducted mainly by members of the faculty. By 1949 we had organized two branches of the East Provo Stake on the campus, the Wymount Branch and the Campus Branch. Both branches were organized with student personnel. Sacrament meetings, Priesthood meetings, Sunday Schools and meetings of all auxiliary organizations were added with a wholesome support by students. From 1200 to 1600 students were attending both Sunday School and Sacrament meeting each Sunday at the Campus Branch. It was a thrill to hear the testimonies of the young men and women attending college. The youth of the Church is strong. I do not fear the outcome.

I regret to say we had a few students who did not conform to the ideals of the Church. This group, however, was small.

I feel that the growth of spirituality developed on the campus between 1945 and 1949 was far more important than all of the physical and material things added during those years.

I hope this gives you the information you desire.

Our graduation here takes place June 18 and 19. As you know, we have 20,000 students on this campus. June 15 is a little too close for Ella and me to attend your Alumni Day. We do extend to you all our love and best wishes.

Sincerely,

Howard McDonald

Appendix 46

P.A. Christensen on Amateur Athletics

In the earlier period of intercollegiate sports in America, educators thought it necessary to justify them in terms of their educational values.* The records of the NCAA show that about forty years ago a Harvard representative at the meetings of the NCAA argued eloquently that college sports in their essence were the physical expression of a spiritual loyalty, a loyalty to institution and to student body. To some of us here today who competed in athletics forty years ago, the value of competition certainly lay not so much in score or ratings or in physical benefits, as in the feeling that, through athletics, we were permitted to ally ourselves with the larger life of the campus and to represent that life in friendly competition with other men similarly devoted.

And it was easy in those days to believe that intercollegiate sports were expressive of and a formative influence in a larger life. They made for student body unity, and they taught fundamental lessons in democratic action. They brought together students with varied backgrounds and purposes in a common loyalty to common causes. In a way they seemed to prepare them for the cooperative loyalties of later life. They extended the spirit of common effort to the conference area. They encouraged the fraternization of student bodies, and stimulated wholesome rivalries in ideas, ideals, and practices.

Such beliefs were made relatively easy in those days by the fact that the young men who played the games were really "fellow students." They had come to the school of their choice, and they expected no special privileges. They were free and eligible to participate in every aspect of student life. They could be editors and valedictorians as well as tackles and second basemen. They expected and desired no compensation beyond the honor and pleasure of representing their school and their student associates.

The men responsible for the athletic programs on the campus were usually regular members of the faculty. They had educational perspective. Many things were to them more important than winning games. Their positions, and the security, happiness, and respectability of their wives and children in the college community were not contingent on the approval of the sporting public, or on the good will of that part of the alumni which somehow we always fail to educate.

Athletic conferences in those days were faculty conferences. They were dominated by men who represented the teaching forces of their institutions. They were pledged to keep athletics subordinate to the larger purposes of education and to preserve it as an activity of students, by students, and for students.

---

*This speech was delivered as the keynote address at a meeting of the Seventh District of the National Collegiate Athletic Association in Denver on 26 December 1950. Dr. Christensen was faculty representative to BYU's athletic council for many years.

No one here today needs to be told that time has brought changes. Few today would welcome the task of proving that athletics as now conducted can be justified in terms of educational value, or that they are still the physical expression of a spiritual loyalty, or that athletes, as we know them, are in a real sense "fellow students" or that they have come to our schools without persuasion or compensation, or that the men in charge of our athletic teams are men of educational perspective to whom winning teams are a matter of secondary importance, or that our conferences are still really controlled by representatives of faculties.

I fear it would be easier to show that athletes as we know them today are rarely "fellow students." By lengthening and intensifying the practice program and by ever widening the schedule of games within and without the conferences we have so monopolized and exploited the energies of the boys as largely to banish them from the larger life of the campus and to make it quite impossible for them to carry the normal academic load with any degree of distinction. Rarely, I fear, are they on our campuses through natural inclination or choice. We have practically forced them to sell themselves to the highest bidders, sometimes in the open market, more frequently, perhaps, in the black one. In the game they are no longer volunteer soldiers fighting out of love for institution and fellow students. Rather they are what the historian calls mercenaries, inspired frequently by no finer motives than a shrewd concern for additional compensation or a feeble sense of present contractual obligations. They are becoming not unlike a group of thoroughbreds, fed, groomed, and stabled apart, exhibited on weekends to ecstatic presidents, faculties, students, alumni, and the sporting public, and, of course, pointed ultimately toward national derbies and sweepstakes.

And this change in the status of the athlete on our campuses is perhaps the inevitable result of a change in administrative attitudes in educational institutions. There is, I fear, too much evidence that school authorities are not so much interested in athletics as a wholesome integral part of a local educative process as they are in athletics as an investment in state and national publicity, or as a bold venture in high finance. And this attitude is, of course, reflected in the administration of conference affairs. So-called faculty representatives are becoming less and less representative of faculties and more and more the automatic voices of athletic councils. Little by little they are surrendering their original powers to athletic directors, coaches, and commissioners. Little more than retainers of the special interests back home, they too frequently offer only a token resistance to tendencies which in their heads and hearts they deplore. In relinquishing their powers to directors and coaches, they appease their consciences with the thought that since these unfortunates have assumed the terrifying responsibility of athletic success, as success is now measured, they should be given every sporting chance to save their lives and reputations as best they can. And such is the civilization of our temples of learning today that failure to produce winning teams usually means that the presidential axe, supplied and sharpened by irresponsible sportswriters and half-educated alumni, will ultimately fall on their exposed and quivering necks.

If the conditions which I have sketched are evils, they are evils born of an inordinate desire for athletic supremacy, a desire that seems at times to have distorted the athletic and educational perspective of everyone on the campus from the janitor up to the president, and, off the campus, from the knot-hole urchin to the governor or state legislature. I see no remedy for these evils except in a return to athletic sanity on the upper levels. There must be a new attempt to appraise intercollegiate sports in terms of educational values. If they can be justified in such terms, then they must be conducted accordingly. To conduct them accordingly will demand that athletics throughout the nation minister to a general educational need and not to a particular institutional ambition. It will demand of presidents the educational statesmanship which asserts that an activity that is fundamentally desirable in college life everywhere must be maintained, not as a private monopoly, but as a common good.

In our present mood no good can come from a further removal of regulations governing methods of procuring and maintaining athletes. Remove the restraining influences of the NCAA while we are still unrepentant, and competitive anarchy will spread both within conferences and between or among them. For every new device for attracting and holding athletic power here, there will be a counter inducement there. Every agreement reached for the conduct of competitive buying in the open market will be nullified by subversive buying in the black market.

And it doesn't take a prophet to see what the final results will be. Intercollegiate athletics will disappear from hundreds of American campuses. Some schools will adopt the Chicago way in order to save what is left of institutional self-respect. Many will be forced out of competition by economic necessity. Monopolies will be established by institutions possessing the greatest competitive advantages — and, perhaps, the least compunction of conscience. Their thoroughbreds will be the best in the world, their food the most sumptuous, their grooming the most deft and meticulous, their stabling the most luxurious that legislatures, alumni, and bowl games can buy.

No one has been a more devoted lover of sports than I have been. I am sorry that my life-long devotion to them and the experiences of nearly twenty-five years as a faculty representative have not enabled me to make a more glowing confession of faith in things as they are. Frankly I see no salvation for athletics in our area and in America as a whole except from a general repentance and a sincere turning away from sin. I fear we are quite incapable of either.

Appendix 47

President David O. McKay to Ernest L. Wilkinson and the BYU Faculty

Dear President Wilkinson:

Recent disturbing events in our country — such as an alarming increase in nearly all categories of crime, divorce, juvenile and adult delinquency, riots at colleges, strikes of school teachers, civil disorders which go far beyond "peaceable assemblies," the resurrection of a pagan philosophy that God is dead, demoralizing movies, television programs which encourage lewd and lascivious conduct, and now a report of a national committee on law enforcement which, instead of recommending the enforcement of our criminal laws, would surrender to the forces of evil by eliminating from the category of crime nearly all sex offenses — have given me great concern and prompt me to write you as to measures which I hope you, as President of Brigham Young University, and the faculty will follow to make sure that the thousands of students under your supervision are receiving the proper teaching and training. I want them to be protected from the seriously increasing evils of the day which past prophets have indicated would come to pass, and which are now upon us.

(1) I want, first of all, to congratulate you, the faculty, and the students of Brigham Young University upon the fact that we have had no riots or other serious disturbances at the "Y" such as have tarnished the reputations of other institutions and brought down public condemnation upon them. In view, however, of current trends and pressures on our young people, as reflected daily by the public press, I wish that you and the faculty would be even more vigilant than you have been in the past to see that only students of acceptable spiritual and academic standards are admitted and retained, and that the reputation of Brigham Young University as a university where the "glory of God is intelligence," and where high standards of moral conduct, sobriety, and order are ever present, are not only maintained, but increasingly improved and enhanced.

(2) In these days when not only religious standards but some of the Ten Commandments themselves are under attack, I hope that you and the faculty will go the extra mile in seeing that the religious doctrines of our Church are taught in their fullness so that students will have proper religious convictions for all decisions which they have to make. The trends of the time in the opposite direction are so strong that it will require extraordinary vigilance on the part of all of us to resist them.

I have been happy over the years to know that the faculty itself some years ago resolved that the first qualification for appointment to the faculty of Brigham Young University is that of an "attitude toward and adherence to the principles of the Gospel of Jesus Christ." I am happy, also, to know that a very large number of faculty members are now serving with general boards, or as stake presidents, bishops, and high council members, and in other Church positions. I would urge all members of the faculty, whether they have a Church position or not, to teach the principles of the Gospel and standards in every class whenever the opportunity arises, whether that class be a class in theology or otherwise.

(3) I cannot help but think that there is a direct relationship between the present evil trends which I have above indicated, and the very marked tendency of the people of our country to pass on to the state the responsibility for their moral and economic welfare. This trend to a welfare state in which people look to and worship government more than their God, is certain to sap the individual ambitions and moral fiber of our youth unless they are warned and rewarned of the consequences. History, of course, is replete with the downfall of nations who, instead of assuming their own responsibility for their religious and economic welfare, mistakenly attempted to shift their individual responsibility to the government.

I am aware that a university has the responsibility of acquainting its students with the theories and doctrines which are prevalent in various disciplines, but I hope that no one on the faculty of Brigham Young University will advocate positions which cannot be harmonized with the views of every prophet of the Church, from the Prophet Joseph Smith on down, concerning our belief that we should be strong and self-reliant individuals, not dependent upon the largess or benefactions of government. None of the doctrines of our Church gives any sanction to the concept of a socialistic state.

It is a part of our "Mormon" theology that the Constitution of the United States was divinely inspired; that our Republic came into existence through wise men raised up for that very purpose. We believe it is the duty of the members of the Church to see that this Republic is not subverted either by any sudden or constant erosion of those principles which gave this Nation its birth.

In these days when there is a special trend among certain groups, including members of faculties of universities, to challenge the principles upon which our country has been founded and the philosophy of our Founding Fathers. I hope that Brigham Young University will stand as a bulwark in support of the principles of government as vouchsafed to us by our Constitutional Fathers.

Again, may I express my gratitude for all that you and members of the faculty have done to give Brigham Young University the reputation it now has. May God bless you to carry it to still greater heights, in the "Mormon" tradition I have set forth above. I remain

Sincerely yours,
David O. McKay

Appendix 48

President Spencer W. Kimball's Second Century Address

My beloved brothers and sisters:

It was almost precisely eight years ago that I had the privilege of addressing an audience at the Brigham Young University about "Education for Eternity." Some things were said then which I believe, then and now, about the destiny of this unique University. I shall refer to several of those ideas again, combining them with some fresh thoughts and impressions I have concerning Brigham Young University as it enters its second century.

I am grateful to all who made possible the Centennial Celebration for the Brigham Young University, including those who have developed the history of this University in depth. A centennial observance is appropriate, not only to renew our ties with the past, but also to review and reaffirm our goals for the future. My task is to talk about BYU's second century. Though my comments will focus on the Brigham Young University, it is obvious to all of us here that the University is, in many ways, the center of the Church's Educational System. President McKay described the University as "the hub of the Church educational wheel." Karl G. Maeser described the Brigham Young Academy as "the parent trunk of the great education banyan tree," and later it has been designated as "the flagship." However it is stated, the centrality of this University to the entire system is a very real fact of life. What I say to you, therefore, must take note of things beyond the borders of this campus, but not beyond its influence. We must ever keep firmly in mind the needs of those ever-increasing numbers of LDS youth in other places in North America and in other lands, who cannot attend this University, whose needs are real and who represent, in fact, the majority of LDS college and university students.

In a speech I gave to many of the devoted alumni of this University in the Arizona area, I employed a phrase to describe the Brigham Young University as becoming an "educational Everest." There are many ways in which BYU can tower above other universities — not simply because of the size of its student body or its beautiful campus — but because of the unique light BYU can send forth into the educational world. Your light must have a special glow, for while you will do many things in the programs of this University that are done elsewhere, these same things can and must be done better here than others do them. You will also do some special things here that are left undone by other institutions.

First among these unique features is the fact that education on this campus deliberately and persistently concerns itself with "education for eternity," not just for time. The faculty has a double heritage which they must pass along: the secular knowledge that history has washed to the feet of mankind with the new knowledge brought by scholarly research — but also the vital and revealed truths that have been sent to us from heaven.

This University shares with other universities the hope and the labor involved in rolling back the frontiers of knowledge even further, but we also know that through the process of revelation that there are yet "many great and important things" to be given to mankind which will have an intellectual and spiritual impact far beyond what mere men can imagine. Thus, at this University among faculty, students, and administration, there is and must be an excitement and an expectation about the very nature and future of knowledge that underwrites the uniqueness of BYU.

Your double heritage and dual concerns with the secular and the spiritual require you to be "bilingual." As LDS scholars you must speak with authority and excellence to your professional colleagues in the language of scholarship, and you must also be literate in the language of spiritual things. We must be more bilingual, in that sense, to fulfill our promise in the second century of BYU.

BYU is being made even more unique, not because what we are doing is changing, but because of the general abandonment by other universities of their efforts to lift the daily behavior and morality of their students.

From the administration of the BYU in 1967 came this thought:

> Brigham Young University has been established by the prophets of God and can be operated only on the highest standards of Christian morality.... Students who instigate or participate in riots or open rebellion against the policies of the University cannot expect to remain at the university.
>
> The standards of the Church are understood by students who have been taught these standards in the home and at Church throughout their lives.
>
> First and foremost, we expect BYU students to maintain a single standard of Christian morality....
>
> Attendance at BYU is a privilege and not a right, and ... students who attend must expect to live its standards or forfeit the privilege.
>
> [Ernest L. Wilkinson, July 1967]

We have no choice at BYU except to "hold the line" regarding gospel standards and values and to draw men and women from other campuses also — all we can — into this same posture, for people entangled in sin are not free. In this University (that may to some of our critics seem unfree) there will be real individual freedom. Freedom from worldly ideologies and concepts unshackles man far more than he knows. It is the truth that sets men free. BYU, in its second century, must become the last remaining bastion of resistance to the invading ideologies that seek control of curriculum as well as classroom. We do not resist such ideas because we fear them, but because they are false. BYU, in its second century, must continue to resist false fashions in education, staying with those basic principles which have proved right and have guided good men and women and good universities over the centuries. This concept is not new, but in the second hundred years we must do it even better.

When the pressures mount for us to follow the false ways of the world, we hope in the years yet future that those who are part of this University and the Church Educational System will not attempt to counsel the Board of Trustees to follow false ways. We want, through your administration, to receive all your suggestions for making BYU even better. I hope none will presume on the prerogatives of the prophets of God to set the basic direction for this University. No man comes to the demanding position of the

Presidency of the Church except his heart and mind are constantly open to the impressions, insights, and revelations of God. No one is more anxious than the Brethren who stand at the head of this Church to receive such guidance as the Lord would give them for the benefit of mankind and for the people of the Church. Thus, it is important to remember what we have in the revelations of the Lord:

> And thou shalt not command him who is at thy head, and at the head of the Church. [D&C 28:6]

If the governing board has as much loyalty from faculty and students, from administration and staff as we have had in the past, I do not fear for the future!

The Church Board of Education and the Brigham Young University Board of Trustees involve individuals who are committed to truth as well as to the order of the kingdom. I observed while I was here in 1967 that this institution and its leaders should be like the Twelve as they were left in a very difficult world by the Savior:

> The world hath hated them, because they are not of the world, even as I am not of the world.
>
> I pray not that thou shouldest take them out of the world, but that thou shouldest keep them from the evil.
>
> They are not of the world, even as I am not of the world. [John 17:14-16]

This University is not of the world any more than the Church is of the world, and it must not be made over in the image of the world.

We hope that our friends, and even our critics, will understand why we must resist anything that would rob BYU of its basic uniqueness in its second century. As the Church's Commissioner of Education said on the occasion of the inaugural of President Oaks,

> Brigham Young University seeks to improve and to "sanctify" itself for the sake of others — not for the praise of the world, but to serve the world better.

That task will be persisted in. Members of the Church are willing to doubly tax themselves to support the Church's Educational System, including this University, and we must not merely "ape the world." We must do special things that would justify the special financial outpouring that supports this University.

As the late President Stephen L Richards once said, "Brigham Young University will never surrender its spiritual character to a sole concern for scholarship." BYU will be true to its charter and to such addenda to that charter as are made by living prophets.

I am both hopeful and expectant that out of this University and the Church's Educational System there will rise brilliant stars in drama, literature, music, sculpture, painting, science, and in all the scholarly graces. This University can be the refining host for many such individuals who will touch men and women the world over long after they have left this campus.

We must be patient, however, in this effort, because just as the City of Enoch took decades to reach its pinnacle of performance in what the Lord described as occurring "in process of time" (Moses 7:21), so the quest for excellence at BYU must also occur "in process of time":

> Ideals are like stars; you will not succeed in touching them with your hands. But like the seafaring man on the desert of waters, you choose them as your guides, and following them you will reach your destiny. [Carl Schurz, 18 April 1975, Address in Faneuil Hall, Boston]

I see even more than was the case nearly a decade ago a widening gap between this University and other universities both in terms of purposes and in terms of directions. Much has happened in the intervening eight years to make that statement justifiable. More and more is being done, as I hoped it would, to have here "the greatest collection of artifacts, records, writings . . . in the world." BYU is moving toward preeminence in many fields, thanks to the generous support of the tithepayers of the Church and the excellent efforts of its faculty and students under the direction of a wise administration.

These changes do not happen free of pain, challenge, and adjustment. Again, harking back, I expressed the hope that the BYU vessel would be kept seaworthy by taking "out all old planks as they decay and put in new and stronger timber in their place," because the Flagship BYU must sail on and on and on. The creative changes in your academic calendar, your willingness to manage your curriculum more wisely, your efforts to improve general education, your interaction of disciplines across traditional departmental lines, and the creation of new research institutes here on this campus — all are evidences that the captain and crew are doing much to keep the BYU vessel seaworthy and sailing. I refer to the centers of research that have been established on this campus, ranging from family and language research on through to research on food, agriculture, and ancient studies. Much more needs to be done, but you must "not run faster or labor more than you have strength and means provided" (D&C 10:4). While the discovery of new knowledge must increase, there must always be a heavy and primary emphasis on transmitting knowledge — on the quality of teaching at BYU. Quality teaching is a tradition never to be abandoned. It includes a quality relationship between faculty and students. Carry these over into BYU's second century!

Brigham Young undoubtedly meant both teaching and learning when he said:

> Learn everything that the children of men know, and be prepared for the most refined society upon the face of the earth, then improve on this until we are prepared and permitted to enter the society of the blessed — the holy angels, that dwell in the presence of God. [*Journal of Discourses* 16:77]

We must be certain that the lessons are not only taught but are also absorbed and learned. We remember the directive that President John Taylor made to Karl G. Maeser "that no infidels will go forth from this school":

> Whatever you do, be choice in your selection of teachers. We do not want infidels to mould the minds of our children. They are a precious charge bestowed upon us by the Lord, and we cannot be too careful in rearing and training them. I would rather have my children taught the simple rudiments of a common education by men of God, and have them under their influence, than have them taught in the most abstruse

> sciences by men who have not the fear of God in their hearts. . . . We need to pay more attention to educational matters, and do all that we can to procure the services of competent teachers. Some people say, we cannot afford to pay them. You cannot afford not to pay them; you cannot afford not to employ them. We want our children to grow up intelligently, and to walk abreast with the peoples of any nation. God expects us to do it; and therefore I call attention to this matter. I have heard intelligent practical men say, it is quite as cheap to keep a good horse as a poor one, or to raise good stock as inferior animals. And is it not quite as cheap to raise good intelligent children as to rear children in ignorance? [*JD* 24:168-69]

Thus, we can continue to do as the Prophet Joseph Smith implied that we should when he said: "Man was created to dress the earth, to cultivate his mind, and to glorify God."

We cannot do these things except we continue, in the second century, to be concerned about the spiritual qualities and abilities of those who teach here. In the book of Mosiah we read,

> Trust no one to be your teacher nor your minister, except he be a man of God, walking in his ways and keeping his commandments. [23:14]

> I have no fear that the candle lighted in Palestine years ago will ever be put out. [William R. Inge]

We must be concerned with the spiritual worthiness, as well as the academic and professional competency, of all those who come here to teach. William Lyon Phelps said:

> I thoroughly believe in a university education for both men and women; but I believe a knowledge of the Bible without a college course is more valuable than a college course without the Bible.

Students in the second century must continue to come here to learn. We do not apologize for the importance of students' searching for eternal companions at the same time that they search the scriptures and search the shelves of libraries for knowledge. President McKay observed on one occasion that "the university is not a dictionary, a dispensary, nor is it a department store. It is more than a storehouse of knowledge and more than a community of scholars. The University life is essentially an exercise in thinking, preparing, and living." We do not want BYU ever to become an educational factory. It must concern itself with not only the dispensing of facts, but with the preparation of its students to take their place in society as thinking, thoughtful, and sensitive individuals who, in paraphrasing the motto of your Centennial, come here dedicated to love of God, pursuit of truth, and service to mankind.

There are yet other reasons why we must not lose either our moorings or our sense of direction in the second century. We still have before us the remarkable prophecy of John Taylor when he observed,

> You will see the day that Zion will be as far ahead of the outside world in everything pertaining to learning of every kind as we are today in regard to religious matters. You mark my words, and write them down, and see if they do not come to pass. [*JD* 21:100]

Surely we cannot refuse that rendezvous with history because so much of what is desperately needed by mankind is bound up in our being willing to contribute to the fulfillment of that prophecy. Others, at times, also seem to have a sensing of what might happen. Charles H. Malik, former president of the United Nations General Assembly, voiced a fervent hope when he said that

> One day a great university will arise somewhere . . . I hope in America . . . to which Christ will return in His full glory and power, a university which will, in the promotion of scientific, intellectual, and artistic excellence, surpass by far even the best secular universities of the present, but which will at the same time enable Christ to bless it and act and feel perfectly at home in it. ["Education and Upheaval: The Christian's Responsibility," *Creative Help for Daily Living,* 21 September 1970]

Surely BYU can help to respond to that call!

By dealing with basic issues and basic problems, we can be effective educationally. Otherwise, we will simply join the multitude who have so often lost their way in dark sunless forests even while working hard. It was Thoreau who said, "There are a thousand hacking at the branches of evil to one who is striking at the root" (1, "Economy," *Walden*). We should deal statistically and spiritually with root problems, root issues, and root causes in BYU's second century. We seek to do so, not in arrogance or pride, but in the spirit of service. We must do so with a sense of trembling and urgency because what Edmund Burke said is true: "The only thing necessary for the triumph of evil is for good men to do nothing" (letter to William Smith, 9 January 1795).

Learning that includes familiarization with facts must not occur in isolation from concern over our fellowmen. It must occur in the context of a commitment to serve them and to reach out to them.

In many ways the dreams that were once generalized as American dreams have diminished and faded. Some of these dreams have now passed so far as institutional thrust is concerned to The Church of Jesus Christ of Latter-day Saints and its people for their fulfillment. It was Lord Acton who said on one occasion,

> It was from America that the plain ideas that men ought to mind their business, and that the nation is responsible to Heaven for the acts of the State — ideas long locked in the breast of solitary thinkers, and hidden among Latin folios — burst forth like a conqueror upon the world they were destined to transform, under the title of the Rights of Man . . . and the principle gained ground, that a nation can never abandon its fate to an authority it cannot control [*The History of Freedom and Other Essays,* 1907]

Too many universities have given themselves over to such massive federal funding that they should not wonder why they have submitted to an authority they can no longer control. Far too many no longer assume that nations are responsible to heaven for the acts of the state. Far too many now see the Rights of Man as merely access rights to the property and money of others, and not as the rights traditionally thought of as being crucial to our freedom.

It will take just as much sacrifice and dedication to preserve these principles in the second century of BYU, and even more than were required to begin this institution in the first place—when it was once but a grade school, and then an academy supported by a stake of the Church. If we were to abandon our ideals, would there be any left to take up the torch of some of the principles I have attempted to describe?

I am grateful, therefore, that, as President Oaks observed, "There is no anarchy of values at Brigham Young University." There never has been. There never will be. But we also know, as President Joseph Fielding Smith observed in speaking on this campus, that "knowledge comes both by reason and by revelation." We expect the natural unfolding of knowledge to occur as a result of scholarship, but there will always be that added dimension which the Lord can provide when we are qualified to receive and he chooses to speak:

> A time to come in the which nothing shall be withheld, whether there be one God or many gods, they shall be manifest.

And further,

> All thrones and dominions, principalities and powers, shall be revealed and set forth upon all who have endured valiantly for the gospel of Jesus Christ. [D&C 121:28-29]

As the pursuit of excellence continues on this campus, and elsewhere in the Church Educational System, we must remember the great lesson taught to Oliver Cowdery who desired a special outcome — just as we desire a remarkable blessing and outcome for BYU in the second century. Oliver Cowdery wished to be able to translate with ease and without real effort. He was reminded that he erred, in that he "took no thought save it was to ask" (D&C 9:7). We must do more than ask the Lord for excellence. Perspiration must precede inspiration; there must be effort before there is excellence. We must do more than pray for these outcomes at BYU, though we must surely pray. We must take thought. We must make effort. We must be patient. We must be professional. We must be spiritual. Then, in the process of time, this will become the fully anointed University of the Lord about which so much has been spoken in the past.

We can sometimes make concord with others, including scholars who have parallel purposes. By reaching out to the world of scholars, to thoughtful men and women everywhere who share our concerns and at least some of the items on our agendum of action, we can multiply our influence and give hope to others who may assume that they are alone.

In other instances, we must be willing to break with the educational establishment (not foolishly or cavalierly, but thoughtfully and for good reason) in order to find gospel ways to help mankind. Gospel methodology, concepts, and insights can help us to do what the world cannot do in its own frame of reference.

In some ways the Church Educational System, in order to be unique in the years that lie ahead, may have to break with certain patterns of the educational establishment. When the world has lost its way on matters of principle, we have an obligation to point the way. We can, as Brigham Young hoped we would, "be a people of profound learning pertaining to the things of this world," but without being tainted by what he regarded as the "pernicious, atheistic influences" that flood in unless we are watchful. Our scholars, therefore, must be sentries as well as teachers!

We surely cannot give up our concerns with character and conduct without also giving up on mankind. Much misery results from flaws in character, not from failures in technology. We cannot give in to the ways of the world with regard to the realm of art. President Romney brought to our attention not long ago a quotation in which Brigham Young said there is "no music in hell." Our art must be the kind which edifies man, which takes into account his immortal nature, and which prepares us for heaven, not hell.

One peak of educational excellence that is highly relevant to the needs of the Church is the realm of language. BYU should become the acknowledged language capital of the world in terms of our academic competency and through the marvelous "laboratory" that sends young men and women forth to service in the mission field. I refer, of course, to the Language Training Mission. There is no reason why this University could not become the place where, perhaps more than anywhere else, the concern for literacy and the teaching of English as a second language is firmly headquartered in terms of unarguable competency as well as deep concern.

I have mentioned only a few areas. There are many others of special concern, with special challenges and opportunities for accomplishment and service in the second century.

We can do much in excellence and, at the same time, emphasize the large-scale participation of our students, whether it be in athletics or in academic events. We can bless many and give many experience, while, at the same time, we are developing the few select souls who can take us to new heights of attainment.

It ought to be obvious to you, as it is to me, that some of the things the Lord would have occur in the second century of the BYU are hidden from our immediate view. Until we have climbed the hill just before us, we are not apt to be given a glimpse of what lies beyond. The hills ahead are higher than we think. This means that accomplishments and further direction must occur in proper order, after we have done our part. We will not be transported from point A to point Z without having to pass through the developmental and demanding experiences of all the points of achievement and all the milestone markers that lie between!

This University will go forward. Its students are idealists who have integrity, who love to work in good causes. These students will not only have a secular training, but will have come to understand what Jesus meant when he said that the key of knowledge, which had been lost by society centuries before, was "the fulness of the scriptures." We understand, as few people do, that education is a part of being about our Father's business and that the scriptures contain the master concepts for mankind.

We know there are those of unrighteous purposes who boast that time is on their side. So it may seem to those of very limited vision. But of those engaged in the Lord's work, it can be truly said, "Eternity is on your side! Those who fight that bright future fight in vain!"

I hasten to add that as the Church grows global and becomes more and more multicultural, a smaller and smaller percentage of all our LDS college-age students will attend BYU, or the Hawaii Campus, or Ricks College, or the LDS Business College. It is a privileged group who are able to come here. We do not intend to neglect the needs of the other Church members wherever they are, but those who do come here have an even greater follow-through responsibility to make certain that the Church's investment in them provides dividends through service and dedication to others as they labor in the Church and in the world elsewhere:

> To go to BYU is something special. There were Brethren who had dreams regarding the growth and maturity of Brigham Young University, even to the construction of a temple on the hill they had long called Temple Hill, yet "dreams and prophetic utterances are not self-executing. They are fulfilled usually by righteous and devoted people making the prophecies come true." [Ernest L. Wilkinson, *Brigham Young University: The First One Hundred Years*]

So much of our counsel given to you here today as you begin your second century is the same counsel we give to others in the Church concerning other vital programs — you need to lengthen your stride, quicken your step, and (to use President Tanner's phrase) continue your journey. You are headed in the right direction! Such academic adjustments as need to be made will be made out of the individual and collective wisdom we find when a dedicated faculty interacts with a wise administration, an inspired governing board, and an appreciative body of students.

I am grateful that the Church can draw upon the expertise that exists here. The pockets of competency that are here will be used by the Church increasingly and in various ways.

We want you to keep free as a university — free of government control, not only for the sake of the University and the Church, but also for the sake of our government. Our government, state and federal, and our people are best served by free colleges and universities, not by institutions that are compliant out of fears over funding.

We look forward to developments in your computer-assisted translation projects and from the Ezra Taft Benson Agriculture and Food Institute. We look forward to more being done in the field of education, in the fine arts, in the J. Reuben Clark Law School, in the Graduate School of Management, and in the realm of human behavior.

We appreciate the effectiveness of the programs here, such as our Indian program with its high rate of completion for Indian students. But we must do better in order to be better, and we must be better for the sake of the world!

As previous First Presidencies have said, and we say again to you, we expect (we do not simply hope) that Brigham Young University will "become a leader among the great universities of the world." To that expectation I would add, "Become a unique university in all of the world!"

May I thank now all those who have made this Centennial Celebration possible and express appreciation to the alumni, students, and friends of the University for the Centennial Carillon Tower which is being given to the University on its one hundredth birthday. Through these lovely bells will sound the great melodies which have motivated the people of the Lord's

Church in the past and will lift our hearts and inspire us in the second century — with joy and even greater determination. As I conclude my remarks now, may I offer a brief dedicatory prayer for the Carillon Tower so that all of you might participate in this dedication rather than moving to that site itself.

Dedication of the Carillon Tower and Bells

Our Father in heaven, we are grateful for this, the gift of thy people, the alumni, the faculty, the staff, and the friends of Brigham Young University, for this collection of fifty-two bells in this carillon tower on the campus of this, thy great University.

We are grateful for the faithfulness and craftmanship of those who constructed the bells, those who have transported them, and those who have placed them into the tower.

Father, we are grateful for the diversity of the bells in their size, versatility, and music-giving tones, for the clavier and the clappers and the magnetic tape and the keyboard, and we ask thee, O Father, to protect this tower, these bells, and all pertaining to them, and we pray that the carillonneur will have the preciseness and the ability to create beautiful music from the bells in this tower.

Father, we thank thee for this institution and what it has meant in the lives of hundreds of thousands of people and their posterity, for the truths they have learned here, for the characters that have been built, for the families which have been strengthened here. Let thy spirit continue to be with the president of this institution and his associates, the faculty, the students, alumni, staff, and friends of this University, and their successors that thy Spirit may always abide here and that stalwarts may emerge from this institution to bring glory to thee and blessings to the people of this world.

Just as these bells will lift the hearts of the hearers when they hear the hymns and anthems played to thy glory, let the morality of the graduates of this University provide the music of hope for the inhabitants of this planet. We ask that all those everywhere who open their ears to hear the sounds of good music will also be more inclined to open their ears to hear the good tidings brought to us by thy Son.

Now, dear Father, let these bells ring sweet music unto thee. Let the everlasting hills take up the sound; let the mountains shout for joy and the valleys cry aloud, and let the seas and dry lands tell the wonders of the Eternal King.

Let the rivers and the brooks flow down with gladness; let the sun, the moon, and the stars sing together and let the whole creation sing the glory of our Redeemer forevermore.

Now, our Father, we dedicate this carillon tower, the bells, the mechanical effects and equipment, and all pertaining to this compound and ask thee that thou wouldst bless it and protect it against all destructive elements. Bless it that it may give us sweet music and that because of it we may love and serve thee even more.

In the name of Jesus Christ. Amen.

Index

C

H

I

M

T

U

DEDICATORY ADDRESS AND PRAYER FOR BUILDINGS CONSTITUTING THE NEW LANGUAGE TRAINING MISSION ADJOINING BRIGHAM YOUNG UNIVERSITY

On 27 September 1976 President Spencer W. Kimball dedicated the various buildings of the Language Training Mission. The administration building was named after President Wilford W. Woodruff; other buildings were named after other great missionaries of the Church, including the Rey L. Pratt, Erastus Snow, Matthew Cowley, Parley P. Pratt, and Jacob Hamblin residence halls and the George Q. Cannon and Heber C. Kimball teaching stations.

These buildings constitute the first series of buildings comprising the Language Training Mission. The second series of buildings is now in the process of construction, and when completed, they will be named after faithful missionaries of the Church. A third series of buildings, it is contemplated, will be built thereafter, and will likewise be named after other great missionaries of the Church.

The dedication of these buildings, which collectively form the Language Training Mission, was not done within the first one hundred years of the history of BYU, if that history dates from the time that Brigham Young, on 16 October 1875, conveyed the first property to BYA, or from the time the first classes were held in January 1876, but the dedication was so near to the one hundredth anniversary and the dedicatory address and prayer were of such supreme significance to the future of BYU and its service to the Church in supplying the language training for the missionaries, that it was thought highly desirable to print the dedicatory address and prayer in this volume.

Beloved brothers and sisters:

This is a happy day. We have been looking forward to it for many months. It is pleasing to be with you wonderful young missionaries and all those who are so interested in what you are doing here.

When the mission training first began, President Heber J. Grant made the statement,

> When you go to remodeling and overhauling it, see that the building is made big enough for all future needs.

He spoke that to Bishop David A. Smith when there were very, very few missionaries going out.

Sixty-two years ago when I came to Salt Lake City to be set apart for my mission to the Central States Mission, there was a long basement tunnel from the gatehouse into the temple in Salt Lake with coats, hats, and shoes lining the long passageway.

I was ushered into a room of the Annex and set apart for my mission. There was no Mission Home or formal instructions and training for the important position I was to have for the next twenty-eight months.

It was nearly ten years later, May 1924, when President Anthony W. Ivins declared,

> I think it's a shame that our boys are permitted to come to this city and wander around as they are doing. It seems to me we should have some place where we can take care of them and look after them while they are in the city.

The west side of North State Street at that time was lined with big two-story residences, where the east entrance to the Church Office Building is now located. These houses had been built in 1888 and 1891 by daughters of President Brigham Young. One of these North State Street buildings behind the Beehive House was set apart for the purpose of preparing missionaries for their fields of labor. I don't think we had even thought about languages at that time; we just went into the mission field and learned the language.

Some remodeling and readjusting was done, and on 3 February 1925, fifty persons or more gathered in the big front room for dedication services. General Authorities and auxiliary leaders were present, and the building was dedicated as a Mission Home by President Heber J. Grant. LeRoi C. Snow, a son of President Lorenzo Snow, was named as director. The first group of missionaries, five in number, came to the home a month later. Classes were held in the LDS High School buildings and in the old Bishop's Building, which were on Main Street, until 1927, when a second house was added to the Mission Home and the two were connected. The missionaries were given a course in Church organization and functions and, hopefully, some spiritual stimulation. I remember those days very well, and also the days that followed. When I came into the Council of the Twelve in 1943, that was still the Mission Home.

On 5 March 1962, and that was just yesterday, you know, the Mission Home was moved to the former New Ute Hotel at 119 North Main Street where space was arranged for 320 missionaries, twenty classrooms, and a large assembly hall. President and Sister Lorin Richards were called to direct these facilities.

We little dreamed that we would some day need and have such a magnificent structure as this.

In October 1970, plans were announced for the purchase of the unused LaFayette Elementary School on North Temple Street for a Mission Home. Extensive repairs were made, and missionaries moved into that building in 1971. Brother and Sister Joe Whitesides were the first directors of the missionary activities in that new location. Other leaders have followed, and tens of thousands of missionaries have answered their calls and then received their training and supervision there.

It was in December 1961 that the Language Training Mission began here at BYU with twenty-nine missionaries. Brigham Young University started to give instruction in Spanish to missionaries going to Mexico prior to their departure, and beginning in June 1963 all missionaries assigned to Spanish-speaking missions were sent to this institute. Soon afterwards, Portuguese was added to the curriculum. Later in 1963 the institute was organized into a regular mission of the Church, with Dr. Ernest J. Wilkins as president, and was given the name of the Language Training Mission. Since that time, approximately 33,500 missionaries have trained in the LTM program here in Provo.

The German program began in March 1964, followed by the Navajo language in 1967, French in October, Italian in 1969, and also in 1969 the language training missions were established at Ricks College in Idaho for the Scandinavian languages and

Dutch, with Ermel J. Morton as mission president, and the South Pacific and Oriental languages at the Church College of Hawaii in Laie were under Brother Kenneth J. Orton as mission president. Instruction in Afrikaans began in Provo in March 1970.

Brother Max L. Pinegar was called to preside at the Provo LTM immediately upon his return as mission president to the Netherlands Mission in 1974. He was preceded by the late Dr. Terrence L. Hansen, who had succeeded Dr. Ernest J. Wilkins in 1970.

The three Language Training Missions—Hawaii, Rexburg, and Provo—were finally consolidated in Provo on 16 July 1975, when the missionaries previously sent to Hawaii were changed to Provo. These were followed by the Ricks LTM missionaries, who began reporting to Provo on 6 May 1976. Prior to the merger of the three LTM's, approximately 5,500 missionaries had been trained in six years at Hawaii and 2,280 in seven years at Ricks. During fiscal year 1973-74, 2,837 missionaries were trained in Provo, and in the calendar year 1975, 4,367 missionaries were trained. It is estimated that 5,500 will receive training at this LTM in 1976.

At this great Language Training Mission, the missionary develops spiritually, learns his mission language, memorizes the proselyting discussions, and develops within himself a sensitivity for the people to whom he is being sent.

The Language Training Mission is considered a reputable and recognized language school and compares favorably with other well known intensive language schools. Perhaps more students are trained in languages per year at this institution than at any other language school in the whole world. The cost for training is approximately $290 per student as compared to the Peace Corps of our government at around $1,000 per student.

There are today 1,350 plus missionaries in this mission. We welcome you and love you and send you forth with our blessings.

This is the largest number of missionaries that has ever been in the LTM at a single time.

Language instructors are recruited from among the BYU students who are returned missionaries or who are foreign students. They are carefully selected and trained and become excellent and capable instructors.

It would be interesting to note that there were 790 missionaries in all the world in 1900; in the year when I was called, 1914, there were 794, about half as many in all the world as there are here today. In 1920, there were 891; in 1930, 854; in 1940, there were 2,145; 1950, 5,164; 1960, 8,211; 1970, 13,768; and in September of this year, there are an estimated 24,306. In the period of forty years from 1900 to 1940 there was an increase of 1,355 missionaries, or 270 percent. Between 1940 and 1976, there was an increase of 22,161, or a 1,033 percent increase. From 1970 to 1976, there has been an increase of 10,538, or 75 percent.

We are greatly pleased with the response of the people outside of the United States who have responded so well to the missionary work. Only four years ago there were but 529 non-American missionaries, and now so far in 1976, we have approximately 2,300, which is nearly a 400 percent increase in four years. This pleases us greatly for the local missionaries have much advantage over the American missionaries since they need no visas, they have the language and the customs of the people, and they know many of the people themselves.

When I was made an Apostle in 1943, there were but 38 missions, and now we have 146 missions. This explains the need for these additional facilities. We now have missions established in fifty-four countries throughout the world, from one pole to the other.

The missionaries in the Language Training Mission have increased from 29 in 1961 to 2,375 in 1970 and 5,500 in this year. That is tremendous!

It might be of interest to you to know that the following languages are being taught in the training school: Afrikaans, Cantonese, Danish, Dutch, Farsi (Persian), Finnish, French, German, Icelandic, Indonesian, Italian, Japanese, Korean, Mandarin, Navajo, Norwegian, Portuguese, Samoan, Serbo-Croatian, Spanish, Swedish, Tahitian, and Thai, a total of twenty-three.

To enhance their spiritual training and attitudes, twenty

branches with local brethren serving as leaders have been organized here. That is a wonderful record.

I would like to bring to your attention the magnificent painting on the wall of the main floor in the Church Office Building portraying the Savior standing upon the Mount of Olives with His eleven apostles (Judas having already gone) and probably pointing to all the world. He said:

> Go ye into all the world, and preach the gospel to every creature.
>
> He that believeth and is baptized shall be saved . . .
>
> (Mark 16:15-16.)

This gives us our constant, everlasting inspiration. We remember a further scripture, which says:

> And the Lord said to Samuel, Behold, I will do a thing in Israel, at which both the ears of every one that heareth it shall tingle. (I Samuel 3:11.)
>
> . . . many shall run to and fro, and knowledge shall be increased. (Daniel 12:4.)

Nineteenth century theologians thought they saw the fulfillment of these predictions in the coming of the steam engine, the sewing machine, the motor car. What they saw was but the dim beginnings of the most spectacular increase of knowledge since men first dwelt upon the earth. Could they emerge from their graves today and behold a giant rocket in flight, a man-made satellite in orbit, and moving pictures of the moon or Mars appearing on a TV set, or a famous choir in South Dakota singing to much of the earth through a satellite off in space, they would recognize in all these and numerous other space-age marvels a fulfillment far beyond their expectations but nonetheless valid for all of that.

The works of God are endless. We stand in awe as we see some of the evidences of increased knowledge, and we tingle and tingle and tingle.

A *National Observer* article written by Michael T. Malloy gives us some information of the tomorrow for language. While all the languages are extremely important, the persons of Spanish background are the second largest minority in the

United States. They are the fastest growing minority, and they are nourished by heavy immigration from the Spanish-speaking world.

The Hispanic tide, which is emerging, is sweeping across the American scene.

It is reported that "there are more than 3 million Chicanos in California, and that New York City, with its 1.5 million to 2.5 million Latinos, has as many as some Latin American countries."

This author says there are more Hispanics in New Jersey than in Arizona and more in Illinois than in New Mexico, and Chicago has a quarter of a million, and Detroit has twenty Spanish-speaking nationalities.

"Spanish is by far the most common second language spoken in the United States." Possibly 8 million of the 197 million Americans older than four speak a language other than English, and of these, some four million speak Spanish. Hundreds of thousands speak Italian, Chinese, French, German, Japanese, Filipino, Portuguese, Korean, and nearly a million speak other languages.

Chicano families are large, frequently extending to seven or eight children, so they are growing faster than the non-Spanish-speaking Americans. There are probably 11,202,000 persons of Spanish origin in the United States, and while that is only five percent, yet their growth shows a twenty percent increase in two years in their population. The fertility rate is about double that of American citizens.

This author further says that there is another huge group of the farm workers in the United States who have crossed the Rio Grande. The Latin American population is growing, the author says, three times as fast percentage-wise as that of the United States, but their income is only one-sixth as large. Mexico alone adds more than two million people to the North American continent each year. Americans add fewer than 1.3 million. The population of Mexico is now about sixty million and will be a hundred million by the year 2000.

That was very interesting to me, and I thought it might be to you because we have long realized, of course, that our neighbor to the south is fast-growing and is very important to us, and perhaps our baptisms are greater there than any place in the world. So you who are going to learn Spanish, build yourself so that it will be a permanent language, so that you can always speak it, because Spanish is coming to the front.

President Ezra Taft Benson mentioned his missionary days, as did President Marion G. Romney.

Just a few words about my missionary days. I was called when I was nineteen. I went to Globe, Arizona, where I was to earn money for my mission. My father had a large family, and he had a difficult time to provide for us. So I decided when I got my call, I would make my own way. I would pay for my own mission. The best job I was able to get was milking cows, and we had about ninety cows in that dairy and we milked them in the middle of the night and the middle of the morning. I would milk about eighteen to twenty-nine cows twice a day, wash the bottles and cans, do the separating, feed the cattle, clean the yards, and do all that goes on in a dairy. When I received my remuneration, it was $47.50 for the month. That wasn't just an hour, that was a month, and then it finally was raised to $62.50 in the third year that I went.

What I am trying to say is that this was *my* mission. One of my closest friends sent me a $5 bill one day, and he said, "I want to have a part of your mission," so I would have to share it with him, of course, but I saved all the money. Every two or three weeks I would get me an ice cream cone for a nickel when I went to town, but I saved practically every penny for three summers while I was going to high school because I wanted to go on a mission, and it took care of me for nearly my whole mission.

My father had given me a little colt which soon became a big, beautiful black stallion. I was able to get a good price for it, and the sale of that horse kept me on my mission for the balance of my time, with just a little help from my father.

I have always been proud that I had taken that attitude toward the mission, for it was mine.

Now, brothers and sisters, this is a glorious occasion to be here in this beautiful, commodious building, to dedicate it to the Lord. I will close my remarks and will now proceed to dedicate this building and the facilities that adjoin it.

DEDICATORY PRAYER

Our Father which art in Heaven, hallowed be thy name, thy kingdom come, thy will be done, on earth as it is in heaven.

Father, we love thee. We love thy Son. We recognize thy great power. We appreciate the part that thou hast permitted us to play in this great movement.

Father, we are grateful for this land, the choicest land above all other lands in the world. We are grateful for it, and we ask thee to help us to continue to beautify it and to appreciate it and to make it worthwhile.

Father, we are grateful that thou didst send thy prophet, Joseph Smith, in this dispensation, to restore the gospel to the earth. We are grateful for his visions and his revelations and the sweetness of his life and for all that came through him to make of this a great and inspired program.

Father, we are grateful that the Prophet Joseph Smith found the Lamanites, because we recognize that with 60,000,000 Lamanites or more in the world, we have a great responsibility to them, and we are grateful that they, in many, many countries, are accepting the gospel and especially in the country of Mexico south of us.

Father, we remember and call to thine attention again the beautiful portrait that is painted in the building in Salt Lake City which is a constant inspiration to us, reminding us that the Lord had great ideas and intended that the gospel should go to all the world, not just to our nearest neighbors.

And Father, we are grateful for that and all other things that thou hast blessed us with.

Father, we are grateful for the duty that thou hast imposed upon us and the privileges that have been coming to us and that we, as missionaries, may continue to spread the gospel far and wide. We wish to take the gospel to every creature and give them the privilege of accepting it if they will.

Father, we are grateful for the inventions of this day, for the airplane, for the train, for the cars, for the television, for all of the things that we know thou hast created and developed for us to take the gospel to the world and realize thou wilt permit others to use these facilities as it seems necessary.

Father, we are grateful for all thy many blessings, for the life and the health and the strength that we enjoy. We are grateful for our delightful families and the desire on the part of our sons and daughters and others to fill missions and to carry forward this great program.

Father, we are grateful for the Language Training Mission that has been developed through these years and for the vision of those who have done this. We are grateful for this land and for the property that we have here, this beautiful area whereon these buildings have been constructed. We are grateful to the architects and to the workers and to all who have contributed toward the building of these structures in which we train our missionaries.

Father, we come to thee now to dedicate to thee these lovely buildings, large and commodious and inspiring. We dedicate these buildings to thee, our Father, and mention individually the buildings which have been constructed—this beautiful building in the name of Wilford Woodruff, remembering he was one of thine holy apostles. He was President of thy Church; he was responsible for the baptism of the writers of the Declaration of Independence in the St. George Temple. This courageous leader according to Thy revelation terminated the program on plural marriage during the time when it was opposed by federal law. His baptisms, Father, have been numerous, and he will be an inspiration to all missionaries for all time to come. We dedicate this building and name it the Wilford Woodruff Building.

Father, we remember George Q. Cannon, who was the first counselor to three presidents of the Church. He had the gift of tongues; he translated the Book of Mormon into Hawaiian. He was a missionary, a leader, a theologian, and we dedicate an adjoining building in honor of President George Q. Cannon and to the proselyting of the gospel and name it the George Q. Cannon Building.

Heber C. Kimball, my own beloved grandfather, opened the door of the gospel to Great Britain in 1837 and baptized 2,000 members in about eight months. He was the first counselor to Brigham Young during a difficult era. He looked after the printing of the Book of Mormon in England. He was a great missionary and a leader and a colonizer, and Brigham Young used to say, "Heber is my prophet." He and Brigham Young never did "lift up their heels" against the Prophet Joseph Smith. We now dedicate and name another adjoining building the Heber C. Kimball Building.

Erastus Snow was an apostle and a missionary and the developer of Utah's "Dixie" country. He went to Scandinavia to spread the gospel in 1850. He translated and published the Book of Mormon and the Doctrine and Covenants in Danish. He was a great missionary and will long be remembered as an example to all missionaries as they go forward to teach the gospel, and so we name and designate one of the halls as the Erastus Snow Building.

Parley P. Pratt and his companions converted Sidney Rigdon and brought a whole congregation into the Church in Kirtland, Ohio. He was a great missionary, and for many long years he served in the United States, Canada, England, South America, and the South Seas. He wrote a number of tracts and many hymns which we still sing. He was killed in Arkansas as a martyr to the Church, and it has been our privilege to visit the scene of his burial. We dedicate another residence hall and name it the Parley P. Pratt Building.

Matthew Cowley was a great missionary to New Zealand and to the Polynesians. He was an apostle with a great, magnetic power with all the people of the South Seas, an associate with whom we traveled over the ocean. We dedicate, then, a residence hall to the memory of Brother Matthew Cowley, our dear friend and brother and a great missionary, and we name it the Matthew Cowley Building.

Jacob Hamblin was designated by Brigham Young as an apostle to the Indians. He was a great missionary to the Indian nations of the Southwest. He loved them and they loved him, and he made a great place for himself among them. We therefore dedicate the building where missionary couples will reside and give it the name of Jacob Hamblin Building.

Rey Lucero Pratt was a great missionary in Mexico. He was presiding there in the dangerous days of the revolution in Mexico. He later became a member of the First Council of Seventy. Brother Pratt we loved for his integrity and his faithfulness to his missionary service, and we give a residence hall building the name of Rey Lucero Pratt and dedicate it as a part of the Language Training Mission.

We are grateful for all these men, our Father, for their lives and their devoted service, and we hope, our Father, that the missionaries by the tens of thousands who will come to this mission home for their training will remember as examples these men for whom the buildings are named.

Now we dedicate all these buildings, our Heavenly Father, for the rich program which has been established, that from here may emanate the gospel, the testimony of thy Son, and the testimony of the Prophet Joseph Smith. May the work go forward that the ultimate work and hope of the first Prophet of this dispensation may be realized, that the nations may finally be proselyted and every nation, kindred, tongue, and people may hear the word of the Lord in their own language. To that end we have established, our Father, this great institution for the teaching of these many languages to the many missionaries who come here.

We ask thee, our Father, to bless the young people who will come that they may fulfill their obligations to teach the gospel to the world.

Now, we dedicate all these buildings and ask thy continued blessings to be upon Brother Pinegar and all those who shall assist him in this great service, and we do this all, dedicating them by the power of the priesthood which we hold, and in the name of Jesus Christ. Amen.